INTELLECTUALS AND THEIR PUBLICS

Intellectuals and their Publics

Perspectives from the Social Sciences

Edited by

CHRISTIAN FLECK
University of Graz, Austria

ANDREAS HESS
University College Dublin, Ireland

E. STINA LYON
London South Bank University, UK

ASHGATE

Published by
Ashgate Publishing Limited
Wey Court East
Union Road
Farnham
Surrey, GU9 7PT
England

Ashgate Publishing Company
Suite 420
101 Cherry Street
Burlington
VT 05401-4405
USA

www.ashgate.com

British Library Cataloguing in Publication Data
Intellectuals and their publics : perspectives from the social sciences
1. Intellectuals 2. Intellectuals - Public opinion
I. Fleck, Christian, 1954- II. Hess, Andreas III. Lyon, E. Stina
305.5'52

Library of Congress Cataloging-in-Publication Data
Intellectuals and their publics : perspectives from the social sciences / by Christian Fleck, Andreas Hess and E. Stina Lyon.
p. cm.
Includes index.
ISBN 978-0-7546-7540-2
1. Intellectuals. 2. Intellectuals--Political activity. 3. Intellectuals--Case studies. 4. Intellectual life--Case studies. I. Fleck, Christian, 1954- II. Hess, Andreas. III. Lyon, E. Stina.

HM728.I5733 2008
305.5'52--dc22

2008038856

ISBN 978 0 7546 7540 2

Mixed Sources
Product group from well-managed forests and other controlled sources
www.fsc.org Cert no. SA-COC-1565
© 1996 Forest Stewardship Council
FSC

Printed and bound in Great Britain by
MPG Books Ltd, Bodmin, Cornwall.

Contents

PART THREE CASE STUDIES

List of Contributors

Jeffrey C. Alexander is Professor of Sociology and Co-Director of the Center for Cultural Sociology at Yale University, USA.

Stefan Auer is Senior Lecturer in History and Politics and Deputy Director of the Innovative Universities European Union Centre at La Trobe University, Australia.

Howard Davis is Professor of Social Theory and Institutions in the School of Social Sciences at the University of Wales, Bangor, UK.

Mary Evans is Professor of Sociology. Until her retirement, she taught in sociology and women's studies at the University of Kent, UK.

Christian Fleck is Professor of Sociology at the University of Graz, Austria.

Tom Garvin is Professor of Politics in the School of Politics and International Relations at University College Dublin, Ireland.

Andreas Hess is Senior Lecturer in the School of Sociology at University College Dublin, Ireland.

Laurent Jeanpierre is Assistant Professor in Political Science at the University of Strasbourg and researcher at the Groupe de sociologique politique européenne, France.

Dirk Kaesler is Professor of Sociology at the University of Marburg, Germany.

E. Stina Lyon is Professor of Sociology and Pro-Dean for the Faculty of Arts and Human Sciences at London South Bank University, UK.

Sébastien Mosbah-Natanson is currenty a teaching assistant in political science at the University Paris-Dauphine and is a research associate at the Centre d'études sociologiques of the University Paris IV-Sorbonne, France.

Stefan Müller-Doohm is Professor of Sociology at Oldenburg University, Germany.

William Outhwaite is Professor of Sociology at Newcastle University, UK.

Anson Rabinbach is Professor of Modern European History and Director of the Program in European Cultural Studies at Princeton University, USA.

Werner Reichmann is Scientific Assistant at the University of Constance, Germany.

Markus Schweiger works as a sociologist in a social welfare organization and is a research affiliate at the Department of Sociology, University of Graz, Austria.

John Torpey is Professor of Sociology at the Graduate Center, City University of New York, USA.

Per Wisselgren is Assistant Professor of History of Science and Ideas at Umeå University, Sweden.

Joseba Zulaika is Professor of Anthropology and Deputy Director of the Center for Basque Studies at the University of Nevada, Reno, USA.

Acknowledgements

The editors would like to express their gratitude to institutions and individuals who helped with the preparation of this book. In the first instance, our thanks must go out to the Directorate of the General Research of the European Commission, which funded a collaborative research project, Analyzing and Overcoming the Sociological Fragmentation in Europe (ANOVASOFIE, contract no. CIT2-CT-2004-506035), which provided the research context from which most contributions to this volume emerged. A final ANOVASOFIE symposium took place at University College Dublin where earlier versions of some of the chapters published here were presented and discussed. UCD supported us with the necessary infrastructure and financial aid. We would like to take this opportunity to thank all our ANOVASOFIE partners and all the other participants who joined the effort. Mara Verlic and Johannes Ebner helped to standardise all the contributions gathered here. Finally, we would like to thank all those at Ashgate who guided us through the complex editorial process.

Introduction

Intellectuals and their Publics: Perspectives from the Social Sciences

Christian Fleck, Andreas Hess and E. Stina Lyon

Reflecting and commenting on their professional calling are two activities intellectuals do regularly – and often they do so with passion. Ever since the term 'intellectual' became defined in more specific terms at the turn of the last century during the Dreyfus Affair,[1] intellectuals have been engaged in debates in which they have tried to position themselves sociologically, politically and culturally. A newly defined modern public has become the space where intellectuals try out their ideas or where they battle out their differences against real and imaginary rivals – sometimes even to the extent of trying to exclude competitors from the *agora*.

Over the years, new groups of intellectuals have entered the public arena while older ones have disappeared. New social differentiations have developed and with the help of new conceptual tools intellectuals have tried to make sense of the changes. Just a look reveals that the twenty-first-century intellectual is very different in his or her aspirations and functioning role when compared to the type that more than a hundred years ago was emerging. Today there exist considerably more agendas and competing views in terms of what defines intellectual life and what intellectuals should or should not do. The latest but certainly not the last invention in a series of such self-creations is that of the so-called 'public intellectual'. (For a working definition and role description of the public intellectual and the role public sociology should play, see Burawoy, 2005).

---

1 The Dreyfus Affair (1898–1904) was named after the French officer Dreyfus, who had wrongly been accused by the authorities of spying for the Germans. The novelist Emile Zola was so outraged by the deeply flawed investigation and the miscarriage of justice that he decided to publish an open letter, 'J'accuse', subsequently signed by 1200 supporters, most of them writers, scholars and teachers. Ever since Georges Clemenceau called this manifestation 'a protest of intellectuals', the term stuck (Collini, 2006, 20f.). However, it would be wrong to suggest that intellectuals did not exist before the term 'intellectuals' was coined. The cases of Alexis de Tocqueville and Gustave de Beaumont, also discussed in this volume, clearly reveal that intellectuals existed a long time before the concept and modern notion and usage of the term became more widespread at the beginning of the last century (for a discussion of this aspect, see Collini, 2006, 17ff., and, more detailed, Charle, 1996). In *La marche des idées* (2003) François Dosse has reminded all participants in this debate that one has to distinguish between the history of intellectuals and intellectual history; the two can overlap, but they are hardly the same.

The aim of this volume on intellectual engagement in the public sphere is threefold. First, we try to identify some of the major issues intellectuals have tried to address and come to terms with, such as the changing public sphere, women intellectuals and just causes. Second, we look at particular complex social and political configurations in which intellectuals situated themselves, taking on positions or defending values, with all the contradictions, dilemmas and risks that engagement entails. Finally, we will study some particular cases, names and academic programmes in order to deepen our understanding of what intellectual engagement meant in the past and what it means today. The editors take this Introduction as an opportunity to establish a few parameters and to introduce some ideas that will help the reader to gain a better overall sense of the arguments presented in this volume. We would also like to draw the reader's attention to Howard Davis's reflections in the Conclusion to this volume, which together with the Introduction provide a frame for the investigations collected here.

Looking back at how intellectuals came into existence as a particular social group, the classic intellectual who entered centre stage towards the end of the nineteenth century is the first type that comes to mind. Being almost always male, he made his mark by usually addressing a single, undivided and usually well-educated audience – in other words, a relatively small portion of the population. The early type of intellectual came in two forms: as a university professor and as a professional writer. The prestige of a university professor was usually high enough to suppress any objections with regards to the authority of their public utterances. Bertolt Brecht once called this *das große Einverständnis*. This 'great consensus' between university-based intellectuals and the powers that be was a very solid one, in the sense that the public engagement of intellectuals was firmly located within the boundaries of the dominant discourse. Pronouncements of a radical, oppositional nature remained the exception. Many of the debates were, so to speak, about the pace of social improvement, not about the general direction society should take or about suggesting radical societal alternatives. Before the labour movement won access to decision-making institutions – in the first instance by democratically increasing their vote and by enlarging their representation in parliament – those few intellectuals who showed solidarity with the early labour movement and the emerging organized left could easily be neglected, marginalized or simply ignored by the majority of the educated public. The prime example of such reaction – or better, non-reaction – has to be Karl Marx, who during his own lifetime never experienced any wider recognition (if we disregard for a second that nucleus of followers and comrades who took his words as gospel). It would take a long time, actually the 'massification' and institutionalization of the labour movement, best expressed and symbolized in the rise of workers' parties, either of the socialist or the social democratic type, before Marx's intellectual contribution could be fully acknowledged.

The second classic group of intellectuals, already briefly mentioned above, consisted of writers. Quite a few of these men of letters could actually make a living from their art or were subsidized in one way or another and were thus in a position to ignore expectations of the public at large. However, while this type of the writer-intellectual deviated more from the overall societal consensus than the first type of the university-based intellectual, most of their transgressing was confined to artistic questions and did not deal specifically with social problems. The great realistic novels of Balzac, Zola and Dickens and the naturalistic plays of Hauptmann and Ibsen portrayed social misery; seldom did their authors speak out in favour of a completely different societal model. Both types have been contemplators, whereas an emerging third type was more active as spokesmen of nations, nations to be, social movements and causes.

Until the period leading up to the First World War, most of the intellectual debates were closely related to particular social forces and their causes, such as the various nationalisms and political projects of self-determination, imperialist and Western ideas of civilization, the battle between religious beliefs and the emerging secularized state, and addressed such important democratic questions as the inclusion of women and workers. Fundamental opposing contributions from intellectuals gaining wider public recognition emerged only after the communist movement had gained power in Russia and with the newly established Soviet regime now trying to connect with and influence the worldwide network of devotees – not a few of them 'intellectual workers' defending obediently the party line.

Between 1917 and 1989, many of the debates among intellectuals were indeed debates about the pros and cons of communism. This unintentionally brought the social democratic left into accord with Western democracy, in some countries arguably quicker than in others. Halfway through this era, in the 1950s, just as Daniel Bell announced the *End of Ideology*, a new ideology-driven movement entered the stage: neo-Marxism and the students and youth movements with their new idols, Che Guevara, Hồ Chí Minh and Mao Zedong. Interestingly, these leaders were very much seen as practical intellectuals by their admirers[2] – even if their own martyr death (as in the case of Che Guevara, Patrice Lumumba or Amilcar Cabral) and the sacrifice of entire parts of the population (as in the case of China's Mao or Kampuchea's Pol Pot) were the net results. The tragic irony was that some of the radicalized intellectuals actually tried to copy their idols, re-enacting or re-creating in their own Western society what their idols had practised under Third World conditions. Fortunately, the majority populations of Western countries resisted following the example of such self-proclaimed revolutionary *avant-gardes* or simply decided to ignore their occasionally bizarre-sounding battle cries.[3]

2 Those people were admired not only by student activists but by well-established social scientists, too. For example, Karl W. Deutsch, John R. Platt and Dieter Senghaas (1986) celebrated Lenin's theory of revolution and his conceptualization of the one-party state together with Mao Zedong's peasant and guerrilla organization as examples of major social science breakthroughs.

3 In this respect, the founding of guerrilla groups in Western countries was maybe not so different or so far away when compared to the present day's suicide bombers –

The audience of classical intellectuals consisted of educated people, and at the turn of the last century this still meant a relatively small portion of the population. However, due to modernization this audience grew steadily. Mass education and an increasing professionalization of occupations produced more and better-educated receivers for intellectual messages; they also contributed to a process that can best be described as a further differentiation in terms of available expectations. This has also created a wider range of critical voices for public intellectuals to engage with. Besides the enlargement of the audience and the developing of a wider spectrum of expectations, the expansion of the education system also offered would-be intellectuals without private means security and a stable income. Until then the normative term 'intellectual' stood mainly for alternative interpretations; now it became a descriptive term and signifier for all those professions that developed, manipulated and disseminated knowledge. Echoing older classifications, but partly also in an attempt to re-conceptualize and re-brand some old-fashioned and outdated Marxism, the new kind of intellectual now became known as the 'knowledge worker', encompassing both normative-emancipatory and descriptive dimensions.

In what may be described as a cunning moment or a twist of reason, the New Left may have unwillingly contributed to the new development in which the old world of bourgeois reasoning became increasingly democratized, shaping intellectuals and their products and perceptions profoundly in the process. Those intellectuals or would-be intellectuals who entered the formal system of higher education as professors or instructors were exposed to new, often competing role expectations. However, it was only after the Second World War and as a result of decolonization that developing countries began to follow the Western trend in higher education by introducing educational policies, often by means of special incentives such as scholarships, bursaries and writers-in-residence schemes, which made entry into higher education possible for future intellectuals. Until then the elites of the decolonized world (including most intellectuals) had mainly received their education at universities in the developed world.

Due to the changes described above, the majority of modern intellectuals across the Western world and in most (but not all) of the developing countries have for some time now encountered and experienced some kind of counter-pressure. It is probably fair to say that expectations of the public at large are no longer fully congruent, neither with the life and logic of academia nor with the rules that determine the success of the professional writer. To paraphrase Niklas Luhmann, while the medium of scholarship is looking for the truth or a scientific explanation, or in the case of the writer, aiming at a 'true' (but somehow unachievable) description of reality, the medium and means of appreciation of the public is applause – the dilemma, of course, being that one rarely gets applause for understanding, telling or revealing 'the truth'. Obviously, seeking truth(s) demands

---

the only difference being perhaps their different ideological backgrounds. Again, a small minority group wants to 'liberate' the majority population from its 'moral downfall' and its 'complicity' with the powers that be.

a completely different set of attitudes and practices, and aiming for widespread public acknowledgment is not one of them (although fame can occasionally be a by-product of good research or scholarship). One way of evading such apparent contradictions is, of course, to concentrate one's energy and motivation and apply them to one field only. In other words, seeking refuge in specialization becomes a realistic option. The price, however, is the retreat of the scholar and researcher from engaging with the larger public sphere.

The engagement of the old-type intellectual rested on three pillars: ideology, an orientation towards the public at large, and the need for subsidies. Each of these pillars began to deteriorate and to crumble during the course of the twentieth century. Ideologies lost their appeal, mass culture diversified the public and created a larger spectrum of voices; finally, the economic base for independent middle-class existences disappeared during recurrent economic crises. However, the new haven for intellectuals, the world of higher education into which even the majority of professional writers now escapes from time to time (or sometimes even permanently) experienced fundamental changes too. Differentiations took place inside all levels of universities, research and scholarship – no stone remained unturned, no department unchanged.[4] As a result, scholars and researchers are now confronted with an increased level of complexity in terms of both defining and finding their role *vis-à-vis* the public and in terms of what is expected of them as full-time university employees. In the first quarter of the twentieth century, university professors could still remain in their proverbial ivory tower, ignoring demands from the outside world or speaking out only if they felt that it was the right moment to do so. If a professor actually spoke to the larger audience beyond the classroom, he could be sure that his authority was never challenged. At a later stage, however, changes in the organization of the scholarly environment forced professors to transgress the boundaries of their professional world when making public announcements; now, they would often find themselves in the position of having to legitimize their status and their views. As a result, particularly the more scientific-oriented disciplines developed specific patterns of dealing with non-academic audiences[5].

The most common relationship with the outside world was and still remains the surveillance and major funding authority, in Europe usually located in ministries or other parts of the state apparatus. In countries with a larger share of private universities, the surveillance authority is usually exhibited by boards of overseers, trustees and so on. Originally, the state provided all the means university professors needed, but step by step, other actors entered the field. Funding bodies such as philanthropic foundations offered additional means for research. Since modern research consists mainly of team efforts – the idea of the lone scholar is not dead yet, but is an outgoing model at least in terms of big funding schemes – the new spenders become even more influential because team effort also means requesting

4 Only the German *Lehrkanzel* survived.

5 Stephen Hawking would be a representative figure in this respect.

and receiving more money. Funding team projects means that contracts have to be carefully negotiated and rules and regulations have to be followed. This in turn means interacting and liaising regularly with people outside the traditional realm of scholarly work. Whereas state or supra-national funding bodies define the wider research agendas while leaving space for individual or group researchers in that they do not set or define all aspects of the research, most of the new funding bodies give money only to well-defined endeavours that are usually to be completed within clearly specified periods. The drift is clear: team effort, outside funding, big science – goals which all reinforce each other and lead not only to a different kind of research but also to a different kind of engagement. A discipline or a particular department can indeed look very different if their leading members are successful in securing such funds. A further effect of this increase in funding opportunities is not only that scholars of one discipline are in competition with each other, but also that there is now also increased competition between neighbouring disciplines, with all the various consequences this entails, such as new role expectations but also new disciplinary hierarchies, envy or misunderstood pride.

New relations between academia and the business world emerged when scientific disciplines either teamed up with or even established themselves as enterprises mainly for the purpose of soliciting patents and/or exploiting intellectual copyrights. Some of these new enterprises were more successful than others, but the important thing to bear in mind in this context is that these new kinds of relationships also impacted on and shaped the functioning of the intellectual process and the disciplines involved. New campus enterprises expect that contractually bound research results or products remain their sole property. Rarely is the public at large aware of those products, although the former helps to fund the latter indirectly through taxpayers' money. The outcome is obvious. We are dealing here with the private appropriation of (partly) publicly funded knowledge. As if that was not problematic enough, very often researchers who are subcontracted as partners are also prohibited from disseminating or sharing their knowledge and their findings with colleagues and the wider scientific community. What stands out here are the influence and power that one sphere (the privately funded enterprise) exercises and holds over and against another (the publicly funded higher education sector and its intellectual workforce). The state or the government that often functions as a mediator or facilitator complicates matters, but does not take away from the fact that this is basically a deeply uneven relationship in which the private enterprise sets the agenda, controls the process and determines what to do with the final product, while the intellectual workforce, albeit at times without enthusiasm, follows and executes the enterprise's will. In terms of seeing those researchers ever engaging critically in the public sphere, the chances seem minimal. Almost by definition, they have become more interested in the sales of their intellectual products than in a genuine public discussion or the distribution of knowledge. Some may be highly visible in the media, but they appear to approach the larger audience in a purely instrumental way, to raise their own prestige and to attract more research funds from public authorities.

The social sciences and those scholars and researchers who still see themselves as intellectuals are in a particularly complicated position *vis-à-vis* potential 'customers' or 'clients' because their ability to feed the wider public's curiosity has, as a result of the changes outlined above, become somehow limited. In the eyes of the public, the social sciences are further undermined by the very fact that they lack an overall consensus. Social sciences and sociology in particular are fragmented enterprises, divided into rivalling schools and approaches. Furthermore, simplifying things is certainly not an attitude that one can encounter when sociologists meet in public. Even worse, those sociologists who regularly contribute to public debates often suffer a decline in terms of their scholarly reputation.[6]

Be all this as it may, and even with all restrictions, ifs and buts, there are still intellectuals who engage in the public sphere. A brief analysis of the various shades and engagements of the public intellectual might help us to understand the complexities involved.[7] The role of the modern intellectual usually encompasses a set of different roles. Each role segment offers, so to speak, some 'rewards', but it also involves some difficulties. The most uncontroversial role is that of the expert. The expert interacts primarily with a set of well-defined players, either from the private or the public sector, or with the media as a commentator on a specific range of issues related to the expertise in question. Major entrepreneurs as well as the media have a strong interest in securing the reputation of the expert because expert knowledge means first and foremost generating or securing authority through credibility. Counsellors and consultants are special cases of this category of experts. Their activity and advice are usually hidden from the wider audience. They are in a way more privatized versions of experts, because they counsel clients exclusively. As a rule, both types of experts provide recommendations towards public policies and avoid what intellectuals regularly do, namely criticizing a given social, political or even cultural condition. As long as experts are giving advice in one policy field only, they can secure their public and scholarly reputation much better than those generalists who critically comment on broader societal conditions.

Experts who leave their narrowly defined fields of competence and offer comprehensive or holistic solutions encounter much stronger responses from other experts, from politicians connected with opposition parties, and the media. The broader an expert's portfolio, the more visible he or she becomes. Professor X is then not only the expert for the reform of the higher education system, but a panellist at the Annual Meeting of an Academy of Fine Arts, regularly writes op-ed commentaries in a widely circulated newspaper, shows up on talk shows, can be persuaded by a publisher to exchange letters with another intellectual or artistic celebrity, earns honorary degrees, and so on. This trajectory of becoming a public

---

6 The examples of Daniel Bell, Ralf Dahrendorf, Ulrich Beck or Anthony Giddens come to mind here.

7 Still readable descriptions of the newly emerging role of the expert can be found in C. Wright Mills's essay collection *Power, Politics, and People* (1963), see particularly 292–304, 405–22 and 599–613.

figure resembles a one-person Matthew effect, almost like an elevator that only knows one direction – upwards.[8] Today the 'public intellectual' role has its dark side too, because of the time limit public figures experience. The expiry dates of public intellectuals comes much faster than those of the scholars, the shelf life of the ideas and publications of the latter definitely lasts longer. The power of the media in its various guises to make or break public intellectuals has greatly increased and is likely to continue and expand.

Experts with a broad portfolio cannot be easily distinguished from public intellectuals, and as a matter of fact, for the audience they often resemble one another, sometimes even to the point of becoming identical. This identical perception reminds us that any public intellectual actually needs to be an expert in something. Strong convictions and fine prose are not enough, and it seems that this distinguishes classical intellectuals from the new type of public intellectuals. Whereas the former needed nothing more than conviction and style, the latter need to speak with some scientific or expert authority.

Evaluation of contributions of expert-intellectuals follows two conflicting patterns. Expert proposals become criticized either according to the terms of scholarship or those of politics. The more a suggested remedy contradicts the political convictions of other experts or interested parties, the more the scholarly standing of the experts will be challenged. The best antidote against annoying policies is to question the scientific fundament on which suggestions have been built. On the other hand, in the case of challenging the scholarly reputation of someone who is not only a social scientist but also a public intellectual, it is sometimes appropriate to say that the person in question no longer takes part in real research, has lost track with developments in the field in which he purports to be knowledgeable, holds outdated views, and so on. However, one also has to concede that the demands experienced by public intellectuals can sometimes be so intense that remaining an active researcher is almost impossible (for more details, see Zuckerman, 1979).

Two crucial incentives to perform the role of public intellectual are that the financial reward can be very high and that status gratification follows almost instantly. While in the past it was not unheard of for a scholar or researcher to

8 There is, however, nothing more embarrassing than having made it to the top and then have nothing more to say, either because one has spent all his intellectual energy and capital and only repeats what everybody knows already, or because one has been found out – that is, the intellectual in question has turned out to be a non-reasoning propagandist or simply a hypocrite who does not act upon his or her own teachings. Noam Chomsky would be a prime example for the first case (nothing new to say); Peter Handke taking sides in the case of the Serbian perpetrators is an illustration of the latter scenario of the propagandist, while Günter Grass and Zygmunt Bauman could serve as prime examples of being hypocrites because of their negative, if not to say embarrassing response concerning the revelations about and discussions of their respective pasts (Grass having been a member of the SS and Bauman a Stalinist informer and agent).

be acknowledged and celebrated only once he or she had passed away (Walter Benjamin is such a case), nowadays the celebrity status of a mass media guru can be reached in a relatively short period. Of course, only a few intellectuals reach this level of appreciation, but the incentives for trying are strong, and the rewards (money and fame) can be reaped immediately.[9]

The last point brings us finally to the topic of the modern mass media and the changing public sphere, and the influence both have on intellectuals. Let us take, for example, the cases of Max Weber and Emile Durkheim. Both acted in the public sphere, but at the time this sphere consisted only of some newspapers and magazines, public appearances in front of a few people, to whom one could speak using one's voice in a shared language of scholarship, and conversations with a handful of public figures who sought advice. There was no telephone, no radio, no TV, no easy-to-use public transport, not to mention Websites, online discussion groups devoted to particular thinkers, and the chance to travel to any place worldwide within 24 hours. Besides the multiplicity of media options, the world of mass media radically transformed the role of public intellectuals. The public to whom one speaks today consists of several audiences, only with a few of whom a speaker might be familiar with regard to their expectations, knowledge and familiarity with one's own thinking. Therefore, voicing ideas can have its communication and transmission problems, probably more so today than in the past. Below the surface of cosmopolitanism, local or subjective knowledge still continues to play a crucial role and mistakes, either on the side of the sender or the recipients, are almost inevitable. The multiplicity of media and places where public intellectuals are visible can sometimes cause severe dissonances. It also puts a premium on the ability to communicate in a popular and accessible style, not always easy when it comes to complex social problems and questions.

The critical attitude exhibited by what has traditionally been referred to as intellectuals lies at the core of their self-understanding. This deserves some closer examination. Over the last hundred years, the majority of intellectuals were on the political left. Their criticism was rooted in the tradition of the Enlightenment; however, some intellectuals developed and used a rather exotic rhetoric and somehow lost the sensibility or capacity to reach out beyond a narrow circle of followers. A feeling of isolation and alienation on the side of those who claimed to offer sound interpretations of the present occurred, which in turn led to further radicalization, sometimes to such an extent that the space ship of critical attitudes lost contact with the Mother Earth of knowledge and scholarship. Antonio Gramsci's organic intellectual, embedded in a social movement, can be found less in those politically challenging constellations Gramsci actually had in mind when he conceived his idea of the organic intellectual than in societies with a relatively high degree of normative integration. In other words, successful intellectuals

9 While in the past intellectuals mainly addressed a national audience, some public intellectuals have now attained such fame that they can reach out to a continental and on occasion – such as the World Social Forum – even a global audience.

were always embedded in their society's cultural and political life. The story of the Myrdals as public intellectuals is so convincing because it shows that getting the message through to both the people and the politicians needs some kind of embeddedness in one's own society. (Michael Walzer has made the same point; Walzer, 1987 and 1988.)

This short overview about some aspects of the old and new role of the public intellectual cannot explain comprehensively all aspects of that complicated relationship between intellectuals and the public. However, we hope that we have provided the reader with some basic ideas. Perhaps the frame itself must be reformulated and refined in response to a changing role and faced with new and pressing social and political circumstances. We hope the reader will share with the editors the excitement of gaining new insights from the contributions to this volume.

The contributions which follow are organized according to a three-step logic ('provocations' – 'complications' – 'case studies'). Seen collectively, the contributors are social scientists broadly speaking; individually speaking, they might see themselves as sociologists, historians, anthropologists, political scientists or they come from some other related discipline and sub-discipline. Whichever label applies and whatever the epistemological vantage point, the contributions reflect the need for an ongoing cross-disciplinary social science debate about the changing and contested role of social knowledge in the civic and public sphere.

Reflecting on the tasks and role of public intellectuals from a social science perspective, the opening discussion in Part One starts with some provocative statements and questions. Our first three contributors, Jeffrey C. Alexander, Mary Evans and Joseba Zulaika, raise crucial questions that go to the very heart of the notion, role and functioning of public intellectuals. In his historical-theoretical reflection 'Public Intellectuals and Civil Society', Jeffrey C. Alexander notes that the public intellectual's role has become fundamental to the civil repair of modern societies. It is rooted in the first public sphere that emerged in Athens, and in the iconic figure of Socrates. These secular origins became folded into the Judeo-Christian trope of prophetic judgement. Public intellectuals criticize society on behalf of the putative, and necessarily unrealized, solidarity that underlies the civil-public sphere, and they do so by pronouncements that refer to the power of truth. Being a public intellectual must be understood performatively. It is an expressive figure organized in sub-genres formed by such political traditions as the revolutionary, reformist, conservative and counter-revolutionary, but it has also expressed itself in the figure of the public psychotherapist initiated by Freud. In real historical time, however, the performance of public intellectual is not as transcendental as it seems. As much denunciation and demonization as idealistic and inspiring, public intellectual discourse engages the binary, bifurcating discourse of civil society. Even while promoting civil repair, public intellectual performance becomes a vehicle for carrying out the excluding and stigmatizing boundary enforcement that also characterizes every civil society.

In the second contribution, Mary Evans asks a question that has been around ever since the term 'intellectual' was first coined: 'Can Women Be Intellectuals?' Referring to Virginia Woolf, Evans questions the degree to which women can maintain for themselves independence from those institutions which have been instrumental in maintaining male dominance. Woolf was writing at a time when women were fighting to obtain access to higher education and the professions, but she realized that the cost of achieving this access was collusion with the values of those institutions. However, Evans's contribution is not primarily concerned with the dominance of one gender in institutional contexts, rather it addresses the gendered dynamic of intellectual life. The 'discovery' of sex differences in the eighteenth century in one sense enlarged the world for women since it allowed them to claim a particular space, yet at the same time it arguably established a pattern in which women have been confined either to the articulation or the defence of women's particularity. When we consider the past two hundred years of intellectual life, we can now perhaps look back and see not the emancipation of women – and certainly not the intellectual emancipation of women – but a much more complex process in which the qualities of masculinity and femininity have become reified into intellectual standards and expectations, leaving little space for that openness of thought and imagination which Woolf wished to defend.

Our third provocative piece comes from Joseba Zulaika. In his contribution, entitled 'Terrorism and the Betrayal of the Intellectuals', Zulaika looks at the current terrorism discourse, and particularly the complex and often problematic role that intellectuals play in that discourse. Zulaika asks what one can do, as an intellectual, when the primary community to which one belongs (family, friends, village, country, occupation) produces terrorists? What exactly is the intellectual task? Should it be to define them, to diagnose them, to condemn them, to persuade them, to understand them, to exorcize them? Should one look at the situation as tragedy, irony, farce, romance or sheer crime? Whether in the Basque Country, Ireland or the United States, intellectual approaches to terrorism are of necessity enmeshed in the writer's self-definitions and ideological investments. Zulaika further questions whether there is a sense in which expertise on the terrorist Other presupposes acceptance of the logic of taboo and wilful ignorance of the actual life conditions of the subjects of research. Zulaika concludes that different readings and approaches to the phenomenon of terrorism are likely to produce antagonistic intellectuals.

The second part of this volume addresses some of the complex issues about which public intellectuals often get passionately exercised. First, William Outhwaite looks at how public intellectuals have shaped and responded to civil society debates. In his contribution, 'European Civil Society and the European Intellectual', he asks: 'What is, and how does one become, a European intellectual?' Outhwaite attempts to relate the idea of the intellectual in contemporary Europe to discussions of the eventual (in either sense of the term) existence of a European civil society or public sphere. He takes a limited informal sample of sociologists and other intellectuals and explores the dimensions of their pan-European resonance and the extent to which this is facilitated or hindered by media, academic and cultural structures.

In her contribution, 'What Influence? Public Intellectuals, the State and Civil Society', E. Stina Lyon addresses the issue of the relationship that exists between public intellectuals, the state and civil society and the production and interpretations of 'social knowledge'. Sociologists, Lyon argues, have since the inception of the discipline been influential agents in the public domain beyond academe in a variety of ways: as politicians, government advisers, social researchers on government-funded projects, critical writers and paradigm shifters, public orators, propagandists for social movements and voluntary organizations, teachers and activists. Lyon's argument starts with the assumption that what constitutes 'social knowledge' in the public domain has over time, and place, been a contested issue with power over its collection, interpretation and dissemination shifting between the state, civil society and the public, each variably receptive to and supportive of exposure, criticism or advocacy by public intellectuals. Lyon then outlines some of the different types of public 'connectivity' that create public platforms, and their implications for sociological influence in these different domains. She argues that the often lamented demise of the public intellectual, the 'man of knowledge' as understood in the past, can from within such a framework be seen as a less interesting question for sociologists when compared with and juxtaposed to attempts to articulate what kinds of sociological intellectuals are needed in the public sphere at present, and how and why they should be supported.

In his chapter 'Public Intellectuals, East and West: Jan Patočka and Václav Havel in Contention with Maurice Merleau-Ponty and Slavoj Žižek', Stefan Auer takes the complex relationship between the state, knowledge and intellectuals a step further. One would think that intellectuals are ideally suited to make a valuable contribution to the political life of their societies. However, more often than not, observes Auer, even the wisest among them have failed dismally. Intellectual sophistication offered no reliable protection against political idiocy. The contention of Auer's contribution is that dissident intellectuals in Central and Eastern Europe proved to be more prudent in their political judgements about important issues of their time than their Western counterparts. To give substance to this argument, Auer restricts himself to a sample of representative figures (Czesław Miłosz, Jan Patočka, Václav Havel *contra* Maurice Merleau-Ponty, Jean-Paul Sartre, Slavoj Žižek) and some key issues, such as their views on power and violence. Auer uses Hannah Arendt as a moderator in this fictional debate.

Auer's discussion clearly points towards those debates that are associated with the fall of the Berlin Wall. Anson Rabinbach takes this event as his starting point too, but gives it a different historical twist and treatment. In 'Public Intellectuals and Totalitarianism: A Century's Debate', he looks at how, since the fall of communism, both the word and to a somewhat lesser extent the concept of totalitarianism has made a significant, and some would argue permanent, comeback. During the 1990s, historians, as Ian Kershaw noted, have been compelled 'to examine with fresh eyes the comparison between Stalinism and Nazism'. More recently, in the atmosphere of heated controversy during the debate prior to the war in Iraq, a number of distinguished commentators once again embraced the word 'totalitarian', extending its scope beyond the historical dictatorships of the 1930s and 1940s to include regimes and movements in the Middle East. Rabinbach asks, 'Why does the comparison between Stalinist communism and Nazism still continue to produce offence or provoke fervour? Can "totalitarianism" serve both as exoneration and as a way of amplifying guilt, as apologia and indictment, depending on how closely the speaker's position might be identified with the victims or perpetrators?' As Rabinbach points out, totalitarianism has always been a protean term, capable of combining and re-combining meanings in different contexts and in new and ever-changing political constellations. A powerful reason for the persistence of 'totalitarianism' can be found in the historicity of the term itself, the importance of 'moments' of totalitarianism, rather than in its conceptual validity, its intellectual 'origins' or its 'heuristic' value. The 'moment' of totalitarian performs a well-established rhetorical political function, defining a horizon of cognitive and intellectual orientations that sharpen oppositions, at the expense of obscuring moral and political ambiguities. As Walter Laqueur shrewdly observed more than two decades ago, the debate over totalitarianism has never been a purely academic enterprise. It has, as Rabinbach concludes, also been about an intensely political concept, defining the nature of enmity for the Western democracies for more than half a century.

Whereas the function of Part One was to raise crucial questions about the tasks and roles of public intellectuals and Part Two dealt with complex and complicated issues linked to those tasks and roles, Part Three consists of case studies in which some of the most prominent public intellectuals and their role and function are being investigated in detail. Some of the greatest public intellectuals actually fulfilled that function before the term 'intellectual' had been coined, as the first two intellectual case studies about Alexis de Tocqueville and his companion Gustave de Beaumont show.

In 'Tocqueville as a Public Intellectual', John Torpey demonstrates that Tocqueville's *oeuvre* admits of a considerable variety of interpretations, is politically polyvocal, and has been enormously influential in the United States and around the world. Despite this massive resonance, Tocqueville's writings are simply not regarded today as crucial to the training of professional sociologists – as opposed to well-read undergraduates or scholars of other kindred disciplines. Torpey argues that Tocqueville's stature as a public intellectual, his apparent concern with countries rather than concepts, and his presumed failure to live up to twentieth-century standards of scientific rigour has left him out of the sociological canon. At the same time, his views on intellectuals have been in line with relatively conservative thinking about the politics of that group that is unappealing to sociologists with world-transforming ambitions. Yet his understanding of the politics of intellectuals is rather more sociological in character than those of Marx. Ultimately, argues Torpey, Tocqueville should be seen as a kind of modern-day Stoic in the mould of Max Weber – someone who regarded certain changes as unstoppably afoot in modern society, whether he liked them or not, and who saw it as his task to make sense of those changes and to do what he could to moderate their more extreme effects.

While *Democracy in America* and its author Alexis de Tocqueville achieved prominent intellectual status, very little is known about his colleague and companion Gustave de Beaumont. In their contribution, 'Tocqueville's Dark Shadow: Gustave de Beaumont as Public Sociologist and Intellectual *Avant la Lettre*', Tom Garvin and Andreas Hess briefly sketch out Beaumont's achievements as a public intellectual in the liberal French tradition who was also an internationalist-minded political sociologist preoccupied with the darker side of societal and political conditions in the United States, France and the United Kingdom and Ireland. While Garvin and Hess's historical reconstruction acknowledges Beaumont's special relationship with Tocqueville, they also argue that there were important differences between the two. This becomes particularly obvious with Beaumont's *Ireland* book. The authors conclude that it is not only important to acknowledge Beaumont as a public sociologist and intellectual *avant la lettre*, they also argue that it is a liberal conception of public sociology – like that of Tocqueville and Beaumont – which is needed at present but which seems to be missing from current debates.

The remainder of Part Three consists mainly of case studies that differ from the more historical Tocqueville and Beaumont studies in that they discuss more contemporary figures and their reputation and public role. The first attempt is that of Laurent Jeanpierre and Sébastien Mosbah-Natanson. In their contribution, 'French Sociologists and the Public Space of the Press: Thoughts Based on a Case Study (*Le Monde*, 1995–2002)', Jeanpierre and Natanson provide a contemporary sociological description and analysis of open editorial pages of France's main national daily newspaper, *Le Monde*. They reason that in France the social sciences have become increasingly the base from which to launch a career as a public intellectual. However, they also argue that the career of the public intellectual and the career of the scientist are clearly differentiated. The majority of the columns written by French intellectuals in the daily press are general viewpoints. They often deal with foreign policy and international problems with no relation whatsoever with the specific professional skills of the writer. The authors conclude by offering a typology of public intellectuals in the press consisting of the universal specialist, the spokesperson, and the specialist who can sometimes be an expert.

In our next case study, 'You Only See What You Reckon You Know: Max and Marianne Weber in the United States of America at the Turn of the Twentieth Century', Dirk Kaesler discusses whether the American experience of Max Weber impacted on his work. Kaesler maintains that the sociologist already had everything worked out about the United States before actually visiting the country, and that the trip functioned more as *post festum* affirmation of the theory than as a completely new experience that would then be conceptualized. Kaesler also maintains that this finding does not take away from Weber's genuine intellectual insight into the functioning of American society. In contrast, it just affirms how intellectually well prepared Weber was before making the Atlantic journey. Kaesler concludes that Weber did not only get America 'right', but that he actually turned out to be a sociological prophet in regard to the future course of American society and politics.

In his case study 'Towards a Sociology of Intellectual Styles of Thought: Differences and Similarities in the Thought of Theodor W. Adorno and Jürgen Habermas', Stefan Müller-Doohm takes a closer look at the function of intellectual style of thought for the public sphere, where we uncover a somewhat surprising feature that is common to Theodor W. Adorno and Jürgen Habermas. While it is true that for Adorno the notion that the process of negation that has dissent as its goal is crucial, Habermas's form of critique is inspired by the idea of communication which – in the best case – can culminate in agreement. But in both men, the appellative function of intellectual critique, whether it addresses morally sensitive subjects, as in Adorno's case, or a politically functioning public sphere, as with Habermas, points to the agonal positionality of the intellectual style of thought. Agonality, in which the battle for meaning is the defining feature of the intellectual style of thought, finds its expression whenever commonly accepted views, convictions, institutional preconceptions and tendencies become the objects of contestation. As an agonal form, Müller-Doohm argues, intellectual critique is an 'incompetent but legitimate form of criticism' (Lepsius), and it follows from this that agonality is an interpersonal characteristic of the intellectual style of thought. It may make its appearance in finely graded and highly divergent versions: in Adorno's case as agonality with the goal of dissent, in that of Habermas as agonality with the goal of deliberation.

Earlier, in Part One of this volume, Mary Evans asks whether there can be women intellectuals. In his detailed study 'Women as Public Intellectuals: Kerstin Hesselgren and Alva Myrdal', Per Wisselgren looks at two of the foremost Swedish intellectuals, both of them women. Wisselgren shows in detailed fashion how Alva Myrdal and Kerstin Hesselgren have influenced public debate and public policies. The aim of Wisselgren's contribution is to argue for the need for a more gender-sensitive understanding of public intellectuals. The first section of the chapter problematizes the concept of the public intellectual in itself; the author points at its inherent ambiguity, historical situatedness and gendered bias. In the second section, this discussion is empirically substantiated by analysing and contextually comparing two of Sweden's most prominent intellectual women in the first half of the twentieth century. Wisselgren pays particular attention to the historically changing spheres of social research, social reform and the public. He concludes that a substantial part of the answer to the question concerning the lack of women among public intellectuals is to be found in exactly those very academic spheres in which traditionally gendered institutional barriers prevailed.

In our final case study, 'How Hayek Managed to Beat Lazarsfeld: The Different Perception of Two Sub-fields of Social Science', Werner Reichmann and Markus Schweiger compare and contrast the work and impact of two different public intellectuals. In their study, Reichmann and Schweiger argue that as academic disciplines, sociology and economics took off almost at the same time. More specifically, in the 1920s business cycle research institutes were founded that enriched economics with very empirical and quantitative works. Around the same time, applied and empirical social research emerged. Comparing the development of the two disciplinary sub-fields, one can observe the existence of many similarities and differences, continuities and discontinuities that finally led to completely different receptions and positions. However, the applied economists were in many respects more successful than the empirical social researchers. The direct comparison and juxtaposition shows that F.A. Hayek, the first scientific leader of the Viennese business cycle research institute, had a much greater impact than Paul F. Lazarsfeld, who is regarded as the founder of empirical applied social research. It is ironic that the intellectual heritage of the less politically engaged researcher Hayek now has much more political influence than the very ideologically driven sociological work of Lazarsfeld. Judging by such perceptions and results, the authors legitimately ask, 'Which factors contribute to making one particular field of scientific work successful and public more respected than another?'

The volume concludes with some reflections by Howard Davis. In 'Revisiting the Concept of the Public Intellectual', the author reconsiders and discusses the strengths and limitations of the various conceptualizations and notions of the public intellectual presented in this volume.

References

Burawoy, Michael (2005), 'Presidential Address: For Public Sociology', *American Sociological Review* 70:1, 4–28.

Charle, Christophe (1996), *Les intellectuals en Europe au XIX siècle* (Paris: Editions du Seuil).

Collini, Stefan (2006), *Absent Minds: Intellectuals in Britain* (Oxford: Oxford University Press).

Coser, Lewis A. (1965), *Men of Ideas* (New York: The Free Press).

Deutsch, Karl W., Platt, John R. and Senghaas, Dieter (1986) 'Major Advances in the Social Sciences Since 1900: An Analysis of Conditions and Effects of Creativity', in *Advances in the Social Sciences, 1900–1980: What, Who, Where, How?* (Cambridge, MA: Abt Books).

Dosse, François (2003), *La marche des idées* (Paris: Éditions La Découverte).

Mills, C. Wright (1963) *Power, Politics, and People* (New York: Oxford University Press).

Walzer, Michael (1987), *Interpretation and Social Criticism* (Cambridge, MA: Harvard University Press).

Walzer, Michael (1988), *The Company of Critics* (New York: Basic Books).

Zuckerman, Harriet (1979), *Scientific Elite: Nobel Laureates in the United States* (New York: Free Press).

PART ONE
PROVOCATIONS

Chapter 1
Public Intellectuals and Civil Society

Jeffrey C. Alexander

In the title to this volume, we find the key words 'public' and 'intellectual'. Both refer to separation and universality, to the capacity for judgement that emerges from the status of being separate and the capacity for universalism.

According to philosophical convention, the public is a space separated from the immediate, particularistic demands, and also the resources, of organizations. It is a space outside of them, in which people can – indeed, are compelled to – exercise their reason, as Kant said, or in Habermas's terms, engage in unfettered critical discourse. The public is, however, something else as well; it is the imagined and widely inclusive community that is both implied and constructed by such putative reasoners and discoursers, the civil sphere evoked by critics and sometimes loyalists as a counterpoint to demands of the market, the state, religion and family.[1]

Intellectuals are actors who can exercise judgement because they themselves are free-floating, independent of particular commitments. They are defined as those motivated by such general categories as justice and truth. They make statements on behalf of humanity, in order to serve Rousseau's general will, the real interests of which everyday actors, because they are prone to bias or irrationality, are not themselves consciously aware. In theoretical terms, then, 'intellectuals' and 'public' are concepts that go hand in hand. This is true in sociological and historical terms as well. The emergence of the public sphere corresponds with the rise of intellectuals.

Structural Analysis: Origins in Ancient Greece and Prophetic Religion

Ancient Greece was where the *polis* first emerged and from which the term 'public' first came into being. The *polis* was, literally, a separate sphere of activity, peopled by every adult male who was not a foreigner or a slave. It was held to constitute the community of the city state, whose activity was discourse, reasoning, rhetoric, argument, and of course, voting, and via delegation, governing.

---

1 I am not entirely happy with the 'public' as a sociological-cum-philosophical category, but I will not pursue these reservations here. In formal terms, however, I would prefer to employ the hyphenated term 'civil-public' in any discourse about public intellectuals (see Alexander, 2006).

Once an actual place, since its demise the *polis* has been a myth, a regulating idea. At the centre of this myth has been an intellectual, Socrates. Socrates was a real person, but we know him only through Plato's construction. As we learn about him in the dialogues, Socrates is the man of truth, who speaks from total disinterest, as an individual with no attachments of a particularistic sort – friendship, *oikos*, city-patriotism, passion. The objective truth-teller, he embodies the ethics of the public sphere. He died because he refused to stop speaking the truth against power, to buckle down to the particular will in a time of war. The story about the death of Socrates has always been at the heart of what the ideals of the public, and the obligations of an intellectual, should be.

This 'republican' tradition has exercised extraordinary power over the last 2500 years. It is noteworthy, and unfortunate, that this legacy was slighted by our discipline's greatest historical and comparative thinker, Max Weber. Still, we can work out what the relation between the Weberian and Socratic understandings of public intellectuals might be. Weber provides a broad religious-cum-cultural understanding of why the West has been so responsive to the myth of public intellectuals and rational-critical judgement. It has been so, he attests, because of the new role of prophecy, which emerged with ancient Judaism and was institutionalized first in Christianity, and later, and much more emphatically, in Protestantism.

In the Weberian scheme, prophets are the religious equivalents of intellectuals. In contrast with public intellectuals, prophets were motivated by *a priori* religious commitments. Yet the abstracted and transcendental status of these beliefs allowed independence and critical distance from the more particularistic institutions, organizations and conventions of the day. It is not entirely surprising, then, that Shmuel Eisenstadt made use of Weber's comparative religion theory to explain the historical rise of the intellectuals in the different civilizations of the Axial Age (see Eisenstadt 1982).

There seems little doubt that Weber implicitly, and Eisenstadt explicitly, are right. The modern public intellectual is, in fact, also a prophet.[2] The performative understanding of 'intellectual' has depended, since the Christian and Roman mixing of the Jewish and Greek, on the background script of prophecy, especially the thundering Old Testament kind.

---

2 It is, none the less, a great misfortune that the Weberian tradition did not itself connect its religious sociology to the origins of philosophy and reason in the Greek public sphere, and it is to Parsons' great credit that he tried to do so, most notably in his *Societies: Evolutionary and Comparative Perspectives* (Parsons, 1966). That Weber himself did not do so betrays his ambivalence about the democratic tradition. He saw prophets not only as the first intellectuals, but also as the first demagogues, and tended to equate modern mass democracy with plebiscitary Caesarism – far from the Socratic ideal.

The Performative Dimension

Before discussing modern examples of public intellectuals and their relationship to the civil-public sphere, I need to introduce one more analytical consideration. What I have presented so far is a 'structural' analysis of the institutional and culture conditions for the emergence of public intellectuals. But the role of public intellectual must also be performed. To be a public intellectual is a matter of making and of convincing. In John Austin's terms, 'public intellectual' is not just constative and descriptive, but connotative and subjunctive. Being a public intellectual is not only locutionary, a matter of linguistic definition, but illocutionary and perlocutionary, a matter of doing things with words. As a performative, it is not just role-taking but role-making.[3]

A good example of this distinction can be found in the life of the great French sociologist Pierre Bourdieu. Throughout most of his career, Bourdieu was content to be a sociologist-intellectual. He pursued the truth through empirical and theoretical studies, studies whose normative reference was the deficits in the modern civil-public sphere. In France, the audiences for Bourdieu's sociology extended into the non-academic public sphere. According to the perspective I am developing here, however, Bourdieu did not become a public intellectual until, in the last decade of his life, he published *La Misère du Monde*, made regular appearances on French television, and ostentatiously associated with *Le Monde Diplomatique* and the ultra-left Gauchist movement that opposed the French Socialist Party and its so-called neo-liberal policies.

Being a public intellectual, in other words, is not just a matter of telling the truth and of being separate and free-floating and truly representing the universal. It is a matter of performing as if one were all these things. Being a public intellectual is symbolic action, a matter of becoming what Emerson called a 'representative man'. To become exemplary in this manner is to dramatically embody the myth of universalism, the binary code of public versus private, and the narrative of progressive triumph.

We know, of course, that this is not how Plato wished to understand Socrates, and certainly it does not accord with the Socratic myth. According to Plato, Socrates hated 'rhetoric'. In the *Gorgias*, Socrates railed against rhetoricians, accusing them, in contemporary terms, of being public relations flacks or spin doctors. He maintained that philosophers spoke truth, that only they had the courage to face facts, and that their influence rested entirely upon their ability to present rational and logical deductions and empirical inductions based on observations. As Detective Joe Friday used to say on the American television drama *Dragnet*: 'We want the facts, ma'am, only the facts.'

3 This is Ralph Turner's early symbolic interactionist distinction, which indicates the influence of Erving Goffman on his thinking, and in this sense the role of performance philosophy and theory *avant la lettre*.

Plato distrusted fiction and mimesis of all kinds. But here we cannot follow either Socrates or Plato. Did not Socrates himself have a 'style'? Was he himself not dramatic and persuasive? On his daily trips throughout the Athenian marketplace, did he not wish to grab and hold the attention of his fellow citizens, to draw an audience around him? Was he not himself surrounded by a supporting cast? Rhetorical performance, in other words, was central to the very origins of the public intellectual. Teachers and schools of rhetoric emerged in Athens, after all, at the very same time as did the new philosophers of truth. Their aim was to allow speakers in the *polis* to be more persuasive, and thus more effective, to supply them with the performative capacity to exercise more illocutionary and perlocutionary force.

How much more performative has been the 'public intellectual' in the millennia since the Greeks. As mythical figures, Socrates and the Old Testament prophets are the principal protagonists in a narrative script that has displayed an extraordinary reproductive power. In this script, the ancient republic is presented as a golden age, in relation to which public intellectuals measure the decline of the civil sphere in modern days.

The Socratic sense of truth-telling as purely constative, as non-performative rational judgement, is a form of philosophical false consciousness which has created problems of self-understanding for modern public intellectuals, and thus, in some instances, for the ideals of intellectuals to have public effect. It is often suggested, for example, that the rational presentation of objective and unbiased knowledge can, and should, be the basis for effective entry into the public sphere.[4] Nothing could be further from the truth. Public intellectuals need to connect with, and speak on behalf of, the great narrative myths of our time, to sing about the possible triumph of progress, to strike the chords of national, regional and ideological myths about equality and democracy. They must strive to become symbolic icons who can embody rationality and universalism in the present day.

The Cry for Civil Repair: Modern Traditions of Public Intellectual Performance

In relation to the civil-public sphere, the role of the public intellectual offers not only the hope but a road map to institutionalizing civil ideals. Ever since their inception, of course, such ideals have been in trouble. They were undermined in

4 This is a major problem in the American sociologist Michael Burawoy's understanding of public intellectuals, which is informed, and deformed, by the Enlightenment, or 'modernist', idea of intellectuals as legislators, as truth-carriers of expert knowledge. As Bauman has suggested, at the core of this latter idea sits an idea of the intellectual as a member of a scientific and objective vanguard. Taken literally, such a particular approach carries some of the elitist dangers that bedeviled left-wing and right-wing revolutionary social movements in the twentieth century.

Ancient Greece, in the Roman republic, in the Renaissance city states. Even as the civil-public sphere first became institutionalized in a national form, by law and democratic procedure, it was accosted on every side, by markets and classes, parties, states, families, religions, regional chauvinism, ethnic and racial ties. To sustain even the semblance of a differentiated and voluntary association of co-operative and deeply identified human beings has been no easy thing. To maintain formal democracies, let alone social democracies, has been perilous, and this is only to speak of conditions inside the nation state. It has been utterly impossible between them.

Such difficulties, and their fateful and often fatal consequences, have created audiences eager for public intellectual performance. Demanding that the fragmented solidarity of the civil sphere be repaired, public intellectuals defend the integrity of, and outline the possibilities for, a more civil society. Their performances have two parts. The first identifies 'destructive intrusions' to the civil ideal. The second recommends how the rents in the fabric of civil solidarity can be repaired.

The Revolutionary Tradition

Michael Walzer has described the post-Marion exiles, the Puritans, as the first public intellectuals of the revolutionary tradition (see Walzer, 1965). Inheritors of Weber's prophets, they also created modern empirical science, were strong believers in truth-telling, and intensely committed to democratic and participatory politics. They framed the English revolution in terms of demands for a more level society, denouncing 'Popist' hierarchies, magic and mystery, and what public intellectuals today might call bullshit of all kinds – except, of course, their own. In Puritan literature, these dangers were constructed as destructive intrusions to civil solidarity.

The first liberal democratic theory, such as Locke's, came out of this Puritan tradition, and the English and Scottish democratic theorists of civil society informed what later became French Enlightenment thought. The Philosophes were the first group of secular public intellectuals in the revolutionary tradition, presenting empirical truth as highly corrosive of corrupt kinships, social divisions and dogma. In the name of rationality, they performed denunciation, and created at least the ideological conditions for the first secular and violent social revolution, which began in France in 1789.

By the 1840s, the revolutionary prophecy carried by public intellectuals became translated into the idioms of socialism, symbolized and stimulated by the publication of *The Communist Manifesto*. The fundamental reference of this version of the prophecy remained the same. It was to abolish unequal social divisions, on the one hand, and repressive domination, on the other, so as to stitch back together a more thoroughgoing solidarity. According to this socialist version, such a natural and spontaneous association could be achieved only if economic life were freed from the destructive intrusion of the market.

This originating moment of anti-capitalist public intellectual performance drew from both the Socratic and biblical traditions. The 'young Hegelians' group from which Marx emerged drew on their master's belief in a god-like and immanent reason, which, while historicizing Kant, was also steeped in spiritual understandings of a life-altering other-worldly force. The émigré communist workers who commissioned Marx and Engels to write their *Manifesto* in London were themselves a chiliastic religious brotherhood, rooted in a version primitive Christianity. In their eloquent and stirring manifesto, Marx and Engels combined all this with the highest truth-telling social science of their time, British political economy.

The iconic figure of the revolutionary public intellectual became a myth, and it powerfully buffeted Western societies well into the later days of the next century. This new performative role became reconfigured in other religio-cultural orders that had emerged from the Axial Age. The revolutionary public intellectual became a hero with a thousand faces. He became Mao Zedung, the Leninist neo-Confucian scholar who emerged as the great prophet of the middle kingdom and exercised near god-like performative authority. He became Frantz Fanon, the prophet, philosopher and therapist of civil repair in its anti-colonial form. Fanon's belief in the transformative power of revolutionary violence to repair psyche and society was rooted not only in his experience as a psychiatrist, but in the teachings of Sartre, which derived from, and itself reconstituted, some of the most esoteric, 'separated' and universalizing intellectuality of the century we have only recently left behind.

From Mao and Fanon were derived the whole repertory of 'Third World revolutionaries', the hero prophets from Che Guevara to Subcommander Marcos. The populist leader of the Zapatista rebellion was outed as having once lived as a privileged philosophy graduate student at *Universidad Nacional Autónoma de México*, which explains his confident claims on secular truth. The former student-intellectual Marcos's commitment to the civil repair of Mexico is genuine, but equally so is the Subcommander's performative sense. This pipe-smoking, mask-wearing and manifesto-writing public intellectual is playing a familiar role. Osama Bin Laden presents a more recent, and non-Western, incarnation of this revolutionary tradition. His aim is to repair the solidarity, not of the ancient Greek Republic, but of the ancient Islamic one. Not only is the terrorism of Al Qaeda highly dramaturgical, but the organization has provided a whole series of videotapes and recordings performing denunciation, ever since they broke onto the global stage on 11 September 2001.

The public–intellectual performance of civil repair does not have to be revolutionary. It is more democratic, if not nearly so exciting, when it is reformist. One thinks here of such great public intellectuals as Bentham and Mill in nineteenth-century Britain, and later of the Fabian Society. Such reformist figures and organizations denounced the corruption, repressions and exclusions of modern society, and through their evocative and impassioned roadmaps laid claim to knowledge about how to repair it. John Maynard Keynes was perhaps the most influential reforming public intellectual of the twentieth century. His performance combined brilliant truth-telling with commitments to solidarity and its repair, and the high dudgeon of moral denunciation with ethereal participation in an ideal aesthetic world far removed from everyday modern life. Keynes condemned capitalists for their demonic and irrational 'animal spirits', but he fervently believed in the singular power of capitalist economies to provide the material means that were necessary, in his view, to facilitate the good life.

Other Traditions

It would be fruitful to explore other genres of the public intellectual role. Radical right-wing revolutionaries have been immensely influential public intellectuals, although the *gemeinschaftlich* solidarities they would restore are definitely not of the civil type. Neo-conservatives are today perhaps the most influential public intellectuals of all. Their opponents' representations of neo-conservatives as anti-civil egoists, as concerned only with wealth and power, should be understood as rhetorical deconstruction rather than an empirical interpretation. Like those on the Left, neo-conservative intellectuals derive their power and authority from their defence of the civil sphere and their promise of its repair. They frame the threat to civil solidarity, however, as emanating, not from the market, but from the state, and indeed, from liberal and secular intellectuals themselves. Following such thinkers as Ludwig von Mises, Milton Friedman and Ayn Rand, they see markets as all about freedom and reciprocity, as civil societies in miniature. Against these claims, other neo-conservative public intellectuals, in the spirit of Burke and Oakeshott, have asserted that traditions and traditional authorities are essential if trust is to be restored to civil life.

Nor are the genres of public intellectual performance exclusively political. There is a psychoanalytic tradition of therapist as public teacher that orients itself to the interactional level of civil society. From Freud and Jung to Erik Erikson and Jacques Lacan, these therapist-prophets have tried to restore the subjective capacity for feeling, balance, confidence and rationality. Through their intellectual performances as public therapists, they have tried to save civilization.

Exposing the Public Intellectual as a Private Person: The Dialectic of Denunciation and Repair

Public intellectuals are not as free-floating and universalizing as they think they are or as we might like to be. The civil sphere is instantiated in real time and space, and it is concerned as much with exclusion as inclusion. Civil discourse is binary, promoting not only liberty, but also repression. As iconic figures of the civil sphere, public intellectuals have reflected its embeddedness in race, nation, religion, ethnicity, gender, sex and civilization. Their cries for civil repair have not only extended solidarity by humanizing others, thus allowing emancipation. These cries have also constituted rhetorics of demonization, constructing certain groups as unworthy of inclusion into civil society and thus as candidates of annihilation.

I do not advance this heretical, and perhaps even perverse, argument as a free-floating proposition. Rather, I am putting into a general and sociological form the actual language of public intellectuals themselves, who are forever denouncing one another, and the putative groups and interests the other represents. Intellectuals paint their opponents as uncivil, and thus as unattractive, so as to undermine their effectiveness in the performances of public life. Napoleon did this famously for the French revolutionaries and radical men of letters, calling them not philosophers or intellectuals, but ideologues, chastising them for promoting dogma rather than truth, and accusing them of thinking not about the public, but about themselves. Since that time, to call somebody an ideologue has been to accuse them of particularistic self-interest, to strip from them of their very quality of publicness.

Such denunciation of public intellectuals as neither universal nor truthful, but as particularistic, self-interested and dogmatic, is a universal trope that takes on many different forms. The Marxist Left denounced civil reformers as middle-class and bourgeois, as merely co-opting the indignation of the lower classes, or even as trying to rise to rulership themselves. Conservatives and reformers, for their part, have 'exposed' revolutionary public intellectuals as actually concerned with class and party rather than with the civic body as such, and as insensitive to the corrosive effects of violence upon their utopia of civil society.

The most sweeping and effective contemporary deconstruction of public intellectuals has been the postmodern. Radicals, reformers and conservatives alike have been condemned as modernists, and thus, whether knowingly or unknowingly, restricted by whiteness, maleness, homophobia, Orientalism and, above all, by their own commitment to universalizing rationality. Presenting modernism as narrow, violent and anti-civil, postmodern public intellectuals make the claim that flexibility, humour and a sensitivity to the particular and concrete can restore the trust and reciprocity upon which civil community depends.

Those who have of late been speaking as global cosmopolitans might be said to represent public intellectuals of a post-postmodernist kind. Speaking on behalf of an imminent global civil sphere, Ulrich Beck accuses all previously existing social science of methodological nationalism, evoking a newly energized discourse of civil idealism on a world-wide scale. Other global public intellectuals, such as David Held and Mary Kaldor, develop roadmaps for global civil repair of a more practical but just as anti-national kind. The performance of these new cosmopolitans is closely related to the public intellectuals of the new Europe, whose civil and Socratic public aspirations have been sharply highlighted by the recent counter-movement of anti-constitutional backlash. But the dialectic turns. Volker Heins has recently accused Habermas and other avowedly cosmopolitan European public intellectuals of 'Orientalizing America', of engaging in a particularistic discourse that divides and ranks the world's civil societies, and privileges Europe as more worthy and pure (see Heins, 2005; for a broader discussion of the issues raised in this paragraph, see Alexander, 2006, 371–82).

Conclusion

Despite these rather sobering considerations, I deeply believe in public intellectuals. They are among the most important carrier groups for the discourse of civil society, which, despite its fragmentation and weakness, remains the closest that human societies have yet come to making the universal concrete. Civil repair is a project, and public intellectuals participate in it in a critical, if often highly ambiguous, way.

References

Alexander, Jeffrey C. (2006), *The Civil Sphere* (Oxford: Oxford University Press).

Alexander, Jeffrey C. (2007), 'Globalization as Collective Representation: The New Dream of a Cosmopolitan Civil Sphere', in Ino Rossi (ed.), *Frontiers Of Globalization Research: Theoretical and Methodological Approaches* (New York: Springer).

Eisenstadt, Shmuel N. (1982), 'The Axial Age: The Emergence of Transcendental Visions and the Rise of Clerics', *European Journal of Sociology* 23:2, 294–314.

Heins, Volker (2005), 'Orientalizing America', *Millennium* 34:2, 433–48.

Parsons, Talcott (1966), *Societies: Evolutionary and Comparative Perspectives* (Englewood Cliffs, NJ: Prentice-Hall).

Walzer, Michael (1965), *Revolution of the Saints* (Cambridge, MA: Harvard University Press).

Chapter 2
Can Women Be Intellectuals?

Mary Evans

The contributions in this volume bear witness to the richness and the diversity of the cultural heritage of Europe. Even if we now raise questions about the extent of 'Europe' and the implicit exclusiveness of the very idea of Europe, most writers recognize that there is an intellectual tradition which we can define as European and which shares the common experiences of cultural transformation in the Renaissance, the Reformation and the Enlightenment. The 'big' dates of European history (1776, 1789, 1848) may relate to events in a particular country (or even, in the case of 1776, to another continent), but all had an impact across Europe, just as the two wars of the twentieth century which we define as 'World Wars' had their origins in European tensions and hostilities. There is therefore no contest here with the 'idea' of Europe; the question which I wish to raise is that of the relationship between gender and European intellectual history, and the issue of whether or not women have taken part and can take part in the European intellectual tradition. It is notable that the one woman whose name occurs with any prominence in these chapters, Alva Myrdal, was the partner of an equally distinguished man, a man who enjoyed considerable prestige and respect within his lifetime.

The question of whether or not women can be intellectuals in the same sense of men is not a question which I wish to locate within an argument about permission or toleration. In one sense, the answer to the question of whether or not women can be intellectuals is that there is no problem, women can be intellectuals just as much as men, in much the same way that women can be academics or fulfil any other kind of occupational role. Indeed, this chapter includes a discussion of the work of notable women intellectuals. The first question is whether or not questions on gender that specifically relate to women can be discussed with the same parity and access to the mainstream of intellectual life as those questions which concern men. The second question is whether or not the absence of explicit gender differentiation in post Enlightenment traditions (or perhaps the taken-for-granted assumption of the male as the definitive human actor) assigns to women the endless responsibility of making evident the two-dimensional nature of the 'human'. Assigning this intellectual role to women then pre-determines (and inherently limits) the role of women intellectuals: it is a role of qualification and the elaboration of difference. The issues, therefore, are about whether or not the 'settlement' in the Enlightenment over the question of gender actually allowed a space for gender difference and for the recognition that not all issues in the social world can be interpreted as matters of a single, and predominantly male, experience.

Second-wave feminism (in the 1970s and early 1980s) made much of the way in which the 'human' was widely interpreted in male terms; this interpretation, it was argued, arose from a long European tradition of both marginalizing the female and the feminine, and excluding women. Thus both actual women, as female human beings, were excluded from intellectual life, and at the same time those issues which seemed to be associated with the feminine were separated from the so-called 'great' traditions. (Although it should be added here that one of the most famous 'great' traditions – that of the English novel – was agreed to have included many women.)

This chapter is not concerned, except in terms of marking the issue, with the question of the structural constraints on the participation (and terms of the participation) of women in European intellectual life. We now know that the general pattern, throughout Europe, is that of equality in the numbers of men and women entering higher education, and yet a domination by men of the established and prestigious positions within the academy. At every stage – other than entry – men outnumber women in university hierarchies: there are more male postgraduate students, more men appointed to university posts and more men occupying senior university appointments. Leaving aside the question of whether or not the present condition of European universities enables us to define securely intellectual life in terms of academic life, there is a clear pan-European phenomenon of the domination by men of 'higher learning'. A considerable number of studies have considered the reasons for this pattern: the usual structural reasons of explicit discrimination, together with more complex explanations related to gendered caring responsibilities. These constraints on the participation by women in the intellectual workforce are undoubtedly important, and significantly alter the life chances of many individuals, but my interest is rather in the gendered pattern of intellectual life, the way in which traditions and paradigms are established. An example of the way in which the gendered pattern of knowledge is manifested is Mozart's *Requiem Mass*. Composed in the final years of the eighteenth century and just before Mozart's death in 1791, the *Requiem* opens with the judgement of men, a judgement which is then taken up by women. What is extraordinary about this masterpiece is not just that it was written by a sick man, but for the purposes of this chapter, that the very structure of the work follows the pattern of the relationship of the different genders to knowledge. A further footnote to the story is that just after creating this final great work, Mozart was hastened to his death – as Peter Gay has pointed out – by the dangerous medicine of the time. A discipline which is often associated with the rise of science and Enlightenment mastery of Nature was – at the very end of the Enlightenment – as dangerous to its patients as it had ever been (see Gay, 1999, 138–9).

The Enlightenment 'settlement' about gender – which I shall argue still dominates European intellectual life – was not one which we can characterize as excluding women. Rather, I shall suggest that the form of the 'settlement' was one in which women (as active participants in intellectual life) were given a place, but excluded, in both the sense of exclusion as particular human beings and exclusion as 'the female/feminine', from the dominant traditions. It is the second issue rather than the first with which I am chiefly concerned here, and my thesis is that in the debates of the period 1780–1820, the terms were set for the patterns of gender and knowledge for the next two hundred years. This pattern was not determined by explicit discrimination against the female or the feminine (although in terms of employment practices, this was certainly the case until relatively recently), but it was determined by the way in which women and men discussed the question of the importance of gender in social life, and the gradual shift towards the assumption that the female/feminine was in an important sense distinct from the universalism of the 'male'.

Many readers of intellectual history (and the history of gender relations) will be familiar with Thomas Laqueur and his work on the way in which, in the eighteenth century, biological gender differences were given a new theoretical meaning (see Laqueur, 1990). What emerged from the transformation in the understanding of differences in biology was a binary distinction between male and female: by the eighteenth century, writers (including Mary Wollstonecraft and Jane Austen) could write with confidence the words, 'as a woman'. But – and here, of course, comes the beginning of a tradition which has largely led to the exclusion of women from 'knowledge' – that sense of personal gendered identity did not take place in a social vacuum. Indeed, it arrived at a point in European history when the Enlightenment, as numerous writers including Zygmunt Bauman, Krishan Kumar and John Jervis have pointed out, became a 'project'. As Jervis suggested:

> Thus Bauman points to the fateful link between rationalism and imperialism here: if I am enlightened, it is my duty to enlighten you; Enlightenment becomes a mission, necessarily intolerant of otherness. The ambition of these programmes – even their grandeur – is captured by Kumar, who writes of the way Enlightenment thinkers 'converted millennial beliefs into a secular idea of progress' whereby 'the millennium becomes scientific and rational, the dawn of an era of unending human progress on earth'. (Jervis, 1998, 232)

It would be wrong to assume from the above that writers on the Enlightenment, and the writers of the Enlightenment themselves, wished to argue a case for the exclusion of women from what became known as the 'Enlightenment project'. Numerous writers of the eighteenth century (among them Hume, Addison, Shaftesbury, Burke, Adam Smith and Carter) all questioned the idea of what can be described as 'arid masculinity'. In their edited volume of essays *Women, Gender and the Enlightenment*, Barbara Taylor and Sarah Knott point out that the key human types of the Enlightenment were the man of feeling and the woman of sensibility (personified by Rousseau and Germaine de Stael's fictional Corinne), but they also point that one of the key themes of the late Enlightenment was woman as an object of study. As they write:

> First is the centrality of Woman to the civilisation paradigm that shaped both the famed optimism and the dark underside of the Enlightenment. Often assumed to have been a marginal concern for the Enlightenment theorists, the status of women was treated by most leading philosophers as a key barometer of social 'improvement'. (Knott and Taylor, 2005, xix)

This use of women (or more specifically, the status of women) as a test of the degree of 'enlightenment' in a society has continued through the nineteenth century (Marx, for example, saw the social status of women as a crucial indicator of how civilized a society is) and into the twentieth and twenty-first. Indeed, references to the subjugation of women have been part of the rhetoric justifying the military intervention of the West in Afghanistan.

However, we need, with reference to the point made above about the status of women as a mark of social enlightenment, to note that the majority of the writers who have accepted this view have seen the emancipation of women in terms of the full participation of women in paid labour (the view of Marx and Engels) and civil society (the view of liberals from John Stuart Mill onwards). The form of female emancipation which is referred to has never been one which assumes the eradication of gender difference and is implicitly located within a paradigm which assumes the male gate-keeping of access to the public social world. Notwithstanding those questions about the difference between the public and the private which Jürgen Habermas has raised, the social world throughout Europe operates with a distinction between the public – which is generally conceived of in terms which are less extensive than those of Habermas – and the private, which is more traditional and more closely related to domestic life than in Habermas's distinction (see Habermas, 1991). Women in contemporary Europe take part in both public and private spheres: the question here is whether or not they take as much part as men in that public sphere, made – as Habermas points out – through our investment since the end of the eighteenth century in the 'private'. Part of the investment which we have made in the private sphere since the Enlightenment has been in the literary public sphere, for it has been through literature, especially the eighteenth- and nineteenth-century psychological novel, that we have deepened that interiority that is at the basis of bourgeois versions of the private and privacy.

The making of the bourgeois, post-Enlightenment self has attracted the attention of numerous writers other than Habermas (for example, Charles Taylor and Zygmunt Bauman) as well as an extensive literature on the links between fiction and gender (see Taylor, 1989).

Within this latter tradition, there has been a recognition, for example in the work of Nancy Armstrong, Mary Poovey, Sandra Gilbert and Susan Gubar, that the tradition of female writers in the nineteenth century was much engaged with putting the case of women to a male world (see Armstrong, 1987; Poovey, 1984; Gilbert and Gubar, 1979). It is precisely that dynamic that is the issue here: the fiction written throughout Europe by women in the nineteenth century is as important in the history of fiction as any fiction written by men. There is no question here that the 'canon' is as much defined by women as it is by men. But if we look at the internal dynamic of the works by women, what we see – with few exceptions – is either a defence by women of a female ethic and a female world, or a claim by women to alteration in the world of men. If we consider fiction by men, what we do not see is the mirror image of this. Thus, that what I propose here is that the Enlightenment 'settlement' (as I have described it) was one which gave to women (as female human beings) and to the female (as a form of subjectivity) a place in the development of the 'interiority' of the public mind, but that that place was one in which the female and the feminine was essentially a position of defence and/or replication. The political slogan much endorsed by second-wave feminism – that every man needs a woman to reflect him as twice his actual size – was something of a parody of the history of the relationship between gender and knowledge. It was not so much that men needed women to accept and sustain their achievements, rather that the place occupied by women in the construction of knowledge was a piece of either confirmation or the defence of the feminine.

This account of the history of knowledge since the end of the eighteenth century suggests that what has happened in the years since the end of the Enlightenment is that although women have gained access to education, the professions, the vote, legal autonomy and – in most European countries – independent control of fertility, there remains an intractable binary division within knowledge which still assumes a division between male and female. Hence, to ask the question of whether or not women can be intellectuals is not to ask the question in the literal sense which the title of this chapter might suggest (the answer to that question is an emphatic 'Yes!'), but to consider whether or not the distinctions between male and female are such entrenched distinctions in the human mind that intellectual work – whether by women or by men – always takes place within this framework. This is not to argue that women will write about the concerns of women, and men of the concerns of men, but that all people (male and female) will write with a sense of gender difference, and that sense has not yet proved itself capable of avoiding the assumptions about the male/masculinity and the female/femininity which are part of our intellectual heritage.

In 1949, in *The Second Sex*, Simone de Beauvoir wrote of women as 'the other' and the sex which is defined throughout the history of European thought as the aberration from the definitive human, which is male. Part of that same generation of European female intellectuals which included Alva Myrdal (1902–1984) and Hannah Arendt (1906–1975), de Beauvoir wrote of women, but (and again like Myrdal and Arendt) with a close public association with a male other. For years after the publication of *The Second Sex*, de Beauvoir was defined in terms which confirmed her own assessment of the gendered hierarchies of knowledge of the culture: she was the lifetime 'companion' of Jean-Paul Sartre, who had come second to him in their final competitive examinations, she was a 'feminist' writer (whereas, of course, Sartre occupied the male, world, stage as a writer and philosopher), and in so many ways and in so many different contexts, she was described as 'fellow existentialist'. Angela Carter once famously remarked that the great question about de Beauvoir was why a nice girl like Simone was spending her time with a horrible man like Sartre, and although the question is flippant, it does suggest something important about social views of the relationship; it invites us to consider de Beauvoir as an autonomous individual, and not as forever associated with a superior male peer.

A considerable amount of energy has now been spent by various writers (for example, Toril Moi) in demonstrating that there is a lot more to de Beauvoir's work than that of the person who in a sense provided the human illustrations for Sartre's philosophy (see Moi, 1994). Moi has shown that de Beauvoir's epistemology was at least as sophisticated as that of Sartre, and played a crucial part in the development of his work. This form of project is further illustrated in more recent work on de Beauvoir. For example, in an introduction to Simone de Beauvoir's *Philosophical Writings*, Margaret Simons wrote:

> A study by Edward Fullbrook of their posthumously published letters and diaries found that Sartre had read a second draft of Beauvoir's *She Came to Stay* just as he was beginning work on *Being and Nothingness* (1943). Thus Beauvoir's novel, long assumed to be an application of Sartre's philosophy in his essay, was instead discovered to be one its sources. (Simons, 2004, 2)

Moi, Simons and others claim that de Beauvoir was a far more original thinker than she has previously been given credit for, and that the conventional assumption that Sartre was the intellectually dominant figure is founded in sexist prejudices about the relative intellectual capacities of women and men. These exercises are important in both the general terms of thinking about gender and the European intellectual heritage, and the more specific terms of re-writing and re-considering the de Beauvoir–Sartre relationship, but they are, arguably, still a part of that binary conceptualization of women, men and knowledge. De Beauvoir has to be defended and claimed to be at least as important as a man, Sartre has to be shown to be dependent upon the creativity of a woman. The process is further complicated by de Beauvoir's claim throughout her life that she wrote only as a human being, and that she did not accept ideas about a 'female language' and a 'female voice' which became part of the ontology of French second-wave feminism in the work of Monique Wittig and Luce Irigaray. Women therefore claimed de Beauvoir for women, while de Beauvoir herself adamantly located herself within a un-gendered world.

The contest over de Beauvoir, and where she belongs, and to whom, will no doubt continue for some time. A prolific and wide-ranging writer such as de Beauvoir inevitably leaves behind a rich resource for future generations. But what the contest illustrates particularly well – and there is probably no other female European writer of such stature who invites such different interpretations – is that the question of gender and knowledge remains as alive as it has ever been, and as much located within a context of a binary opposition between the female and the male. When we read *The Second Sex* in the early years of the twenty-first century, we read of a world which has in part become part of history – the impact of biology on women of which de Beauvoir writes (the problems about fertility, the rigid codes about sexual behaviour and so on) is now far from the reality of much of the West. But what remains is the argument which de Beauvoir wants us to consider: that of whether or not women (and she means literally women) can take the same part as men in the creation and articulation of knowledge. De Beauvoir certainly recognizes those categories of masculinity and femininity, and she is perfectly aware that both biological sexes can, consciously or otherwise, exhibit these behaviours, but she does not depart from a recognition of the impact of biological difference on the human person. In the final pages of *The Second Sex*, she advocates the assumption by women of male patterns and behaviours: choose paid work, reject motherhood and claim autonomy is her message. As Margaret Walters has suggested, there is much that is redolent of Calvin's Geneva about these pages: it is not the dissolution of gender that we see here, but its replication (see Walters, 1976, 304–78). It might be claimed that for women of her generation, de Beauvoir had no option except to choose those ways of life associated with men: in France in the first half of the twentieth century (in common with much of the rest of Europe), there simply were few options for women except marriage and motherhood.

The enlargement and the re-writing of the social roles of women and men is part of the map of Europe which has been re-made since the end of the Second World War. Europe – and particularly the United Kingdom – led the way in the legal and civil changes related to marriage, sexuality and fertility which collectively constituted the institutional framework of what became known as the 'permissive society'. In the early years of the twenty-first century, parts of Europe have moved to accept marriage between partners of the same sex, and many moral codes relating to sexual behaviour have been revised. Thus we can observe that since the time when *The Second Sex* was written, the social context of relations between women and men has shifted dramatically. Yet the question remains of whether this shift in the personal and institutional arrangements of the social world has had – and will have – any impact on the way in which we think about the world, and here, whether or not that binary division between male and female and feminine and masculine will erode as the social world has changed and will undoubtedly go on changing. Materialist explanations of the nature and structure of knowledge would assume that as the material world changes, so will the 'knowledge' that develops within it, but to argue that would imply considerable confidence that gender relations in the world have changed as fundamentally as is sometimes argued.

There have, however, been important attempts to speed up the rate at which the binary divisions of gender change. Foremost among these attempts in the past twenty years is the work or Judith Butler, which has argued for a theory of sexuality that asserts the primacy of sexuality in the social structure and proposes a theory of sexuality which separates the 'performance' of sexuality ('doing' masculinity or femininity) from actual biological sex (see Butler, 1990). Whatever our biological status, we are all able, Butler argues, to choose the kind of gendered persona that we become. Using evidence (largely anthropological) which demonstrates that throughout the world there are numerous different ways or learning and exhibiting gender, Butler suggests that what is important in the twenty-first century is a rejection of those often brutal assumptions that impose 'normal' expectations of gender on women and men. Butler, in effect, wishes to dissolve gender, so that neither men nor women are expected to perform particular kinds of gendered behaviour. It is a theory which has been hugely influential, not least because in the 'real' world it seems to offer a way out of the impasse of traditional forms of masculinity and femininity, and because in the interpretation of diverse forms of representation, it seems to offer a way of understanding literature and the visual arts which highlights the sexual ambiguity of much of that work.

Butler, as the above hopefully suggests, is very far from an essentialist in terms of the discussion of sexuality and gender difference. Indeed, her work is an important discussion of how we might move beyond the binaries of male and female. It is notable that her work has had a huge impact across disciplines, although the part of her work which probably remains the most contentious is her assumption that gender is the key form of social stratification and social difference. Nancy Fraser is one of those who have taken issue with this idea, and argued that late capitalism (postmodernism, whatever social label for our society we use) can easily accommodate itself to whatever individuals choose to make of their biology (see Fraser, 1997). It is apparent from evidence throughout the West that this is entirely true, just as evidence from the same world shows the huge, vocal resistance to anything approaching a re-writing of traditional gender expectations and the social arrangements that accompany them. Feminist writers have described the resistance to feminism as 'backlash'; in parts of the United States, a stronger vocabulary would be needed to describe the physical threats to female autonomy in the shape of murderous assaults on abortion clinics.

It is impossible, therefore, to conclude that the West has moved beyond a position in which there is no social concern about gender and behaviour. There are many contexts in which 'gender-blind' policies have been introduced; equally, there are many social situations in which gender difference is fiercely maintained.

The aspect of Butler's work which remains most problematic for writers on gender is the extent to which her thesis about gender allows us to move beyond the 'Enlightenment Settlement' about gender and begin to think in ways which do not invoke the essentialist categories of male and female. The 'settlement' achieved at the time of the Enlightenment was, as Kate Soper has suggested, one in which women were allowed a place, and in which the emotional possibilities of 'feeling' and 'sentiment' were de-sexualized and allowed a prominent and positive place in the range of human behaviour. But – and it is a very important qualification – she also argues that:

> The radical, feminist moment had passed by 1800 … Women after 1800, it seems, continued to be confined to educational writing (now including political economy made simple) and to novels; the fields of history, philosophy, political economy, and political

> theory remained beyond them. But if the outcomes of Enlightenment are measured against the aspirations of the late eighteenth -century feminist radicals – those who sought an intellectual world unmarred by 'sexual distinctions' – then much remained to be achieved. (Soper, 2005, 711)

Whether or not the two hundred or so years after 1800 have seen many achievements that can suggest the lessening of gender distinctions in the intellectual world remains an intensely problematic question. The contribution of de Beauvoir – who was the first modem writer to problematize the question of the relationship of gender to knowledge – remains as crucial a landmark in the first half of the twentieth century as that of Judith Butler does in the second. But in two important ways, neither of these authors, important as their work is in the way we think about gender, systematically address the question of both the part that women play in intellectual life and the part that gender plays in the construction of knowledge. Leaving aside those explanations which define differences between male and female forms of participation in intellectual life in terms of differences in the constitution of male and female brains, and those psychoanalytical theories which posit different accommodations for women and men with language and subsequently with knowledge, we are left with a history of intellectual life in Europe which is marked by that pattern identified in Mozart's *Requiem* at the beginning of this chapter: a pattern in which men state and women qualify. If we look at the history of intellectual and cultural life in Europe over a two hundred-year period from the Enlightenment, what we can see is a pattern in which in all disciplines – with the exception of the novel – male contributions have been dominant. Nor, until very recently, was this difference in terms of gendered participation an issue for cultural historians: it was taken as read (and still is in many contexts today) that there was no 'problem' about the gender of the person constructing knowledge. We can take from this the innate assumption that the gender of the person involved in intellectual life is insignificant, or we can think of it in terms of the refusal of the dominant norms of intellectual life to entertain the view that the gender of the person might be relevant. The former possibility is a reading of the intellectual world which deconstructs gender somewhat in advance of Judith Butler: her work leaves us in the same position as those theories which had refused to 'see' gender in previous historical periods.

Among those people who had most emphatically refused to see 'gender' in intellectual life in the past were those cohorts of women who worked hard and long for the integration of women into higher education and the professions. Much of the energy of these women – who informed the practices of those enclaves of entryism into professional life on both sides of the Atlantic – was devoted to the demonstration that women could do just as well as men in all forms of competition. Reaction to what many women saw as the advocacy of the de-sexualization of women was often vehement: a tradition from Dorothy Sayers (in the novel *Gaudy Night*) to Sylvia Plath (in *The Bell Jar*) which caricatured and lampooned the spinsters who devoted their lives to the higher education of women. The tensions between expectations of female sexuality (both imposed and internalized) were such as to create a continuous post-Enlightenment tradition of the fear of women intellectuals. 'Bluestockings' became the butt of jokes, and served to entrench the commonplace idea that only men were the legitimate occupants of the academy and the higher learning.

The woman writer who most fiercely resisted the idea that the route to female intellectual emancipation lay in the replication of male patterns was Virginia Woolf. Writing at about the same time as Dorothy Sayers, Woolf was (and is) notable for her resistance to the idea that women should take part in the institutions and culture of the academy and intellectual life. In *Three Guineas*, Woolf argues the case against this choice: look at these institutions, she argues, see who occupies them, and consider the links of these institutions to other, politically suspect, aspects of the social world. What she does, in effect, is to take up an aspect of intellectual life which is as seldom discussed today as it was in 1938: the aspect of the social power of the academy. Do not join in, says Woolf: there is no way of joining certain institutions which will allow you to control your own actions or indeed your thoughts. As a theory of social integration, it assumes the complete power of institutional life to absorb and control the individual; yet as a theory of the integrative power of institutions, it is not radically different from most of the sociological findings on the same subject.

Woolf is generally regarded – with Proust and Joyce – as one of the great writers of modernism and the subjectivity of the modern. If she is 'placed' within this tradition, her politics are of course marginalized and her political writing becomes a footnote to her fiction. But the reality of Woolf's work – and life – is that she had an intense sense of the political, and a particularly intense sense of the gendered polities of subjectivity. As we have seen, Jürgen Habermas has written of 'the literary' as the form through which modern (post-Enlightenment) bourgeois society considers its internal self; however, what it does not do is to discuss the gendered nature of that subjectivity and consider the ways in which the 'modern self' (as unsexed to Habermas as it is to Charles Taylor and other writers) simply assumes the 'male'. Indeed, much contemporary social theory, concerned as it is with the decline of 'respect' (Richard Sennett) or 'community' (Robert Putnam), does not 'gender' these ideas. It is not to diminish the important contributions made by these writers to say that their work does not take account of the different meanings which 'respect' and 'community' might have for women and men: doing this in a very real sense demonstrates only too clearly the intellectual position which women occupy – a position of qualification and the articulation of difference. Critics of this relatively limited intervention in the intellectual world would argue that this qualification is itself pointless: simply pointing out that gender differences exist does not in itself constitute a theoretical contribution or an insight into the working of contemporary world on a par with that of Putnam or Sennett or any other figure who has written about the world of the late twentieth and early twenty-first century.

But the example above – of important work which is then qualified by women – exemplifies the theoretical problems faced by those (of whatever biological sex) who want to include gender as an issue to be taken account of in our considerations of the social and intellectual world. 'Women' therefore becomes a term which might well (and indeed, in reality generally does) refer to people who are biologically female, but it can also refer to those who want to extend our understanding of the world in which we live. Alasdair MacIntyre, Claudia Johnson and the present author have all written of Jane Austen's Fanny Price as the definitive heroine of the Enlightenment: a heroine who becomes independent of all expectations except those of her conscience. But Fanny Price is not the usual personification of the Enlightenment 'settlement' about women that usually belongs to the explicit recognition of women. Paradoxically, it was precisely that recognition which has led, arguably, to the consistent marginalization of women and the feminine in intellectual traditions, and which remains a position from which women still have to achieve emancipation.

References

Armstrong, Nancy (1987), *Desire and Domestic Fiction* (Oxford: Oxford University Press).

Bauman, Zygmunt (1991), *Modernity and the Holocaust* (Cambridge: Polity Press).

Butler, Judith (1990), *Gender Trouble* (London: Routledge).

Fraser, Nancy (1997), *Justice Interruptus* (London: Routledge).

Gilbert, Sandra and Gubar, Susan (1979), *The Madwoman in the Attic: The Woman Writer and the Nineteenth Century Literary Imagination* (New Haven, CT: Yale University Press).

Gay, Peter (1999), *Mozart* (London: Weidenfeld and Nicolson).

Habermas, Jürgen (1991), *The Structural Transformation of the Public Sphere: An Inquiry into a Category of Bourgeois Society* (Cambridge, MA: MIT Press).

Jervis, John (1998), *Exploring the Modern* (Oxford: Blackwell).

Knott, Sarah and Taylor, Barbara (eds) (2005), *Women, Gender and Enlightenment* (London: Palgrave).

Laqueur, Thomas (1990), *Making Sex* (Cambridge, MA: Harvard University Press).

Moi, Toril (1994), *Simone de Beauvoir: The Making of an Intellectual Woman* (Oxford: Blackwell).

Poovey, Mary (1984), *The Proper Lady the Woman Writer: Ideology as Style in the Works of Mary Wollstonecraft, Mary Shelley and Jane Austen* (Chicago, IL: Chicago University Press).

Simons, Margaret (ed.) (2004), *Simone de Beauvoir: Philosophical Writings* (Chicago, IL: University of Illinois Press).

Soper, Kate (2005), 'Feminism and Enlightenment Legacies', in Knott, Sarah and Taylor, Barbara (eds), *Women, Gender and Enlightenment* (London: Palgrave).
Taylor, Charles (1989), *Sources of the Self* (Cambridge: Cambridge University Press).
Walters, Margaret (1976), 'The Rights and Wrongs of Women', in Oakley, Ann and Mitchell, Juliet (eds), *The Right and Wrongs of Women* (Harmondsworth: Penguin).

Chapter 3
Terrorism and the Betrayal of the Intellectuals

Joseba Zulaika

What do you do, as an intellectual, when your primary community of family, friends, village, or country produces 'terrorists'? What is your intellectual task – to define them, to diagnose them, to condemn them, to persuade them, to understand them, to exorcise them? Should you look at it as tragedy, irony, farce, romance, or sheer crime? Whether in the Basque Country, Ireland or the United States, intellectual approaches to 'terrorism' are of necessity enmeshed in the writer's self-definitions and ideological investments. The result is that various readings and approaches to the phenomenon of terrorism are likely to produce antagonistic intellectuals. Given the logic of taboo and association by contagion that is typical of terrorism discourse, we might even ask whether 'expertise' on the terrorist Other presupposes a wilful ignorance of the actual life conditions and subjectivities of the violent actors.

Yet nothing seems to define a Spanish or Basque intellectual as much as his or her view of Basque terrorism and how it is related or unrelated to a Spanish political impasse. In the small world of Basque politics, every writer appears to be compelled to provide a diagnosis, a solution, a condemnation, a jeremiad or some sort of commentary on the problem of terrorism. It is a sort of Rorschach Test of where you stand as an intellectual. For Caro Baroja, the great social historian, the whole thing became an incomprehensible 'labyrinth'. For some of the best-known Basque/Spanish intellectuals, such as Fernando Savater, the whole thing is nothing but criminal terrorism. You also have the phenomenon of noted former ETA members who later became the most militant anti-ETA and anti-nationalist writers. Then you have political scientists, sociologists and anthropologists who try to place the phenomenon in a historical and cultural context. You also have the figure of the 'terrorism expert', who applies to the phenomenon a technical-juridical language and treats all various forms of terrorism as being ramifications of the very same thing.

An Ethnographer in the Field: Subjugated Knowledge for Subjugated and Violent People

As an Anthropology graduate student in the United States, I overcame my ambivalence to returning home and decided to write an ethnography of ETA. What else was there worth writing about when you have people killing and being killed for the sake of an idea? After all, I had friends who had been and still were members of ETA, and my youth had been haunted by the spectre of unending violence. In particular, I could never forget the case of the bus driver in my own Basque village, murdered one Saturday morning by ETA in front of his neighbours, housewives who had gone shopping to the town four miles away. My mother was on the bus. On their ride back home, she saw the two young men, pistols in hand, advance towards the driver, shouting at him, 'You are a dog!', before killing him. The screaming housewives got out of the bus and were brought to the village by passer-by drivers. I found my mother in shock, sitting on the stairs, unable to walk home. Other women who had witnessed the crime were on the street, still sobbing, when I went out. 'But how can that be?' is all they could say, their faces in horror.

I composed an ethnography trying to make sense of the 'But how can that be?' I provided historical, sociological and cultural models of performance that could help contextualize, never explain, the perplexing phenomenon of murder. Even if not your usual European ethnography of the time on small village life or ritual fiestas, it was well within the paradigms of American academic anthropology; it had positive reviews in the discipline's major journals, and was even nominated for a Margaret Mead Award. Yet this same ethnography was also furiously contested by combatant anti-ETA intellectuals. One of them, Jon Juaristi, himself a former ETA operative, regaled me with a full page on a Sunday in the main Spanish newspaper, *El Pais*, accusing me of cowardice and of heroifying vulgar murderers.

Hence the initial unsettling question: are you allowed to weave an ethnography around murder? Is it morally and politically correct to be a detached ethnographer when murder is at stake? This is the question that was put to me when my ethnography came out. Nobody in the discipline would question that you could write on infanticide, regicide or headhunting and produce a valuable monograph without anyone questioning whether you favoured killing infants or kings or cutting the heads of outsiders. But could you use the anthropology trade as a distancing device to study 'terrorism'? You were always allowed to be a policeman, a judge, a moralist, a counter-terrorist. But an anthropologist?

The question brings into relief the role of knowledge when confronted with something we could call foundational violence and which goes at the heart of situations such as the Basque political impasse. You could practise ethnographic distance, say, when you study murder in a tribe in the Philippines. But are you allowed to make an ethnography of headhunters in your own society?

The intellectual and moral issue has to do with you positioning 'inside' or 'outside' of the realm of the crime that is being committed. You are allowed a position of utmost externality to the crime, signalled by strong condemnation and moral indignation at the perversity of murder. If you are an ethnographer who is describing 'their' institutionalized murder, in a foreign culture with strange customs, nothing is being risked. Knowledge of their madness is all legitimate, particularly if it is drowned in vats of moral indignation.

But assume now you are doing an ethnography of your own society and from a subject position that is internal to the phenomenon. Imagine you are studying the unsavoury consequences of nationalism and you are nationalist, or the paradoxes of Catholic dogma and you are a Catholic, or as in my case, the murder in your village and you are a villager. You can always claim that, even if you are a nationalist or a Catholic or a villager, you do not agree with a certain aspect of your identity. But still, the issue of your belonging to that identity does not disappear. If you are an American and you don't like what your army is doing in Iraq, are you free from any responsibility by simply saying, 'I don't agree with it'? Your country, your institution, your ideology are also part of your identity.

In the case of the murdered bus driver in my village, I knew him quite well. By the time I was 11, he had taught me how to dance and prepared me for an *aurresku* performance in the plaza of the village. I used to visit his shoe repair shop while I was still a child. He gave me career advice and he was fond of me. Yet later, when polarization took place in the village, I disagreed with his pro-Franco politics. Still, I knew the man, and I did not approve of his killing. (His killing was celebrated with champagne.) In short, this was murder I could not deal with in merely 'objective' terms and from a purely 'external' position. I could not reduce the situation to the polarity 'they/us', the murderers always being 'they', never 'us'. If you are an American and if you realize that it is the army paid with your taxes that is doing the killing in Iraq, it is inconsistent to then say that 'they' are the killers, not you.

This is all related, of course, to what subject position you choose for yourself when confronted with violence or poverty or injustice in the world. Is it the hegemonic position or the subaltern one, the First World position or the Third World, the existing power or the marginal or emergent one?

At a level of disciplinary practice, the intellectual may be in the position of having to work with what Foucault named 'subjugated knowledges'. These are the types of knowledge that have no centre of authority behind them, be it a state, an established scientific institution or a historic tradition. These situations are not that uncommon for an anthropologist. The claims to sovereignty, history, truth and other universal narratives are slim when you are a tribe with no written tradition and no army. Confronted with the power of colonial and sovereign states, the claims to historical legitimacy coming from their former dominions or sub-state polities are not likely to be at the same level of authority. Do they even have a right to narrate their own histories, have a literature of their own, write down their laws?

What should be the authentic location of knowledge when we are dealing with crimes that have fallen inside the heavily tabooed discourse of terrorism? In the case of the murder in my village, to take an example, whose truth could claim to be final? The one by the police, the judge, the moralist, the counter-terrorist, the killer? For the ethnographer, there is one place of knowledge that is not insignificant: the primary community of the village – that is, the first neighbours and their elaborate formal and informal networks of relationship among families in the traditional culture; the group of friends who went back to the schoolboy years and who knew him intimately, including the falling out he had had with his 'milk brother' (the nationalist friend who was his political opponent, but orphaned as a child, and following traditional neighbour relations, had been nursed by his own mother); the recent history of political resistance in the village, including the religious group of which he had been a member. Does such 'subjugated knowledge' have a place in contextualizing the murder?

Legality is, of course, a key theme. Is it there any other legality but the one derived from the state? Should an intellectual stride aside from the established legality? Can you study the outside-law Zapatistas as if they were a legitimate political group? History is filled with revolutionary and transgressive movements of all sorts. What sort of intellectual legitimacy do they have?

Obviously, you might be a lifelong member of a party, an ideology, a community, and then, cutting all ties, decide to take the positions that are contrarian to your group. You can claim that you no longer have any responsibility with what you did as a member of that party, ideology of community. But things are not that clean. If you are a European, aren't you complicit with Europe's colonial history? If your party, while you were a member, was involved, say, in 'dirty war' and as a result murdered scores of people, now that you have cut all ties with that party, are you totally 'innocent' from your former affiliation? Or, say, you were a member of a terrorist group such as ETA, and then later on you position yourself as an anti-ETA activist, does that entail that you have no responsibility whatsoever for the terrorist actions committed by ETA while you were a member? These are very real situations in the debates, say, between Basque/Spanish intellectuals. They question the validity of the 'us/them' divide regarding the ongoing violence. In short, once we are 'post' some ideology or party – post-Marxists or post-nationalists or post-Christians – what is our relationship to the 'before'?

Foucault distinguished the 'universal intellectual' versus the 'specific intellectual'. Regarding the murder in my village, we know what the universal intellectual has to say: murder should always be illegal, wrong, a crime. What should the specific intellectual who studies the event *in situ* have to say? Well, maybe he should not study it in the first place. Maybe there are areas where a specific intellectual – an ethnographer, perhaps – should not trade.

The relationship between the individual and the group (organization, society, culture) is one of the sticking points at the outset. Is the murder in question the personal act of a murderer, or is it motivated by political goals and group ideology? One of the decisive traits of military institutions is that the individual has to surrender to the collective organization and will. Soldiers in the Spanish military are not allowed to pronounce the pronoun 'I'. Typically, the individual is not personally responsible for carrying out orders that have been decided at a higher level in the hierarchy. An organization such as ETA shares this military culture. But if you accept the obvious fact that a terrorist organization has a military command structure and that operatives in it are subject to a hierarchical culture, you are perhaps granting too much already. For those who will not see in ETA militants anything but criminal murderers, postulating an organization and a hierarchy that somehow waters down the individual responsibility of the murderer is thus unwelcome. Furthermore, any links between the activist and his or her nationalist community are also unwanted.

Anthropologists of my generation, informed mostly by the works of Marx, Durkheim and Weber, have taken for granted the profound interaction between individuality and collectivity. We easily sympathize with Gramsci (1959) when he wrote in his essay 'What is Man?' that 'it is essential to conceive of man as a series of active relationships (a process) in which individuality, while of the greatest importance, is not the sole element to be considered'. Gramsci's view was that 'the individual does not enter into relations with other men in opposition to them but through an organic unity with them, because he becomes part of social organisms of all kinds from the simplest to the most complex'. His conclusion is most telling:

> If individuality is the whole mass of these relationships, the acquiring of a personality means the acquiring of consciousness of these relationships, and changing the personality means changing the whole mass of these relationships. (Radhakrishnan 1990, 82)

This might be reasonable for ordinary social relations, but when you are dealing with the taboo of terrorism, can you postulate that the terrorist has some ties and dependencies with his or her community, his or her culture, his or her political party, his or her organization? Still, the inter-dependence between the individual and the collective does not deny agency. Even if humanity is shaped in a social process, it does not mean that these relationships are mechanical. The subject can in fact change those relations. There is no denying of human intentionality. Gramsci posits an interplay between 'man as structure' and 'man as intentionality'.

An ethnographic approach to the phenomenon of political terrorism will in fact put emphasis on both sides of the equation: on the structure that conditions the militant's actions; and on the purposes that guide and fool the actor. Both moves are unwelcome for the intellectual who would not grant the terrorist any leeway. The mere assertion that the terrorist harbours some political intentionality appears to be too much of a concession. He or she should be treated not only as a person totally alone and thus unrelated to his or her social condition, but also as a person with no further purpose, programme or vision; the terrorist is merely a mechanical madman, a criminal and nothing else, someone almost incapable of subjectivity or intentionality.

Faced with such a polarizing taboo, the intellectual is faced in the end with the dilemma of demonizing or normalizing the terrorist. We anthropologists have long studied the phenomenon of taboo. It serves to categorize and localize danger.

Once you have something tabooed, you feel you are in control. Demonization and tabooization are central to the dominant discourse of international terrorism. But what if, after framing everything in such discourse, the logic of taboo comes back to haunt you?

If we look at the contemporary discourse of terrorism promoted by the US, there is the extraordinary sight of the ongoing 'war on terror' used as justification for claiming for oneself all sorts of states of exception at home and abroad. There is nothing like counter-terrorism to rekindle the age-old mutual dependence between demonizing the enemy while claiming exemption from legal accountability for oneself. The true exceptionality of 'normal' realities such as Guantanamo, Abu Ghraib or the Patriot Act have even raised, in the opinion of some commentators, the spectre of proto-fascism. Henry Giroux has summarized the symptoms as follows: the cult of traditionalism and reactionary modernism; the diminishing of public space and corporatization of civil society; the building of a culture of fear and patriotic correctness; the attempts to control the mass media through regulation, corporate ownership or spokespeople; the rise of the Orwellian version of Newspeak, and the collapse of the separation between church and state (see Giroux, 2004, 14–32).

In the end, as Aretxaga notes:

> A war against Terrorism … mirrors the state of exception characteristic of insurgent violence, and in doing so reproduces it ad infinitum. The question remains: What politics might be involved in this state of alert as normal state? Would this possible scenario of competing (and mutually constituting) terror signify the end of politics as we know it? (Aretxaga, 2001, 149)

The terrorist enemy plays a pivotal role in such a redefinition of politics as we know it and that is at stake in the war on terror.

Experts and Journalists: Writing Terrorism

There is another approach to terrorism that is at the antipodes of the ethnographer: the so-called 'terrorism expert'. While I wrote my ethnography of Basque political violence, a group of such experts was meeting for months in a London hotel in order to issue a much trumpeted 'report' that would dictate what Basque violence was and what should be done about it (see Zulaika, 1991). It had been commissioned by the Basque government, frustrated by the negative resonance that 'terrorism' had for Basques in the international media, and clearly hoping that the experts would recognize the anti-Francoist dictatorship context in which ETA had originated, as well as the ultimately political basis to its violence.

The terrorism experts' fundamental claim about Basque violence was that it *is* terrorism, which means that it belongs to the same category that includes other European and non-European groups. Thus, two-thirds of the report are given to describing such other terrorist groups, the assumption being that this amounts to describing to ETA, since they all belong to the same category of behaviour. The reminder was devoted to the 'ought' of a Basque anti-terrorist crusade, including legal measures, security provisions, various social policies, as well as a 'Plan for Consciousness-Raising'. And social science was needed 'in parallel with the implementation of the counter-measures recommended later in this report', and therefore 'such research will enable action to combat terrorism' (Rose, 1986, 35–6). The entire enterprise was premised on ideological and moral imperatives, and stated detailed steps for indoctrination against nationalist values at all social and educational levels. This was all done in the name of scientific 'expertise' and of 'international' scholarship. This raises a fundamental question: how does a foreign expert know what is best for the educational curriculum, political parties or moral consensus of a given society? Some of the same experts who diagnosed the Basque situation were also at the time influential in the United States (Zulaika and Douglass 1996, 51).

In order to grasp the claims of such international discourse on terrorism, one needs to start by paying attention to the writing itself of the counter-terrorist text. There is a world of difference about what constitutes a fact, depending on whether the writer is a journalist, an ethnographer, a sociologist, a novelist or an expert. Writing terrorism itself becomes 'inaugural' of the contents of the discourse. Far from being a mere mirror of the facts on the ground, discourse may *create* its own reality. The media confronts us daily with the realities of terrorism, as well as with the discoursive nature of many of the 'facts'. The plot to blow up as many as ten airplanes over the Atlantic with liquid explosives uncovered by the British police in London in August 2006 will suffice to illustrate the point. Having arrested 21 people, the alarm could not have been more ominous. Paul Stephenson, the Deputy Chief of the Metropolitan Police in London, declared on 10 August that the plotters were intent on 'mass murder on an unimaginable scale'; John Reid, the British Home Secretary, predicted that as the result of the 'highly likely' attacks, the loss of life would have been on an 'unprecedented scale'. I had to fly from Spain to the USA with my family ten days after the plot had become front-page news; the anticipation for the flight became dreadful as daily news detailed the hours of waiting at the airports, the prohibition to carry handbags, the repeated cases of flights aborted or returned to their destination because of the hysteria provoked by some unruly passenger. After we made it home safely, a report by the *New York Times* detailed that the plotters had left 'a trove of evidence', thus fully confirming the initial alarm. Yet a careful reading of the report provided a very different picture of the events. It admitted that, according to five senior British officials:

> the suspects were not prepared to strike immediately. Instead, the reactions of Britain and the United States in the wake of the arrests of 21 people on Aug. 10 were driven less by information about a specific, imminent attack than fear that other, unknown terrorists might strike.

That is, fear that some unknown terrorists might strike, not the ones they had arrested, had been the true reason for the apocalyptic alarm that turned the world's air traffic into chaos. In fact, 'despite the charges, officials said they were still unsure of one critical question: whether any of the suspects was technically capable of assembling and detonating liquid explosives while airborne'. Some of the suspects had been under police surveillance for over a year, and what had triggered the police action was that one of the key suspects, Rashid Rauf, who holds dual British and Pakistani citizenship, had been arrested in Pakistan. Initially, it was said by one official, and later disclaimed by another, that upon Rauf's arrest an explicit message to the plotters to 'go now' had been issued. This prompted the decision by Scotland Yard to go ahead and arrest the entire group, when in fact British investigators would have wanted to monitor the suspects for longer. In short, the group was under close police surveillance; having installed video cameras and audio recordings in their 'bomb factory', the police knew the group was not ready to attack (some of them did not even have passports yet, let alone tickets to fly), and by the police's own admission, they even questioned whether any of the group members had the capacity to detonate an explosive. So we are left with the question: was the threat, which must have cost billions to the aviation industry, so alarming as to create the world-wide air traffic chaos? The same senior officials characterized the apocalyptic remarks of two weeks earlier as 'unfortunate'. After his dire predictions of 10 August, Mr. Reid sought to calm the public by lowering the threat level from critical to severe and acknowledging that: 'Threat level assessments are intelligence-led. It is not a process where scientific precision is possible. They involve judgments.'

Here we have a typical case of terrorism's hyper-reality, in which the facts are there (the alleged plotters were clearly up to something), but they take shape against a background of threats and fears that then become constitutive of the events themselves. That is, the scare was as much the product of the *interpretation* of messages as of the actual immediacy of the threat. This is an example of how discourse remakes reality. After all, how is it that there was no major terrorism chapter in the terrible history of the first half of the twentieth century, a period unparalleled in military brutality? If during the period of world-wide wars, in which tens of millions of soldiers and civilians were dying in Europe, terrorism was a footnote, how is it that currently, in a strategic reversal of priorities, conventional wars such as the ones in Afghanistan and Iraq appear to have become substitutes for fighting terrorism, deemed to be now the ultimate threat to civilization? Newspapers did not need to make use of the term 'terrorism' until the 1970s; you will not find 'terrorism' as a heading in the *New York Times Index* or the *London Times Index* prior to 1970. The assassination of President Kennedy was just that, an 'assassination'. The attack on President Reagan was something quite different – a 'terrorist' act. We are not doubting the existence of assassinations, but making the obvious point that whether a given assassination is covered as terrorism or not, such a discursive decision has stark political and legal connotations. In this sense, the discourse creates its own reality. The existence of Guantanamo is unthinkable without the discourse of terrorism.

In short, we are confronted with a new epistemic space, a new act of naming that was deemed to be necessary for a new historical reality. Awareness that reality is up for grabs, and that the US administration's rationales for the war on terror have only the most tenuous connections to reality, has become a staple of the mainstream political debate, as reflected in the daily media's coverage of the administration's political agenda. The big scare produced by the uncovered British plot in the end had to do as much with the *rhetorical* dimension of terrorism as with the actual danger posed by those arrested on 10 August, half of whom were later released without charges. We are not denying that the evidence for the plot was there, only that its apocalyptic nature became credible because of the rhetorical power of terrorism. To talk of its rhetorical dimension means that the link between actions and goals is mediated by interpretations; that is, the primary persuasions that matter to the terrorist are the reactions themselves. Counter-terrorism is equally rhetorical, in that a primary concern for officials in their 'war against terror' is how the public perceives and interprets their actions. There is a long history of politicians using terrorism to their advantage. The 2006 British terror case, for example, is credited with having revamped President Bush's approval ratings by several points, certainly not a negligible result for a president whose numbers were below 40 per cent. Now, imagine the temptation when such rhetorical power, by which you can largely control the public's interpretation of a certain threat or potential action, is available to power. Such a rhetorical dimension becomes even more critical in a situation in which the activities of the terrorist as well as those of the counter-terrorists are clouded in secrecy and classified information. This can produce the not uncommon situation in which the alleged enemies feed rhetorically into each other's interests, as each side perceives political advantages in the existence of the other.

An assessment of the rhetorical aspects of the discourse requires close attention to the writing of terrorism and the narrative plots in which the arguments are couched. Hayden White called this 'tropic', namely, the presence of tropes (metaphor, metonym, synecdoche, irony) used in 'the process by which all discourse *constitutes* the objects which it pretends only to describe realistically and to analyze objectively' (White, 1978, 154). The dominant tropic space in contemporary political and journalistic discourse is 'terror'. Thus, such tropics of terror, by which attention is paid to the conceptual premises, emplotted stories and the very 'illusion of sequence' of narrativity, should be of primary concern to Critical Terrorism Studies.

Camus on the Betrayal of the Intellectual

What concerns us is how contemporary terrorism is turned into narrative, and how the various kinds of narrative affect actual history by dissolving or magnifying the violence. Shoshana Felman has devoted incisive essays to discussing the ways in which history as holocaust had affected the relationship between history and narrative. She does this following Hegel's perspective that 'the term history unites the objective and the subjective side, and denotes … not less what *happened* than the *narration* of what happened. This union of the two meanings we must regard as of a higher order than mere outward accident' (Felman and Laub, 1992, 93). And she takes the work of Albert Camus, of whom it can be said that he created the new form of *narrative as testimony,* as exemplary to examine such relationship. She concentrated on two of his novels, *The Plague* (1948) and *The Fall* (1958).

The Plague describes a town stricken by an epidemic. The mass murder of about a hundred million people by the contagion of a plague is a clear allegory of the Second World War epidemic that had just ended. Camus was a member of the French Resistance, and wrote the novel as an underground testimony and as an actual intervention in the conflict. The protagonist of the novel is a doctor who fights against the plague with dignity and determination. As testimony, the novel is in itself a document of primary, unproblematic data echoing history. Since the narrator is well informed and an honest witness, history appears to speak for itself. The narrative is self-evident, the events are literal, and the witness's only task is to not get in the way of the events themselves by simply stating, 'this is what happened' (Felman and Laub 1992, 101). Still, why does Camus write a novel and use the metaphor of the plague if things are so literal? Such a plague is an 'impossible' thing, something that had vanished from the Western world, the novel tells us. There is thus a tension between an event that was supposed to have banished and its actual occurrence that is conveyed by the allegory. 'Camus' testimony is not simply to the literality of history, but to its *unreality*, to the historical vanishing point of its unbelievability' (Felman and Laub, 1992, 103).

The events of the Holocaust were also disbelieved for years by the Allies, and are still persistently denied by revisionists of history. The 'crisis of witnessing' brought about by the Holocaust springs precisely from the fact that the victims/witnesses were vanished, and that therefore the event itself could not be witnessed. This requires a testimony that goes beyond the journalistic; it requires the imaginative powers of literature, the total condemnation of unqualified testimony. The reader becomes a witness by means of the literary testimony's capacity to elicit a perception of history in one's own body in the manner that the doctor protagonist has to be a witness of the events though his own death, so that he is 'radically transformed by the very process of witnessing' (Felman and Laub, 1992, 109). Witnessing teaches the doctor about the stark facts of history by means of his own crisis and transformation. In the end, the doctor, summoned to give evidence, becomes the narrator who is going to speak for everyone. He is the one who 'has deliberately taken the victim's side and tried to share with his fellow citizens the only certitudes they had in common – love, exile, and suffering. Thus he can truly say there was not one of their anxieties in which he did not share, no predicament of theirs what was not his' (Camus, 1948, 272).

Thus, confronted with the horrors of the twentieth century, Camus's work introduces us to urgencies of a new literature of witnessing as the new cultural and political imperative of what Elie Wiesel and others have deemed an 'Age of Testimony'. The act of literary witnessing requires for Camus not a simple statement of the facts, but an act of commitment aimed at transforming the relationship between history and its various forms of narrative consciousness. The writer's task is to constantly find new forms to intervene in that narrative space. As Camus writes, 'To create today is to create dangerously. Any publication is an act, and that act exposes one to the passions of an age that forgives nothing,' while he complains about 'the feeling the contemporary artist has of lying or of indulging in useless words if he pays no attention to history's woes' (Felman and Laub, 1992, 115). Bearing witness becomes in the end an act of survival. But at the very end of the novel there is a sniper who has gone mad, proof that not even the honest witness can speak for all, and who raises the question of whether a healing testimony is possible in the contemporary times of the Holocaust and international terrorism. Camus would respond to that very question nine years later by writing *The Fall*.

'I must repeat: we, the survivors, are not the true witnesses,' writes Primo Levi, a survivor of Nazi concentration camps. 'Those who … have not returned to tell about it or have returned mute, … they are … the submerged, the complete witnesses' (Levi, 1989, 83–4). It is the failure of the witness which concerns us here, her inability to be sure of the value of her narrative knowledge. In the background of *The Fall*'s plot there is an emblematic event: the narrator saw by chance the suicide of a woman who suddenly jumps into the Seine river. Unlike in *The Plague*, where the narrator experiences directly the evil he is going to speak against, in *The Fall* the narrator witnesses a missed event, the absence of a face-to-face, which reduces the witness to silence. In *The Fall*, the death of the Other lacks significance, and the protagonist does not share his act of witnessing with the community.

'*The Fall*,' suggests Felman, 'in opposition to *The Plague*, explores the roots of the disasters of contemporary history not in the evil of the enemies (some external bacillus of Plague) but, less predictably, in the betrayal of the friends' (Felman and Laub, 1992, 171). This is based on the well-known facts regarding the falling out between Sartre and Camus as the result of the publication of *L'Homme revolté* (1951), where Camus denounced dogmatic Marxism and Stalinism in particular, and which earned him a negative review in Sartre's journal *Les Temps modernes*. Their controversy centred on the role of history; in Sartre's view, the process of dialectical totalization explained Stalin's rule. Camus thought that the totalitarian impulse of historicism was as deluded as its opposite ideology, idealist anti-historicism. It is only by denying reality that one may consider history to be a totality into itself. One should not believe that there is 'nothing but history' nor that there is 'nothing of history'. 'There are two sorts of impotence,' he concludes, 'the impotence of Good and the impotence of Evil' (Felman and Laub, 1992, 174). Sartre accused Camus of negative anti-historicism, and recalled his past exemplary testimonial role, best expressed in *The Plague* – a healing task of 'personal salvation' made 'accessible to all'. But it is such ideology of salvation and its corresponding witnessing authority that Camus wants to question in *The Fall*.

The Camus that denounced 'the plague' was a heroic witness upholding the promise of communal salvation. But the Camus who concentrated on a suicide with the mere possibility of a missed rescue was now a witness of loss and perdition. This is not the Camus who celebrated the incoming history of redemption at the end of *The Plague*, the totally new beginning after the Second World War. While Sartre thinks that Camus is a man of the past by failing in his role to recognize the progress and thus be a witness to the cure, Camus thinks that it is Sartre who lives in the past by neglecting to be a witness to the atrocities of the Soviet Union inspired by his own prophetic Marxism – denies the present and its continuation of the unceasing plague. Camus charges that even if Soviet communism was the most important revolution of the twentieth century, one still has to denounce the terror of the concentration camps it has brought about.

'There are always reasons for murdering a man,' the narrator observes in *The Fall* (Camus, 1958, 112). The Nazis did it in their search for a 'final solution'. What else could it be but its double, such salvation ideology that rationalized murder in search of a final socialist utopia? Thus, 'Camus now realizes that the very moral core that gave its momentum to *The Plague* – the establishment of a community of witnessing – was itself in some ways a distortion, a historical delusion' (Felman and Laub, 1992, 181). The very notion of 'alliance' he had formed with Sartre and his group breaks down, and Camus comes to the conclusion that the witness has no ally. The true witness is beset in the end with issues of knowledge and silence. When Sartre accuses Camus that he is merely 'looking' at history from Hell rather than 'making history', Camus replies that he is 'making silence' by refusing to look at the horrors of Stalinism.

This interplay between historical action and writers' reflection was echoed two weeks before the 2004 US presidential election when an aide, who sounded like the all-powerful Karl Rove, scorned at journalists and their 'reality-based community'. He informed his interviewer, Ron Suskind, that 'a judicious study of discernible reality' is 'not the way the world really works anymore'. He added:

> We're an empire now, and when we act, we create our own reality. And while you're studying that reality – judiciously, as you will – we act again, creating other new realities, which you can study too, and that's how things will sort out. We're history's actors … and you, all of you, will be left to just study what we do. (Rich, 2006, 4)

Camus would reply that not only are they making history by their actions, but also by their non-actions; they are 'making silence' by their refusal to see and hear other views, by shrouding in secrecy what they don't want the public to know.

It was systematic deafness and muteness to the realities of the concentration camps that made possible the extermination of the Jews. This was the secret shared by all the sides of the war, and around which the genocide happened. It is well known that the present American government has a network of secret jails around the world in which alleged terrorists are being kept under unknown conditions with no access to lawyers and human rights groups. The Guantanamo prison has been compared to a modern concentration camp. Are the political realities of 'the view from Hell' discussed by Camus over? What made such realities possible in the past was their minimization through systematic silence. Isn't the very fact that a Guantanamo and such a shadowy network of secret prisons is tolerated by the American public proof of Camus's argument regarding the betrayal of the witness by 'making silence' and in the end turning all of us into accomplices of the jailers?

The conclusion we are led to is that the very unmediated access to the evidence of *The Plague* and the very nature of the unqualified testimony given there 'fails precisely to account for the specificity of a disaster that consisted in a radical failure of witnessing, an event to which the witness had no access, since its very catastrophic and unprecedented nature as event was to *make the witness absent*' (Felman and Laub, 1992, 194). Thus, witnessing itself can hardly be made present to consciousness. The witness, as I recount in my ethnography of Itziar, sees a man being murdered and asks in horror: 'But how can that be?' What happened? What is the event itself? A vulgar murder? An act of justice? A revolutionary demand? An act of madness? Just tell us, what is it? Should we act as witnesses? Is there anything we can say or do? Nobody knows for sure how to react. But how can that be? But what is it?

A cryptic theft is narrated in *The Fall*: a painting entitled *The Just Judges*. It is the allegory of those who speak from a position of moral rightness; this is also the case of the honest witness of *The Plague* who has a clear picture of what is going on. It is this complacency of the witness who assumes for himself untainted innocence that *The Fall* wants to unmask. Because if the witness is truly aware of the modern history of crime in which he lives, including the Holocaust, there is no place of complete innocence –'innocence can only mean lack of awareness of one's participation in the crime' (Felman and Laub, 1992, 196). Camus's point echoes Dostoevsky: 'We cannot assert the innocence of anyone, whereas we can state with certainty the guilt of all. Every man testifies to the crimes of all the others – that is my faith and my hope' (Camus, 1958, 110). Since in this perspective there is no longer a place of innocence from which to testify, we are guilty of our own innocence. Guilt thus becomes not a state opposed to innocence, but a process of awakening.

There was a clear separation between crime and testimony in *The Plague*. But in *The Fall*, the witness is a lawyer who can take either side of an issue and who is only representing the victim. 'And don't forget, moreover,' warns Camus, 'that *today the judges, the accused and the witnesses are permuted*' (Felman and Laub, 1992, 198). This is the case, for instance, with the Basques, former victims of Nazi/Francoist aggression in Guernica, now victimizers through ETA's terrorist actions (see Zulaika, 1991).

The Fall refers to the turning point marked in history by the events of the Holocaust and the crisis of witnessing it brings forth. Whose fall is being narrated when the narrator witnesses the fall of the suicide woman off the bridge – the woman's, or the narrator's who did not tell anyone about what he saw? It is this fall/failure of the witness that we are confronted with in *The Fall*. Previously, in 1946, Camus had written in *Neither Victims nor Executioners*:

> The years we have gone through have killed something in us. And that something is simply the old confidence man had in himself, which led him to believe that he could always elicit human reactions from another man if he spoke to him in the language of a common humanity. (Camus, 1986, 27–8)

After Auschwitz, the radical crisis of witnessing forces narrative to become the writing of such impossibility.

Contemporary terrorism is one more proof that Camus's early warning that something fundamental has died in us has lost none of its urgency. He wrote this faced with the Nazi death camps, but also with the Hiroshima, Nagasaki and the systematic bombings of European cities by both sides. The war showed not only the capacity for genocidal murder, but also, as pacifists have insisted, the use of massive violence in the name of a just cause. Camus broke with the centuries-old tradition of the Just War – a thinking that is untenable during the nuclear era, when the very idea of war in any classical military sense has become simply obsolete. Camus came to abhor especially the abstract state's role in serving to legitimize murder, and the ominous role of technology in the national security system. We live, he writes, 'in a world of abstractions, of bureaus and machines, of absolute ideas and of crude messianism. We suffocate among people who think they are absolutely right, whether in their machines of in their ideas' (Camus, 1986, 29). Technology not only increases the lethality of the weapons, but obliterates the witnessing function by distancing the executioners from their deeds:

> The Allied bomber squadrons could obliterate block after block of German cities and return to their officers' clubs to celebrate. Today, hundreds of thousands of engineers design and produce weapons of mass destruction such as the Trident submarine, described by Archbishop Raymond Hunthausen as 'the Auschwitz of Puget Sound'. This work is done in the comfort of air-conditioned offices, where weapons are tested, war games played, and mega-deaths calculated at computer terminals. (Camus, 1986, 9)

It is the bureaucracy that makes the decisions, so individuals are free to deny their responsibility in the potential consequences of such weapons. Mass destruction is thus planned *with no witness for it* and everyone innocent. To this Camus replies: 'We are all guilty.' The righteous ideologies in the defence of democracy and Western civilization, and supported by reason and science, were in the end masks for murder, since 'there are always reasons for murdering a man'.

Camus is no conventional pacifist: 'People like myself want not a world in which murder no longer exists … But rather one in which murder is not legitimate' (Camus, 1986, 31). Friends reacted by telling him that he 'was living in Utopia'. But he confronts his critics by retorting whether, in the present infernal world, aren't they also living in Utopia by agreeing with the logic of murder that endlessly and more perilously than ever 'throws us back on murder'? It is not a matter of Utopia versus reality, but one between a Utopia that makes common sense and a Utopia that is nourished by the nightmare fantasy of competing bureaucratic systems of violence in an era of nuclear technology and a state of terror that is legitimized with the principle that the end justifies the means (Camus 1986, 34). Is it asking too much, Camus contends, that in such a nuclearized world, moral justifications for violence (always with God on our side) be cut off from the reality of war?

Contemporary terrorism brings a new urgency to the central issue dealt with by Camus, which he phrased thus:

> Do you, or do you not, directly or indirectly, want to be killed or assaulted? Do you or do you not, directly or indirectly, want to kill or assault?' All who say No to both these questions are automatically committed to a series of consequences which must modify their way of posing the problem. (Camus 1986, 30)

This breaks entirely new moral and political ground. It amounts to the recognition that whoever does not want to be a victim must also refuse to be executioner by never justifying that killing is legitimate. This is, of course, utopian, since for most of us the killing will be done by a professional army that represents a nation state, in a distant land, and with the remoteness of technological means.

The discourse of 'the terrorist' adds a new dimension to the ideological justifications for the legitimate war: it provides the figure of an almost sub-human being who has no moral, legal or political grounds to claim whatsoever, bent on murderous, arbitrary and random violence, which prompts the immediate reaction, widely justified in public opinion, that the taking of his or her life is not only legitimate, but the only sensible thing to do. It could be argued that currently, the creation of such discourse is in itself a strategic ideological construct to condone murder. The terrorist is the new signifier, as was 'Hitler' during the Second World War, that demands all out war by whatever means. Thus, the dangers seen in the ideology that the ends justify the means, that our killings are unlike their killings, that a conspiracy of silence is warranted because of the nature of the enemy, in short, that we are more than justified to murder them and still be, not only innocent, but heroes are nowhere as real as in 'the war on terror'. What summed up Camus's indictment of the unfortunate circumstances that 'have killed something in us' was 'simply the old confidence' we had 'in the language of a common humanity' (Camus, 1986, 27–8). The one figure in contemporary political discourse of an enemy who is wholly unlike us, with whom we would never share our sense of humanity, is of course the loathsome terrorist. This is the discourse that demands we totally separate ourselves from him or her, that we treat him or her with the logic of all-out contagion, that we simply taboo him or her as an entity of utter danger and unmitigated evil. From this lack of common humanity and the inability to witness the other's suffering sprung for Camus all the moral and political dangers of the post-war period, a deadlock that rendered the state of humanity 'closed to the future'. Even in the horrors of the Second World War, and while himself committed to clandestine resistance, he was still able to see the moral bankruptcy of both sides using wholesale military violence against the other, and had the courage to speak up against the simplistic choices between what he called 'the impotence of Good' and 'the impotence of Evil'.

References

Aretxaga, Begoña (2001), 'Terror as Thrill: First Thoughts on the "War on Terrorism"', *Anthropological Quarterly Journal* 75:1 (Winter 2001), 149.

Camus, Albert (1948), *The Plague*, trans. Stuart Gilbert (New York: Alfred A. Knopf).

Camus, Albert (1958), *The Fall* (New York: Alfred A. Knopf).

Camus, Albert (1986), *Neither Victims Nor Executioners*, trans. Dwight Macdonald (Philadelphia, PA: New Society Publishers).

Felman, Shoshana and Laub, Dori (1992), *Testimony: Crisis of Witnessing in Literature, Psychoanalysis, and History* (New York and London: Routledge).

Giroux, Henry A. (2004), *The Terror of Neoliberalism: Authoritarianism and the Eclipse of Democracy* (Boulder, CO: Paradigm Publishers).

Gramsci, Antonio (1959), 'What is Man?', in *The Modern Prince*, trans. Louis Marks (New York: International Publishers).

Grey, Stephen; Sciolino, Elaine and Van Natta Jr, Don (2006), 'In Tapes, Receipts and a Diary, Details of the British Terror Case', *New York Times*, 28 August, front page.

Levi, Primo (1989) *The Drowned and the Saved* (New York: Vintage Books).

Radhakrishnan, R. (1990), 'Toward an Effective Intellectual: Foucault or Gramsci?', in Bruce Robbins (ed.), *Intellectuals: Aesthetics, Politics, Academics* (Minneapolis, MN: University of Minnesota Press).

Rich, Frank (2006), *The Greatest Story Ever Sold: The Decline and Fall of Truth: From 9/11 to Katrina* (New York: Penguin Press).

Rose, Carl et al. (1986), *Report of the International Commission on Violence in the Basque Country* (Vitoria, Spain: Eusko Jaurlaritza,), 9.1.21 and 9.1.14.

White, Hayden (1978), *Tropics of Discourse: Essays in Cultural Criticism* (Baltimore, MD: John Hopkins University Press).

Zulaika, Joseba (1991), 'Terror, Totem, and Taboo: Reporting on a Report', *Terrorism and Political Violence* 3:1, 34–49.

Zulaika, Joseba (1998) 'Tropics of Terror: From Guernica's "Natives" to Global "Terrorists"', *Social Identities* 4:1, 93–108.

Zulaika, Joseba and Douglass, William A. (1996), *Terror and Taboo: On the Follies, Fables, and Faces of Terrorism* (New York and London: Routledge).

PART TWO
COMPLICATIONS

Chapter 4
European Civil Society and the European Intellectual: What Is, and How Does One Become, a European Intellectual?

William Outhwaite

> Whether … a forum for communication will arise ironically depends mostly on intellectuals as a group who unceasingly talk about Europe without ever doing anything for it. (Habermas, 1996, 16)

> In the world today, we are already perceived and addressed not only as 'French' or 'German', but as 'European' intellectuals. (Balibar, 2004, 205)

> In Europe we have a conception of the political that includes an educative role; it isn't so robotized as in the United States. (Kristeva, 1993, 179)

I have been concerned for some time with questions around the possible existence of something one might call a European civil society (see Outhwaite, 2000 and 2006), and this chapter continues these reflections. By 'European' I mean for these purposes Europe-wide, or at least common to several countries of Europe. So in the case of civil society, if the term means anything at all, it is clear that there are civil societies in the UK, Germany and so on, but whether there is a European-level civil society is much more questionable.

There is in fact a kind of Dutch auction in much thinking, including my own, about these issues, where we start by asking whether there is a European-wide civil society, retreat to a conception in which there may not be that but at least there may be a European public sphere, and finally, if disappointed in that expectation,[1] to my present theme, whether at the *very* least we can talk about a smallish number of transnationally recognized European intellectuals, including sociologists, or at least social theorists.[2] Intellectuals might then be seen as the vanguard of a

1 It is, of course, a simplification to pose the issue simply as one of the existence or non-existence of a European public sphere. As Risse (2002, 1–2) and others have suggested, it makes more sense to distinguish between different types of public spheres and different dimensions of 'transnationalness'. For a more optimistic analysis, see, for example, Trenz and Eder (2004).

2 Richard Münch (1999, 249), for example, has suggested that the bearers of a European identity will primarily be 'the elites of top managers, experts, political leaders and intellectuals …'.

European public sphere or civil society *à venir*, rather as they were in Germany and elsewhere for the national societies of the nineteenth century.[3] They would, of course, be dependent on existing national and transnational structures, notably syndication arrangements and other transnational media forms.

When I began to draw up a list of possible candidates, the number of contemporary or recently active intellectuals with a genuinely Europe-wide resonance revealed itself as rather small. Many of these, moreover, could be argued to owe their prominence in part to their contributions to questions about Europe. To exclude them for this reason, however, would have left me without a list at all. More seriously, it would be natural to expect European intellectuals to be interpellated, by themselves or by others, to comment on European issues.

The lists in the Appendix to this chapter are therefore a provisional, and no doubt biased,[4] suggestion of some likely suspects (almost all, I fear, male). What I have in mind in distinguishing between the A and B lists is the feeling that those on the former are pretty much household names, and the latter rather less prominent and/or with a reputation confined to a narrower field.

Of my A List, I shall concentrate in particular on a sub-set of eight social theorists: Bauman, Bourdieu, Derrida, Eco, Foucault, Giddens, Habermas and Žižek. These are probably sufficient to illustrate some characteristic differences in trajectory. Despite the untimely death of three of them, all continue to be central to social and cultural theory in the early twenty-first century, as well as holding or having held significant roles as public intellectuals. Each is firmly grounded in their native or, in Bauman's case, adopted country, while having a major presence in the rest of Europe. (I am ignoring here the otherwise important Algerian connections of all three Frenchmen.)

Bauman, of course, was driven out of Poland in 1968, and returned, so far as I know, only in 1988. He has probably been the most reluctant to embrace the role of public intellectual, which accrued partly as a result of his accelerating output of stunningly original and stimulating work in social theory, and partly also because of the transformation of Eastern Europe and Russia from the late 1980s onwards. He received the Amalfi European Prize in 1990, and the Adorno Prize in 1998. He has written substantially on the topic of Europe, most recently in a short book (Bauman, 2004).

3 For the German case, see for example Bernhard Giesen (1993). Even in the nineteenth century, of course, there was a good deal of trans-European activity by public intellectuals. As Christophe Charle (2004, 187) notes, Zola and the other French Dreyfusards, whose intervention is widely seen to have launched the word 'intellectual', received widespread support from the rest of Europe. The Second World War was also a powerful impetus to pan-European intellectual as well as (other) political activity. Klaus Mann (quoted by Hartmut Kaelble, 2004, 304) wrote in 1949 that intellectuals are: 'Europeans now. Shared suffering has a unifying force.'

4 Less biased, perhaps, than John Lechte's *Fifty Key Contemporary Thinkers* (1994), of whom only six are both really contemporary (for example, not Freud or Bakhtin) and not French (or primarily active in France). To be fair, the subtitle of the book makes clear that he is concerned with structuralism and its opponents.

The case of Bourdieu is rather particular. About his prominence there can be little doubt. His death, like Derrida's, made the lead story and most of the front page of *Le Monde*, and was substantially covered elsewhere in the European press. Although his first book, on Algeria, was inevitably a focus of major public controversy, he was also reluctant to embrace the role of intellectual in a field which he was more concerned to deconstruct. In his later, more militant period, nastily characterized by Luc Boltanski in *Le Monde* as 'a kind of agitprop', he made up for lost time with a host of public interventions and initiatives. His Centre de Sociologie Européenne, founded in 1968, speaks to his pan-European concerns. In 1997, he received the Ernst Bloch Prize in Ludwigshafen; Ulrich Beck's *laudatio* (Beck, 1997) specifically addressed the issue of European intellectuals. Beck himself appears on my B List, but is a plausible candidate for promotion to A; again, he has become increasingly concerned with European issues.

Giddens's trajectory has been different, but comparably dramatic. From being very much a professional sociologist (indeed, the doyen of UK sociology), though spectacularly well travelled and with an unrivalled ability to speak without notes, he went on to develop the intellectual rationale for Blair's 'third way', to make LSE a major centre of public as well as scholarly debate, and to performatively illustrate his conception of globalization with a series of Reith Lectures at sites around the world. He is now, of course, a Labour peer and active in a number of major European initiatives, particularly in the area of social policy (Giddens, 2007).

Foucault, Derrida, Eco and Žižek seem to have slipped less problematically into their public intellectual roles, though Derrida's seems to have been relatively slow to develop (Lamont, 1987). Habermas, too, was pugnaciously involved in controversy from the beginning of his career, with his outraged response to Heidegger's unwillingness to address his complicity with Nazism (Habermas, 1953) and his active involvement in the later student movement. His first publication in English (Habermas, 1971) included two essays on this subject. In 2001, he received the German publishers' Peace Prize[5] and was described in one commentary on this event as the 'Hegel of the Federal Republic' (Ross, 2001). His joint statement with Derrida in 2003 was a particularly prominent transnational intervention. He is also, of course, the author of some ten volumes of 'political writings' which he is careful to distinguish from his other scholarly work. He has become increasingly concerned with European issues, notably the constitution, whose vicissitudes in France and the Netherlands he commented on with a powerful combination of passion and cool analysis. (He had earlier, of course, argued unsuccessfully for a new German constitution in 1990.)

What can we conclude from these instances? All these thinkers have massive scholarly reputations. All of them, even if in some cases their theoretical works

5 The list of recent recipients of this prize itself a useful indicator of Europe-wide resonance. As well as Habermas in 2001, it includes the Hungarian Peter Eszterházy in 2004 and the Turkish writer Orhan Pamuk in 2005.

are sometimes dense and difficult, have written superbly for a broader public. If I am right that the names of most if not all of them would be familiar to the readers of serious newspapers and journals across Europe, what does this tell us about a putative European public sphere?

Let us look a bit more closely at media structures across Europe. Very crudely, print and electronic media have experienced opposite developments: concentration in the first case, massive diversification in the latter. In both, however, ambitious projects of Europeanization in the 1970s tended to be abandoned or scaled down in the latter part of the twentieth century. Morley and Robins (1995, 52) note, for example, 'the retreat of many of the entrepreneurial enthusiasts of "European" satellite television, away from their original pan-European ambitions, towards a revised perspective which accepts the limitations and divisions of separate language/cultural markets in Europe'. There is also no genuinely European newspaper published in the major languages, and *The European* (1990–98), published in English and owned for most of its brief life by the notorious Robert Maxwell, made a poor showing compared to the *Herald Tribune*, *Financial Times* or *Economist*. Schlesinger and Kevin (2000, 222–9) give a somewhat more positive analysis of the substantial pan-European presence of these three publications.[6] They point also to Euronews, launched in 1993 on a transnational public service broadcasting base and transmitting in the major West European languages; this, however, is very uneven in its European reach. More recently, *France 24* broadcasts in English as well as French, but is solidly and explicitly French in its basis and orientation.

Most discouraging, perhaps, is the abandonment of automatic syndicalization of mainstream newspapers, as opposed to the production of specialized cosmopolitan editions such as *Le Monde*'s weekly/monthly in English or the *Guardian Weekly*: 'Thus there are hardly any transnational media that have the potential to reach the majority of European citizenry' (Adam, Berkel and Pfetsch, 2003, 70).

Those taking a sceptical view of the existence of a European public sphere, particularly media theorists, have tended to conclude that Europe has not got past first base. Marianne van de Steeg (2002, 499–500) cites three typical examples from Philip Schlesinger (1995, 25–6), Peter Graf Kielmansegg (1994, 27–8) and Dieter Grimm (1995, 294–5). For Kielmansegg and Grimm, linguistic division more or less rules out the possibility of Europe forming a communicative community. Schlesinger sets the stakes fairly modestly as 'the minimal establishment of a European news agenda as a serious part of the news-consuming habits of significant European audiences who have begun to think of their citizenship as transcending the level of the nation-state'. He goes on, however, to suggest that 'even a multilingual rendition of a single given European news agenda is more likely to be diversely "domesticated" within each distinctive national or language context … than it is likely to reorient an audience towards a common European

6 See also Preston (2005), who cites an overseas sales figure of 300,000 for *The Financial Times*.

perspective'. And what for Schlesinger is a hypothesis becomes for Grimm a matter of definition:

> A Europeanized communication system ought not to be confused with increased reporting on European topics in national media. These are directed at a national public and remain attached to national viewpoints and communication habits. They can accordingly not create any European public nor establish any European discourse. (Schlesinger, 1995)

As Van de Steeg argues, this is both theoretically and empirically dubious. Theoretically, it overlooks the ways in which a communicative community may not just be the product of an existing substantive community, but may help to bring it into existence.[7] Empirically, it seems to rule out interesting elements of Europeanization within existing national media structures. As she shows in a modest but suggestive study of the discussion in 1989–98 of the prospects of the EU's eastern enlargement in four European weeklies, there are significant differences between the four. Whereas *Der Spiegel* and the *New Statesman* tended to relate most clearly to their respective national frameworks, the Spanish *Cambio 16* reprinted articles from similar German, Italian and French journals, and the Dutch *Elsevier* engaged more directly with pan-European debates (Van de Steeg, 2002, 514). The *New Statesman* stands out for its relative lack of attention to the concrete implications of enlargement for the EU's institutions and procedures (Van de Steeg, 2002, 515).

Although she does not discuss intellectuals explicitly, Van de Steeg's conception of the public sphere is loaded in that direction; she defines it as 'consisting of actors who debate in public a topic which they consider to be in the public interest, i.e. of concern to the polity'. More importantly, a media analysis of this kind would be highly relevant to assessing the structural opportunities for Europeanizing intellectuals.

Three further distinctions might be useful in mapping the area: those between the domestic and the international, the multinational and the transnational, and between invited contributions (speeches, articles, interviews, debates) and spontaneous interventions by intellectuals in the public sphere. Newspapers and journals may be multinational, like the *Financial Times*, with its modified overseas editions, or (more rarely) genuinely transnational, like *Lettre International*

7 There are, of course, parallels with Habermas's position on these issues, and more specifically, with his dispute with Grimm; and also with Ulrich Beck and Edgar Grande's more speculative argument in *Cosmopolitan Europa* (2004) that a reflective and cosmopolitan conception of Europe can to some extent escape the dilemmas of in/out, us/them, nation state/federation. The undeniable elitism of the EU is here given a positive spin: the EU embodies the paradox of a civil society *from above* aiming to establish one from below (Beck and Grande, 2004, 196). More optimistically, they suggest, the concept of European civil society offers the EU the opportunity of opening up a transnational space in such a way that it organizes itself.

(which, however, has a home base in Germany) or the academic journals of the ISA (International Sociological Association) and ESA (European Sociological Association), which migrate to follow their editorial teams from site to site, even if they have a home base for publishing and printing.

Invitations may be nationally based, as when the BBC invites Giddens to deliver a lecture series, international, as when the German Book Trade invites the Polish/British Bauman to receive its prize or the Polish paper *Polityka* invites Michnik and Habermas to a debate published there and in *Die Zeit* (Habermas and Michnik, 1993), or transnational/European, as in the case of the Charlemagne Prize. Interventions will most often be national, but may be transnational in their origin and/or destination, as in the joint declaration by Habermas and Derrida (2003), or an appeal on human rights in Turkey, published in the *Guardian* in September 2005. Any shift towards the internationalization or Europeanization of such activities will therefore be of interest.

What, in conclusion, can one say about a European public sphere? I have cited some of the more sceptical commentators on this, but I shall close with a recent statement by Klaus Eder (2005), from the more optimistic pole to which I would also in the end attach myself, at least with the will and part, at least, of the intellect. For Eder, an emergent public sphere and demos are evolving together:

> A transnational public … exists in Europe as a cross-cutting of elite publics, citizens' publics and popular publics, related to each other by some supranational institutional environment … A European public is not a chimere but a thing that already turns up in critical times … [he mentions Habermas's intervention in the Iraq war protest] A transnational public sphere … is one which is no longer tied to a reified body of people such as the nation, but to a latent demos that can be there when time requires it. (Eder, 2005, 341–2)

References

Adam, S., Berkel, B. and Pfetsch, B. (2003), 'Media Opportunity Structures: A Brake Block for the Europeanisation of Public Spheres?', <http://europub.wz-berlin.de>.

Bauman, Zygmunt (2004), *Europe: An Unfinished Adventure* (Cambridge: Polity Press).

Balibar, Étienne (2004), *We, The People of Europe? Reflections on Transnational Citizenship* (Princeton, NJ: Princeton University Press).

Beck, Ulrich (1997), 'Mißverstehen als Fortschritt. Europäische Intellektuelle im Zeitalter der Globalisierung', <http://www.homme-moderne.org/societe/socio/ubeck/laudaD.html>.

Beck, Ulrich and Grande, Edgar (2004), *Das kosmopolitische Europa* (Frankfurt: Suhrkamp).

Böröcz, József and Sarkar, Mahua (2005), 'What is the EU?', *International Sociology* 20:2, 153–73.

Charle, Christophe (2004), 'Intellectuals in Europe in the Second Half of the Nineteenth Century', in Hartmut Kaelble (ed.), *The European Way* (Oxford: Berghahn), 186–204.

Collini, Stefan (2006), *Absent Minds: Intellectuals in Britain* (Oxford: Oxford University Press).

Crowley, John (2003), 'The European Public Space: Assembling Information that Allows the Monitoring of European Democracy', <http://europub.wz-berlin.de>.

Delanty, Gerard (2003), 'The Making of a Post-Western Europe: A Civilizational Analysis', *Thesis Eleven* 72, 8–24.

Delanty, Gerard (2005) 'Cultural Translations and European Modernity', in Ben-Rafael, Eliezer (ed.), *Comparing Modern Civilizations: Pluralism versus Homogeneity* (Leiden: Brill).

Della Porta, D. (2003), 'Dimensions of Political Opportunities and the Europeanisation of Public Spheres', <http://europub.wz-berlin.de>.

Eder, Klaus (2005), 'Making sense of the public sphere', in Gerard Delanty (ed.), *Handbook of Contemporary European Social Theory* (London: Routledge), 333–46.

Eriksen, E.O. (2005), 'An Emerging European Public Sphere', *European Journal of Social Theory* 8:3, 341–63.

Eriksen, E.O. and Fossum, J.E. (eds) (2000), *Democracy in the European Union: Integration through Deliberation?* (London: Routledge).

Giddens, Anthony (2007), *Europe in the Global Age* (Cambridge: Polity Press).

Giesen, Bernhard (1993), *Die Intellektuellen und die Nation* (Frankfurt: Suhrkamp).

Goussault, Bénédicte (2002), 'La mort de Pierre Bourdieu dans la presse', EspacesTemps.net (15 October), <http://espacestemps.net/document499.html>.

Grimm, Dieter (1995), 'Does Europe Need a Constitution?', *European Law Journal* 1:3, 282–302.

Habermas, J. (1953), 'Mit Heidegger gegen Heidegger denken. Zur Veröffentlichung von Vorlesungen aus dem Jahre 1935', *Frankfurter Allgemeine Zeitung*, 25 June; reprinted in Habermas, J. (1981), *Philosophisch-politische Profile* (Frankfurt: Suhrkamp).

Habermas, J. (1971), *Toward a Rational Society* (London: Heinemann).

Habermas, J. (1991), 'Europe's Second Chance', trans. Habermas, J. (1994), *The Past as Future* (Cambridge: Polity Press).

Habermas, J. (1996), *Die Einbeziehung des Anderen* (Frankfurt: Suhrkamp), trans. Habermas, J. (1998), *The Inclusion of the Other* (Cambridge: Polity).

Habermas, J. (2008), *Ach, Europa* (Frankfurt: Suhrkamp).

Habermas, J. and Derrida, J. (2003), 'February 15, or what binds Europeans together', *Constellations* 10:3, 364–70.

Habermas, J. and Michnik, A. (1993), 'Mehr Demut, weniger Illusionen', *Die Zeit*, 17 December, 9–13.

Hjerm, Michael (2003), 'National Sentiments in Eastern and Western Europe', *Nationalities Papers* 31, 4.

Kaelble, Hartmut (ed.) (2004), *The European Way* (Oxford: Berghahn).

Kielmansegg, Peter Graf (1994), 'Läßt sich die Europäische Gemeinschaft demokratisch verfassen?', *Europäische Rundschau* 22:2, 23–33.

Kögler, H.-H. (2005),'Constructing a Cosmopolitan Public Sphere: Hermeneutic Capabilities and Universal Values', *European Journal of Social Theory* 8:3, 297–320.

Kristeva, Julia (1993), 'Foreign Body: Conversation with Scott L. Malcolmson', *Transition* 59, 172–83.

Lamont, Michele (1987), 'How to Become a Dominant French Philosopher: The Case of Jacques Derrida', *American Journal of Sociology* 93:3 (November), 584–622.

Lamont, Michèle (1992), *Money, Morals, and Manners: The Culture of the French and American Upper-middle Class* (Chicago, IL: University of Chicago Press).

Lechte, John (1994), *Fifty Key Contemporary Thinkers: From Structuralism to Postmodernity* (London: Routledge).

Lepenies, Wolf (2007), *Qu'est-ce qu'un intellectuel européen?* (Paris: Seuil).

Morley, David and Robins, Kevin (eds) (1996), *Spaces of Identity: Global Media, Electronic Landscapes and Cultural Boundaries* (London: Routledge).

Müller, Jan-Werner (2000), *Another Country: German Intellectuals, Unification and National Identity* (Newhaven, CT: Yale University Press).

Müller-Doohm, Stefan (2005), 'Theodor W. Adorno and Jürgen Habermas – Two Ways of Being a Public Intellectual: Sociological Observations Concerning the Transformation of a Social Figure of Modernity', *European Journal of Social Theory* 8, 269–80.

Münch, Richard (1999), 'Europäische Identitätsbildung', in Viehoff, R. and Segers, R.T. (eds), *Kultur, Identität, Europa* (Frankfurt: Suhrkamp), 223–52.

Nederveen Pieterse, Jan (2002), 'Europe, Traveling Light: Europeanization and Globalization', in Kempny, Marian and Jawlowska, Aldona (eds), *Identity in Transformation: Postmodernity, Postcommunism, and Globalization* (Westport, CT and London: Praeger).

Outhwaite, William (2000), 'Towards a European Civil Society?', *Soundings* 16 (November), 131–43.

Outhwaite, William (2006), 'Is There a European Civil Society?', in Rogowski, Ralf and Turner, Charles (eds), *The Shape of the New Europe* (Cambridge: Cambridge University Press), 87–103.

Preston, Peter (2005), 'Serving up continental short shrift', *The Guardian*, 26 June, p. 7.

Reed-Danahay, Deborah (2005), *Locating Bourdieu* (Urbana, IL: Indiana University Press).

Risse, Thomas (2002), *How Do We Know a European Public Sphere When We See One?*, <http://web.fu-berlin.de/atasp/texte/pi5s1otn.pdf>.

Ross, Jan (2001), 'Hegel der Bundesrepublik', *Die Zeit*, Feuilleton, 42.

Schlesinger, P. (1995), 'Europeanisation and the Media: National Identity and the Public Sphere', <http://www.arena.uio.no/publications/working-papers1995/95_07.xml>.

Schlesinger, P. and Kevin, D. (2000), 'Can the European Union Become a Sphere of Publics?', in Eriksen, E. and Fossum, J. (eds), *Democracy in the European Union* (London: Routledge), 6–29.

Trenz, H.-J. and Eder, K. (2004), 'The Democratizing Dynamics of a European Public Sphere: Towards a Theory of Democratic Functionalism', *European Journal of Social Theory* 7:1, 5–25.

Van de Steeg, Marianne (2002), 'Rethinking the Conditions for a Public Sphere in the European Union', *European Journal of Social Theory* 5:4, 499–519.

Appendix

A List

Giorgio Agamben
Raymond Aron
Raymond Barthes
Jean Baudrillard
Zygmunt Bauman
Pierre Bourdieu
Ralf Dahrendorf
Régis Debray
Gilles Deleuze/Félix Guattari
Jacques Derrida
Umberto Eco
Hans Magnus Enzensberger
Michel Foucault
Anthony Giddens
Günther Grass
Jürgen Habermas
Václav Havel
Julia Kristeva
Jean-François Lyotard
Adam Michnik
Antonio Negri
Andrei Sakharov
Jorge Semprún
Alexander Solzhenitsyn
George Steiner
Slavoj Žižek

B List

Tariq Ali
Rudolf Bahro
Étienne Balibar
Ulrich Beck
Norberto Bobbio
Alain Finkielkraut
Timothy Garton Ash
Germaine Greer
Michael Ignatieff
Václav Klaus
Leszek Kołakowski
György Konrád/I. Szelényi
Karel Kosik
Claude Lévi-Strauss
Michel Maffesoli
Roy and Zhores Medvedev
Edgar Morin
Serge Moscovici
Jean-Luc Nancy
Conor Cruise O'Brien
Jacques Rancière
Milan Šimečka
Tzvetan Todorov
Alain Touraine

Chapter 5
What Influence? Public Intellectuals, the State and Civil Society

E. Stina Lyon

> D.B.: 'The minute you have something individual to say, by definition, it will strike consonance in some and dissonance in others. I think that only mediocrity gets an uncontroversial reaction. And controversial has become almost a swear word in today's world, you know "He's controversial."'
>
> E.W.S.: 'They always say that about me.'
>
> D.B.: 'I would take that as a great compliment.'
>
> E.W.S.: 'Oh, I do, I do. But it is not meant that way. It's meant that this is a person who troubles the status quo in some way, which we want to preserve at all costs. But on the other hand, one also wants an audience. One does not want to be so repellent.'
>
> (Daniel Barenboim and Edward W. Said in conversation, 2004)

Introduction: Troubling the Status Quo

This chapter aims to develop a framework for understanding the relationship between 'public intellectuals', the state, civil society in all its manifestations and the public at large. Sociologists have since the inception of the discipline been influential agents in the public domain beyond academe in a variety of ways: as politicians, government advisers, social researchers on government funded projects, critical writers and paradigm shifters, public orators, propagandists for social movements and voluntary organizations, teachers and publicists. On the one hand, questions about social relations in the public domain lie at the core of the sociological enterprise, both theoretically and empirically. On the other, the behaviour of sociologists and the reception of what they say by society at large in all its workings exemplify those very relations of power, organization, networks and social influences as well as those of exclusion, failed aspirations and disappointments. What, and who, has had influence over 'social knowledge' in the public domain has over time and place been a contested issue with power over its collection and interpretation shifting between the state, civil society and a populace variably receptive to exposure and criticism by 'public intellectuals'.

It is not the aim of this chapter to attempt to draw up a rigid typology of public intellectuals. Nor is it that of engaging in critical debate with a long tradition of sociologists who have written on the nature of intellectuals as a social stratum or class in relation to other elites (see Brym, 1980; Karabel, 1996). Rather, the intention here is to attempt and outline of some of the different types of 'connectivity' that create public platforms, the dimensions that characterize these relationships and their implication for sociological influence. It will conclude with a brief discussion of the contemporary fragmentation of sociological knowledge as an academic discipline, and its impact on the public role of its protagonists and their status in the public domain. As the focus of my own recent work has been the intellectual and political contribution of a very public pair of intellectuals, Alva and Gunnar Myrdal, they will figure strongly in the following. So will their shared conception that attempts to reconcile individual and social values with the day-to-day realities of power and its consequences present a range of dilemmas, the nature of which it is the responsibility of intellectuals to deconstruct and investigate.

The concept of 'public' has many meanings: as an adjective, it is commonly used to describe something which is by or for a whole community or nation or people 'in general', but also to that which is known and accessible to all. To do something in public is to do something openly, not secretly or privately. As a noun, it refers to a community or nation or any section of the community considered in some way as an audience for information and communications. The expression of 'publicness', as Ryan writes, can flourish in a range of distinctive places, not only in literary or political clubs and in the culture of print, but also in a wide array of open public spaces where matters of general interest are discussed in 'styles of debate that defy literary standards of rational and critical discourse' (Ryan, 2003, 390). The concept of a 'public sphere' is thus a fluid one, with changing boundaries depending on the nature of particular economic and political processes, but also on the vagaries of fashion and culture. As Hess argues, what counts as the public sphere is a social sphere with social boundaries, the definition and inclusivity of which are themselves a matter for debate among public intellectuals (see Hess, 2000, 114).

An 'intellectual' is a person having a powerful and trained intellect who is inclined to the activities or pleasures of the intellect with a fondness for the scholarly activities of thought and reasoning. 'Thought' is both an activity and the product of such an activity which when written down may remain long after its originator has departed, what Popper described as the 'third world' of ideas not reducible to either mind or matter. I chose the word 'reasoning' rather than 'rationality' since the latter is a characteristic of a particular kind of reasoning, not always or necessarily an attribute of someone regarded as an 'intellectual'. A 'public intellectual' is thus someone who applies intellectual activities for a whole community, or nation, in a way that is open and accessible to the members of that community or nation, however defined. This, of course, also means that a public intellectual can at times, if his or her views are seen to be dangerous to the community by strong opposing interests within that community or nation, easily become seen as a public enemy. Most often both concepts have also come to have honorary connotations. A 'public-minded' person is someone seen to put the interests of the larger community above narrow selfish personal interests. The title of 'intellectual' is also seen only to accrue to persons whose reasoning is believed to display evidence of a *good* intellect, whether defined as well trained in the art of scholarship or in socially acceptable insights perceived to be of value whatever the reasoning underpinning them. As there is also a critical dimension, controversy, inherent in scholarship and reasoning, a public intellectual is also understood as being one who as was once said of the German professor, 'ist ein Mann, der anderer Meinung ist' – a man or a woman who troubles the status quo. Sociology might be a relatively young discipline, but as Walzer argues, public social criticism is as old as society itself and complaint 'one of the elementary forms of self-assertion, and the response to complaint is one of the elementary forms of mutual recognition' (Walzer, 1989, 3).

Intellectuals have a paradoxical status in democratic societies between enlightened intellectual ideals and egalitarian ones. On the one hand, they are expected, at times even required, to contribute their special knowledge, creative capacities and communicative skills. On the other, the professed egalitarian tenets of democracies also have an inborn tendency to view them with suspicions for their intellectual skills with reasoning and words. Democracies need both expertise and 'normative' insights as provided by intellectuals and the opportunity for public deliberations created by 'intellectual contestation'. Thus intellectuals should participate in public life for the sake of good judgement and good governance. But when they do, and when push comes to shove, the 'people' will choose among themselves those they will listen too, and it may not be those with the wisest or most informed judgement (see Goldfarb, 2003).

In the social sciences, such intellectual and scholarly reasoning relates to what we might call 'social knowledge', the production of descriptions, explanations and perhaps more importantly interpretations of society and its workings. Varieties of such knowledge has always been part of state-formation and nation-building, for military as much as for civilian purposes, but through the diversification of production and democratization processes, it has also increasingly become part of the everyday activities of citizens, producers, consumers and interest groups of various kinds. However, there has always been a tension within intellectual reasoning in general and social science particularly between on the one hand the search for universal principles and abstract conceptualizations, and on the other some passionate commitment to the minutia of local issues and times. When Said and Barenboim were asked where they felt they 'belong', Barenboim answered, 'Wherever there is music,' and Said chose 'cosmopolitan New York', because 'I can be "in it" but not "of it"'. But whatever generalities Barenboim and Said mentioned as their universal intellectual home, their passions have also been very clearly directed at creating a language of discourse across their own conflict-ridden local places of identification. As Geertz notes about anthropology, much sociology is a 'craft of place' and as much social knowledge is context-dependent and 'local' as is cumulatively universal and long-term (see Geertz, 1983).

All this, of course, begs the question what, and who, is the 'public', the community or nation to be served, and what the nature of the influence exerted might be. If by intellectual influence we mean having an effect, direct or indirect, on the beliefs and actions of persons in power and authority, and thereby on the institutions they represent, or on the attitudes and behaviour of sections of the public at large, the question similarly arises of which social groupings are involved and how these are defined as funding, supporting, intended or affected audiences, whether in a narrow sectarian or nationalistic way, or in a broader perspective of humanity in general. Finally, if we overlay this with the traditional political value perspectives of radicalism, progressivism, conservatism, socialism, liberalism, feminism, nationalism, racism, imperialism and varieties of 'globalism' and religious standpoints, each of which has created its own 'public intellectuals', we can begin to see some of the complexities in trying to develop a framework for understanding the real and imagined influence of public intellectuals.

I will in the following structure this chapter around the three core 'legitimators' and 'sponsors' of public intellectuals and their activities – the state, civil society and the public at large – and within each section, see how the dilemmas generated by different dimensions of sociological 'localism' versus 'universalism', the 'centre' and 'periphery' location of power relations, and top-down and 'expert' polemic versus bottom-up 'partisan' or cross-community 'dialogical' modes of relating to 'the public' intersect with each other and the allusive factor of 'influence'.

The State

The state in its varieties of forms has always used and paid for public intellectuals as technical strategists and ideological legitimators. The Prince has always needed his Machiavelli to give advice on the furtherance of his powers, though not all of them have necessarily been 'Machiavellian' in outlook. Public intellectuals have always obliged, whether as a Leonardo da Vinci with imaginative military machines, or a Giddens with ideas of how to manage welfare states in a capitalist economy. Systematic social knowledge about the ruled realm first gained significance for taxation and military purposes that required detailed information about the population from which levies and footsoldiers were to be drawn. With nation-formation, industrialization and democratization processes, other aspects of the quality and social well-being of populations arising from the needs for military and economic strength and political and social cohesion became important across Western societies, culminating in welfare state systems. Such systems depend for their administration and function as well as for political legitimacy on 'social knowledge' as a major part of political governance. Much of this knowledge now appears in the form of social statistics of various kinds to the collection and analysis of which public intellectuals contribute in a variety of ways, directly and indirectly. In a book on applied social research which is useful for these purposes, Bulmer outlines different modes that exist and are possible between the social analyst and public policymaking. He distinguishes between the 'engineering model' of such a relationship, more favoured by government for obvious reasons, and the 'enlightenment model' in which the social scientist contributes also to goal and agenda setting, not just through information about various means by which goals set elsewhere can be achieved (see Bulmer, 1982). There has in the social sciences been a lively debate on the advantages and disadvantages of such different models.

Modernity relies on rationality as the main means for making democracy work. The ideal of rationality prescribes that first we must know about a problem, then we can decide about it. Democracy demands that decisions are made only after open and evidenced debate. So, first the civil servants and commissioned researchers investigate a policy problem, then the minister is informed, who in turn informs parliament, who decides on the problem. Power is brought to bear on the problem only after we have made ourselves knowledgeable about it. But rationality is in itself a weak form of power, and the administration of rational planning and implementation is itself a political process. In reality, power often ignores or designs knowledge at its convenience, 'the blind spot of modernity' to use Flyvberg's expression (see Flynbjerg, 2001). While power may produce rationality, and rationality power, their relationship is asymmetrical. Power has a clear tendency to dominate rationality and knowledge in the dynamic and overlapping relationship between the two. If knowledge is power, then power also defines what gets to count as knowledge. The interpretation of social evidence is not only a summary and a commentary, but an attempt to present a definitive picture, a Foucaultian way of 'mastering' the evidence available. It is also in the very nature of social knowledge that evidence collected to disprove something can all too easily be reinterpreted to prove its very opposite. Booth's path-breaking empirical work on poverty in Victorian East London was originally prompted by his desire to refute evidence discussed in Parliament on the extent of poverty in London. Using his own funds, he in the end irrefutably proved them right. But the postmodernist position that therefore 'it is all political' obscures the real observable differences between types of political systems in how social knowledge is collected, used and understood, and how public intellectuals enter the political decision-making process, differences worthy of analysis. At present, sociological debates on intellectuals and politics, though important, are short of real evidence of how knowledge systems work in a complex democratic state rich in contradictory interests and aspirations (see, for example, Furedi, 2004). British Royal Commissions, Swedish Government Investigative Committees and Congressional Hearings in the US, though similarly evidence-seeking, all are very different animals when it comes to who gets access to the construction of interpretations, and how.

The concept of 'social engineering', a term often associated with the Myrdals, is of relevance here. At the turn of the last century, the concept of 'engineer' was associated with the activities of public professionals engaged in making the world a better place through the application of reason and technology. After the Holocaust and the Gulag, the term took on more sinister connotations necessitating a reformulation of the role of intellectuals in their relationship to the state. Public intellectuals, in serving the state, has served totalitarian dictators in their social visions as well as the more enlightened democratic rulers envisaged in the Federalist Papers. Intellectuals, argues Bauman, can no longer see themselves as 'legislators' over the behaviour and aspirations of the publics they research and write about in the same way as before, but need to take more democratic stances as social 'interpreters' to retain their legitimacy in the public domain (see Bauman, 1987). Myrdal saw the social scientist as having a twofold relationship to state policymaking. On the one hand, the social scientist needed to develop a 'prognosis' based on theoretical analysis of empirical evidence of social and economic trends to give a picture of what is and is likely to happen. But when working in political contexts it is also necessary to contribute to the development of 'programmes', plans for action based additionally on political and economic feasibility in terms of conflicting values over both goals and the means acceptable to achieve them. The latter might require a different kind of social research to establish what public acceptability is and might be. However, in neither case, he argued, can the values of a 'working scientists' be neatly dispensed with or put aside. That being the case, they should be honestly declared in open debate rather than hidden behind abstract rhetoric. But as Myrdal learned at a cost when over time he became seen as a political liability both in Sweden and in the US, the power of rationality is not always the rationality of power (see Lyon, 2004). Other 'public' sociologists have been caught in the same dilemma. So for public intellectuals, from the point of view of influence *vis-à-vis* the state, both knowledge of the principles of the rationality of knowledge and knowledge of the rationality of power become important to be able 'to hang on' in there. Men such as Daniel Moynihan, Robert Reich and Henry Kissinger in the US, all three with some claim to being 'public intellectuals', are not just razor-sharp in the interpretative skills of turning opposing pieces of evidence into supportive ones, they are also tough power brokers in presidential back rooms. Razor-sharp major public intellectuals such as Sartre and Foucault, though laudable in their academic contribution and radical zeal, have not always been successful in their attempts to become a politically effective force (see Lilla, 2001).

The sharpening of disciplinary boundaries between the different social sciences after the Second World War and the institutionalization of their definition in a growing university sector in some ways changed the nature of what public intellectuals in the social domain felt qualified to talk about in the public sphere. With the concept of 'expertise' more narrowly defined, and the discipline of sociology itself fragmenting into narrowly defined specialisms, 'generalist' social commentators involved in public debates about issues such as welfare, immigration, crime, family policy and so on face a greater risk of putting their own status as reasoning academics on the line within their own specialist community of experts (see Ennis, 1992). This, one can argue, also makes it easier for governments to ignore them, given that the nature of economic and social problems faced by states and their governments do not fall within neat disciplinary boundaries. In modernity's claim to rationality, sociology has never had a strong space of its own in comparison to the 'harder' social sciences of economics, and even geography. The British sociologist Ray

Pahl tells a revealing story from the early days of the redevelopment of the old docklands in London. When the chair of the development corporation was asked if there was a woman on its board, he answered: 'No, but we have a sociologist.' If academics and public intellectuals are paid to produce social knowledge at the highest perceived validity and rationality and that is defined as 'scientistic', then the credibility of the status of the sociological contribution may easily be undermined, as well as leading to continuing temptations for public intellectuals to withdraw from the state and its various apparatuses into a more sympathetically grounded and more specialist and academically 'local' dialogical domains.

For intellectuals in the scientific enlightenment tradition, there ultimately has to be some kind of a tension between the 'local' and the 'general'. If the principles of reasoning are universal, and social relationships can be explained in ways that have some universal applicability, then loyalty to the 'nation' and the state in and for itself has to be limited, in that it creates the wrong boundaries, accidental as they are. States and governments do not remain the same for long. They change due to both internal and external forces, which creates a problem for public intellectuals, whatever their relationship to the state. States occasionally change rapidly, either through the internal institutionalized transfer of power, or through socio-economic crises and political revolutions or through the threat of war. During the twentieth century, major wars, the Depression, the rise in fascism, the Cold War and more recently the fall of the Soviet bloc and the rise of aggressive world-wide terrorism all impacted on thinkers and researchers. By the very nature of their public position, intellectuals become called upon to remain loyal or to break the relationship and risk public dethronement and a fall from grace alongside their work and ideas. Occasionally, the nature of the severance has remained secret until revealed in secret service records. One can here think of Talcott Parsons, Isaiah Berlin, Sartre and Myrdal as examples of public intellectuals who have been shown either to be closer to the state or more subversive of it in their activities than was apparent at the time. They were, I am sure, not alone in this. And works directed at the state, such as, for example, Durkheim's work on the French education system or Weber's more political writings, may as a result disappear into the obscurity of history alongside the state to which they directed their polemics (see Kaesler, 1988).

In commentaries on the work of Gunnar Myrdal, the strength of both his patriotism and his internationalism is noted as a contradiction (see Appelqvist and Andersson, 1988; Eliæson, 2000). One might argue that from the point of view of a writer such as Fukuyama and his work on 'the end of history', such a combination of sentiments equates with a form of intellectual imperialism. From both Myrdal's perspective, the legal and social rights for individual citizens were fairer and Swedes led, and continue to lead, materially better lives than in most other countries, and propagating ideas about the means for achieving this for all could not be regarded as entirely suspect. An origin in a small country no longer known for its imperial pretensions allows a different context for the interpretation and dissemination of ideas about justice and social and political governance than those emanating from the heart of an empire with aspirations of global political and economic control.

Finally, the close relationship between states and secular rationality is a Western phenomenon. We owe some greater attempts at understanding the role of public intellectuals in the Islamic tradition, in which a strong integration between political and religious life has always been present, in their efforts to carve out a space between the economic demands for democratization and secularism of modernity, and the political and religious forces pressuring for the rights of culturally based nation-building (see Ramadan, 2001). The process of secularization since the Enlightenment has been very different in the Western Christian world, conceived of as a new and better way of being religious, since freedom from state control enabled religion to be more true to its spiritual ideas. In the Muslim world, secularism developed differently and has, on the other hand, often consisted of a brutal attack upon religion and the religious, as in Egypt or Turkey and early twentieth-century Iran (see Armstrong, 2001). The position of public intellectuals in many developing and middle-income countries similarly shows the tenuous relationship between public critical debate, evidence-based governance and state power and repression, making their dilemmas as harsh and impossible as those faced by intellectuals in Western Europe during periods of totalitarianism (see Altbach, 2003).

Civil Society

Whatever definition we choose to give to the concept of 'civil society', it has always been a locus for the funding and legitimization of the activities of intellectuals, and it has often been an important base from which ideas have entered the public sphere. Civil society has facilitated and does facilitate the role of public intellectual as 'partisan' involved with the 'local' or the 'sectional' as an alternative way of exercising power and influence. This has been especially so for social thinkers and analysts with a critical and reform-oriented agenda. There can be said to be at least three kinds of civil service organizations. First, there is a 'communitarian' one of social groupings for togetherness and the sharing of responsibility for others than ourselves, the loss of which is bemoaned in the West, and the need for which is propagated in the post-communist societies. Recent research into the history of civil society throws some doubt on such assumptions, most societies having some form of social groupings for community affairs and influence outside the remit of the state with which public spokespersons are associated (see Arjomand, 2004; Ryan, 2003). There are also interest group organizations such as trade unions, employer organizations, political parties, chambers of commerce and specialist interest groups, all on the assumption of strengthening a collective voice against the state and state policy. The Myrdals' close association with the reformist Swedish Social Democratic Party and the platform this provided for their ideas is well documented (Eyerman, 1985). In the history of sociology, 'the woman question', 'the black question', 'the poverty question', 'the homosexuality question', to name but a few, have been social issues that have formed the discipline. What were initially objects of social research and analysis have over time become participating subjects in the development of the discipline itself. With globalization, the organization of sectarian interests is no longer confined within the borders of the nation state, but also reflected in the lobbying work of international organizations and NGOs in areas such as human rights, environmentalism and anti-poverty movements (see Iriye, 2002). Alva and Gunnar Myrdal's fame as public intellectuals stemmed partly from their eagerness to see fundamental social issues as having a global – or as Alva Myrdal called, it a 'planetary' – dimension, and from their many intellectual and public activities to further their ideals and passions in the international domain.

Finally, there are and have been varieties of societies for mutual benefit and financial support, such as mortgage societies, charitable trusts, funeral and insurance societies. Each has spawned its own intellectual advocates and spokespersons on issues of social relations, community, class, welfare and environmentalism. Some of these have been major funders of critical social research, such as the Carnegie Corporation (which funded Myrdal's critical study of race relations in the US, much to the displeasure of many of its citizens), the Ford Foundation (which funded Bowles and Gintis's very influential critical Marxist analysis of the education system in the US), and in Britain the Rowntree and Leverhulme Trusts (which have done much to keep the issue of poverty on the public agenda), and the Runnymede Trust (which has done the same for immigrant and minority communities in Britain). Such funding has in many instances enabled public intellectuals, and ordinary academics, to speak with a voice independent of the state. As Gunnar Myrdal argued, such independence is a crucial factor in the pursuit of intellectual critical debate about social affairs (see Myrdal, 1970). If such freedom is curtailed, or censored and over-managed in academic context, the presence of alternative sources of funding is crucial for vigorous informed debate.

It is in this context important to note that the route to fame through the organizations and institutions of civil society has been particularly important for women intellectuals, for a long time excluded from the state and its various administrative apparatuses as well as from sociological discussions about the role and social location of public intellectuals. Women philanthropists, in their concern about social problems and social reform, have played an active role in the laying the foundations for what was to become the discipline of sociology (see Wisselgren, 2000). Dale Spender has argued that modern feminist theorists have repeatedly reinvented their feminist rebellion, largely because women have had so little control over the knowledge produced about them in its many misrepresentations. Women must first, she argued, unlearn what society has taught them about themselves, to reject prevailing wisdoms and begin afresh with their own experiences. As late starters, they have sought to question, reject and re-conceptualize. Women intellectuals have repeatedly been confined to cycles of the lost and found, only to be lost and found again (see Spender, 1983; Deegan, 1991). In her work on women's public access to politics in the nineteenth-century US, Ryan rejects Habermas's account of the decline of the public sphere during this period. She shows how the women's movement 'injected considerable feminist substance into public discourse, articulating concerns once buried in the privacy of one sex as vital matters of public interest' (Ryan, 2003, 389). By occupying scattered 'public spaces' outside regular political organizations, women enlarged the range of issues that weighed into the 'general interest', opened up the public space to a vast new constituency and found circuitous routes to public influence. The tenacious efforts of women and other groups to subvert restrictions on full citizenship in the public sphere and to be heard in public, in her words, 'testify to the power of public ideals, that persistent impulse to have a voice in some space open and accessible to all where they could be counted in the general interest' (Ryan, 2003, 393).

Like many marginalized populations, the empowerment of women has necessitated the construction of a separate identity and the assertion of self-interest through the development of a civil society of their own. Famous women sociologists have disseminated their work and gained fame through varieties of women's organizations, trade unions, political parties and professional interest groups. Not all of these have shared the same goals, purposes and visions for female emancipation, but the public debates generated have themselves brought female intellectuals and thinkers into the public domain. The political power and influence of the women's movement as a whole, and of social science women within it, is perhaps best evidenced in the way in which the European Union has taken on board issues of equal opportunities, especially in the domain of labour market regulations and parental rights. In the case of Alva Myrdal, this route to public fame also involved her in creating new national and international networks, voluntary organizations, and movements for mothers, teachers and pre-school educators. When her influential book *Nation and Family* (1941) was published in the US, there was already a rich network of organizations ready to disseminate its ideas for a more women- and family-friendly welfare state. The ideas presented in the book have passed in and out of academic favour, but continue to frame an ongoing debate about the role of women and childbearing and rearing in democratic socictics aiming for gender equality. But by bringing aspects of the female condition into the public domain, women intellectuals such as Alva Myrdal with her work on children and the family, Simone de Beauvoir on gender roles and ageing, and Susan Sontag on caring, cancer and AIDS have also suffered the experience of intellectual marginalization precisely because of their emphasis on issues seen to lie outside the core business of intellectual affairs. Similarly, the involvement of 'minority' intellectuals such as Stuart Hall, Paul Gilroy and Patricia Collins, whose work on the complexities of identity and identity politics has transformed the debate on race relations in Britain and the US, and William Julius Wilson in the US on the social and economic geography of race, have been strongly anchored in the experiences of the communities they see themselves as representing. Like the work of du Bois before them, their intellectual work has not always been equally recognized by the majority communities of which they are part.

The sociologist as partisan is a folk hero or heroine, and his or her perceived power base's closeness to the 'people' has led to a fair amount of sociological romanticism about the moral virtues of 'local' and 'participatory' social science knowledge-making. 'Local knowledge' easily turns into 'universalizing' knowledge without the required universalizing evidence, even when it comes to the analysis of that local community itself, its internal social fault lines, self-perceptions and understandings. Conversely, the claim to universal scholarly rationality can collapse when 'local' interests can be shown to have contributed to the use of rationalizing evidence in favour of a particular cause. The strongest critics of female public intellectuals such as Alva Myrdal and Simone de Beauvoir have come from within the feminist movement itself. This has often invoked aspects of their personal lives and its relationship to their writings about the private sphere of women they worked so hard to make a legitimate object for public concern (Lyon, 2000). Many public intellectuals in social science like the Webbs and the Myrdals in the early half of the last century were tainted in some way or other by their real, or assumed, association with, for example, the eugenics movement, now seen as a precursor of later more sinister racist organizations (see Ekerwald, 2001).

The Public

With the advance of communication technologies, the opportunities for 'publicness' have grown dramatically. But when it comes to critical intellectual debate on matters social, the position of intellectuals remains a privileged one, whether defined by communality of education, status, class, power position or celebrity. Access to platforms for the dissemination of ideas and information depends not only on relationships to networks of power and to information 'gatekeepers', but also on varying degrees of public receptivity to critical thought and new ideas. Legitimacy with the public at large has to be earned, and what is seen to accrue such legitimacy varies with social and political contexts. Part of this relates to being at the scene at the right time when there is a hunger for new ideas and new solutions. In a recent BBC interview, Putnam, the author of the famous book *Bowling Alone* (1999), expressed great surprise that his scholarly and argumentative book on what he saw as the major change in social and community relations in the US brought him such immediate fame, not only in the US but across the world. There were continuing invitations to talk not just to high-powered politicians and governments, but to the press and the media. His ideas were obviously timely and struck a chord with policymakers and a populace facing varieties of problems over the funding of care and an economic desire for the community and families in the provision for it. Giddens's writings on the 'third way' similarly hit the British and American public at a time when both societies were reeling under the social shock of harsh conservative free market economics, yet aware of the economic gains it had brought to ossified labour markets. They both write in an easily accessible style, and were both helped by the media and the press, in Giddens's case by the publishing house of his own creation. Economic depression and a national hunger for social change in the 1930s formed the background against which the Myrdals' easily accessible writings on the welfare state reached initially national and later international fame. Marx's *Communist Manifesto* may not have been a great work of sociological thought, but its timely arrival, aided by its rousing language and an improved printing technology, made it a bestseller with some impact.

Not all societies value intellectual debates in equal measure. The public debates generated in France by Sartre, de Beauvoir, Foucault and Bourdieu, and I believe in Germany by Adorno, Horkheimer and Habermas, have no equivalence in, for example, Britain, where intellectuals traditionally have less of a social standing. But academic status undoubtedly helps in much of the public domain. Chomsky's work on linguistics bears little relationship to his very public and much disseminated views on the future of the world and the negative role of the US within it, but it has afforded him a social status with some right to the pulpit. It has been said that thinkers like Berlin and Popper in Britain and Marcuse in the US gained some of their status in the Anglo-Saxon world by virtue of the German accent, and occasionally the idiom in which they spoke. They were, of course, also helped by the ease with which they spoke and wrote in English, making their writings accessible to a wider audience than had they stayed within their language of origin only. The rise of English as a world language enabled Giddens's lecture series on globalization to be broadcast simultaneously on networks across the globe. The theoretical and professional specialization of sociology as a discipline has not only led to a fragmentation of social knowledge, but also to a greater specialization of language creating obstacles to the ease with which new ideas can be understood by a general public. Alva and Gunnar Myrdal's public fame and influence must partly be explained by their shared conviction that popular dissemination and accessible forms of writing were vital preconditions for intellectual influence with the public. Their archive is astonishingly rich in pamphlets, articles and essays written for the popular press and public meetings in a variety of contexts. In his large study of American race relations, Gunnar Myrdal adopted the strategy of leaving academic debate, methodological and theoretical depth discussions, to footnotes and appendices, making the main text one that could easily be read by politicians, policymakers and the public at large (see Lyon, 2004).

In the knowledge society, the premium on knowledge and knowledge-producers is high. In management speech, it is seen as an organizational challenge to generate value from knowledge, and that knowledge and knowledge-production needs to be managed for maximum effect and return on investment. But as organizations go through life cycles, so does knowledge. As contexts change, so knowledge ages, particularly so when it comes to social knowledge. Evidence becomes out of date, and theories no longer politically or socially acceptable. Knowledge progresses through several stages: creation and acquisition, sharing, mobilization, diffusion and media commoditization. It is not equally exciting to a public audience at each stage. Ideas can lose their excitement once widespread and well known, as much as for reasons of having been proven wrong or useless. In sociology, it is often new concepts in terms of which social phenomena are described that remain (see Merton and Wolfe, 1995). The founding fathers, and a few mothers, would have been amazed to discover how key concepts in longstanding arguments on the causes and consequences of social inequality such as class, gender roles, status, and more lately, social capital, at one time new, socially threatening, politically mobilizing and diffused with missionary zeal by many a public intellectual, have entered common parlance to the point where they now go unnoticed. Another area in which sociological works have infiltrated the public domain is that of research methods techniques, now part and parcel of the regular activities of most organizations in the public and private sphere of the economy as well as in organizations of civil society. In the light of recent work by the UN in disseminating good research practice in development contexts, Alva Myrdal's dream of an international bank of social sciences information and a methodological 'tool kit' capable of serving policymakers in all fields and across all national boundaries today seems less of a utopian fantasy than her faith that politicians would make effective use of it (see Myrdal, 1955; United Nations Development Programme, 2000).

Public Intellectuals and Knowledge Values

The attempt above to look sociologically at the many and varied dimensions that make up the construct of a public intellectual leaves us in the end with the problem of values and the danger of too cynical an approach to the relationship between temporally confined power structures, ever-changing popular aspirations and ideological fashions, and intellectual fame and influence. Seeing the intellectual and academic work of reasoning as an increasingly professional activity, its public face ought to be a concern for the profession as a whole, and that includes a more publicly shared understanding of the core values that underlie this activity of 'reasoning'. In his famous essay on the social rules and norms of the scientific community, Merton worked on the underlying assumption that the principle of competitive transparency and openness to critical scrutiny was ultimately the best guarantee for the progress of truth – or perhaps we should, with Popper, say, maximized avoidance of falsehoods, errors and the idols of the marketplace. Much of what has remained as 'classic' in sociology has been repeatedly exposed to critical scrutiny, and survived, albeit not always as intended, but refined and reworked within new conceptual frameworks and methodological practices. The concepts of class, status, structure, social power and inequality, bureaucracy, citizenship and theories about the inter-relationship between the social structural and the personal and biographical all originated with critical thinkers putting their ideas in the public domain for open scrutiny and debate. Even founding fathers such as Marx, Weber, Durkheim, Parsons, Du Bois, Mills and Titmuss, for example, have all at times been intellectually and politically 'demoted' or even politically repressed, but also re-read and resurrected to frame the more contemporary discourses of Bourdieu, Giddens and others.

But the professional contexts of knowledge-production are changing. Sapiro has argued that the prophetic mode of politicization of intellectuals is being replaced by a more professional stance and a re-conceptualization of academic and intellectual work as defined by a more limited conception of 'competence' (see Sapiro, 2003). With universities globally changing towards a more corporate and market-driven system of managerially driven organization, the role of the academic as public intellectual is under considerable pressure (see King, 2004). What has been called the 'accountability movement' in the public sphere demands more immediate political and economic returns for money invested in the development and dissemination of 'social knowledge'. The nature of publishing has changed in a similar direction. In the 'knowledge society', public intellectuals have become not only increasingly socially and economically important as feeding the economy and the complex systems of social administration and welfare on which political support depends, they are also increasingly asked to 'account for themselves' and provide measures of their own performance (see O'Neill, 2002). This indicates a lack of trust in intellectuals as valued public spokespersons. Such lack of trust might limit their capacity to be 'free-floating', but also their role as protectors of the conditions necessary for critical knowledge-producing processes. Academics are also, not unrelated, becoming more professionalized and organized in order to carve out a space for themselves as independent knowledge-producers with their own interests and commitments to autonomy and intellectual independence to protect. They are thus also in themselves, as a collective, coming to form an important part of civil society in the sense of an intermediary grouping between the state and the public at large.

Recently in Britain, a large number of professional associations representing social science academics, social researchers and varieties of social practitioner researchers set up an Academy for Social Sciences. There are a large number of such associations in Britain. When, in preparation for the next quality evaluation of research in British universities, requests for nominations for membership on subject panels across all subjects were sent out, they went to over 400 different such organizations, ranging from the ancient and august Royal Society to the Viking Society for Northern Research. The new Academy for Social Science has over forty societies as members, and aims to reduce 'fragmentation' of influence and to act as an umbrella organization enabling a more collective, non-elitist, social science voice to be heard *vis-à-vis* government and the press. This new organization was a response to a long period of political hostility to the social sciences, especially sociology, by the Thatcher government and the popular press. It soon commissioned a report on the state of social sciences in Britain that included a set of recommendations to government, leading funding bodies, the universities, but also to the academic community itself (see Academy for the Social Sciences, 2002). On the shared assumption that social life might be conducted more sensibly, and public policies might be better founded, if social science research were more widely disseminated and understood, the report notes the deficit in public knowledge about the social sciences. There is a lack of correlation between academics who are highly regarded by their peers and those who make frequent contributions to the media. The public take-up of ideas was noted, with, for example, the concept of 'social capital' mentioned more often in a major British national newspaper than 'productive growth'. But the general acquaintance with the products of social knowledge research was seen as limited, and the very phrase 'social research' does not seem to mean much, even to well-informed persons. The social scientists interviewed for the report complained of journalistic lack of interest in social scientific methods and intolerance of conceptual sophistication, riding roughshod over the fine details of research.

It calls for a greater collective presence of social scientists in government activities, better accessible national database systems, the development of more supportive media networks, and improved education of politicians, journalists and young people in the protocols and methods of social inquiry. It also calls for more 'thinking time' and better funding for academics and researchers, especially in the context of higher education, to foster greater innovativeness and originality. In other words, here is an instance of 'intellectuals', a few of them 'public', organising themselves as part of civil society to protect and take forward their own interests as knowledge seekers and providers with a strong commitment to the quality of that knowledge and the conditions necessary for its production. But important as all this is, if what drives a 'public intellectual' is having 'something individual to say' in the competitive marketplace of ideas, then it is perhaps unlikely that we will see intellectualism itself, as opposed to the profession of knowledge producers, a 'social movement' of any magnitude or force. Interestingly, the new Academy also created the honorary status of 'Academician' to woo support, and a higher membership fee, from some of its more august members – a strategy not without internal conflict and competition.

Whither Public Intellectuals?

Concerns about the decline of the public intellectuals are yet again being expressed, some of the reasons for which have been outlined above (see Posner, 2001; Furedi, 2004). Whether we take an 'optimistic' or 'pessimistic' and more cynical approach to the task, value and influence of public intellectuals, their 'success' or 'failure' in the end depends on the nature of those very ideas themselves, and whether the public at any one time see their impact on the state, civil society and public debates as a useful move 'forward' or not. This is especially so when the state and political and economic administration is taking a more managerial, incremental and pragmatic turn. This means that a single 'public intellectual', such as Weber, Durkheim, Myrdal or de Beauvoir or Bourdieu, can go through different stages of fame and influence, both in his or her own lifetime and in the *Nachruhm* they leave behind. The polemics may be lost, outmoded and surpassed, and the context of the dialogue may be lost. But by being at times interestingly wrong rather than trivially true in what they write, their ideas will remain useful bones for future thinkers to cut their teeth on. It is also the case that ideas and theories are regularly rediscovered when political climates change to re-incorporate them, as has recently began to happen to the Myrdals and their once premature global perspective on fundamental and universal aspects of social human rights.

But leaving content aside for a moment, there are many interesting sociological questions that need to be asked about the nature of knowledge governance and about what kinds of state structures are capable of negotiating the tension between the desire of power for secrecy and control, and the demands of reasoning, and democracy, for openness, controversy and debate, and the dilemmas to which this tension gives rise. There are also questions that can, and need to be, asked about the role of different types of organizations in civil society when it comes to the production, funding and interpretation of social knowledge and the tensions raised between interest group and community serving 'local' knowledge and the risks of political and social fragmentation in a larger nation-building and international context. Finally, the explosion of information technology, and changes in the processes by which the public get to hear about, understand and disseminate social knowledge, calls for some investigation. This includes issues of how the public gets to learn about the processes of evidence-collection and reasoning in social science scholarship. Maybe in the end the influence of the 'soundbite', that particular word or phrase that captures a social mood at a particular time, is the most public sociological intellectuals can hope for. But it may be a 'soundbite' they did not initially choose themselves. Socrates knew that when he refused to write down his ideas. We will never know whether he would have appreciated Plato's doing so on his behalf, only that it ensured his fame and influence, for better or for worse.

As Goldfarb notes, making sense to the public has always been difficult. Between the blind ideological commitment of prophetic speculation and the arrogance of 'legislation' on the one hand and alienated indifference and withdrawal on the other there is a still a possibility of principled critical action, more than mere 'interpretation', with the specific task of fostering productive evidence-based deliberation (see Goldfarb, 2003). The changing ideological political landscape with its recent uncertainty about what counts as left and right, coupled with contemporary political issues of human rights and diversity, provides an opportunity yet again to rediscover the discursive responsibilities of intellectuals. This may mean a decline in the role of the public intellectual as prophetic 'guru'. It does not mean a decline in the importance of the role of the intellectual in public. Jaspers' collection of lectures presented to German academics immediately after the Second World War reminds us of the seriousness of this responsibility and the consequences of its abdication (see Jaspers, 1961 [1947]).

Troubling the status quo in a variety of public modes, both political and intellectual, have brought women into the mainstream of academe, intellectual life, politics and the discipline of sociology. It might therefore be appropriate to conclude with a note of optimism about the role of the public intellectual:

> Because everyday politics inevitably falls short of standards of perfect rational discourse, a chimera even in the heyday of the bourgeois public sphere, the goal of publicness might best be allowed to navigate through wider and wilder territory. That

is, public life can be cultivated in many democratic spaces where obstinate differences in power, material status and hence interest can find expression. (Ryan, 2003, 394)

References

Academy for the Social Sciences (2002), *Great Expectations: Report of the Commission for the Social Science* (London: Academy for the Social Sciences).

Altbach, Philip G. (ed.) (2003), *The Decline of the Guru: The Academic Profession in Developing and Middle-income Countries* (London: Palgrave Macmillan).

Appelqvist, Orjan and Andersson, Stellan (1998), *Vagvisare: Texter av Gunnar Myrdal* (Stockholm: Norstedts Forlag).

Arjomand, Said (2004), 'Coffeehouses, Guilds, and Oriental Despotism: Government and Civil Society in Late 17th–Early 18th-century Istanbul and Isfahan, and as Seen from Paris and London', *Archives européennes de sociologie/European Journal of Sociology* 45:1, 23–42.

Armstrong, Karen (2001), *Islam: A Short History* (London: Phoenix Press).

Azmanova, Albena (2004), 'Europe's novel political cultures in the early twenty-first century', *Contemporary Politics* 10:2, 111–25.

Barenboim, Daniel and Said, Edward W. (2004), *Explorations in Music and Society* (London: Bloomsbury Publishing).

Bauman, Zygmunt (1987), *Legislators and Interpreters: On Modernity, Postmodernity and Intellectuals* (Cambridge: Polity Press).

Brym, Robert J. (1980), *Intellectuals and Politics* (London: George Allen and Unwin).

Bulmer, Martin (1982), *The Uses of Social Research: Social Investigation in Public Policy Making* (London: George Allen and Unwin).

Deegan, Mary J. (ed.) (1991) *Women in Sociology: A Bio-bibliographical Sourcebook* (New York: Greenwood Press).

Ekerwald, Hedda (2000), 'Alva Myrdal: Making the private public', *Acta Sociologia* 43:4, 343–52.

Ekerwald, Hedda (2001), 'The modernist manifesto of Alva and Gunnar Myrdal: Modernisation of Sweden in the thirties and the question of sterilisation', *International Journal of Politics, Culture and Society* 14, 555–71.

Eliæson, Sven (2000), 'Gunnar Myrdal: A theorist of modernity', *Acta Sociologica* 43:4, 331–41.

Ennis, James G. (1992), 'The Social Organisation of Sociological Knowledge: Modeling the intersection of specialties', *American Sociological Review* 57, 259–65.

Eyerman, Ron (1985), 'Rationalising Intellectuals: Sweden in the 1930s and 1940s', *Theory and Society* 14:6, 777–807.

Eyerman, Ron (1994), *Between Culture and Politics: Intellectuals in Modern Society* (London: Polity Press).

Flynbjerg, Bent (2001), *Making Social Science Matter: Why Social Inquiry Fails and How It Can Succeed Again* (Cambridge: Cambridge University Press).

Fukuyama, Francis (1992), *The End of History and The Last Man* (Harmondsworth: Penguin).

Furedi, Frank (2004), *Where Have All the Intellectuals Gone?: Confronting 21st Century Philistinism* (London: Continuum).

Geertz, Clifford (1983), *Local Knowledge: Further Essays in Interpretative Anthropology* (New York: Basic Books).

Giddens, Anthony (1994), *Beyond Left and Right: The Future of Radical Politics* (Cambridge: Polity Press).

Giddens, A. (1998), *The Third Way: The Renewal of Social Democracy* (Cambridge: Polity Press).

Goldfarb, Jeffrey C. (2003), 'Civility and Subversion: The Intellectual in Democratic Society', in Hess, A. (ed.) *American Social and Political Thought: A Reader* (New York: New York University Press), 368–73.

Hess, Andreas (2000), *American Social and Political Thought: A Concise Introduction* (New York: New York University Press).

Iriye, Akira (2002), *Global Community: The Role of International Organisations in the Making of the Contemporary World* (Berkeley, CA: University of California Press).

Jaspers, Karl (1961 [1947]), *The Question of German Guilt* (New York: Capricorn Books).

Kaesler, Dirk (1988), *Max Weber: An Introduction to his Life and Work* (London: Polity Press).

Karabel, Jerome (1996), 'Towards a theory of intellectuals and politics', *Theory and Society* 25:2, 205–23.

King, Roger (2004), *The University in the Global Age* (London: Palgrave Macmillan).

Lilla, Mark (2001), *The Reckless Mind: Intellectuals in Politics* (New York: NYRB).

Lyon, E. Stina (2000), 'Biographical constructions of a working woman: The changing faces of Alva Myrdal', *European Journal of Social Theory* 3, 407–28.

Lyon, E. Stina (2001), 'Education for Modernity: The Impact of American Social Science on Alva and Gunnar Myrdal and the "Swedish model" of School Reform', *International Journal of Politics, Culture and Society* 14, 513–37.

Lyon, E. Stina (2004), 'Researching Race Relations: Myrdal's American Dilemma from a Methodological Perspective', *Acta Sociologica* 47:3, 203–17.

Merton, Robert K. (1957), *Social Theory and Social Structure* (New York: The Free Press).

Merton, Robert K. and Wolfe, Alan (1995), 'The cultural and social incorporation of sociological knowledge', *The American Sociologist* 26:3, 15–38.

Myrdal, Alva (1941), *Nation and Family: The Swedish Experiment in Democratic Family and Population Policy* (New York: Harper and Brothers).

Myrdal, Alva (1955), 'A Scientific Approach to International welfare', in Myrdal, A., Altmeyer, A.J. and Rusk, D., *America's Role in International Social Welfare* (New York: Columbia University Press).

Myrdal, Gunnar (1944), *An American Dilemma: The Negro Problem in Modern Democracy* (New York: Harper and Brothers).

Myrdal, Gunnar (1953), 'The relation between social theory and social policy', *British Journal of Sociology* 4, 210–42.

Myrdal, Gunnar (1970), *Objectivity in Social Research* (London: Duckworth).

O'Neill, Onora (2002), *A Question of Trust* (Cambridge: Cambridge University Press).

Posner, Richard (2001), *Public Intellectuals: A Study of Decline* (Cambridge, MA: Harvard University Press).

Putnam, Robert (1999), *Bowling Alone: The Collapse and Revival of American Community* (New York: Simon & Schuster).

Rabinow, Paul (ed.) (1984), *The Foucault Reader* (Harmondsworth: Penguin Books).

Ramadan, Tariq (2001), *Islam, the West and the Challenges of Modernity*, trans. S. Amghar (Leicester: The Islamic Foundation).

Ramadan, Tariq (2003), *Western Muslims and the Future of Islam* (Oxford University Press).

Reich, R.B. (1990), *The Power of Public Ideas* (Cambridge MA: Harvard University Press).

Ryan, Mary P. (2003), 'Gender and Public Access: Women's Politics in 19th-Century America', in Hess, A. (ed.), *American Social and Political Thought: A Reader* (New York: New York University Press), 389–95.

Sadri, Ahmad (1992), *Max Weber's Sociology of Intellectuals* (Oxford: Oxford University Press).

Sapiro, Gisele (2003), 'Forms of politization in the French literary field', *Theory and Society* 32, 633–52.

Spender, Dale (1983), 'Modern feminist theorists: Reinventing rebellion', in Spender, D. (ed.), *Feminist Theorists: Three Centuries of Women's Intellectual Traditions* (London: The Women's Press), 366–80.

United Nations Development Programme (2000), *Human Development Report* (New York and London: Oxford University Press).

Walzer, Michael (1989), *The Company of Critics* (London: Peter Halban).

Wisselgren, Per (2000), *Samhallets Kartlaggare* (Stockholm: Brutus Östlings Bokforlag).

Chapter 6
Public Intellectuals, East and West: Jan Patočka and Václav Havel in Contention with Maurice Merleau-Ponty and Slavoj Žižek

Stefan Auer

Ever since Plato wrote the Allegory of the Cave in his *Politeia*, philosophers have found easy excuses not to engage with politics. According to Hannah Arendt, Plato describes 'the sphere of human affairs – all that belongs to the living together of men in a common world – in terms of darkness, confusion, and deception which those aspiring to true being must turn away from and abandon if they want to discover the clear sky of eternal ideas' (Arendt, 1961a, 17; see Arendt, 1982, 21). However, Arendt's reading of Plato is incomplete. The philosopher's mission in life was not accomplished by his freeing himself from the cave of ignorance. Once he had seen the *agathon* (the ultimate source of the Good, but also the source of all existence), he had to return to the cave. In other words, he had to apply his acquired wisdom to the political sphere. If Socrates is seen as one of the first famous public intellectuals in European history, Plato could be seen as one of the first theorists postulating the duties of public intellectuals. He even foresees the dangers that public intellectuals would be exposed to: people would try to kill them (Plato, 1993, 243).[1]

As Plato understood, public intellectuals were vulnerable, because they were forced to think and act outside their area of expertise. In modern times this old insight has found its latest expression in the normative view that intellectuals should participate actively in more than one defined social field. It is not surprising that many intellectuals have failed to live up to this task. That is a danger that even Plato recognized in his *Politeia*. More often than not, even the wisest among them

1 This is not the place to defend Plato against the kind of accusations that Karl Popper made in his *Open Society and its Enemies* (Popper, 1962). It suffices to say that Plato's aim was not primarily to design a political order, as is misleadingly implied in the English translation of the title *Republic*, but rather to discuss the fundamental principles of morality. It was Aristotle who developed Plato's insights further and turned them into a distinctly *political* philosophy. By doing this, Aristotle revolutionized Plato, yet at the same time, he also remained truthful to his former teacher. As Patočka observed: 'for Aristotle all of philosophy is within the Platonic cave. You know that Plato himself forces the philosopher to return to the cave' (Patočka, 2002, 189).

failed when they entered the political sphere. Intellectual sophistication offered no reliable protection against political idiocy. The paradigmatic example of this failure is Martin Heidegger's engagement with Nazism. Yet this chapter is not primarily about the failings of Heidegger and his spiritual children.[2]

The contention of this chapter is that dissident intellectuals in Central and Eastern Europe proved to be more prudent in their political judgements about important issues of their time than a number of their West European counterparts. This is, of course, a vast generalization. To give more substance to this argument, I will restrict my presentation to a couple of representative figures (Czesław Miłosz, Jan Patočka, Václav Havel *contra* Maurice Merleau-Ponty, Jean Paul Sartre, Slavoj Žižek). I will frame my analysis around historic snapshots (1956, 1968, 1977), I will contrast their views about political power and the legitimacy of revolutionary violence, and I will use Arendt as a moderator in this fictional debate.

Arendt described how twentieth-century intellectuals were drawn into politics in the times of crises. For example, the Nazi occupation of France forced poets, writers and philosophers into the Resistance. Overnight, these intellectuals were forced to become *public* intellectuals who sought to challenge the tyrannical regime 'in deed and word'. 'The men of the European Resistance', Arendt argued, 'had begun to create that public space between themselves where freedom could appear' (Arendt, 1961a, 4). Political engagement in times of crises, such as revolutions, may be dangerous, but potentially also very rewarding. Revolutions were those rare moments in human history which enabled intellectuals to participate in the public realm on the level of intensity never experienced before. In other words, 'the revolution came to play, as Malraux once noticed (in *Man's Fate*), "the role which once was played by eternal life": it "saves those that make it"' (Arendt, 1961a, 8).

Yet it is important to note that Arendt's fascination with revolutions is tempered by her critical attitude to revolutionary violence. Her search for 'the lost treasure of revolution' (Arendt, 1961a, 5) was an attempt to identify political constellations which would allow for radically new beginnings, without descent into anarchy and violence. This is also the reason why she considered the American rather than the French Revolution to be more successful in creating conditions for political freedom (see Arendt, 1965). While Arendt's account of the American Revolution might have been rather idealized, her insights into the relationship between power and violence proved remarkably astute, especially for the communist regimes in Central and Eastern Europe. She believed that political actors who had to resort to the use of violence showed weakness rather than strength. Not surprisingly, Arendt's thinking found resonance among the dissident intellectuals in Central

2 Richard Wolin's argument that thinkers influenced by Heidegger 'remain afflicted by many of [his] oversights and conceptual imbalances' and that 'the sins of the father will be visited upon the daughters and sons' is overblown (Wolin, 2001, 20). But I share his concern with the decline of moral sensitivity amongst a number of postmodern philosophers (Wolin, 2004).

Europe, and influenced, among others, Jan Patočka.[3] Arendt's conception of politics illuminates the dynamics of the collapse of communism and the role of intellectuals in this process (see Auer, 2004).

Maurice Merleau-Ponty and Revolutionary Violence

If we accept the Arendtian understanding of politics as the opposite of violence, then Maurice Merleau-Ponty's *Humanism and Terror* (1969) and Slavoj Žižek's eulogies of Lenin (see Žižek, 2001, 113–16; Žižek, 2002a) and Robespierre (see Žižek, 2007), by definition, betrayed politics. They betrayed politics by employing their outstanding rhetorical skills in defence of Leninist, or even Stalinist, revolutionary terror. They convinced themselves and many of their readers that the radical political alternative which emerged in Eastern Europe offered more hope to mankind than anything Western Europe could ever offer. They believed that the communist regime in the Soviet Union and its satellites, despite its revolutionary violence (or, in Žižek's case, *because* of its revolutionary violence), could be seen as superior to liberal democracy and its rhetoric of human rights.

For Merleau-Ponty, violence was a necessary part of political life. Hence, there was no point in rejecting it. Instead, what was important was to identify its progressive application. 'If Marxism is a theory of violence and justification of Terror,' argues Merleau-Ponty, 'it brings reason out of unreason, and the violence which it legitimates should bear a sign which distinguishes it from regressive forms of violence' (Merleau-Ponty, 1969, 98). Merleau-Ponty invites us to differentiate between progressive and reactionary forms of violence, between good and bad terror.

Merleau-Ponty's *Humanism and Terror* develops a bizarre hypothesis: What if Stalin and his henchmen really managed to deliver a society that would be free of conflict, free of exploitation – a society that would create possibilities for genuine individual emancipation? Maybe then, all that violence, all those victims of terror, might be justified; they would have helped to bring about a better and more humane future:

> Neither Bukharin nor Trotsky nor Stalin regarded Terror as intrinsically valuable. Each one imagined he was using it to realize a genuinely human history which had not yet started but which provides justification for revolutionary violence. In other words, as Marxists, all three confess that there is a meaning to such violence – that it is possible to understand it, to read into it a rational development and to draw from it a human future. (Merleau-Ponty, 1969, 97)

3 For Arendt's influence on Patočka, see Findlay (2002, 96–9). For her influence on Polish dissident circles, see, for example, Spiewak (2003, 170–73).

According to Merleau-Ponty, 'life, discussion, and political choice occur only against the background of violence. What matters and what we have to discuss is not violence but its sense or its future' (Merleau-Ponty, 1969, 109).

This is the negation of politics in the Arendtian sense, as for Arendt, speech and rhetorical acts were the defining features of politics. Arendt criticized Marx and his glorification of violence, because 'it contains the more specific denial of λόγος, of speech, the diametrically opposite and traditionally most human form of intercourse. Marx's theory of ideological superstructure ultimately rests on this anti-traditional hostility to speech and the concomitant glorification of violence' (Arendt, 1961a, 23). In her view, violence was pre-political; in its pure form it was actually the opposite of power and the opposite of politics (see Arendt, 1969, 56).

While Merleau-Ponty defended violence merely as a necessary evil that will bring about a better, more humane future, Žižek went one step further. For him, revolutionary violence *is* already a part of the better future, because he sees violence as 'an authentic act of liberation, not just a passage à l'acte' (Žižek, 2002a, 261). Žižek bemoans the fact that these days, Merleau-Ponty's argument in favour of humanism *and* terror finds little support even within the remnants of the radical Left. The 'sensitive liberal' left-wing intellectuals, according to Žižek, delude themselves by believing that it is possible to opt for humanism *or* terror. By advocating non-violent political struggle, they want to have 'a decaffeinated revolution, a revolution which doesn't smell of revolution' (Žižek, 2007, vi). In contrast, Žižek urges his readers to consider:

> The choice 'humanism *or* terror', but with *terror*, not humanism, as a positive term. This is a radical position difficult to sustain, but, perhaps, our only hope: it does not amount to the obscene madness of openly pursuing a 'terrorist and inhuman politics', but something much more difficult to think through. (Žižek, 2007, xiii)

To think through this 'obscene' proposition, Žižek's intellectual acrobatics rely on the wisdom of Agamben, Althusser, Badiou, Deleuze, Foucault, Lacan and Levinas, in addition to the classic writings of Robespierre and Lenin, and a number of examples from contemporary popular culture 'from the Schwarzenegger-figure in *Terminator* to the Rutger-Hauer-android in *Blade Runner*' (Žižek, 2007, xv).

Merleau-Ponty's argument in favour of revolutionary violence does not go far enough for Žižek. It is linked too closely to the outcome of the revolutionary process. Because we can never be sure what the final outcome of any revolution might be, we must have the courage to endorse 'divine violence', argued Žižek. Violence was justified not primarily by its outcome, but rather by the conviction and fervour of the actors involved in this process – their revolutionary 'authenticity'.[4] In other words,

4 Žižek recalls the following episode to illustrate the point: 'when Brecht, on the way from his home to his theatre in July 1953, passed the column of Soviet tanks rolling towards the Stalinallee to crush the workers' rebellion, he waved at them and wrote in his diary later that day that, at that moment, he (never party member) was tempted for the first time in his

Lenin's and Robespierre's violence is good because Lenin and Robespierre are good revolutionaries – whatever the actual outcome of their (failed?) revolutions. The question, to what extent these violent revolutions succeed in delivering on their promise of a truly just society, becomes for Žižek largely irrelevant.

Slavoj Žižek in Hollywood

To be sure, Slavoj Žižek is a strange candidate for the label of a typical 'Western' intellectual. He spent his formative years in Eastern Europe, having grown up in communist Yugoslavia, where he even worked in 1977 'at the Central Committee of the League of Slovene Communists', and later as 'Researcher at the University of Ljubljana's Institute for Sociology' (Myers, 2003, 8). However, it is worth noting that Yugoslavia was one of the few communist countries that was really *outside* the Soviet-dominated bloc. It was the most 'Western' and liberal of all the communist countries, which might also explain why so many intellectuals in the former Yugoslavia felt no urge to deal seriously with the legacy of their totalitarian past(s). The country that produced the internationally acclaimed philosopher-ironist Žižek also gave the world its artistic musical equivalent in the form of the group Laibach (which also calls itself NSK: Neue Slowenische Kunst), a group of artists appropriating the imagery of both Nazi and Stalinist-style propaganda.

Like Laibach, Žižek is an arch-manipulator. Just as Laibach seeks to provoke by imitating old totalitarian propaganda, Žižek attempts to subvert the ruling ideology of his day – whether it be Yugoslav communism or Western liberalism – by provocatively endorsing terrorist revolutionary ideologies, even as he joins the intellectual establishment of the liberal-democratic West. Recipients of both Žižek's philosophy and Laibach's music might be confused about the 'real political meaning' of these works, the message behind the ironic gestures, but their confusion is simply the first step towards overcoming their blind acceptance of the ruling ideology. As Žižek observed:

> The first reaction of the enlightened Leftist critics was to conceive of *Laibach* as the ironic imitation of totalitarian rituals; however, their support of *Laibach* was always accompanied by an uneasy feeling: 'What if they really mean it? What if they truly identify with the totalitarian ritual?' – or, a more cunning version of it, transferring one's own doubt onto the other: 'What if *Laibach* overestimates their public? What if the public takes seriously what *Laibach* mockingly imitates, so that *Laibach* actually strengthens what it purports to undermine?' (Žižek, 1993)

According to Žižek, this subversive tactic is effective precisely because its aims are not clear:

---

life to join the Communist Party. It was not that Brecht tolerated the cruelty of the struggle in the hope that it would bring a prosperous future: the harshness of the violence as such was perceived and endorsed as a sign of authenticity' (Žižek, 2002b, 5).

> In this sense the strategy of *Laibach* appears in a new light: it 'frustrates' the system (the ruling ideology) precisely insofar as it is not its ironic imitation, but over–identification with it – by bringing to light the obscene superego underside of the system, over–identification suspends its efficiency. (Žižek, 1993)

Is *this* clear now? I hope not. To think that one can really understand Žižek is certain proof of *not* getting him right. His strategy of 'over-identification', like the one used by Laibach, requires ambiguity and uncertainty. Is Žižek really a Stalinist and a passionate defender of Robespierre? Is he really as relaxed, not to say enthusiastic, about the attacks on 11 September 2001 and irreverent towards its victims as it seems (Žižek, 2002b)? Or is he just pretending, the better to offend bourgeois sensitivities? We do not know. And we shall never know for certain. As one of many commentators on Žižek's growing body of work observed: 'what Žižek is doing is to pretend to pretend to be a Stalinist' (Parker, 2007).[5]

Žižek, the cultural critic, freely admits that he has never seen about half of the movies that he wrote about. He said that he was an 'absolute Hegelian' there, and was simply afraid that to watch a movie he had heard or read about 'may spoil [his] theory' (Taylor, 2005). In a similar vein, he boasted that when he used to work for the Slovenian magazine *Mladina*, he routinely wrote book reviews about non-existent books. I cannot help but think that Žižek's approach to history is not all that different – not in the sense that he writes about non-existent events, on the contrary, he writes about events which naive people like you and me find frighteningly real as he would write about Hollywood movies (whether they be real, or invented). Žižek writes with equal ease about the perpetrators (and their victims!) of the Holocaust, Stalinism and September 11 as he writes about Hitchcock or snuff pornography. It is almost as if these events merely occurred in order to help him to illustrate some of the more intricate points of Lacanian theory. The West with its 'passion for the [Lacanian] Real', for example, called for a terrorist attack, just as sado-masochists desire self-inflicted pain:

> And was not the attack on the World Trade Center with regard to Hollywood catastrophe movies like snuff pornography versus ordinary sado–masochistic porno movies? … we can perceive the collapse of the WTC towers as the climactic conclusion of twentieth-century art's 'passion for the Real' – the 'terrorists' themselves did not do it primarily to provoke real material damage, but for the spectacular effect of it. … That is the rationale of the often-mentioned association of the attacks with Hollywood disaster movies: the unthinkable which happened was the object of fantasy, so that, in a way, America got what it fantasized about, and that was the biggest surprise. (Žižek, 2002b, 11 and 15–16)

---

5 Or as Žižek put it in his inimitable style: 'When I appear to be sarcastic and so on, the point is not to take [this] seriously. What is not to be taken seriously is the very form of sarcasm, [it] is the form of the joke, which must not be taken seriously' (Taylor, 2005).

There is probably no more entertaining rendition of both Nazism, Stalinism and their respective victims as the one delivered by Žižek's creative genius. How come so very few readers are disgusted by it? As perplexing as Žižek's theories is the phenomenon of his ever-growing popularity that reaches far beyond his homeland. There may not be many enthusiastic followers of Žižek's intellectual adventures in the countries of Central Europe, but he has certainly acquired star-like status in Western academia. If any formal confirmation of his status in the West was needed, in the summer of 2005 Žižek was appointed International Director of the Birkbeck Institute for the Humanities in London, which seeks to promote the role of a public intellectual.[6]

The Captive Mind

Whence the fascination of Western intellectuals with violence and terror? According to Czesław Miłosz, Western intellectuals are simply bored, or in his words:

> suffer from a special variety of *taedium vitae*; their emotional and intellectual life is too dispersed. Everything they think and feel evaporates like steam in an open expanse. Freedom is a burden to them. No conclusions they arrive at are binding: it may be so, then again it may not. The result is constant uneasiness. (Miłosz, 1962, 79)

This is what Miłosz suggested half a century ago in *The Captive Mind*. Published roughly at the same time as *Humanism and Terror*, Miłosz's study remains one of the best accounts of the allure of totalitarian ideologies. It deals with the difficulties intellectuals encounter when they engage with politics. Even though his primary subject was the position of Eastern not Western European intellectuals, his insights were applicable to both groups.

Miłosz was puzzled by the fact that so many people in Poland and elsewhere in Central and Eastern Europe were unable to resist the allure of the communist ideology. He explained it partly by their sense of alienation and the kind of existential *Angst* that befalls intellectuals after the Heideggerian 'death of metaphysics'. The communist project offered a way out of these difficulties by providing people with transcendental hope (with history becoming a new God), and by allowing intellectuals to reconnect with the working classes. The supposedly superior insight of Marxist intellectuals into the logic of history

6 There was no sign of false modesty in Žižek's response to this new challenge. As he stated on the official Website of the Institute: 'I like what was offered to me by Birkbeck, that is, to promote the role a public intellectual, to be intellectually active and to address a larger public. It's not only good for me, but also for Birkbeck and the country' (see <http://www.bbk.ac.uk/news/20060201i>). Another testimony to Žižek's growing popularity is a documentary feature movie that follows the famous philosopher on a lecture tour around the globe (see Taylor, 2005).

enables them to condone suffering (of others!). There can be no progress without suffering, no victories without victims:

> Let a new man arise, one who, instead of submitting to the world, will transform it. Let him create a historical formation, instead of yielding to its bondage. Only thus can he redeem the absurdity of his physiological existence. Man must be made to understand this, by force and by suffering. Why shouldn't he suffer? He ought to suffer. Why can't he be used as manure as long as he remains evil and stupid? If the intellectual must know the agony of thought, why should he spare others this pain? (Miłosz, 1962, 10)

Miłosz identified different strategies by which intellectuals complied with, or even actively supported, repressive Stalinist regimes. However, he did not foresee, and probably could not have foreseen, the possibility of independent thought in the communist part of Europe; the emergence of dissident intellectuals that was later made possible thanks to the partial de-Stalinization of communist regimes.

Ironically, the emergence of his own political thought showed that his assessment was too pessimistic. If the regimes of Central and Eastern Europe were truly as totalitarian as Miłosz seems to have suggested in his *Captive Mind*, no one, not even Miłosz himself, would ever have been able to oppose it. If everyone internalized 'the eternal wisdom' of the ruling ideology, no dissenting voice could ever have been articulated. We know now that this was not the case. The series of revolts against communism – 1953 in East Germany, 1956 in Poland and Hungary, 1968 in Czechoslovakia, 1980–81 in Poland – seem in hindsight like a long march towards the final collapse of the Soviet empire in 1989–91. The series of revolts also marks different stages in a slow process, in which ever more Western intellectuals sought to distance themselves from schematic ideological thinking.

Merleau-Ponty, for example, had become increasingly disenchanted with Marxism even before the violent suppression of the Hungarian uprising of 1956.[7] Events in Hungary reinforced his earlier concerns and resulted in further critical reflections on the Soviet experiment. While Merleau-Ponty half a century ago disowned the main arguments of his *Humanism and Terror* (Merleau-Ponty, 1955, 227–33), and called for a thorough de-Stalinization – 'a de–Stalinisation which is unchecked, consequential, and extended beyond the frontiers of communism to the whole left that communism has "frozen"' (Merleau-Ponty, 1964, 308) – his contemporary Jean-Paul Sartre needed another decade to move away from these positions. In contrast, Žižek continues to argue that 'Stalinist ideology even at its most "totalitarian" still exudes emancipatory potential' (Žižek, 2001, 131). Back in 1956, Jean-Paul Sartre maintained that the defence of the achievements of the communist revolution in Hungary required tough measures. At this point in time at least, Sartre seems to have been more concerned with the slight potential

7 The turning point is possibly marked with the publication of the collection of essays *Adventures of the Dialectic*, which also contains a polemical attack on Sartre and his alleged 'Ultrabolshevism' (Merleau-Ponty, 1955, 95–201).

for a revival of a reactionary regime in Hungary rather than with the obvious deficiencies of the communist model (see Sartre, 1968).

The next serious challenge to the communist order in Eastern Europe and the communist illusion in the West (see Furet, 1999) was the suppression of the Prague Spring in 1968. This marked Sartre's departure from his earlier position towards the 'really existing socialist regimes'. Yet it took another decade and the publication of Solzhenitsyn's *The Gulag Archipelago* in 1974 for the French intellectual Left to denounce communism, Marxism and Leninist-style revolutionary politics and to re-discover the political relevance of human rights discourse (see Lefort, 1986). This was 'the anti-totalitarian moment of the 1970s', which culminated in France in 1977 (see Christofferson, 2004), the very same year that gave rise to the Charter 77 human rights movement in communist Czechoslovakia. This is no coincidence, as the radical shift in Western debates about human rights was partly triggered by the emergence of dissident movements in Central and Eastern Europe, as well as the adoption of the 1975 Helsinki accord (see Horvath, 2007).

The year 1977 also propelled to political prominence a distinguished Czech philosopher, Jan Patočka, who, despite not being sufficiently known to Western audiences, was undoubtedly one of the most influential dissident intellectuals in Czechoslovakia.[8] Patočka, a student of Heidegger and Husserl, shared a number of the pessimistic assumptions about modern societies, East *and* West, made both by Žižek and Merleau-Ponty. He went even further by saying that 'man always is essentially in a hopeless situation. Man is a being committed to an adventure, which, in a certain sense, cannot end well. We are a ship that necessarily will be shipwrecked' (Patočka, 2002, 2). But he drew radically different lessons from this insight. He did not see the need to abandon the language of human rights. On the contrary, Patočka's political philosophy offers a sophisticated defence of fundamental values of liberal democracy (human rights and freedom) without resorting to the temptations of dogmatic ideological thinking. Patočka accepted Heidegger's lesson about the death of metaphysics, but this did not prevent his asking whether we can salvage something from our common European heritage – something that would still 'be believable even for us, that could affect us in a way so that we could again find hope in a specific perspective, in a specific future, without giving in to illusory dreams and without undervaluing the toughness and gravity of our current situation' (Patočka, 2002, 12).

8 It is telling that a recent study that devotes a whole chapter to the impact that East European dissidents had on French intellectuals refers erroneously to 'Pantocka' (Christofferson, 2004, 168 and 291). Christofferson underestimates the influence of dissident intellectuals. There has been a growing interest in Patočka's work reflected in a number of recent studies and commentaries (see Findlay, 2002; Rorty, 1991; Szakolczai, 1994; Tucker, 2000) and translations into English (see Kohák, 1989; Patočka, 1996; Patočka, 2002). Patočka even had a major influence on Derrida (see Derrida, 1995), and is said to have triggered the ethical turn in his philosophy (Lom, 2002, xix).

Jan Patočka and Socrates

Patočka grounded his agonistic philosophy of human rights in Socrates. For Patočka, Socrates was struggling with the same set of dilemmas that plague modern intellectuals. Acting and thinking before 'the birth of metaphysics', Socrates' ideas seem relevant to our current predicament. Socrates, 'the great questioner', challenged the force of tradition and of all received wisdom. No moral doctrine could be accepted without rational scrutiny. 'He formulates his new truth', Patočka argued, 'only indirectly, in the form of a question, in the form of a sceptical analysis, of a negation of all finite assertions' (Patočka, 1989, 180). Socrates' project focuses on the following question: How to live a good life without any certainties, or firm metaphysical foundations? In this existentialist uncertainty, in this 'problemacity of being', Patočka located the possibility of freedom.

Building on Husserl, Patočka conceives of human life as a movement towards a horizon that constantly presents us with new possibilities and changing perspectives:

> This positive principle of freedom is hidden in the contingency of principles of human action. And what belongs to human freedom? That man can find or not find himself in the choice of his life and in the realization of what follows from that choice, that he can, so to say, seize or miss himself, that he can seize his – what? In this we see the problemacity of freedom, the problemacity which no one and nothing can take away from man. (Patočka, 2002, 205)

It follows that with freedom comes responsibility, the very thing that Žižek seems unable to take seriously. The idea that one can, in Patočka's terms, 'find, or miss himself' is a reformulation of the specifically human possibility of 'living in truth', popularized by Václav Havel. Patočka explained this concept some years earlier:

> Humans are the only beings which, because they are not indifferent to themselves and to their being, can live in truth, can choose between life in the anxiety of its roles and needs and life in a relation to the world, not to existing entities only. (Patočka, 1995)[9]

In contrast to Merleau-Ponty in his *Humanism and Terror*, Patočka develops an understanding of the political that is very much in line with Arendt's thinking.[10] Like Heidegger, Patočka is a philosopher concerned with fundamental problems of human existence; he knows about the tragic nature of our predicament. But while Heidegger sought escape in German Romanticism and his country retreat in the Black Forest, Patočka, not unlike Arendt before him, seeks salvation in the political.

9 For an English translation and commentary, see Findlay (2002, 47).

10 Ironically, it is also not too far from Merleau-Ponty's political thinking developed later. The further away he moves from the premises of *Humanism and Terror*, the more affinity his political philosophy displays in relation to Arendt and Patočka.

If we are to live our lives carrying the burdens of knowledge of our finitude and of knowledge that there is no possibility of salvation through religion or metaphysics (or German Romantic poetry), we must endow our lives with meaning by other means. Even after the death of God, or the death of metaphysics, there must be *something* more to life than egotistic pursuit of material self-interest (or ironic gesturing of postmodern philosophers). We don't know what this *something* is, just as we do not know and will never know what the final purpose of our existence is. But this must not prevent us from asking, and acting responsibly.

Patočka's political philosophy is as interesting as his political actions. Both his thinking and his personal biography resonate with the life of Socrates. As in the case of Socrates, Patočka's actions should be seen as an integral part of his philosophical project. Just as Socrates pursued philosophy outside any institutional framework simply by confronting his fellow Athenians with difficult questions, Patočka spent many years outside the official academia engaging young students in covert seminars conducted in private apartments. Clearly, when politics is about 'inserting ourselves into the world by word and deed' (Arendt, 1961b, 263), their projects were as much political as they were philosophical.

But can philosophy ever be so closely linked with politics? Arendt argues that 'since philosophical truth concerns man in his singularity, it is unpolitical by nature' (Arendt, 1961b, 246). According to Arendt, Socrates only really made a political impact when he accepted his execution. Žižek, by contrast, is happy to contemplate the execution of others. Arendt believed that Socrates gave an example that vindicated his doctrine that 'it is better to suffer wrong than to do wrong' (Arendt, 1961b, 247). I am not persuaded by Arendt's dismissive remark about philosophy (surely Socrates was not really in the business of establishing a 'philosophical truth'?), but nobody can doubt that the best test of credibility of a moral philosopher is his capacity and willingness to live up to his own moral demands. At any rate, it is clear that Socrates reinforced his influence by setting an example. The same can be said about Patočka.

Charter 77 and Human Rights

Even though Patočka was not directly involved in politics for the most part of his life, he had the opportunity to demonstrate that he was willing and capable to take a stance. This came at the beginning of 1977, when he joined a small group of intellectuals to create a human rights movement, Charter 77. The situation in Czechoslovakia in the late 1970s was grim. After the suppression of the Prague Spring in 1968, very few people had any hope that the repressive political system could be improved. Most Czechs and Slovaks passively complied with the regime they detested. Modest hopes were raised with the Helsinki Agreement of 1975, in which all the signatories, including the countries of the Soviet bloc, pronounced their commitment to the ideals of human rights. Communist leaders never really took this commitment all that seriously, and were taken by surprise once a number of dissident intellectuals started asking them to 'keep their promises'. This was the background to Charter 77.

Patočka was instrumental in Charter 77, both as a thinker and a political activist. It was Patočka who articulated one of the most eloquent defences of human rights:

> The idea of human rights is nothing other than the conviction that even states, even society as a whole, are subject to the sovereignty of moral sentiment: that they recognize something unconditional that is higher than they are, something that is binding even on them, sacred, inviolable, and that in their power to establish and maintain the rule of law they seek to express this recognition. (Patočka, 1990, 32)[11]

On the surface, the demands of Charter 77 were very moderate, even by the standards of the communist part of Europe at that time. After all, the signatories of the Charter only demanded that the communist authorities comply with the obligations that they endorsed in Helsinki in 1975. However, the communist leaders understood the initiative (rightly) as a serious threat to the regime, and persecuted all the crucial actors. Patočka became the first prominent victim. On 13 March 1977, Patočka died as a consequence of a heart attack incurred during prolonged interrogation (Lom, 2002, xiv).

This was a Socratic end to a truly Socratic life, and was understood as such by many of his followers. Regardless of Patočka's outstanding intellectual achievements, it is plausible to argue that his thinking would not have been as influential as it was in Czechoslovakia, were it not for this Socratic engagement that tested his commitment. The best-known student of Patočka was Václav Havel, who also popularized his notion of 'living in truth' (Findlay, 1999). It required Žižek's theoretical sophistication to charge this relentless advocate of human rights with 'religious fundamentalism'. In Žižek's eyes, Havel betrayed the true cause of Western intellectuals, which is to fight against 'the knaves of capitalism'. As he put it: 'there is no escape from the conclusion that his [Havel's] life has descended from the sublime to the ridiculous' (Žižek, 1999, 3).

The same Žižek who in 1977 produced political speeches for Slovenian party apparatchiks (Myers, 2003, 8), and who in the late 1980s boasted to one of his English academic colleagues about being appointed as a commissar 'to monitor and control dissident activity' in his workplace (see Parker, 2007), is these days appalled by Havel's lack of sound political judgement. In contrast, Havel actively defied the communist regime in Czechoslovakia and shared Patočka's conviction that a life without freedom is not worth living. As Ivan Chvatík, one of the guardians of Patočka's philosophical heritage, commented:

11 For an English translation, see Kohák (1989, 341).

> The maintenance of this life [in freedom] is worth dying or killing for – it even becomes a duty. The free person cannot be responsible for life beneath the level of the free life – such a life has no sense for him. (Chvatík, 2003, 8)

It may well be questioned whether Chvatík's interpretation of Patočka to the effect that freedom might be worth 'killing for' goes too far. At any rate, the choices for people living in communist Czechoslovakia in the 1970s and 1980s, and possibly even more so in the former Yugoslavia, were seldom as dramatic as this quote suggests. As Havel famously argued in his astute analysis of power dynamics in post-totalitarian regimes, the demands on ordinary citizens were rather modest. Even a superficial level of conformity sufficed to sustain the regime. In fact, the main argument of Havel's influential essay 'The Power of the Powerless' was to say that the regime was sustained by people complying with the rules of the game, regardless of whether they internalized or whether they were cynical about the ruling ideology (see Havel, 1985). For Havel, the only way out of this situation was to openly reject the lies of the ruling ideology by attempting to 'live in truth'. While Žižek appears to be in agreement with Havel's diagnosis in the 'Power of the Powerless' (Žižek, 2001), he clearly considers his prescriptions as far too naive. In contrast to Havel, Žižek seems to believe that the most effective way to subvert communism was to behave *as if* one was more communist than the communists.

The intellectual trajectories of these two thinkers could not be more different. Havel has moved away from his earlier existentialist critique of both communism and the West (see Havel, 1985) to a position that amounts to a reluctant endorsement of Western-style liberal democracy (see Havel, 1992).[12] Žižek, on the other hand, moved from his (ironic?) endorsement of the reality of communism in Yugoslavia through Stalinism to a position that seems close to an endorsement of 'heroic gestures' of perpetrators of September 11.

Radical intellectuals like Žižek in stable liberal democracies are outraged by the perceived stability of their political systems. They detest the long-lasting discursive hegemony of political liberalism, and see no other way of changing it but by another violent revolution. They see humans in contemporary Western societies as having found themselves in (or – as Heidegger would have it – being *thrown* into) an intolerable situation which can only be overcome by an authentic act of liberation. This must be by definition violent:

> Today's 'mad dance' … awaits its resolution in a new form of Terror. The only 'realistic' prospect is to ground a new political universality by opting for the *impossible*, fully assuming the place of the exception, with no taboos, no a priory norms ('human

12 And Žižek is not the only left-wing intellectual in the West bemoaning this move. Consider, for example, John Keane's rather sensationalist biography of Havel, which argues that his ascendancy to power in post-communist Czechoslovakia (and then the Czech Republic) was accomplished through Havel's betrayal of his earlier political ideals (see Keane, 1999).

> rights', 'democracy'), respect for which would prevent us from 'resignifying' terror, the ruthless exercise of power, the spirit of sacrifice … if this radical choice is decried by some bleeding–heart liberals as *Linksfaschismus*, so be it! (Butler, Laclau and Žižek, 2000, 326)

So, I hear you say, what's the big deal? Many intellectuals made foolish judgements. Heidegger supported the Nazis, Merleau-Ponty justified Stalinism in Russia, Žižek still celebrates Lenin and Robespierre. There isn't anything surprising about this. In fact, you might say, it is naive to assume that philosophers, social scientists or intellectuals in general possess some kind of key to understanding all the problems of morality that would make them somehow better people, or at any rate more astute politically. They have no special knowledge, special insights. It is naive to assume that they are better people (than the rest of us). In contrast to Marx, who urged philosophers to make their world a better place ('philosophers have only interpreted the world, the point is to change it'), some contemporary political thinkers, such as the late Richard Rorty, urged philosophers to shut up (see Rorty, 1999). Against the background of twentieth-century philosophizing that did not protect mankind from the terrible crimes of both Nazism and Stalinism, this proposition seems plausible.

For ancient Greeks, the same proposition would have seemed nonsensical. For Socrates, Plato and Aristotle, philosophy basically had no other purpose than to show the way to the good life, both for individuals and societies. This was then – before the death of metaphysics (or in Socrates' case, before metaphysics was even born), before the death of God. The likes of Miłosz, Patočka and Havel showed with their actions and political thinking that even post-Heideggerian philosophy can give rise to responsible and prudent intellectuals. *Their* experience with the twin evils of totalitarianism in Europe taught them that this must remain the ultimate purpose of all genuine political philosophizing. Miłosz's poem about the meaning of poetry makes this point:

> What is poetry which does not save
> Nations or people?
> A connivance with official lies,
> A song of drunkards whose throats will be cut in a moment,
> Readings for sophomore girls.[13]

Miłosz is probably expecting too much from poetry (and yes, even Miłosz managed to write poems about love). But is it too much to expect from public intellectuals that they display integrity and political prudence in their thoughts and actions?

---

13 From 'Dedication', Warsaw 1945, cited in Michnik (2005, 19).

References

Arendt, Hannah (1961a), *Between Past and Future: Eight Exercises in Political Thought* (New York: Viking Press).

Arendt, Hannah (1961b), 'Truth and Politics', in *Between Past and Future: Eight Exercises in Political Thought* (New York: Viking Press), 227–64.

Arendt, Hannah (1965), *On Revolution* (New York: Viking Press).

Arendt, Hannah (1969), *On Violence* (London: Penguin Press).

Arendt, Hannah (1982), *Lectures on Kant's Political Philosophy* (Chicago, IL: University of Chicago Press).

Auer, Stefan (2004), 'The Paradoxes of the Revolutions of 1989 in Central Europe', *Critical Horizons* 4, 361–90.

Butler, Judith, Laclau, Ernesto and Žižek, Slavoj (2000), *Contingency, Hegemony, Universality: Contemporary Dialogues on the Left* (London: Verso).

Christofferson, Michael Scott (2004), *French Intellectuals Against the Left: The Antitotalitarian Moment of the 1970s* (New York and Oxford: Berghahn Books).

Chvatík, Ivan (2003), 'The Heretical Conception of the European Legacy in the Late Essays of Jan Patočka', <http://www.cts.cuni.cz/reports/2003/CTS-03-14.pdf>, accessed 28 May 2007.

Derrida, Jacques (1995), *The Gift of Death* (Chicago, IL: University of Chicago Press).

Findlay, Edward F. (1999), 'Classical Ethics and Postmodern Critique: Political Philosophy in Václav Havel and Jan Patočka', *The Review of Politics* 61, 403.

Findlay, Edward F. (2002), *Caring for the Soul in a Postmodern Age: Politics and Phenomenology in the Thought of Jan Patočka* (Albany, NY: State University of New York Press).

Furet, François (1999), *The Passing of an Illusion: The Idea of Communism in the Twentieth Century* (Chicago, IL: University of Chicago Press).

Havel, Václav (1985), 'The Power of the Powerless', in Keane, John (ed.), *The Power of the Powerless: Citizens against the State in Central-Eastern Europe* (Armonk, NY: M.E. Sharpe.), 125–214.

Havel, Václav (1992), *Summer Meditations* (New York: Alfred A. Knopf).

Horvath, Robert (2007), 'The Solzhenitsyn Effect: East European Dissidents and the Demise of the Revolutionary Privilege', *Human Rights Quarterly* 29, 879–907.

Keane, John (1999), *Václav Havel: A Political Tragedy in Six Acts* (London: Bloomsbury).

Kohák, Erazim (1989), *Jan Patočka: Philosophy and Selected Writings* (Chicago, IL: University of Chicago Press).

Lefort, Claude (1986), 'Politics and Human Rights', in Thompson, John B. (ed.), *The Political Forms of Modernity* (Oxford: Polity Press), 239–72.

Lom, Petr (2002), 'Foreword', in *Jan Patočka, Plato and Europe* (Stanford, CA: Stanford University Press), xiii–xxi.

Merleau-Ponty, Maurice (1955), *Adventures of the Dialectic* (London: Heinemann).

Merleau-Ponty, Maurice (1964), 'On De-Stalinisation', in McCleary, Richard C. (ed.), *Signs* (Evanston, IL: Northwestern University Press), 293–308.

Merleau-Ponty, Maurice (1969), *Humanism and Terror* (Westport, CT: Greenwood Press).

Michnik, Adam (2005), 'An Uncaptive Mind', *East European Politics and Societies* 19, 12–20.

Miłosz, Czesław (1962), *The Captive Mind* (London: Mercury).

Myers, Tony (2003), *Slavoj Žižek* (London: Routledge).

Parker, Ian (2007), 'Žižek: Ambivalence and Oscillation', <http://www.nskstate.com/appendix/articels/zizek_ianparker.php>, accessed 28 May 2007.

Patočka, Jan (1989), 'Negative Platonism: Reflections Concerning the Rise, the Scope, and the Demise of Metaphysics – And Whether Philosophy Can Survive It', in Kohák, Erazim (ed.), *Jan Patočka: Philosophy and Selected Writings* (Chicago, IL: University of Chicago Press), 175–206.

Patočka, Jan (1990), 'O povinnosti bránit se proti bezpráví', in Prečan, Vilém (ed.), *Charta 77* (Bratislava: Archa), 31–4.

Patočka, Jan (1995), *Tělo, spoločenství, jazyk, svět* (Prague: Oikoymenh).

Patočka, Jan (1996), *Heretical Essays in the Philosophy of History* (Chicago, IL and La Salle, IL: Open Court).

Patočka, Jan (2002), *Plato and Europe* (Stanford, CA: Stanford University Press).

Plato (1993), *Republic* (Oxford: Oxford University Press).

Popper, Karl (1962), *The Open Society and Its Enemies* (London: Routledge and Kegan Paul).

Rorty, Richard (1991), 'The Seer of Prague: The Influence of Czechoslovakian Philosopher Jan Patočka', *New Republic* 205 (1991), 35–9.

Rorty, Richard (1999), *Philosophy and Social Hope* (Harmondsworth: Penguin).

Sartre, Jean-Paul (1968), *The Ghost of Stalin* (New York: G. Braziller).

Spiewak, Pawel (ed.) (2003), *Anti-Totalitarismus. Eine polnische Debatte* (Frankfurt am Main: Suhrkamp).

Szakolczai, Arpad (1994), 'Thinking Beyond the East-West Divide: Foucault, Patocka and the Care of the Soul', *Social Research* 61, 297–324.

Taylor, Astra (2005), *Žižek!* (Zeitgeist Films).

Tucker, Aviezer (2000), *The Philosophy and Politics of Czech Dissidence from Patocka to Havel* (Pittsburgh, PA: University of Pittsburgh Press).

Wolin, Richard (2001), *Heidegger's Children: Hannah Arendt, Karl Löwith, Hans Jonas, and Herbert Marcuse* (Princeton, NJ: Princeton University Press).

Wolin, Richard (2004), *The Seduction of Unreason: The Intellectual Romance with Fascism from Nietzsche to Postmodernism* (Princeton, NJ: Princeton University Press).

Žižek, Slavoj (1993), 'Why are Laibach and NSK not Fascists?', *M'ARS* 3–4, 3–4.
Žižek, Slavoj (1999), 'Attempts to Escape the Logic of Capitalism', *London Review of Books* 21, 3–7.
Žižek, Slavoj (2001), *Did Somebody Say Totalitarianism? Five Interventions in the (Mis)use of a Notion* (London: Verso).
Žižek, Slavoj (2002a), *Revolution at the Gates* (London: Verso).
Žižek, Slavoj (2002b), *Welcome to the Desert of the Real: Five Essays on September 11 and Related Dates* (London: Verso).
Žižek, Slavoj (2007), 'Robespierre, or, the "Divine Violence" of Terror', in *Virtue and Terror* (London: Verso), vi–xiii.

Chapter 7
Public Intellectuals and Totalitarianism: A Century's Debate

Anson Rabinbach

Totalitarianism's Return

Since the fall of communism, both the word and the concept of totalitarianism have made a significant, and some would argue permanent, comeback. This is somewhat surprising since more than three decades ago, the exhausted polemics and vagaries of definition led many Anglo-American historians and political theorists to confidently predict that the 'totalitarian construct will be overtaken, if not by oblivion, at least by creeping desuetude' (Barber, 1969, 39). After a long period of decline, the concept revived during the 1970s and 1980s, as Soviet and Eastern European dissidents and reformers made totalitarianism the 'common denominator' for the opposition throughout Eastern Europe (Rupnik, 1996). As the weaknesses of the classical totalitarianism theory developed by Friedrich Hayek, Carl J. Friedrich, Zbigniew Brzezinski and Hannah Arendt in the 1950s became apparent to Western historians and political theorists, the normative significance of the concept for those living under Soviet hegemony outweighed all such analytic difficulties (see Gleason, 1998, esp. ch. 9). Only in France, as Pierre Hassner pointed out, did the decline of the concept among Western social scientists not inhibit its acceptance among public intellectuals and political philosophers, who valued it all the more as the antipodes to human rights and democracy. 'The inscrutable banality of the social sciences *à l'américaine*', Hassner wrote, 'confronted the equally inscrutable heights of philosophy *à la française*' (Hassner, 1984).

The collapse of communism reinvigorated the concept for obvious reasons, chief among them the historical confirmation of the inability of Soviet-type societies to reform from within or accomplish any substantial modernization of their disintegrating planned economies. The domino effect of the Eastern European protests and the eventual end of the Soviet regime in 1991 accentuated the similarities, rather than differences (which were none the less considerable), among the countries of what was almost anachronistically referred to as the 'Soviet bloc'. For this reason, the disappearance of 'real socialism' compelled historians, as Ian Kershaw noted, 'to examine with fresh eyes the comparison between Stalinism and Nazism' (Kershaw, 1994). The problem of totalitarian violence was the moral and political dilemma of our age, wrote the historian Tony Judt (1998, 96). And the late François Furet, fully aware of the enmity (that also drew them closer to each other) between communism and Nazism, argued in his influential study of the communist ideal, *The Passing of an Illusion: The Idea of Communism in the Twentieth Century*, that Stalinist Bolshevism and National Socialism were not simply comparable, but constituted a 'political category of their own' (Furet, 1990, 180). The obduracy of philo-communism, especially in the French intellectual milieu, Furet maintained, could only be explained by its positive association with anti-Fascism, the Resistance, and above all with the Jacobin phase of the French Revolution, from which Furet drew a direct line to the revolutionaries of 1917. In short, until 1989, to criticize communism in France was almost unpatriotic.

Renewed interest in the moral, philosophical and historical dimensions of the concept were not restricted to scholars of the Nazi and Soviet regimes. In the heated controversy during the debate prior to the war in Iraq, distinguished commentators once again embraced the word 'totalitarian', extending its scope beyond the historical dictatorships of the 1930s and 1940s to include regimes and movements in the Middle East (see Stephenson, 2003; Cushman, 2005). Respected former dissidents such as Václav Havel and Adam Michnik, and supporters of them like André Glucksmann and Jose Ramos-Horta supported the war on liberal-humanitarian grounds, invoking the imperative of resisting totalitarianism (see Cushman, 2005, 14). In the US, the editor of the liberal *New Republic*, Peter Beinart, complained that 'three years after September 11 brought the United States face-to-face with a new totalitarian threat; liberalism has still not been fundamentally reshaped by the experience' (Beinart, 2004). British Foreign Secretary Jack Straw called terrorism a synonym for the 'new totalitarianism … the world's greatest threat to democracy'.[1]

Totalitarianism has always been a protean term, capable of combining and re-combining meanings in different contexts and in new and ever-changing political constellations. The major theorists of totalitarianism were the systematizers of a term that had a long history before it acquired the patina of academic respectability. Yet it is notoriously difficult to pin down what precisely is distinctive about 'totalitarianism'. Is it compelling shorthand, as some of its first theorists insisted, to demonstrate that modern tyranny is unique because it is more invasive, more reliant on the total assent of the 'masses' and on terror than old-fashioned despotism? Is it a 'project', as Hannah Arendt famously argued – an experiment in 'fabricating' humanity according to the laws of biology or history, or is it an 'ideal type' (in the Weberian sense) to which no 'real' dictatorship actually conforms? Is it a concept that can only be defended negatively, as the ultimate rejection of pluralism, legality, democracy and Judeo-Christian morality?

---

1 See <http://news.bbc.co.uk/1/hi/uk_politics/3507730.stm>.

Moral Uproar: French Neo-humanism and the War on Terror

Among those who have been most eloquent and prolific in calling for a serious re-examination of totalitarianism's lessons is Tzvetan Todorov, the Bulgarian-born French literary scholar and public intellectual. 'For me,' writes Todorov in his *Hope and Memory: Lessons from the Twentieth Century*, 'the central event of the century was the emergence of the unprecedented political system called *totalitarianism,* which at its peak, ruled a substantial part of the planet' (Todorov, 2003, 2). Having lived in communist Bulgaria until 1963, Todorov established his reputation in France as a structuralist literary critic, but soon turned from formal aspects of language to ethics and politics, from what he calls 'a historical and anthropological perspective'.[2] In 1982, he published *The Conquest of America*, a remarkable investigation of how in attempting to 'obliterate the strangeness of the external other, Western civilization found an interior other', an experience which led both to egalitarianism and absorption, the acknowledgment of difference and the sanctioning of hierarchy (see Todorov, 1987, 248–9). His more recent works, beginning in the 1990s, were concerned with ethical behaviour in the Holocaust. *Facing the Extreme: Moral Life in the Concentration Camps* (1996) argued that moral acts, including heroism, caring and self-sacrifice, are virtually ineradicable, even under the worst of circumstances, while *The Fragility of Goodness* (2001) documented Bulgarian resistance to Nazi deportation orders. His *Imperfect Garden: The Legacy of Humanism* is a reinterpretation of Montaigne, Montesquieu, Rousseau and Constant as thinkers who offer a moderate and fallible humanism more appropriate to our own modernity than the more dogmatic figures of the eighteenth-century Enlightenment (see Todorov, 2002b). Rousseau figures for him not as a proto-totalitarian, but as a modern who inaugurated a dialogue between the solipsistic individual and the social world. *Hope and Memory* is in many respects a synthesis of both of these preoccupations, a confrontation with the moral and ethical dilemmas that continue to persist after the eclipse of the totalitarianisms that dominated the century, and a plea for a new, moderate and responsible, critical humanism. In this regard, Todorov's re-invention of liberal political thought in France is contemporaneous with that of a number of other well-known critics of the Stalinist Left and the so-called 'philosophy of the 60s' (*Imperfect Garden* is dedicated to the philosopher Luc Ferry, France's former Minister of Education) (Strenski, 2004, 100).

At the core of Todorov's neo-humanism is the view that individual autonomy, solidarity and the recognition of difference within universality constitute the basic values of any democratic polity. 'The grammar of humanism', he writes, 'has three persons: *I*, who exercises his or her autonomy; *thou*, who is equivalent to an *I* but totally distinct from *me* (each *thou* can also be an *I*, and vice-versa) … and *they*,

---

2 Todorov recounts his intellectual and personal development in a book of interviews, *Devoirs et Delices d'une vie passeur: Entrietiens avec Catherine Portevin* (Todorov, 2002a). Recent works on Todorov include Scott and Zaretsky (2001b); Golsan (2004b), and Strenski (2004).

who form the community to which an *I* belongs' (Todorov, 2003, 39). Of course, the problem is not so much in articulating these principles as in judging where one draws the line between the liberty of the individual, the demands of the community and the culture of minorities in any liberal society.

The concept of totalitarianism, Todorov argues, is essential not merely as a historical trope, but for demonstrating that 'the instinct for freedom is part of humanity's biological nature'. Totalitarian states could not, despite their formidable tools, 'mutate the species so as to eradicate its yearning for freedom' (Todorov, 2003, 70). The basic premise of totalitarianism, he contends, is that war is the natural state of man, a worldview that legitimizes annihilation and violence in so far as the absolute good is always justified in extirpating the bad. For that reason, terror is 'a basic and integral part of totalitarian societies', because they are always oblivious to otherness, plurality and difference. Totalitarianism is characterized by a 'cult of science combined with utopian thinking', a radical belief in the transparency of all human life and history, the eradication of individual will and contingency (Todorov, 2003, 30). Totalitarianism is 'always Manichaean, dividing the world into two mutually exclusive parties, the good and the bad, aiming to annihilate the latter' (Todorov, 2003, 33). Neither Nazism nor communism were universalist: 'the only difference is that in one case the division of humanity is "horizontal," based on national frontiers, and the other it is "vertical," between the different layers of a single society: national and racial war for Nazism, and the class struggle for communism' (Todorov, 2003, 37).

Hitler and Stalin each merged nation and socialism, persecuted national minorities, replaced conviction with submission and destroyed democracy. Perhaps Todorov's most original insight reveals the need for a theatrical pseudo-democracy (Hitler's plebiscites, Stalin's 'constitution'), a gigantic charade through which totalitarian rulers unwittingly acknowledged, however perversely, the truth of democracy by acting 'as if' they adhered to it.

This assertion presents something of a difficulty since communism, as Raymond Aron acknowledged long ago, also makes a strong claim to universalism by virtue of its rejection of class difference, its Enlightenment belief in human reason, and its goal of human emancipation. Todorov contends that Aron failed to distinguish adequately between the original communist ideal and Lenin's decisive ideological turn, which declared communism's intent to destroy its enemies by systematic violence. Consequently, he claims, Aron could 'turn a blind eye to various features of communism' (Todorov, 2003, 36). Unlike Aron, who came to the conclusion that 'whatever the similarities, the difference [between Nazism and communism] is fundamental', Todorov argues that the similarities are more fundamental:

> The ideals of both regimes jettison universal ambitions: Hitler wanted to create a nation, and eventually a whole world free of Jews; Stalin clamored for a society without classes, that is to say, without the bourgeois. In both cases, one segment of humanity was written off. The only real difference lies in the techniques used to achieve these identical policy aims. (Todorov 2003, 37)

If Todorov had been satisfied with this distinction, his book would be flawed by an approach that elides the essential differences between the dictatorships and their crimes. One can still argue that as different as Western liberalism and Soviet communism may have been, the ideals of Enlightenment reason united them, however imperfectly or temporarily. 'Class struggle' hardly has the same ontological status as 'racial struggle'; in Nazism, the racial struggle is substituted for the political, class antagonism reduced to the invasion of a foreign (Jewish body) that undermines and destroys the natural harmony of the Aryan community (see the instructive comments on this point in Žižek, 2005). At other points, however, Todorov acknowledges that the distinctions are essential. He points out that in many respects, the Nazi programme was closer to the truth of National Socialism than the communist program was to Soviet reality. Nazism more openly acknowledged its imperial ambitions and racial ideology, while the Soviets were more duplicitous, illusory and deceptive about their aims. Consequently, Nazi victims could more easily understand why they had been chosen to suffer than could Communist victims. Communism also saw itself as the logical conclusion of ideas first preached by Christianity, while Nazism had no respect for that tradition, and saw itself rather as the heir of paganism. This too is debatable, since despite its Nordic and racial precepts, there were also strong Christian elements in Nazi ideology, for example the secularization of the Fall in the theory of degeneration, and the secularization of the history of salvation in the emphasis on racial regeneration and charismatic redemption (see Bärsch, 1998).

Somewhat surprisingly, Todorov does not analyse in any detail the extraordinary French debate over the *Black Book of Communism*, published in 1997, though his approach is obviously informed by it and it surely accounts for some of the contradictions elaborated above. Todorov carefully steers clear of its editor Stéphane Courtois's questionable effort to produce a moral arithmetic according to which communism was responsible for 'four times as many' deaths than Nazism, ergo communism was both historically and juridically more condemnable than Nazism. Courtois's egregious introduction to the *Black Book* was an undisguised indictment, undermining several of the important contributions to what was the collective work of half-a-dozen historians, a number of whom publicly repudiated his views (see Courtois et al., 1997).[3] The ensuing polemics called into question the legitimacy of the Nazi–communist comparison, since Courtois insisted – falsely – that communism's crimes (over the entire century and in half-a-dozen countries) had been systematically ignored in favour of the Holocaust. Todorov rejects Courtois's claim of '100 million dead' (under communism) by noting (but not elaborating) that 'although the numbers of dead were approximately equal, the Nazis' systematic destruction of the Jews and other groups deemed undeserving of life has no real parallel'. In the Soviet Gulag, death was not an end in itself,

3 The controversy over *The Black Book* is discussed in Rabinbach (1998) and Aronson (2003), 222–45. A refutation, relying on the different modalities of international communism, can be found in Pudal, Dreyfus, Groppo et. al. (2000).

Todorov emphasizes, 'only in Nazi extermination camps did putting people to death become an aim in itself' (Todorov, 2003, 88). This caveat seems rather to call into question Todorov's aforementioned claim that only the 'techniques' distinguish Nazism from Stalinism; there is a difference between a state that commits genocide and a genocidal state.

If the two dictatorships are ultimately morally but not historically identical, why does the comparison between Stalinist communism and Nazism still continue to produce such offence or provoke such fervour? Why did the *Black Book of Communism*, which caused a sensation in France, have so much less of an impact elsewhere in Europe or in the US? How do the historical distinctions that Todorov ultimately affirms affect his claim that 'the two totalitarian regimes were not like each other in all respects but each was as bad as the other'? Todorov offers an ingenious explanation for why accepting or rejecting the comparison has been so morally and politically charged. Depending on the context, the comparison, he observes, can both serve as exoneration and as a way of amplifying guilt, as apologia and indictment, reflecting how closely the speaker's position might be identified with the victims or perpetrators. For those more closely identified with Nazi murderers, for example, the comparison is welcome since it looks like something of an excuse, while for those closer to the Communists it is pejorative because it looks more like an accusation. For victims of communism, the reverse is true: the comparison is more acceptable because it reinforces the guilt of the perpetrators, while for Nazi victims it is rejected since it appears as an exoneration (Todorov, 2003, 75). This approach helps explain why there is so little public engagement with the memory of Stalinist crimes in the former Soviet Union (which would taint the victory in 1945). Ultimately, however, it amounts to a zero-sum game, which entirely depends on Nazi crimes always being regarded as the greater evil. Indeed, without the moral hierarchy implicit in the schema itself, the comparison is entirely superfluous. Yet the very divergence of reactions, even within the former Soviet imperium, points to a problem, if not with the category of totalitarianism, with the dramatic changes that the Nazi–Soviet comparison undergoes as it traverses a geography of memory that has been etched out different historical landscapes across Europe. Shifting the focus from history to memory, it becomes apparent that the forms of memorialization of the Holocaust that have taken place in the US and in Western Europe since 1945 have virtually turned the Nazi murder of the Jews into a kind of universal ethical 'codex' (despite all medialization and trivialization), a 'cosmopolitan' form of memory and a metaphor for modern evil that bears directly upon post-Holocaust ideals of justice (see Levy and Sznaider, 2001, 151). Almost the opposite could be said of the former Soviet Union, while in East Central Europe, most importantly in Poland, preoccupation with the 'double burden' of Nazi and Soviet rule has led to sustained confrontations over the nature of collaboration and even criminal complicity (see Gross, 2001; Polonsky and Michnic, 2004).[4]

4 On the memorialization of Soviet crimes, see the pioneering article by Etkind (2004). Even today, Russian historians are reluctant to regard 'the Great Patriotic War' in anything

The weakest section of the book is Todorov's theoretical discussion of the relationship between memory and history. He rightly points out that confrontations with memory often proceed from establishing facts to interpreting them, and finally to making them useful for the present; hence no constraints should limit establishing facts, though interpretations are not all of equal value. But to conclude that 'scholarship, being a human activity, has a political finality, which may be for good or bad' is to allow a truism to pass for what has long since become a fertile field of analysis (see Rév, 2005). Todorov's assertion that it is the duty of historians to establish precise facts while sequestering 'experience' to personal testimony and literature is at best an affront to historians, who have long been aware of the difficulties in transforming testimony (archives, memoirs, oral history) into the singular and collective voices of those who actually experience history – in other words, of historical actors, in both 'ordinary' and 'traumatic' circumstances. Even more questionable is Todorov's distinction between 'memory' (solely individual) and 'collective memory' (not memory at all, but discourse in the public arena), which raises the question of why some individuals choose to experience their own history through the lens of totalitarianism while others just as emphatically refuse such an optic. Even in the most subjective accounts, personal, communal or national 'trauma' and the political configuration of potent memories in the public sphere are always simultaneously at play (see LaCapra, 1994, and more recently, LaCapra, 2004). More persuasively, Todorov questions the pedagogical impact of what Henry Rousso calls the 'cohabitation of history and justice' in the sensational trials of Paul Touvier, Klaus Barbie and Maurice Papon, which confronted the 'duty to remember' with the complexities – and in the latter case, with the 'grey areas' – between complicity with Vichy and the Resistance. To be forced to choose – as the legalities of the trials made it seem – between a 'pure' Holocaust memory and a more complex memory that includes Vichy and the Second World War is, of course, deeply problematic (see especially the trenchant comments in Rousso, 2002, 48–84). Yet, one can also argue that these trials did not only pose such stark choices, but that each shed light on different dimensions of complicity and therefore of remembrance, while at the same time leaving others in the shadows.

Totalitarianism is an elastic concept. As Todorov defines it, it includes the denial of the autonomy of the individual, the absence of any division between a free private sphere and a regulated public sphere, the presence of a party that takes place of God, the concentration and personalization of power, the creation of new social hierarchies, and the creation of an illusory world in which plenitude, happiness and harmony are projected into the future. Combined with a hypertropic belief in the transparency of nature and history (scientism), totalitarianism is an 'ideal-type construct' which is, in Todorov's words 'the exact opposite of a democratic state'. Todorov scrupulously avoids the word 'liberal' (which might suggest free market

---

but a positive light. The St Petersburg Institute of History took notice of the Molotov–Ribbentrop Pact only in 1989, while uncomfortable facts about the 22 June invasion (only 8 per cent of the defenders survived) were buried until the last days of the regime.

economics to a French reader), but this also creates the problem that he does not distinguish between liberalism and democracy as 'opposites' of totalitarianism (see Minogue, 1998). This question too has a long history, since totalitarian societies often claimed to be higher and more complete forms of democracy, while liberal institutions and the protection of rights were always lacking (though their pseudo-forms were preserved in constitutions and in some legal norms). Some observers have even suggested that while liberalism or individualism is always the natural enemy of totalitarianism, democracy can be suspected of harbouring totalitarian potentials in the age of 'mass society' (Barber, 1969, 18).

No doubt, Todorov clearly means liberal democracy, drawing from John Locke and Benjamin Constant, in order to combine the Anglo-American emphasis on the autonomy of the individual with the French republican emphasis on the autonomy of the community. Todorov rejects the arguments of thinkers who have regarded totalitarianism as a form of democracy, such as Carl Schmitt, Jacob Talmon, and most recently, Furet. Each in his own way argued that communism followed the logic of revolutionary Jacobinism, combining the ideals of democratic egalitarianism and popular sovereignty with ruthless terror. The French Revolution, Todorov avers, did not link the use of force to the cult of science. Instead, the revolutionaries seized power from monarchs and passed it to the people's representatives, who remained just as absolute (in their collective authority) as the king, if not more so. Consequently, Todorov is quite vague about when we can actually begin to see the first glimmers of modern totalitarian ideology (he unconvincingly suggests the anarchist Sergei Nechayev's *Revolutionary Catechism* of 1869 or Ernest Renan's obscure third *Dialogue philosophique* of 1871 as potential candidates). In any case, he argues that 'only when the three strands of violence, millenarianism, and the cult of science come together can we talk of totalitarianism proper' (Todorov, 2003, 27).

Todorov's narrative is interspersed with six literary biographies, each portraying an exemplary figure who either resisted the totalitarian temptation or found an inner compass by which he or she could reflect on and judge their own experience apart from its logic. These portraits – Vassily Grossmann, Margarete Buber-Neumann, David Rousset, Primo Levi, Romain Gary and Germaine Tillion – are the most effective chapters of *Hope and Memory* – precisely because they pinpoint the 'fragile goodness' which Todorov argues is possible even *in extremis*. Levi is, of course, the best-known, and his experience in Auschwitz provides the moral template against which Todorov views the legacy of totalitarianism:

> Forty years of thinking about Auschwitz taught him that the real culprits, apart from a number of individuals with direct responsibility were the indifference and apathy of the German people. Save for a few exceptions, the Germans as a whole allowed themselves not to know for as long as possible; and when ignorance ceased to be an option they kept their heads down. So how can we justify our own voluntary ignorance today, and our choice of doing nothing: Is that not tantamount to complicity in new disasters, no less painful for being different from the past ones? (Todorov, 2003, 185)

Grossmann, known for his magisterial novel *Life and Fate*, was a communist whose mother was murdered by the Nazis and who fought in the Red Army. The massacre of the Jews was the occasion for his personal transformation, but 'it started him on a path that led him to open his heart to all others, to comprehend and love all human beings' (Todorov, 2003, 60). Another witness is Margarete Buber-Neumann, whose husband, the second-in-command of the German Communist Party, Heinz Neumann, was arrested and murdered by Stalin in 1937. Buber-Neumann was herself arrested in June 1938 and sent to the concentration camp at Karaganda in Kazakhstan. In 1940, after the Molotov–Ribbentrop Pact, she was handed over to the Gestapo, along with other German anti-fascist fighters, Jews and communists who Stalin dispatched via Brest-Litovsk. She was incarcerated at Ravensbrück, which she miraculously survived: 'Her new vocation was to be an exemplary, not to say unique, witness of the inhumanity of both kinds of totalitarianism' (Todorov, 2003, 103). David Rousset was a resister and an inmate at Buchenwald, who suffered insult, ostracism, a libel suit and the vilification of Sartre and Merleau-Ponty for condemning the horror of the Soviet camps and devoting himself to investigating all camps, including those still functioning in the 1950s. Romain Gary fought for the Free French and became a well-known novelist. His emphatic lack of interest in heroism, or in what Todorov sees as a kind of moral exhibitionism of the victor, permitted him to redefine courage as weakness, pity and love. Similarly, Germaine Tillion, also a Buchenwald survivor who tried to negotiate an end to the terror during the Algerian war, represents the kind of courage and selflessness that interests Todorov. It is not the totalitarian experience *per se*, but the ways in which each of these figures transcended their own suffering to embrace the suffering of others, or as in the case of Tillion, as 'she managed to "journey through hell" without being contaminated by evil, she even passed on to us a feeling of exhilaration' (Todorov, 2003, 307).

What attracts Todorov to these figures is not their suffering, but that each rejected the moral righteousness of their own victimhood (or victory, in Gary's case) and abandoned exclusive ways of apportioning good and bad without losing the capacity for moral judgement. These biographical chapters make it apparent that Todorov is above all a moralist who is impatient with, though not himself entirely free of, moralizing. Hence his admiration for 'people of great courage and selflessness' (Tillion) who do not abuse their power. Justice and democracy may be simple virtues; all the same, they are, he writes, 'the only political forces that can stop totalitarianism, by arms if necessary, and make it possible to exercise kindness and freedom' (Todorov, 2003, 73). This admission, however, poses a serious question of how to determine when 'force of arms' is justified and whether the antinomy of democracy and totalitarianism is still meaningful in the post-totalitarian era. Most importantly, it is not really clear what political 'lessons', if any, Todorov believes can be drawn after the defeat of Nazism and communism. And even if lessons can be drawn from the conflict between totalitarianism and democracy, he acknowledges that 'it does not follow that democracy invariably embodies the realm of the good' (Todorov, 2003, 237).

Instead, Todorov turns his attention to what he calls a new form of 'evil done in the name of the good – not only a good that was by definition equivalent to the desire of those who performed it, but a good to which we always aspire, peace and democracy' (Todorov, 2003, 236). His most controversial argument is that there is no such thing as human rights interventionism, and especially as it occurred in Kosovo, such actions demonstrate that even if totalitarianism is the 'empire of evil', imposing human rights or democracy by force violates the principle that there should no infliction of human rights without consent, and makes US efforts on behalf of human rights 'tainted' (Todorov, 2003, 283). He contends that NATO air strikes against Serbia in 1999 created an 'even greater tragedy' than the crimes committed before the intervention, a moral failing exacerbated by Václav Havel's 'cynical' phrase, 'humanitarian bombs'. One of the longest sections of *Hope and Memory* deals with the atomic bombing of Hiroshima and Nagasaki, which Todorov condemns as an even greater 'moral mistake' (than Soviet or Nazi crimes?) since it is still openly defended by 'people who killed in the name of democracy' (Todorov, 2003, 237).

Some commentators saw the powerful effect of memory in the contrast between German and French reactions to the bombing of Belgrade in 1999. The protracted debates over whether to act militarily to prevent what might have become the first European genocide since the Second World War, it seemed, led to a confrontation between German anti-fascism and French anti-totalitarianism. For the majority of Germans, who remembered *Wehrmacht* crimes, 'no more war' trumped 'anti-totalitarianism'. For the French, on the other hand, timely intervention could morally redeem the historical complicity of Vichy and the Holocaust (Ackermann, 2000, 49). Yet, appealing as this sounds, this reading is too simplistic. In Germany, there were significant exceptions among an enlightened Left, including Peter Schneider, Daniel Cohn-Bendit, Claus Leggewie, and most importantly, Joschka Fischer, at the time leader of the Green parliamentary faction (Harpprecht, 2001). Todorov's strong dissent from his compatriots also complicates the picture of a German–French *querelle*. But it was largely French intellectuals – Pascal Bruckner, Claude Lefort, Cornelius Castoriadis, François Furet, Edgar Morin, Maurice Gauchet, André Glucksmann, Bernard-Henri Levy and Alain Finkielkraut – who most resolutely called for intervention against the ethnic cleansing that appeared to be, if not totalitarian, then 'total-nationalism' (Morin, in Ackermann, 2000, 47). In this respect, Todorov seems to be an exception.

Although *Hope and Memory* was written before the second Iraq War (it appeared in France in 2000), Todorov includes a preface to the English-language edition in which he calls US efforts to impose democracy in Iraq 'dangerous' and 'frightening' because of its claim 'to embody the good and impose it on the world by any means' (Todorov, 2003, viii, ix). Men, he argues, cannot be freed from the evil within them. Are we left with only the commonplace that the only ideal truly compatible with the idea of democracy 'is the right of every people to choose its own path, provided that it does no harm to others'? Todorov too often remains content with a moralizing anti-politics that sits uneasily with his democratic convictions. (On this tendency among French intellectuals, see Howard, 2002, 134). His passionate rhetoric against humanitarian interventionism in general, and against the US in particular, is in part the result of his difficulty thinking politically or historically – rather than morally – about the 'lessons' of totalitarianism. Opponents of the Iraq war quickly recognized that the issue is hardly the 'empire of the good', but rather the empire of the incoherent and the incompetent. The unfortunate legacy of militarized neo-conservatism, and its emphasis on pre-emptive war, which in some ways intersects with the French critique of totalitarianism, proved to be a blunt-edged weapon in the arsenal of US foreign policy.

Ironically, other political commentators, most notably Paul Berman, who also wholly embrace the philosophy of 'anti-totalitarianism' as 'the grandest tradition of the left' have drawn entirely opposing conclusions. According to Berman, 'Al Qaeda (and the broader radical Islamist current, of which it is the most radical part) and Saddam's Baath Party are two of the tendencies within a much larger phenomenon, which is a Muslim totalitarianism' (which arose as a reflection of European totalitarianism) (see Stephenson, 2003). Not surprisingly, Berman's list of the writers and intellectuals who produced the new literature on the 'totalitarian passions' of the twentieth century overlaps somewhat with Todorov's. He is especially indebted to Camus for his insight that at a deep level, 'totalitarianism and terrorism are one and the same'. Like Camus, Berman focuses on the gratuitous, even absolutist and metaphysical, violence that he locates in Baudelaire, the nineteenth-century murderous nihilists and today's suicide bombers: 'On the topic of death,' he writes, 'the Nazis were the purest of the pure, the most aesthetic, the boldest, the greatest of executioners, and yet the greatest and most sublime of death's victim's too – people, who in Baudelaire's phrase knew how to *feel* the revolution in both ways' (Berman, 2003, 45). Where he finds the link to the European cult of violence, which was, it should be emphasized, far more 'satanic' than 'sacred' in its inspiration (the anti-Judeo-Christian dimension is lost in this portrait), is in the writings of Sayyid Quatb, the Egyptian-born Islamist philosopher who was a leading figure in the Muslim Brotherhood until he was hanged in Egypt in 1966. According to Berman, Quatb is a totalitarian not merely because of his condemnation of the 'hideous schizophrenia' of the West with its disenchantment and diminished spirituality, but because of Quatb's identification with the European conviction that the liberal project of the nineteenth century was 'a gigantic deception foisted on mankind in the interest of plunder, devastation, conspiracy and ruin' (Berman, 2003, 118). Despite the decades of war and enmity between the secular Baathist socialists and the Ayatollah Khomeini's Islamist revolutionaries, Berman regards both as 'death-obsessed' and 'apocalyptic rebellions against liberalism'; from them, he claims, Al Quaeda, inherited its 'chiliastic' and 'totalitarian cult of death'.

What is perplexing is not simply the parallel between the bloody dictatorships of the 1930s and 1940s and contemporary Islamist terror, but the way in which 'totalitarianism' can be mobilized for or against the analogy. Todorov rejects any comparison between totalitarianism and the Islamist radicals:

> To my mind, however, the differences are far more significant than the similarities; whereas now, you have the exaltation of religion and the cult of the past, earlier you had the rejection of religion and the cult of the future; whereas now you have the action of stateless individuals and the willingness to sacrifice oneself, earlier you had the actions of all-powerful states and the willingness to sacrifice the lives of others. Nor does the damage caused respectively by the terrorists and totalitarianism belong to the same scale of magnitude. (Todorov, 2003, xiv)

Each of these writers, anti-totalitarian liberals to the core, come to diametrically opposed conclusions. The reason, one suspects, lies not so much in their anti-totalitarian convictions as in their evaluations of European and US policies in the late 1990s. Todorov calls the NATO bombings of Yugoslavia 'catastrophic' (Todorov, 2003, 255). Berman, by contrast, considers the US-led but NATO-supported intervention in the Balkans a 'Lincolnian test' of Europe's capacity to overcome its pacifism and 'lofty isolationism' (Berman, 2003, 173). For supporters of the war, Europeans were 'recycling arguments used by Stalinist "peace movements"; for its opponents the peace movements were the new face of the 'avant-gardist core of Europe', which 'could serve as an example of a post-national constellation' (see Glucksmann, 2003; Habermas and Derrida, 2003, 291–7)

In fact, neither position has much to do with totalitarianism. Although it can plausibly be argued that the end of the Cold War also ended the idea of the 'West' that dominated the post-Second World War world, it is a caricature (on both sides) to regard the United States as unilaterally dangerous and Europe as having unilaterally failed the test. The 'great divide', one hopes, may be a temporary political constellation, and not, as both Todorov and Berman believe, two distinct moral universes.

The Great Dictators: A Genealogy of a Comparison

These public contestations underscore only a few of the troubling dilemmas posed by the comparison between Nazism and communism. The question is not whether such comparisons are in any sense historically and intellectually legitimate, though to some degree comparisons are always subject to the constraints of the present and to shifting political and ideological contexts. However, the extent to which comparison in this domain has been continuously undermined by polemic, scandal and sensation presents a serious obstacle that should be foregrounded before any serious parallels or differences can be discerned. Henry Rousso rightly distinguishes between historical and 'politico-memorial' uses of the comparison (this difficulty is discussed by Rousso in his Introduction to Golsan, 2004a, 3). Yet until recently, few systematic comparisons based on the current state of historical research have actually been undertaken. Among the exceptions are the volumes edited by Ian Kershaw and Moishe Lewin, *Stalinism and Nazism: Dictatorships in Comparison*, *Stalinism and Nazism*, edited by Henry Rousso, and the remarkable *The Dictators* by Richard Overy (Kershaw and Lewin, 1997; Rousso, 2004; Overy, 2004).

All three of these books are free of the multiple sins of Courtois's introduction to the *Black Book*, and all restrict comparison to the era of the dictators Stalin and Hitler (though the period of Lenin's rule is not entirely eliminated). In their joint introduction to the first part of the Rousso volume, Philippe Burrin and Nicolas Werth (whose contribution the *Black Book* was the most significant), historians of Nazism and Soviet communism respectively, underline a distinction that confronts anyone concerned with this subject: the relative paucity of archivally based research on the USSR compared to the decades of monographic and synthetic research on National Socialism. Despite this lacuna, they provide illuminating parallel accounts of the nature of the state, violence and society under both dictatorships. The formative stage of Stalinism, Werth shows, was one of increasing tension between an expanding, disorganized, inefficient hypertrophic state apparatus and the clan-like directorship of Stalin's paladins, resulting in a permanent state of crisis, emergency and mobilization. He embraces a modified version of totalitarianism theory, but stresses that Stalin and his mini-Stalins responded to the 'uncontrolled set of social crises put in motion by the voluntarist politics' of the early 1930s by massive repression and terror, taking on different forms – de-gulagization, famine, deportation, forced labour, imprisonment, culminating in the Great Terror of 1937–38 – and consuming more than a generation of Soviet citizens from a wide variety of social groups (not solely the party elite). These measures did not halt despite the relative stabilization of 'second Stalinism' during and after the Second World War – they were displaced onto ethnic minorities and occupied populations. Unlike Stalinism, which employed violence, however extreme, as a means to an end, Burrin claims that violence was 'at the heart of National Socialism', which espoused a doctrine and ideology of racial warfare from the outset. Victims of Nazi violence included political opponents, social outcasts and groups deemed racially or hereditary unfit, though as Burrin writes, 'the racist logic penetrated and over determined the first two' (Rousso, 2004, 102). Whereas the Gulag system was embedded in the Stalinist logic of criminalizing imagined and real resistance to Soviet society, the Nazi camps were secret, attesting to their radical aim of exterminating those who represented the racial enemy. Historians of Nazi Germany have developed a complex schema to distinguish popular reactions to the regime, ranging from enthusiasm, accommodation, compromise, dissension (*Resistenz*) and disaffection. Most historians of Nazism regard the Third Reich as a consensual society. Still, the question of the extent and effectiveness of the party in welding together the desired *Volksgemeinschaft* remains disputed (see Gellately, 2001; for a critical dissent, see Eley, 2003, 550–83). Hitler's charismatic leadership (Kershaw) certainly promised national unity and community, along with a better life for all Germans. According to Götz Aly, in this respect, propaganda and reality actually coincided, since the regime's promise of greater equality for the German *Volk* was largely realized through a system of social security, tax incentives, marriage and child allowances, pension reform and other redistributionist schemes that ensured a high level of satisfaction among the 'little people' and compliance in the exclusion of all 'so-called elements hostile to the Volk' (Aly, 2005; see the critical remarks in Tooze, 2005). Studies of Soviet social behaviour have revealed, as Werth points out, a rather different picture: the existence of a regime attempting to expand control over ever-increasing domains of social life, and a society that 'opposed this control through an infinite range of diverse forms of resistance, generally passive in nature' (hooliganism, insubordination, malingering), undermining to a great extent the totalitarian model of control and domination.

To date, the best single volume devoted to comparing Hitler and Stalin's dictatorships is Richard Overy's *The Dictators: Hitler's Germany and Stalin's Russia* (2004). Overy devotes only a few lines to the term 'totalitarianism', which he rightly notes has been misunderstood as 'total' domination as opposed to domination that aims at the 'totality' of society. However, his carefully constructed chapters examine the crucial aspects of Hitler and Stalin's rule, including the nature of their respective ruling styles, their cults of personality, the party-state, their utopian aspirations, their Manichean 'friend–foe' propaganda, their cultural revolutions, the economy, their conduct of the war, and finally, the 'empire of the camps'. Overy scrupulously distinguishes the divergences between Hitler and Stalin in all of these areas, pointing out, for example, that whereas under Stalin the party atrophied as the state grew in power, the reverse was true in Hitler's Germany, where the 'fiefdoms' of party rule constituted a more powerful apparatus than the atrophying state. In ideology, he writes:

> difference remains fundamental. For all the similarities in the practice of dictatorship, in the mechanisms that bound people and ruler together, in the remarkable congruence of cultural objectives, strategies, of economic management, utopian social aspirations, even in the moral language of the regime, the stated ideological goals were as distinct as the differences that divided Catholic from Protestant in sixteenth-century Europe. (Overy, 2004, 636)

Yet there can be little doubt, he concludes, that in the aftermath of the Second World War, two unique and extreme forms of dictatorship emerged, both of which were popular and both of whose leaders 'preached the idea of an exclusive, holistic community bound collectively in the pursuit of an absolute utopia'. Both embraced science, both pursued the extermination of social and racial enemies, and both rejected the bourgeois-liberal age. Both used methods that required a new morality that was absolute in its departure from 'conventional moral scruples'. Yet even here, he notes that they differed substantially: Hitler said in March 1941 that he was waging a 'war of extermination'; 'Soviet camps were prisons of a particularly brutal and despairing character,' writes Overy, 'but they were never designed or intended to be centers of extermination' (Overy, 2004, 513 and 608).

These are works of solid scholarship and serious research. Burrin, Werth, Kershaw, Rousso and Overy reprise what has been a productive decade for scholars of the dictatorships. Yet it is not likely that these works will greatly influence the debates over totalitarianism. Whereas Overy sees both striking similarities and a multitude of disparities, Kershaw still maintains that 'a modern state system directed by "charismatic authority", based on ideas, frequently used by Hitler, of a "mission" (*Sendung*) to bring about "salvation" (*Rettung*) or "redemption" (*Erlösung*) – all, of course, terms tapping religious or quasi religious emotions – was unique' (Kershaw, 2004, 249–50). The careful comparison of regimes, however central to the framing of the concept, is not the sole reason for the persistence of 'totalitarianism'. Pierre Hassner has suggested that 'totalitarianism' is a concept that illustrates the principle that literature or philosophy 'periodically presents evidence which demonstrates that *something* escapes the conceptualizations and the empirical research of the applied sciences' (Hassner, 1984). This is certainly a plausible explanation. But I believe a more powerful reason can be found in the historicity of the term itself, the importance of 'moments' of totalitarianism, rather than in its conceptual validity, its intellectual 'origins' or its 'heuristic' value.

Totalitarianism as a Semantic Bridge

Despite these scholarly disputes, the work performed by invoking the word 'totalitarianism' has remained remarkably stable. The word (as opposed to any variant of the concept or theory) has served to bridge changing political affiliations at several crucial historical moments (in the 1930s, 1950s and 1970s) by suspending the ambiguities and political reservations that might otherwise inhibit the creation of new political constellations and alliances. In other words, the 'moment' of totalitarian performs a well-established political function, defining a horizon of cognitive and intellectual orientations that sharpen oppositions, at the expense of obscuring moral and political ambiguities. This is not to wholly dismiss the validity of the concept; 'totalitarianism' certainly is not meaningless, but the meaning it conveys is often quite different from the rhetorical work performed by invoking the word. As Walter Laqueur shrewdly observed more than two decades ago, the debate over totalitarianism has never been a purely academic enterprise (Laqueur, 1985, 29–34). It has also been about an intensely political concept, defining the nature of enmity for the Western democracies for more than half a century.

'Totalitarianism' can be productively regarded as a 'semantic stockpile' that combines the content-oriented logic of the academic disciplines (history, philosophy, political theory) with flexible strategies for calculating public resonance (on the concept of 'semantic stockpiles', see Bollenbeck, 1994, 315–16; Knobloch, 1992, 7–24). As a rhetorical trope, 'totalitarianism' is especially serviceable for bridging any number of political orientations because it fundamentally serves not so much as a 'heuristic' concept, but as a 'consolidator' of any number of '-isms' – most obviously, anti-fascism and anti-communism – that can supply it with meaning at any given moment, as long as it remains opposed to another '-ism', liberalism, or liberal democracy. For at least three generations now, it has operated as a temporal signifier for a certain kind of political 'arrival and departure' (to borrow Arthur Koestler's felicitous title) reconfiguring and restructuring political and ideological constellations within liberalism. Focusing on these moments of totalitarianism can sidestep the inevitable debates that emerge, because totalitarianism is by definition a comparative category, and historical comparisons are always fraught with danger and ambiguity.

The semantic model for anti-totalitarianism was anti-fascism or anti-fascist anti-totalitarianism, a concept that began to galvanize European intellectuals during the 1920s.

The term 'totalitarianism', or *sistema totalitaria*, was invented by one of Mussolini's earliest opponents and victims, the Socialist Giovanni Amendola, who tried to forge a coalition between the democratic centre and the communists. By 1928, the grand old man of Italian socialism, Filippo Turati, could write of the 'worldwide conflict between fascistic totalitarianism and liberal democracy' (Gleason, 1998, 15–16). During the 1930s, anti-fascist anti-totalitarians created a Europe-wide alliance against fascism and quasi-fascist regimes from the Iberian peninsula to Hungary. A decade later, anti-fascism provided a springboard for the Grand Alliance, figuring (for example, in the film *Casablanca*) as the vehicle that brings the 'isolationist' American ex-radical Rick and the Vichy opportunist Louis to the Free French Garrison in Brazzaville after saving the Resistance hero Viktor Laszlo. Anti-fascist attitudes were by no means homogenous, embracing liberals as well as socialists, all of whom hoped to avoid the political mistakes of the 1920s and early 1930s. As William David Jones has pointed out, the Cold War version of totalitarian theory all but obscured this 'lost debate' on the Left that included intellectuals who began their careers in the SPD, the Austrian Socialists or the Neu Beginnen, a non-communist movement constituted after 1933, well before the change in Comintern policy in 1935. German exile opponents of Hitler – Herbert Marcuse, Franz Neumann, Ernst Fraenkel, Arthur Rosenberg, Rudolf Hilferding, Franz Borkenau and Richard Löwenthal – produced the first extensive literature on the totalitarian threat (see the excellent account in Jones, 1999). During this period, European liberals and socialists were the most prominent anti-fascists, including Carlo Rosselli in Italy, Otto Bauer in Austria and Rudolf Hilferding in Germany. They articulated a strategy for the European Left that embraced (though was hardly welcomed by) communists and liberals.

In the United States, the Protestant theologian Reinhold Niebuhr first employed the term in a way that would become characteristic of its American usage, as hegemonic control over all aspects of life, the very antithesis of the liberal state. *Time Magazine* adopted the term in 1934, demonstrating that it functioned far more effectively as a bridge between Christians, New Deal liberals and even a few conservatives than as a conceptually reliable idea (see Alpers, 2003, 67). In France, after the abortive attempt of rightist forces to overthrow democracy during the 'night of the Leagues' on 6 February 1934, a new face of anti-fascism was launched by a group of intellectuals who rejected the rigid 'class against class' strategy of the communists and presented a 'pact of unity of Action' to 'bar the way to fascism', signed by 30 prominent figures including André Malraux, the philosopher Alain Breton and the Surrealists André Breton and Paul Eluard (Winock, 1997, 244).

Between the wars, anti-fascism inspired a generation of intellectuals who were charged by the prospect of mobilizing all their resources for the 'defence of culture' and ending (however illusory that proved to be) the internecine quarrels of the past. For these dedicated opponents of Nazism and fascism, the anti-fascist struggle was premised on the idea that there could be no middle ground, no neutral space and no non-combatants in the global confrontation. Anti-fascism was the binary of binaries, the geopolitical and cultural bifurcation between *Geist* and *Macht*, humanism and terror, reason and unreason, past and future, that framed the first half of the twentieth century as much as anti-communism (in its anti-totalitarian form) can be said to have framed the second. As Klaus Mann wrote in 1938:

> Fascism – however paradoxical this sounds – makes it easier for us to clarify and define the nature and appearance of what we want. Our vision will oppose, point for point, the practice of Fascism. What the latter destroys, socialist humanism will defend; what the latter defends, it will destroy. ('Der Kampf um den jungen Menschen', cited in Wilkinson, 1981, 21)

Popular Front organizations embraced anti-fascists from intellectual luminaries like Roman Rolland, André Gide and Heinrich Mann to the countless footsoldiers who attended Soviet dance recitals, lectures by the Archbishop of Canterbury or tea-parties for Spain. The rhetoric of anti-fascism became a political lingua franca that obliterated all differences among 'progressives'. Christians, socialists, Jews, communists, liberals, even vegetarians (Scott Nearing), could link arms against the 'common enemy'. The everyday culture of anti-fascism sustained the mood of polarized perception. The historian Richard Cobb, who lived in Paris during the 1930s, summed up the mood when he recalled that 'France was living through a moral and mental civil war … one had to choose between fascism and fellow traveling' (Caute, 1988, 165). As George Mosse also recalled in his memoir,: 'the lines between enemy and friend were clearly drawn, this war presented the first chance to fight openly against the fascists other than in newspaper articles and debating societies' (Mosse, 2000, 161). At issue here is the political tunnel vision, the underside of Klaus Mann's clarity, that accompanied the attraction of many Western intellectuals during the 1930s to the aura of resistance and heroic sacrifice that enshrined anti-fascism as the noblest of political enterprises.

With the collapse of communism, scholars and writers have come to regard anti-fascism in a less hallowed light. As Furet rightly emphasized, Stalinist anti-fascism changed the public face of communism; the doctrinal shift in 1935 transformed dedicated Bolsheviks into champions of liberty, marching hand-in-hand with democrats under the banner of humanity and hatred of Hitler (see Furet, 1990, 224). with the watchword of anti-fascism, communists and fellow travellers justified Stalin's crimes while decrying Hitler's. The German émigré philosopher Ernst Bloch, for example, wrote a powerful defence of the Moscow Trials, exemplifying the political blindness that allowed so many Western intellectuals to sacrifice their judgement and principles to Soviet power (on Bloch, see Zudeick, 1985, 146; Rabinbach, 1977, 5–21). Brecht's cynical retort, 'The more innocent they are, the more they deserve to be shot', expressed the powerlessness of those who certainly knew better (cited in Hook, 1987, 493). Even the most orthodox Communists could easily fall prey to Stalinist accusations, exemplified by the terrifying fate of the exile communist intellectuals in Moscow (see Müller, 1991). However, it is not sufficient to simply condemn anti-fascism as political blindness, illusion and duplicity. It was not only fellow travellers who avoided mention (whether out of disbelief or conviction) of Stalinist crimes, because one could not fight fascism by opposing or doing without the support of the communists or the Soviet Union (Traverso, 2004, 91–103). Most liberals also defended Soviet foreign policy as supporting democracy against fascism. In March 1936, the *New York Times* commented on the spread of the idea of totalitarianism by equating it entirely with right-wing regimes – Germany, Italy and Paraguay. Only a few stalwarts in the US, among them John Dewey and Charles Beard, the conservatives Max Eastman, William Bullitt and Eugene Lyons, and the pacifist Dwight MacDonald remained sceptical of the Soviet Union and the popular front (Alpers, 2003, 132 and 139).

By the late 1930s, however, the word 'totalitarian' increasingly and more explicitly began to mean the equivalence of the two dictatorial systems. As Franz Borkenau wrote in his 1940 book *The Totalitarian Enemy*, the Hitler–Stalin Pact and the invasion of Poland by Germany and the USSR shattered the commonly held view 'that Fascism and communism were deadly enemies, and that their hostility was the crux of world politics today' (Borkenau, 1982 [1940], 7). Anti-totalitarianism, especially as it emerged on the Left during the period of the Hitler–Stalin Pact, signalled a commitment to remain an anti-fascist when the Comintern had banned the use of the very term 'fascism' and when remaining an anti-fascist was synonymous with anti-communism (on responses to the pact, see Combe, 1990, 99–102; Regler, 1959; Leonhard, 1989, 173; Sator, 1990). For the writer Manès Sperber, the pact was no tactical 'trick', but in fact brought to light the real symmetries between Hitler's and Stalin's rules. Sperber's judgement that 'for the entire anti-Fascist movement and for all leftists the Hitler–Stalin pact meant the greatest political and moral defeat that they had ever suffered' (Sperber, 1994, 154) was not widely shared at the time. For the most part, those who most emphatically opposed the pact tended to be ex-communists whose experience with the party had already led them to a breach, as was the case with Comintern impresario Willi Münzenberg and the writers Gustav Regler, Arthur Koestler and Sperber, all of whom were already estranged from the party when the pact confirmed their worst fears.

By 1937, not only the anti-Stalinist Left of *Partisan Review* but the secular Right in the United States, and also Christian periodicals like *Commonweal* and the *Christian Century* as well as the *Catholic World*, were all using the term 'totalitarianism' to link, if not equate, fascism and communism (Alpers, 2003, 141). When the philosophers Sidney Hook and John Dewey formed the Committee for Cultural Freedom in May 1939, they brought together socialists (Norman Thomas), liberals (Dorothy Thompson and Elmer Davis) and conservatives (Max Eastman and Eugene Lyons) to oppose what all agreed was the rising tide of totalitarianism. In this new constellation, a cross-pollenization of formerly incompatible intellectuals, the American political spectrum was reconfigured, presaging the undoing of the anti-fascist consensus of the 1930s and reassembling the forces that would eventually unite under the banner of liberal anti-totalitarianism after the Second World War. In 1939, when the American Philosophical Society held a 'Symposium on the Totalitarian State' in Philadelphia, the argument had evolved from the nature of the dictators or the economy to a new focus on 'ideology', not to any specific orientation, but conformity to the will or worldview of the state. As the political scientist Robert MacIver succinctly put it: 'Totalitarianism will not allow difference to be different' (Alpers, 2003, 150).

Despite the effervescence of anti-totalitarian literature in the late 1930s, the German invasion of Russia on 22 June 1941 and the creation of the Grand Alliance quickly placed on hold the moral and political arguments elaborated by ex-communists and social democrats in favour of a consensual understanding of the war that occluded any criticism of the Soviet ally (even the Katyn massacre of some 15,000 Polish officers could be excused if it weakened Allied unity and helped Hitler). Communists who just two years earlier been staunch anti-interventionists, aggressively mobilized for the war against 'Nazi fascism'. Dedicated anti-communists like Raymond Aron and Sidney Hook turned down the volume of their criticism until the end of the war (see Aron, 1990).

In his unjustly forgotten novel *Arrival and Departure* (dated July 1942–July 1943), Arthur Koestler imagined an encounter between an ex-fascist and an ex-communist, each of whom discovers that they were patients of the same psychoanalyst who had cured them of their respective need for ideological 'crusades'. Each is aware he had fled into his political commitments from his night terrors and traumas, each is marooned in a neutral country (Neutralia) as the war rages in the rest of Europe, and each is about to embark for the safety of the US. The ex-communist, utterly disillusioned, weakly tries to mobilize his old beliefs in justice, equality and the international solidarity of the working class against the arguments of the fascist, who accuses him of an excessive attachment to the logic of universalism, of failing to recognize that to succeed, 'an idea has to mobilize the latent tribal force of its sponsor race'. The fascist explains bluntly that the breeding of a new racial aristocracy is under way, that the extermination of the Gypsies is practically finished and 'the liquidation of the Jews will be completed in a year or two' (Koestler, 1943, 126). But Koestler does not end his story as one might expect by reducing the political to the psychological. In an interesting twist, he accuses the analyst of 'tearing out of her garden the tree of knowledge of good and evil'. In other words, the hero discovers that psychoanalysis, which allowed him to resist the original fall into the 'totalitarian temptation', provides no moral compass when faced with the problem of a 'second fall' into the political realm of choice between lesser evils. The novel ends with the hero fleeing the ship seconds before departure in order to enlist in the Royal Air Force. In the final scene, he parachutes into Germany.

During the Second World War, former left-wing intellectuals, just recently gone 'up from communism or Trotskyism', had to face the same choice as Koestler's hero. *Arrival and Departure* is an allegory of these 'premature' anti-totalitarians. Hook described the utter isolation of the small circles that continued to attack the wartime ally, but even he tried to persuade his fellow New York intellectuals to accept the 'lesser evil' (Hook, 1987, 304). After the Red Army broke through the German blockade of Leningrad in January 1943 and began to move westward, *New Republic* editor Malcolm Cowley wrote that 'Russia today is saving the democratic world because she wants to save Russia' (Alpers, 2003, 240). Even George Orwell, who criticized the leading Labour Party intellectual Harold Laski for turning a blind eye to Russian 'purges, liquidations, the dictatorship of a minority, suppression of criticism and so forth', was a strong supporter of the war effort (Kramnick and Sheerman, 1993, 471).

Totalitarianism was by no means a concept forged during and for the Cold War, but it returned with new vigour before the postwar deterioration of US relations with the Soviets. Postwar anti-totalitarianism became the semantic bridge between anti-Nazi and anti-communist liberalism; it enabled former 'progressives' to turn from anti-Nazism to anti-Sovietism. Its revival during the 1950s led to its academic canonization in the classic texts of Hannah Arendt (1951) and Carl J. Friedrich and Zbigniew Brzezinski (1956). Just one month after war's end, in early June 1945, Winston Churchill set the tone for his re-election campaign when he claimed: 'Socialism is inseparably interwoven with totalitarianism and the object worship of the state' (Kramnick and Sheerman, 1993, 481). Churchill lost, of course, but 1948 marked the heyday of the return of 'totalitarianism' and its corollary, 'totalitarian liberalism', which referred to those fellow travellers who refused to accept the new approach to the Soviets demanded by the Truman Doctrine. Hook best expressed the meaning of the moment when he wrote:

> Whoever believed that Nazi expansionism constituted a threat to the survival of democratic institutions must conclude by the same logic and the same type of evidence that Soviet communism represents today an even greater threat to our survival, because the potential opposition to totalitarianism is now much weaker in consequence of World War II. (cited in Whitfield, 1980, 15).

As Norman Podhoretz recalled: 'Whereas the anti-Communist liberals were full of the dynamism, élan and passion that so often accompany a newly discovered way of looking at things, the fellow travelers could marshal nothing but boring clichés and tired arguments' (O'Neill, 1982, 161). In Europe too, liberals could no longer afford to hold onto the misalliance with totalitarianism. Berlin became the 'front-line city' of the cultural Cold War, scene of the famous Congress for Cultural Freedom International in June 1950, a German–American enterprise organized by Melvin Lasky under John McCloy and Shepard Stone's stewardship (see Berghahn, 2001, 130–31). Anti-totalitarianism became the official ideology of the Federal Republic of Germany (as anti-fascism did in the GDR). Although communism still held on to a measure of its intellectual hegemony, it was never a serious challenger in European politics after 1947 (despite the brief flare-up of Euro-communism in the 1970s). After the invasion of Hungary in November 1956, Communist Party membership at the École Normale Supérieure dropped from 25 per cent of the students in 1945 to 5 per cent.

During the late 1940s, the debate over the meaning and applicability of the term 'totalitarianism' was far more intense on the Left than among conservatives, who for the most part avoided the term, or at best regarded the totalitarian order as 'the pathological development of certain reigning forces in the nineteenth century: nationalism, mass democracy, plebiscitary government, individual alienation from traditional dogmas, etc.' (see Nisbet, 1983, 187). Despite the ferocity of hard-line anti-communism, in the 1950s and 1960s most conservatives were isolationists, especially US Republicans, who were more willing to make do with rhetorical opposition than with active intervention. In a scathing article, John Patrick Diggins recently pointed out that the party that the neo-conservatives tout as having 'won' the Cold War actually appeased communism whenever possible – Korea, Hungary, Vietnam and Tiananmen Square. Opposition to communism was initially a project of the anti-Stalinist Left of anarchists, Trotskyites and liberals; it was the Democrats who launched both major anti-communist wars, and for whom the Cold War became an ideological crusade. It is a persistent myth of neo-conservative history that it was the Democrats, who were 'soft' on communism and sold out Poland at Yalta (see Diggins, 2003). Kissinger, not Kennedy, embodied the compromising disposition of conservatism that proved willing to 'accommodate itself to communism'. Still worse, the obsolete neo-conservative obsession with communism and its defeat (which even Ronald Reagan saw could be handled differently in the 1980s) created a mentality, Diggins writes, 'which did much to lead America into making the dangerous decision to arm the Afghan resistance, the muhajideen' (Diggins, 2003).

Liberal anti-communism, for all its moral clarity *vis-à-vis* the Soviet Union, was fatally incapable of coming to grips with the 'grey' areas of US foreign policy, not with the authoritarianisms – Greece, Argentina, Philippines, Indonesia, Chile – supported on behalf of anti-totalitarianism, nor with the difficulties of sustaining 'containment' in Asia and Africa, and most certainly not with McCarthyism. Hook notoriously became trapped in his own web of moral casuistry when he tried to justify *both* academic freedom and support for faculty committees charged with rooting out 'unfit' faculty staff (Hook, 1987, 504). Years later, in the film *Arguing the World*, another New York intellectual, Nathan Glazer, admitted that this was not the New York intellectual's finest hour (Dorman, 1998). The antipathy of '1968ers' to Cold War anti-communism (the notorious debates on anti-communism versus anti-anti-communism that split the New York intellectuals from the 'SDSers', for example) was as justified as Orwell's refusal to countenance the simplicities of anti-fascism in the 1930s. By the 1970s, the Vietnam War had eroded the purported moral clarity of anti-totalitarianism to the point that even supporters of the war did not risk the word to justify it.

During the late 1960s, 'totalitarianism' was abandoned by the majority of Sovietologists as terror ceased to be the defining feature of Soviet rule and as détente replaced containment as US policy. The concept notoriously failed to distinguish a developmental trajectory over different stages, especially during the post-Stalinist era. A mere ten years after its broad acceptance, one of its former defenders could admit that 'it does not serve the cause of comparative political analysis or of political understanding to cling to the concept of totalitarianism' (Curtis, 1969, 116). In 1984, the year of a major mid-course re-evaluation occasioned by George Orwell's 1948 book of that title, its future was in doubt. For the Left, it was especially suspect because during the Reagan era, conservatives like Jeanne Kirkpatrick resurrected the term to distinguish (friendly) autocracies that were presumably reformable from those that were incorrigible and unchangeable enemies. Michael Walzer rightly pointed out that this distinction was not merely self-serving: 'totalitarian ambition bred by authoritarian politics and terror … seems more likely to figure in the future of old-fashioned tyrannies than in the future of failed totalitarianisms' (Walzer, 1983, 121). Two years after the appearance of Kirkpatrick's article, Brezhnevism and gerontological oligarchy gave way to Gorbachev, who set out to do what conservatives said could not occur – reform communism. During that final decade, a variety of 'epicycles' were introduced to keep aspects of the theory on life support: 'enlightened totalitarianism' (Adam Ulam), 'dysfunctional totalitarianism' (Zbigniew Brzezinski), 'failed totalitarianism' (Michael Walzer), 'authoritarian totalitarianism' (Juan Linz) (see Howe, 1983, 121, and the articles in Jesse, 1996).

A Unifying Concept for Exiles, Refugees and Dissidents

The concept of totalitarianism was invented and nurtured by exiles from countries overrun by one or another, and sometimes both, of the totalitarian superpowers. Not accidentally, its main protagonists were German refugee intellectuals or those born in East Central Europe – Hayek, Friedrich, Arendt, Brzezinski – and more recently, Hassner, Todorov, Michnik and Havel, all from countries whose fate was buffeted by *both* totalitarian empires, and whose formative years were spent under the yoke of occupation.[5] Václav Havel's 'The Power of the Powerless' (1985) articulated the persistence of totalitarian behaviour under the relaxed conditions of late communism, and Polish dissident Adam Michnik defended its unalloyed worth when he remarked: 'there is no non-totalitarian communism. Either it is totalitarian or it ceases to be communism' (Michnik, 1985, 47). There may be a

5 During the war, Friedrich served on the Central and Eastern European Planning Board, founded in New York in 1942 by representatives of the exiled governments of occupied Czechoslovakia, Greece, Poland and Yugoslavia. From 1942 to 1945, the Board conducted research and formulated plans for postwar reconstruction in the four countries, with the goal of forming a democratic Central and Eastern European federation.

good deal of irony in the fact that the word 'totalitarianism' emerged politically as its conceptual star was falling, but as a Russian colleague who had emigrated during the early 1990s, remarked: 'Once we started to use the word "totalitarian", the Communist regime was finished.' What he meant was that under Gorbachev, once the Soviet regime could be legitimately considered akin to fascism, its legitimacy (which drew on its anti-fascism) was fatally undermined.

The most striking return of 'totalitarianism' has been in France, which until the end of the 1970s proved most resistant to the concept in Europe (see Hassner, 1984). Under the influence of Solzhenizyn, the end of Maoism and the rise of Eastern European movements like Solidarnosc and Charter 77, a sea change occurred in the French Left, for which Claude Lefort's essay on the dissidents, 'La première revolution anti-totalitaire', is an important marker (Lefort, 1977). In a sense, the French debate over totalitarianism was neither new nor technically a debate on 'totalitarianism', since it focused almost exclusively on communism. It began with the famous Sartre–Camus debate in the 1950s, the Rousset Affair described by Todorov, continued in the 1960s with the intellectual heresies of 'Socialisme et Barberie' and its intellectual lights, Cornelius Castoriadis, Marcel Gauchet and Lefort, who aimed their polemics against the PCF, and continued with the new philosophers of the 1970s, André Glucksmann and Bernard-Henri Levy. All of these figures attempted to historicize and critically expand the notion of totalitarianism by introducing such qualifying terms as the 'totalitarian complex' (Edgar Morin) or 'totalitarian logic' (Lefort), or by emphasizing the congealment of bureaucracy and de-ideologized power, which Castoriadis called *stratocratie* (Hassner, 1984). Characteristically, much of the French controversy was bound up with the historical and political debate over what Furet called the 'phantoms' of the French Revolution, especially since the year of the revolution's two hundredth anniversary coincided with the demise of communism in East Central Europe and the defection of a generation of left-wing intellectuals from the philo-communist camp. Both communism and Nazism could legitimately be viewed as products of democracy, Lefort claims, since each drew its strength from the indeterminacy of modern democracies, in lieu of which totalitarianism provides homogeneity, the identity of ruler and ruled, and transhistorical meaning. Lefort claims that recent accounts of the collapse of the Soviet Union and communism, like Martin Malia's *The Soviet Tragedy* and Furet's *The Past of an Illusion*, which stressed a 'secularized form of messianism' or the 'illusion' of a theory of history, were too narrowly focused on the instantiation of an idea rather than on communism's attempt to fill democracy's endemic void for those lost in history (see Lefort, 1999; Flynn, 2002, 436–44).

Whereas in France a campaign in support of the suppressed Solidarnosc took to the streets in 1981, in Germany most Social Democrats and intellectuals regarded the Polish uprising as a impediment to the policy of 'small steps' that marked the SPD's *Ostpolitik*. When the Berlin Wall fell in 1989, both East and West German writers, most prominently Christa Wolf and Günter Grass, opposed unification, in part because, as Grass formulated it, the division of Germany was necessary and just punishment for Auschwitz (see Huyssen, 1991, 109–43; Müller, 2000). Only in 1993, in a conversation with KOR founder and Polish dissident leader Adam Michnik, did philosopher Jürgen Habermas admit that he had avoided any fundamental confrontation with Stalinism because he did not want applause from the 'wrong side' (Habermas and Michnik, 1994). This silence, Ljubljana philosopher Slavoj Žižek uncharitably argues in his *Did Somebody Say Totalitarianism?*, was the only way for the Frankfurt School to maintain an inconsistent position of underlying solidarity with Western liberal democracy without losing their official mask of 'radical' leftist critique (see Žižek, 2001, 93).

In the recent debate on totalitarianism, Žižek has been a steadily dissenting voice. The very title of his book *Did Someone Say Totalitarianism?* addresses the distinction between the word and the concept. For Žižek, anti-totalitarianism has become a 'kind of Kantian parlogism of pure political reason, an inevitable "transcendental illusion"' that in fact inhibits thought: 'the moment one accepts the notion of "totalitarianism"', he claims, 'one is firmly located within the liberal democratic horizon' (Žižek, 2001, 3). Žižek's polemic is interesting because it is not aimed at the level of the theory or concept of totalitarianism, but directly at what I have been calling its 'moment'. Žižek is most impressive when he works through the distinctive *logic* of Stalinism, which he reads as a symbolic sacrifice that inverts the standard relationship of guilt and responsibility. Unlike Nazi terror, which at least sought 'real' enemies of the regime (communists, resisters and so on), he argues, the Stalinist police were engaged in patent fabrications (invented plots and sabotage, and so on). The ritualized confessions at the Stalinist show trials are the perfect enactment of an imperative that requires the accused to publicly sacrifice their subjectivity for the higher good of the party. Although all actors are aware of the absolute innocence of the accused and the absurdity of the charges, they all (including the accused) behave *as if* the charges were true, symbolically sacrificing the individual. However, Žižek himself wilfully perverts this perversion of ethics when he argues that since Stalinist communists were neither ruthless automata nor merely actors in the staged drama of a higher historical necessity, they were essentially 'right' in so far as they confessed to having 'betrayed' the revolution. Individually they were not guilty, but even at worst, these trials bear witness to the 'authentic' revolutionary project through the ritual of purging the accused of 'betrayal' (Žižek, 2001, 129). Lenin, Žižek contends, was aware of what Georg Lukács called the actuality of the revolutionary 'moment' (*Augenblick*) in which everything must wagered, despite the absence of objective conditions, despite the premature situation, despite, despite, because as Lenin said, 'History will never forgive us if we miss this opportunity' (Žižek, 2001, 116 and 117). This act of intervention, this 'eventness' of the revolution, symbolically reappears in the inverted logic of Stalinism precisely because the Politburo in the 1930s *lost* control of the revolution, perverting the *authentic revolution*, and permitting irrationality – purges, denunciations, paranoia – to 'reinscribe the betrayal of the Revolution within itself' in the form of mass murders that act out the punishment of those who 'objectively' betrayed the revolution. Hence, Žižek concludes, even at its worst, Stalinist ideology was radically ambiguous because it 'still exudes an emancipatory potential' (Žižek, 2001, 131). Todorov, who, it can be assumed, fundamentally disagrees with Žižek, makes almost the same point when he argues that because communism was so much more removed from reality than Nazism, it was therefore more prone to greater violence and camouflage to hide the gap between world and its representation (see Todorov, 2003, 84).

The Iraq War of 2003: A New Moment of Totalitarianism

It is not insignificant that in the intense debate during the months leading to the US invasion of Iraq in 2003, one of the leading supporters of the war was none other than the former Polish dissident Adam Michnik, editor of Warsaw's leading paper, *Gazeta Wyborcza*. Michnik invoked the 'moment' of totalitarianism as the centrepiece of his argument:

> Just as the murder of Giacomo Matteotti revealed the nature of Italian fascism and Mussolini's regime; just as 'Kristallnacht' exposed the hidden truth of Hitler's Nazism, watching the collapsing World Trade Center towers made me realize that the world was facing a new totalitarian challenge. Violence, fanaticism, and lies were challenging democratic values. (Michnik, 2003, 8–15)

This powerful argument semantically bridges the turn from the anti-totalitarianisms of the 1930s and 1950s to the anti-totalitarianism of today. As he put it:

> We take this position because we know what dictatorship is. And in the conflict between totalitarian regimes and democracy you must not hesitate to declare which side you are on. Even if a dictatorship is not an ideal typical one, and even if the democratic countries are ruled by people whom you do not like. (Michnik, 2003, 8–15)

Michnik may well be right to claim that most of those who demonstrated in Europe and America on 13 February 2003 did not take Islamist radicalism seriously enough. But anti-totalitarianism, as I have argued, can both illuminate as well as obscure; the danger is to lose sight of the moral absolutism of the 'moment' and the absence of nuance that always seem to accompany the anti-totalitarianism moment. The complex quilt of Middle Eastern Islam as well as the paradoxical combination of American power and political idealism cannot be subsumed under categories which – however imperfectly – described twentieth-century European realities.

That 'totalitarianism' belongs thankfully to the past. But if it is possible, indeed necessary, to engage in the comparison between Hitler and Stalin's dictatorships, Tzvetan Todorov fares no better and no worse in his attempt to draw moral lessons from the comparison than many of his forebears in this enterprise. One consequence of the end of totalitarianism is the multiple memories and narratives that have begun to surface throughout Europe. The war is being remembered and commemorated through new and old myths as well as through new and old images that encapsulate the end of the war (see Krzeminski, 2005). I vividly recall seeing for the first time the photographs of the public execution in September 1945 of the Nazi Mayor of Prague, Josef Pfitzner, a Sudeten German, and by chance a historian, whose death in a sports stadium was witnessed by some 50,000 jubilant spectators. I was struck by the grim callousness, but also by the euphoria of the spectacle, which runs counter to myths of heroism and resistance or the staged photographs and public monuments devoted to the Soviet liberation characteristic of the era.

In contemporary Russia, the Second World War is publicly sanctified in new museums of the Great Patriotic Victory and in the official 9 May celebrations in 2004 which combined the iconography of the Soviet era with the myths and mystique of Imperial Russia. In Estonia, Latvia and Lithuania, that celebration became a scandal when leaders of those countries demanded that the Soviets not claim the right of liberator when it came to their fate. Issues of occupation, collaboration and complicity, virtually unknown east of Warsaw, are increasingly an essential part of the public memory of Central and Western Europe, both in the occupied and the neutral countries. During the 1990s, Europeans seemed to be gravitating, however haltingly, towards what might be considered a cosmopolitan understanding of the Holocaust as a pillar of identity in European memory (see Diner, 2000, 190–92; Diner, 2003, 68). More recently, however, a variety of new, and to some degree problematic, counter-discourses to such universal memorialization have appeared across Europe, even in Germany, where the memory of the Holocaust, enshrined in the Memorial to the Murdered Jews of Europe opened on 10 May 2005, seemed most secure. Adam Krzeminski, editor of the Warsaw journal *Polityka*, has even voiced doubts that a unified European memory is possible (see Krzeminski, 2005). But is the very idea of a 'unified' European memory desirable? Much more than any unified memory, it is has been the *contestations* over memory – the memorial debate in Germany, the Touvier, Barbie and Papon trials in France, the Jedwabne debate in Poland – that have heightened public awareness of both the local and the universal dimensions of the European catastrophe (see Stavginski, 2002; Golsan, 1996 and 2000; Polonsky and Michlik, 2004). The existence of multiple, even competing, narratives of the past, of which the 'moment' of totalitarianism is just one symptom, reminds us that the landscape of European (and American) memory remains treacherous, and in many respects still uncharted. The return of totalitarianism evinces nostalgia for the clarity of the old enmities: anti-fascism, Cold War liberalism and the anti-communist revolt of the 1970s and 1980s. In the United States, it looks back longingly to the 'fighting faith' of the 1940s and 1950s. But enmities change, and so do enemies; what is distinctive about the current situation is that the clarity is elusive, complexity is with us once again. 'Totalitarianism' remains as ambiguous today as ever: as a historical concept, it is insecure and contested; as memory, it is geographically promiscuous, unstable and nebulous; only as a semantic marker of new political constellations, identities and ideological alliances is it, as ever, indisputable.

References

Ackermann, Ulrike (2000), *Sündenfall der Intellektuellen. Ein deutsch-französisches Streitgespräch von 1945 bis heute*, with Introduction by Francois Bondy (Stuttgart: Klett-Cotta Verlag).

Alpers, Benjamin (2003), *Dictators, Democracy, and American Public Culture: Envisioning the totalitarian enemy, 1920s-1950s* (Chapel Hill, NC and London: University of North Carolina Press).

Aly, Götz (2005), *Hitlers Volksstaat, Raub, Rassenkrieg und nationaler Sozialismus* (Frankfurt am Main: S. Fischer Verlag).

Arendt, Hannah (1951), *The Origins of Totalitarianism* (New York: Harcourt, Brace).

Aron, Raymond (1990), *Memoirs: Fifty Years of Political Reflection*, trans. George Holoch (New York: Holmes and Meier).

Aronson, Ronald (2003), 'Communism's Posthumous Trial', review article, *History and Theory* 42 (May), 222–45.

Barber, Benjamin (1969), 'Conceptual Foundations of Totalitarianism', in Friedrich, Carl J., Curtis, Michael and Barber, Benjamin R. (eds), *Totalitarianism in Perspective: Three Views* (New York: Praeger).

Bärsch, Claus-Ekkehard (1998), *Die Politische Religion des Nationalsozialismus: Die religiöse Dimension der NS-Ideologie in den Schriften von Dietrich Eckart, Joseph Goebbels, Alfred Rosenberg und Adolf Hitler* (Munich: W. Fink).

BBC News (2004), 'Terror "is new totalitarianism"', <http://news.bbc.co.uk/1/hi/uk_politics/3507730.stm>.

Beinart, Peter (2004), 'An Argument for a New Liberalism: A Fighting Faith', *New Republic* (13 December), 13.

Berghahn, Volker R. (2001), *America and the Intellectual Cold Wars in Europe: Shepard Stone between Philanthropy, Academy, and Diplomacy* (Princeton, NJ: Princeton University Press).

Berman, Paul (2003), *Terror and Liberalism* (New York: W.W. Norton).

Bollenbeck, Georg (1994), *Bildung und Kultur. Glanz und Elend eines deutschen Deutungsmusters* (Frankfurt am Main and Leipzig: Insel).

Borkenau, Franz (1982 [1940]), *The Totalitarian Enemy* (New York: AMS Press).

Caute, David (1988), *The Fellow-travelers: Intellectual Friends of Communism* rev. edn (New Haven, CT: Yale University Press).

Combe, Sonia (1990), 'Erinnerungen an den Hitler-Stalin-Pakt in der DDR', in Bisovsky, Gerhard, Schafranak, Hans and Streibel, Robert (eds), *Der Hitler-Stalin-Pakt: Voraussetzungen, Hintergründe, Auswirkungen* (Vienna: Picus Verlag).

Courtois, Stéphane et al. (eds) (1997), *Le livre noir du communisme: crimes, terreurs et répression* (Paris: R. Laffont).

Curtis, Michael (1969), 'Retreat from Totalitarianism', in Curtis, Michael, Friedrich, Carl J. and Barber, Benjamin R. (eds), *Totalitarianism in Perspective* (New York: Praeger).

Cushman, Thomas (2004), 'Anti-totalitarianism as a Vocation: An Interview with Adam Michnik', *Dissent* (Spring 2004), <http://www.dissentmagazine.org/article/?article=368>.

Cushman, Thomas (ed.) (2005), *A Matter of Principle: Humanitarian Arguments for War in Iraq* (Berkeley and Los Angeles, CA: University of California Press).

Diggins, John Patrick (2003), 'The -ism that Failed', *American Prospect* 14:11 (1 December), 22–7.

Diner, Dan (2000), *Beyond the Conceivable: Studies on Germany, Nazism, and the Holocaust* (Berkeley, CA: University of California Press).

Diner, Dan (2003), 'The Destruction of Narrativity: The Holocaust in Historical Discourse', in Postone, Moishe and Santner, Eric (eds), *Catastrophe and Meaning: The Holocaust and the Twentieth Century* (Chicago, IL: University of Chicago Press).

Dorman, Joseph (1998), *Arguing the World* (DVD) (New York: Empire).

Eley, Geoff (2003), 'Hitler's Silent Majority: Conformity and Resistance under the Third Reich', *Michigan Quarterly Review* 42 (Spring), 389–425.

Etkind, Alexander (2004), 'Hard and Soft Cultural Memory: Political Mourning in Russia and Germany', *Grey Room* 16, 36–59.

Flynn, Bernard (2002), 'Totalitarianism after the fall', *Constellations* 9:3, 436–44.

Friedrich, Carl J. and Brzezinski, Zbigniew K. (1956), *Totalitarian Dictatorship and Autocracy* (Cambridge, MA: Harvard University Press).

Furet, François (1990), *The Passing of an Illusion: The Idea of Communism in the Twentieth Century*, trans. Deborah Furet (Chicago, IL: University of Chicago Press).

Gellately, Robert (2001), *Backing Hitler: Consent and Coercion in Nazi Germany* (Oxford and New York: Oxford University Press).

Gleason, Abbott (1998), *Totalitarianism: The Inner History of the Cold War* (New York: Oxford University Press).

Glucksmann, André (2003), 'France's Five Cardinal Sins Over Iraq', *International Herald Tribune*, 26 February, <http://www.frontpagemag.com/Articles/ReadArticle.asp?ID=6335>.

Golsan, Richard (ed.) (1996), *Memory, the Holocaust, and French Justice: The Bousquet and Touvier Affairs*, trans. Lucy Golsan and Richard J. Golsan (Hanover, NH: University Press of New England).

Golsan, Richard (ed.) (2000), *The Papon Affair: Memory and Justice on Trial*, trans. Lucy B. Golsan and Richard J. Golsan (New York; London: Routledge).

Golsan, Richard J. (ed.) (2004a), *Stalinism and Nazism: History and Memory Compared*, trans. Lucy B. Golsan, Thomas C. Hilde and Peter S. Rogers (Lincoln, NB and London: University of Nebraska Press).

Golsan, Richard J. (2004b), 'Tzvetan Todorov, the "Responsible Intellectual" and the New World Disorder', *Modern and Contemporary France* 12:3, 299–311.

Gross, Jan T. (2001), *Neighbors: The Destruction of the Jewish Community in Jedwabne, Poland* (Princeton, NJ: Princeton University Press).

Habermas, Jürgen and Michnik, Adam (1994), 'More Humility, Fewer Illusions – A Talk between Adam Michnik and Jürgen Habermas', trans. Rodney Livingstone, *New York Review of Books* 41:6 (24 March), 24–9; first published in *Die Zeit*, 17 December 1993.

Habermas, Jürgen and Derrida, Jacques (2003), 'February 15, or what binds europeans together: A plea for a common foreign policy, beginning in the heart of Europe', *Constellations* 10:3 (September), 291–7.

Harpprecht, Klaus (2001), 'Die geistige Resistance nach 1945', *Neue Gesellschaft – Frankfurter Hefte* 48:5, 314–16.

Hassner, Pierre (1984), 'Le totalitarisme vu de l'ouest', in Hermet, Guy, Hassner, Pierre and Rupnik, Jacques (eds), *Totalitarismes* (Paris: Economica), 15–41.

Havel, Václav (1985), 'The Power of the Powerless', trans. Paul Wilson, in Keane, John (ed.), *The Power of the Powerless: Citizens against the State in Central-Eastern Europe* (London: Hutchinson).

Hook, Sidney (1987), *Out of Step: An Unquiet Life in the 20th Century* (New York: Harper and Row).

Howard, Dick (2002), *The Specter of Democracy* (New York: Columbia University Press).

Howe, Irving (ed.) (1983), *1984 Revisited: Totalitarianism in Our Century* (New York: Harper and Row, Perennial Library).

Huyssen, Andreas (1991) 'After the Wall: The Failure of German Intellectuals', *New German Critique: An Interdisciplinary Journal of German Studies* 52 (Winter), 109–43.

Jesse, Eckhard (ed.) (1996), *Totalitarismus im 20. Jahrhundert: Eine Bilanz der internationalen Forschung* (Baden-Baden: Nomos).

Jones, William David (1999), *The Lost Debate: German Socialist Intellectuals and Totalitarianism* (Urbana, IL: University of Illinois Press).

Judt, Tony (1998), *The Burden of Responsibility: Blum, Camus, Aron, and the French Twentieth Century* (Chicago, IL: University of Chicago Press).

Kershaw, Ian (1994), 'Totalitarianism Revisited: Nazism and Stalinism in Comparative Perspective', *Tel Aviver Jahrbuch für deutsche Geschichte* 38, 23–40.

Kershaw, Ian (2004), 'Hitler and the Uniqueness of Nazism', *Journal of Contemporary History* 39:2, 239–54.

Kershaw, Ian and Lewin, Moshe (eds) (1997), *Stalinism and Nazism: Dictatorships in Comparison* (Cambridge and New York: Cambridge University Press).

Knobloch, Clemens (1992), 'Überlegungen zur Theorie der Begriffsgeschichte aus sprach- und kommunikationswissenschaftlicher Sicht', *Archiv für Begriffsgeschichte* 35, 7–24.

Koestler, Arthur (1943), *Arrival and Departure* (New York: Macmillan).

Kramnick, Isaac and Sheerman, Barry (1993), *Harold Laski: A Life on the Left* (London and New York: Penguin).

Krzeminski, Adam (2005), 'As Many Wars as Nations: The Myths and Truths of World War II', *Polityka* (23 March); re-published in *Perlentaucher* (6 April 2005), available online in English at <http://www.signandsight.com/features/96.html>.

LaCapra, Dominick (1994), *Representing the Holocaust: History, Theory, Trauma* (Ithaca, NY: Cornell University Press).

LaCapra, Dominick (2004), *History in Transit: Experience, Identity, Critical Theory* (Ithaca, NY: Cornell University Press).

Laqueur, Walter (1985), 'Is There Now, or Has There Ever Been, Such a Thing as Totalitarianism?', *Commentary* (October), 29–35.

Lefort, Claude (1977), 'La première revolution antitotalitaire', *Esprit* 1, 13–19.

Lefort, Claude (1999), *La complication: Retour sur communisme* (Paris: Fayard).

Leonhard, Wolfgang (1989), *Betrayal: The Hitler–Stalin Pact of 1939*, trans. Richard D. Bosley (New York: St Martin's Press).

Levy, Daniel and Sznaider, Natan (2001), *Erinnerung im globalen Zeitalter: Der Holocaust* (Frankfurt am Main: Suhrkamp).

Michnik, Adam (1985), *Letters from Prison and Other Essays*, trans. Maya Latynski, with Foreword by Czesław Miłosz (Berkeley, CA: University of California Press).

Michnik, Adam (2003), 'We, the Traitors', *World Press Review* 50:6 (June), 8–5.

Minogue, Kenneth (1998), 'What is the Opposite of Totalitarianism?', Centre for Political Thought, Krakow, <http://www.omp.org.pl/minogue_ang_ang.php>.

Mosse, George L. (2000), *Confronting History: A Memoir* (Madison, WI: University of Wisconsin Press).

Müller, Jan Werner (2000), *Another Country: German Intellectuals, Unification and National Identity* (New Haven, CT: Yale University Press).

Müller, Reinhard (ed.) (1991), *Die Säuberung: Moskau 1936, Stenogramm einer geschlossenen Parteiversammlung: Georg Lukács ... [et al.]* (Reinbek bei Hamburg: Rowohlt).

Nisbet, Robert A. (1983), '1984 and the Conservative Imagination', in Howe, Irving (ed.), *1984 Revisited: Totalitarianism in Our Century* (New York: Harper and Row, Perennial Library).

O'Neill, William L. (1982), *A Better World: The Great Schism, Stalinism and the American Intellectuals* (New York: Simon and Schuster).

Overy, Richard (2004), *The Dictators: Hitler's Germany and Stalin's Russia* (New York: Norton).

Polonsky, Antony and Michlik, Joanna B. (2004), *The Neighbors Respond: The Controversy Over the Jedwabne Massacre in Poland* (Princeton, NJ: Princeton University Press).

Pudal, Bernard, Dreyfus, Michel and Groppo, Bruno et al. (eds) (2000), *Le Siècle des communismes* (Paris: Editions de l'atelier/Editions ouvrières).

Rabinbach, Anson (1977), 'Ernst Bloch's Heritage of our Times and Fascism', *New German Critique* 11 (Spring), 5–21.

Rabinbach, Anson (1998), 'Communist Crimes and French Intellectuals', *Dissent* (Fall), 61–6.

Regler, Gustav (1959), *The Owl of Minerva: The Autobiography of Gustav Regler*, trans. Norman Denny (New York: Farrar, Straus, and Cudahy).

Rév, István (2005), *Retroactive Justice: Prehistory of Post-communism* (Palo Alto, CA: Stanford University Press).

Rousso, Henry (2002), *The Haunting Past: History, Memory, and Justice in Contemporary France*, trans. Ralph Schoolcraft (Philadelphia, PA: University of Pennsylvania Press).

Rousso, Henry (ed.) (2004), *Stalinism and Nazism: History and Memory Compared*, English-language version introduced by Richard J. Golsan (ed.), trans. Lucy B. Golsan, Thomas C. Hilde and Peter S. Rogers, European Horizons Series (Lincoln, NB and London: University of Nebraska Press).

Rupnik, Jacques (1996), 'Der Totalitarismus aus der Sicht des Ostens', in Jesse, Eckhard (ed.), *Totalitarismus im 20. Jahrhundert. Eine Bilanz der internationalen Forschung* (Baden-Baden: Nomos), 389–415.

Sator, Klaus (1990), 'Das Kommunistische Exil und der deutsch–söwjetische Nichtangriffspakt', *Exilforschung* 8:31.

Scott, J.T. and Zaretsky, R.D. (2001a), 'Translator's Introduction', in Scott, J.T. and Zaretsky, R.D. (eds), *Tzvetan Todorov, Frail Happiness* (University Park, PA: Pennsylvania State University Press).

Scott, J.T. and Zaretsky, R.D. (eds) (2001b), *Tzvetan Todorov, Frail Happiness* (University Park, PA: Pennsylvania State University Press).

Sperber, Manès (1994), *Until My Eyes are Closed with Shards*, trans. Harry Zohn (New York and London: Holmes and Meier).

Stavginski, Hans-Georg (2002), *Das Holocaust-Denkmal. Der Streit um das, 'Denkmal für die ermordeten Juden Europas' in Berlin (1988–1999)* (Paderborn: Ferdinand Schönigh Verlag).

Stephenson, Wen (2003), 'An Interview with Paul Berman', <http://www.pbs.org/wgbh/pages/frontline/shows/blair/liberal/berman.html>.

Strenski, Ivan (2004), 'Nous et les Autres: The Politics of Tzvetan Todorov's "Critical Humanism"', *French Politics* 2, 97–109.

Todorov, Tzvetan (1987), *The Conquest of America: The Question of the Other*, trans. Richard Howard (New York: Harper and Row).

Todorov, Tzvetan (1996), *Facing the Extreme: Moral Life in the Concentration Camps*, trans. Arthur Denner and Abigail Pollak (New York: Henry Holt).

Todorov, Tzvetan (2001), *The Fragility of Goodness: Why Bulgaria's Jews Survived the Holocaust: A Collection of Texts*, trans. Arthur Denner (Princeton, NJ: Princeton University Press).

Todorov, Tzvetan (2002a), *Devoirs et Delices d'une vie passeur: Entrietiens avec Catherine Portevin* (Paris: Les Editions de Seuil).

Todorov, Tzvetan (2002b), *Imperfect Garden: The Legacy of Humanism*, trans. Carol Cosman (Princeton, NJ: Princeton University Press).

Todorov, Tzvetan (2003), *Hope and Memory: Lessons from the Twentieth Century*, trans. David Bellos (Princeton, NJ: Princeton University Press).

Tooze, J. Adam (2005), 'Einfach verkalkuliert', *Die Tageszeitung*, 12 March.

Traverso, Enzo (2004), 'Intellectuals and Anti-fascism: For a Critical Historization', *New Politics*, 9:4 (Winter), 91–103.

Walzer, Michael (1983), 'On "Failed Totalitarianism"', in Howe, Irving (ed.), *1984 Revisited: Totalitarianism in Our Century* (New York: Harper and Row, Perennial Library), 103–21.

Whitfield, Stephen J. (1980), *Into the Dark: Hannah Arendt and Totalitarianism* (Philadelphia, PA: Temple University Press).

Wilkinson, James D. (1981), *The Intellectual Resistance in Europe* (Cambridge, MA: Harvard University Press).

Winock, Michel (1997), *Le Siècle des intellectuels* (Paris: Seuil).

Žižek, Slavoj (2001), *Did Someone Say Totalitarianism? Four Interventions in the Misuse of a Notion* (London, New York: Verso Books).

Žižek, Slavoj (2005), 'The Two Totalitarianisms', *London Review of Books*, 27:6 (17 March), available at <http://www.lrb.co.uk/v27/n06/zize01_.html>.

Zudeick, Peter (1985), *Der Hintern des Teufels: Ernst Bloch, Leben und Werk* (Moos: Elster).

PART THREE
CASE STUDIES

Chapter 8

Tocqueville as a Public Intellectual[1]

John Torpey

The eminent political theorist Sheldon Wolin recently argued that Alexis de Tocqueville was 'perhaps the last influential theorist who can be said to have truly cared about political life' (Wolin, 2001, 5).[2] Tocqueville's indispensable account of *Democracy in America* has been praised as 'at once the best book ever written on democracy and the best book ever written on America' (Mansfield and Winthrop in Tocqueville, 2000). To this day, one can encounter Tocqueville's ideas concerning the peculiarities and peccadilloes of American life and politics on a weekly basis, if not daily, in mass-circulation newspapers and magazines, as well as in the scholarly literature. The extension of his comparative study of the roots and character of modern democracy, *The Old Regime and the Revolution*, has been central to the re-thinking of the French Revolution that took place in France around the time of its bicentennial in 1989. The Tocqueville-inspired historical revisionism of that episode was an intellectual-political development of major political import, dovetailing as it did with the collapse of communism in the Soviet Union and Eastern Europe and giving rise to what has been called (at least in France) the 'Tocquevillean moment'.[3] Meanwhile, supporters of China's so-called 'New Left', who oppose those they view as the country's neo-liberal market fundamentalists, quote the French nobleman often because 'Tocqueville made clear that democracy, not capitalism alone, was the key to America's success, shaping not just its politics but its society, law, culture and economy' (Kahn, 2002, A17). In the United States, the charitable organization United Way created the Tocqueville Society in 1984 'because of Alexis de Tocqueville's admiration for the spirit of voluntary association and voluntary effort for the common good'.[4] His opposition

1 This is an expanded and revised version of a paper previously published under the title 'Alexis de Tocqueville, Forgotten Founder', *Sociological Forum* 21:4 (December 2006), 695–707.

2 For a vigorous critique of Wolin's often harsh views of Tocqueville's perspectives, see Drescher (2003).

3 The writings of François Furet are critical to the re-thinking of the French Revolution that led to the notion that 'the French Revolution is over' as a source of inspiration for later movements and struggles; see, for example, *Interpreting the French Revolution* (Furet, 1981). The first issue of the French journal *Raisons Politiques: Etudes de pensée politique* (February 2001) was titled 'Le moment Tocquevillien'.

4 <http://national.unitedway.org/tocqueville/history.cfm>.

to state-funded 'welfare' – a view that would hearten many contemporary American conservatives – comes through clearly enough in his recently translated *Memoir on Pauperism* (Tocqueville, 1997). These examples, which could be expanded almost at will, demonstrate that Tocqueville's oeuvre admits of a considerable variety of interpretations, is politically polyvocal, and has been enormously influential in the United States, in his native France and around the world.

Despite this massive resonance, Tocqueville's writings are simply not regarded today as crucial to the training of professional sociologists – the field in which his works might arguably be thought most relevant – as opposed to well-read undergraduates or scholars of other kindred disciplines. For example, along with other classic works on society and politics, Tocqueville's writings are a staple of Harvard's Social Studies Program 10, but not of its graduate programme in Sociology. The Tocqueville of *Democracy in America* has been appropriated chiefly by the political scientists, who have become major contributors to public discourse of late with Tocquevillean (which is to say, sociological) analyses of the decline of 'social capital' and of 'voluntary associations' in contemporary American life. The most important writer in this genre is Robert Putnam, whose *Bowling Alone: The Collapse and Revival of American Community* became a best-seller for sounding the alarm. Symptomatically, the *Publishers Weekly* review of the book posted on Amazon.com mistakenly identifies Putnam as a professor of sociology at Harvard (he is in the Government Department) (see Putnam, 2000).[5] Tocqueville's study of the revolution in France represents a major milestone in the comparative analysis of modern revolutions, deeply influencing such important scholars of these matters as Hannah Arendt and Theda Skocpol. Yet the historians generally pay more attention to Tocqueville's writing on the Revolution and on French politics than do sociologists (see Arendt, 1963; Skocpol 1979). In short, Tocqueville is simply not part of the sociological 'canon', which – despite recent efforts to shake up the very idea of a canon and to add new names and voices to it – remains very much built around the venerable 'holy trinity' of Marx, Weber and Durkheim. How can this be?

Part of the answer undoubtedly lies with the extraordinary influence of Talcott Parsons' codification of the sociological canon in *The Structure of Social Action* (1937). The principal players here are Pareto, Marshall (Alfred, for those who may have forgotten), Durkheim, and, of course, Weber. Tocqueville receives nary a mention; then again, neither do the concepts of democracy or of revolution. Instead, Parsons' treatise is oriented towards social life as a 'system' that is 'integrated' in various ways and (said to be) governed above all by norms. Of course, Parsons' functionalism was subjected to a thoroughgoing demolition as the 1960s witnessed a politics (around the globe) that was more conflictual than consensual, and the United States – widely thought to be the society reflected in Parsons' putatively timeless approach – received a certain comeuppance in

5 A similar endeavour by a (group of) sociologist(s) was Bellah et al. (1985). One might characterize these anti-individualists as 'left Tocquevilleans'.

Southeast Asia. Parsons wrote *Structure* on the edge of a precipice, in a context in which capitalism faced its most severe challenge in American history, and his elaboration of systems and norms seemed almost a wilful refusal of the threats to social order that pervaded the time of its writing. As things seemed to be falling apart, Parsons insisted, against considerable evidence, that they simply must hang together. Yet by the time of writing *The Evolution of Societies* (Parsons, 1977), in which Parsons directly engaged with the more radical critics of American society and claimed that the latter 'attains fairly successfully the equality of opportunity stressed in socialism', Tocqueville is invoked as 'an alternative interpretation to recent portrayals of the United States as the prototype of bureaucratization and the concentration of power' (Parsons, 1977, 207 and 215).

For his part, Tocqueville stood on the cusp of the multiple transformations that ushered in European modernity – capitalism, industrialization, revolution, democracy – and sought to make sense of what it all meant, from a long historical and broadly comparative perspective. Mucking around in the feudal (or, in the case of America, the non-feudal) past in search of an explanation for the events of his day, Tocqueville must have seemed to Parsons to possess a maddening lack of the systematic, scientific qualities that he thought essential to an adequate social theory. Yet his exploration of the things that make 'democratic' society such a departure from the preceding 'aristocratic' world – including those 'habits of the heart' that lie somewhere between Parsons' 'norms' and Weber's 'traditional action' – had the virtue of flesh and blood rather than the arid qualities of Parsons' 'systems'. As Tocqueville himself once put it: 'I hate all those absolute systems that ... succeed, so to speak, in banishing men from the history of the human race' (Tocqueville, 1971, 78).

In part, of course Tocqueville's exclusion from the sociological canon was simply a matter of timing, as the Frenchman wrote before the development of modern universities in the Anglophone world, with their jealous divisions of disciplinary fields, more sophisticated notions of methodology, and commitment to newer definitions of what constituted 'science'. (This tendency is reflected clearly in the differences between the requirements of the Harvard Social Studies undergraduate course and those of the Sociology Department's graduate programme.) Moreover, Tocqueville seemed to be writing more about countries than concepts; as sociology developed more scientific pretensions (sometimes derided as 'physics envy'), concern with particular countries and their histories became less and less acceptable. Sociologists thus wrote about concepts, not countries, except in so far as the latter constituted 'cases' of 'societies' that could be neatly disentangled from their larger environments and studied in isolation from one another.[6] Partially for nationalist reasons, and partially because of its traditional preoccupation with

6 For a critical discussion of this development, see Wolf (1982), 3–23. Michael Mann has argued with growing vigour that 'comparative' sociology is almost impossible because the 'units' ('societies') are insufficiently disentangled from one another to make comparison viable (see Mann, 1986, 502–3).

more idealist considerations, German sociology has also evinced little interest in Tocqueville's work, although this may be changing. The neglect of Tocqueville in Parsons' *Structure* is repeated, for example, in Jürgen Habermas's updating of Parsons via a theory of language, *The Theory of Communicative Action*. Yet Claus Offe's recent treatment is respectful, and even enthusiastic (see Habermas, 1984 and 1987; Offe, 2005).[7]

In contrast to the abstruseness of much of Parsons' (and Habermas's) grand theory, Tocqueville wrote about modernity both as a kind of continuous (democratic) revolution and as a place in which old-fashioned revolt would gradually be relegated to the margins of history. The sweep of the revolutionary tide would be located predominantly in the political sphere, however, and would thus end up being principally the concern of political scientists once their field split off from sociology around the turn of the twentieth century. Meanwhile, Tocqueville's conservative interpretation of modern society as one in which equality was on the march and major revolutions would become a thing of the past has been as unsatisfactory to most recent sociologists as it was salutary to Parsons in his arguments with the radicals of the New Left. The fact that Tocqueville was rather hard on political intellectuals has not helped either.

Tocqueville's attitude towards modern politics and the role of intellectuals in it reflected his own ambivalence about the priority of the *vita activa* and the *vita contemplativa*.[8] As he advanced in years and in the level of his political involvement, Tocqueville confronted with increasing dismay a situation in which revolution was very much on the historical agenda, both in terms of a political legacy and in terms of a possible future for his own and other societies. As a young man, reflecting on the meaning of America for his own declining aristocratic European society, he famously argued that 'great revolutions' would become rarer as a result of democratization and the more egalitarian distribution of property that would go with it. Like those who promoted the sale of houses on credit beginning in the nineteenth century, Tocqueville believed in his earlier years that those who had a little something would be especially loath to risk it on the abstract prospect of a revolutionary transformation of society (see Tocqueville, 2000, vol. II, Part 3, Ch. 21).[9]

By 1848, however, Tocqueville intuited that the wolf of socialist revolution was at the door. By then, he was a member of the French Chamber of Deputies, the representative of his home district in Normandy, and soon to be Foreign Minister

7 Habermas (1989 [1962]), does devote several pages to Tocqueville in *The Structural Transformation of the Public Sphere*, dealing mainly with *Democracy in America*. For a more extensive treatment of Tocqueville and his (unacknowledged) impact on Weber, see Hecht (1998).

8 The theme of Tocqueville's ambivalence on this matter runs throughout Wolin's *Tocqueville Between Two Worlds* and is addressed at various points in Brogan (2007). The alternatives of *vita activa* and *vita contemplativa* are discussed in Arendt (1958).

9 For the anti-radical effects of home ownership, see Jackson (1985), 51.

(though only briefly). Alarmed both by the mood that was developing outside and by the apparent obliviousness of his parliamentary colleagues in the face of this challenge, he chided them:

> It is said that there is no danger because there is no riot, and that because there is no visible disorder on the surface of society, we are far from revolution. Gentlemen, allow me to say that I think you are mistaken … It is true that [the working classes] are not now tormented by what may properly be called political passions to the extent they once were; but do you not see that their passions have changed from political to social? Do you not see that opinions and ideas are gradually spreading among them that tend not simply to the overthrow of such-and-such laws, such-and-such a minister, or even such-and-such a government, but rather to the overthrow of society, breaking down the bases on which it now rests? Do you not hear what is being said every day among them? Do you not hear them constantly repeating that all the people above them are incapable and unworthy to rule them? That the division of property in the world up to now is unjust? That property rests on bases of inequity? And do you not realize that when such opinions take root and spread, sinking deeply into the masses, they must sooner or late … bring in their train the most terrifying of revolutions? Gentlemen, my profound conviction is that we are lulling ourselves to sleep over an active volcano … (Tocqueville, 1848, 16–17)

Needless to say, Tocqueville was disturbed by the revolutionary scenario he believed was in the offing, and would do his utmost to ensure that it would not actually come to pass.

Here arises an intriguing historical coincidence of some relevance to the later development of sociology as a field. Shortly before giving the above speech to the French parliament, Tocqueville had been asked by a colleague to pen a 'manifesto' outlining his political position and that of his 'friends' in the legislature; the document was not published at the time, but Tocqueville reproduced relevant snippets in his 'Recollections' (1985). Almost simultaneously, another pair of authors had similarly been commissioned by *their* comrades to draft a statement adumbrating the group's political vision. That document, *The Communist Manifesto*, would eventually become 'the most widely read and influential single document of modern socialism' (Tucker, 1978, 469). Of course, its attitude concerning the revolutionary propensities of the working classes was rather more enthusiastic than was Tocqueville's. Despite their divergent perspectives, however, the authors of the respective manifestos share a great deal in terms of their analysis of what exactly was taking place in the society in which they lived.

Whether there is any textual basis for this resemblance, I do not know. I have not been able to determine whether Tocqueville was aware of Marx and Engels' literary production, but it seems difficult to imagine that this was not the case at least to some degree – though when this awareness might have arisen is unclear. Despite extensive discussion of socialist doctrine in the *Recollections*, Tocqueville does not mention Marx. Yet Marx knew about Tocqueville, we can be certain, for he cites *Democracy in America* in his 1843 essay 'On the Jewish Question' (see Tucker, 1978, 31).[10] Whether or not Tocqueville became familiar with Marx's writings later, however, Tocqueville's analyses already in *Democracy in America* of the polarization of classes and of the worker's 'alienation' from his product in an industrial society bear a striking resemblance to Marx's discussions of these matters in the so-called 'Economic and Philosophic Manuscripts of 1844' and in the *Manifesto* itself. Thus, for example, Tocqueville wrote:

> When an artisan engages constantly and uniquely in the manufacture of a single object, in the end he performs this work with singular dexterity. But at the same time he loses the general faculty of applying his mind to the direction of the work … [T]he man in him is degraded as the worker is perfected. (Tocqueville, 2000, 530)

Embellished with the Hegelian language of the dialectic, this would soon prove very much Marx's own understanding of the consequences of the capitalist labour process as detailed in the 1844 manuscripts.

This is not to say that their analyses of the work process under capitalism (Marx's term, not Tocqueville's) and of the consequences of that system entirely overlapped. On one key point, indeed, Tocqueville's understanding differed sharply from Marx's perspective about the consequences of 'industry' for the economic well-being of workers. According to the Frenchman, 'the slow and progressive rise in wages is one of the general laws that regulate democratic societies. As conditions become more equal, wages rise, and as wages go higher, conditions become more equal' (Tocqueville, 2000, 556). Marx's so-called 'immiseration thesis' would directly dispute the claim of a general rise in wages for workers. Yet on this point, even if it can hardly be said that economic inequality has been eradicated, the verdict of history must be given to Tocqueville.

Still, his analysis of the capitalist system suggested that Marx was onto something the possibility of which Tocqueville also already foresaw in Volume Two of *Democracy in America*. In Tocqueville's words, 'the friends of democracy ought constantly to turn their regard with anxiety in this direction [that of the magnates of manufacturing]; for if ever permanent inequality of conditions and aristocracy are introduced anew into the world, one can predict that they will enter by this door' (Tocqueville, 2000, 532).[11] Marx believed that this aristocracy had already arrived, or at least that it was an iron fact of capitalist social organization that there were some who owned – and others who were dispossessed of – the 'means of production', and that this entailed a society that only appeared to be based on 'free labour'. Accordingly, this social order drew its sustenance from a new form of slavery, disguised as contractually agreed wage labour. Its affront to

10 Brogan mistakenly suggests that Marx's only mention of Tocqueville was in *The Eighteenth Brumaire of Louis Bonaparte* (Marx, 1963 [1852], 101).

11 Brogan neglects to mention the striking similarity between Tocqueville's discussion of the 'aristocracy of industry' and Marx's critique of capitalist inequality and alienation, but it is noted approvingly in Offe (2005), 23.

modern principles of autonomy and equality, in the Marxist view, earned it the just obloquy of those disadvantaged by it.

Marx thus drew the conclusions about 'modern industry' that Tocqueville refused to countenance. While Tocqueville's unpublished manifesto worriedly observed that 'soon the political struggle will be between the Haves and the Have-nots' (Tocqueville, 1985, 15), Marx called for the revolutionary overthrow of the rule of 'capital'. With his privileging of the sphere of material life in making sense of society, Marx's understanding of politics amounted to the notion, to paraphrase Clausewitz, that politics was merely an extension of economics by other means: 'the State is the form in which the individuals of a ruling class assert their common interests' (Marx in Tucker, 1978, 187). The abolition of economic inequality would thus herald the end of any need for a state, which was merely the unavoidable bureaucratic apparatus of rule based on inequality. Marx's view, paralleling that of Saint-Simon, was that the realm of freedom would be marked by a shift from the administration of people to the administration of things.

But not right away, of course; for a time, a 'dictatorship of the proletariat' would be necessary to consolidate the gains of the revolution. Marx's view of the course of the revolutionary transformation ridding the world of capitalism opened the door to sceptical views. Hence, the Russian radical Bakunin would in due course ask of Marx, 'If the proletariat is ruling, over whom will it rule?' Bakunin had hit upon a central difficulty in Marx's conception of the revolution. According to Marx, 'The *class domination* of the workers over the resisting strata of the old world must last until the economic foundations of the existence of classes are destroyed' (Marx in Tucker, 1978, 547). Yet Marx had written frequently enough about theory as the 'head' and the proletariat as the 'heart' of the revolution to raise questions about who would really be in command of the revolution. He argued in *The Communist Manifesto* that:

> In times when the class struggle nears the decisive hour ... a small section of the ruling class cuts itself adrift, and joins the revolutionary class ... in particular, a portion of the bourgeois ideologists, who have raised themselves to the level of comprehending theoretically the historical movement as a whole. (Marx and Engels in Tucker, 1978, 481)

Marx's analysis of the behaviour of the intellectuals in a revolutionary situation is as unsociological as Tocqueville's, written several years later, would be sociological. This difference between the two authors is particularly striking in view of the fact that it was Marx who developed the seminal insight that 'life is not determined by consciousness, but consciousness by life' (Marx in Tucker, 1978, 155). His whole theoretical edifice had been built on the notion that the social situation of the proletariat would lead them to the insight that capitalism was antithetical to their interests. Yet, at the crucial time, it seemed, 'a portion of the bourgeois ideologists' who had come to comprehend 'the historical movement as a whole' would switch allegiances and side with 'the class that holds the future in its hands'. This was as 'idealist' an understanding as one could imagine.

Were these bourgeois likely to give up their positions of dominance simply because they had achieved the necessary level of theoretical understanding about the path of historical development? In contrast to Marx's apparent insouciance – or, at least, lack of critical awareness – about which 'proletarians' would run the 'dictatorship' of their class, Bakunin insisted that the domination in question would be exercised by a new 'regime of the learned' (Marx in Tucker, 1978, 546). Bakunin had not derided Marx as the 'Bismarck of socialism' for nothing. It would take another 35 years for Robert Michels to suggest the existence of an 'iron law of oligarchy' on the basis of his analysis of the domination of educated leaders in the German Social Democratic Party (see Michels, 1959 [1910]). For Michels, however, the 'intellectuals' would rule over the masses because their academic training gave them abilities that would be unavailable to the less educated members of society, who would thus be poorly equipped to challenge the better-schooled. By contrast, Tocqueville viewed the literary abilities of the lettered as precisely their problem.

In his celebrated study of the historic wrong turn that was, for him, the French Revolution, Tocqueville argued that 'men of letters' – the term 'intellectuals' had to await the Dreyfus Affair of the late nineteenth century – had come to be the 'leading politicians' of their day, despite their innocence of practical politics. His analysis of the reasons for the impractical bent of these thinkers' ideas was straightforwardly sociological:

> The very situation of these writers prepared them to like general and abstract theories of government and to trust in them blindly. At the almost infinite distance from practice in which they lived, no experience tempered the ardors of their nature; nothing warned them of the obstacles that existing facts might place before even the most desirable reforms; they didn't have any idea of the dangers which always accompany even the most necessary revolutions. (Tocqueville, 1998 [1856], 197)

Tocqueville thus advanced a line of conservative criticism of intellectuals that would resonate through the works of authors such as Joseph Schumpeter and the neo-conservatives of the last third of the twentieth century (see Schumpeter, 1942, 147; Podhoretz, 1979). This perspective took intellectuals to task for the abstractness of their thought and its divorce from practical life. The underlying assumptions are Burkean views about the historical 'rootedness' of ways of life and their refractoriness *vis-à-vis* 'social engineering' of a rationalist kind. Tocqueville's analysis raises important questions about the degree to which it is possible to 'leap out of history', as the French revolutionaries and the Marxists seemed to want to do, or the extent to which one must recognize that 'the real is rational' and hence unwise to change.[12] It was this propensity towards defending aspects of feudal

12 The notion that the 'real is rational' is Hegel's, but cf. also Aristotle's comment that 'change is a matter which needs great caution' because 'the improvement likely to be effected may be small' (Aristotle, 1958).

society that incited so much of Sheldon Wolin's ire in his *Tocqueville Between Two Worlds*.

From the perspective of Tocqueville's fate in contemporary sociology, it is perhaps worth comparing Tocqueville's views on intellectuals and the Revolution with those of his countryman Emile Durkheim. In a critical review of a book called *The Principles of 1789 and Social Science*, Durkheim notes that the author objects to the 'immoderate taste for the absolute' evident in those principles. Durkheim responds that:

> This taste for the absolute is not peculiar to the Revolution [but] is found in all creative eras, in all centuries of new and hardy faith … Moreover, they have survived over time and have extended themselves far beyond the countries where they were born. A good part of Europe believed in them, and believes in them still. (Durkheim, 1973b, 41)

These comments seem almost directly aimed at Tocqueville, even though he is not the author of the book under review. In a later discussion of 'Individualism and the Intellectuals' in the heat of the Dreyfus Affair, Durkheim cheerfully endorsed a version of rationalism and humanism that would surely have been too much for Tocqueville, despite his mature rejection of the doctrines of the Catholic Church: '[M]an has become a god for man and … he can no longer create other gods without lying to himself.' The intellectuals played a key role here, promoting a notion of legitimacy derived from Enlightenment principles: 'my reason requires reasons before it bows before someone else's', he wrote. 'Respect for authority is in no way incompatible with rationalism as long as the authority is rationally grounded.' The echoes here of Kant's '*sapere aude!*' are unmistakable, and go beyond Tocqueville's lifelong appreciation of the venerability of legitimate (that is, properly earned) aristocratic dominance. In what appears a final slap at Tocqueville, Durkheim insisted that 'not only is individualism not anarchical, but it henceforth is the only system of beliefs which can ensure the moral unity of the country' (Durkheim, 1973a, 49, 50 and 52). Despite this engagement with what might appear to be central aspects of his predecessor's oeuvre, there seems to be no evidence that Durkheim ever addressed Tocqueville's writings head-on.[13] None the less, Durkheim clearly stakes out a position to Tocqueville's left, belying the frequently held notion in sociology that Durkheim was a mere conservative preoccupied chiefly with what would come to be known as 'the problem of order'.

Durkheim's 'progressive' position relative to Tocqueville has been reinforced by more recent appropriations of Tocqueville in France. The French interest in Tocqueville today is dominated by historians and political scientists, presumably because one of his two major works was on France and the history of its revolution. Against the background of the arguments of *Democracy in America*, the later

13 There is no entry for Tocqueville in Lukes (1985). My teacher Robert Bellah once told that me he, too, had sought in vain for references to Tocqueville in Durkheim's writings.

volume on *The Old Regime* suggested that France's political waters were troubled because it did not have the good fortune of the untroubled birth that democracy had had in America: 'The great advantage of the Americans is to have arrived at democracy without having to suffer democratic revolutions, and to be born equal instead of becoming so' (Tocqueville, 2000, 485). This claim raises important questions about the extent to which the 'democratic revolution' could be said to have similar effects on all societies, and to strengthen the perception of American society as unique and 'exceptional'. If the 'point of departure' is everything, how could the French (or anyone starting without the 'immaculate conception' of democracy enjoyed by the Americans) expect to have a successful democracy?[14]

Based on his insights into the differences between France and the US, Tocqueville's study of *The Old Regime* has served as an indispensable source of ammunition for recent intellectual-cum-political struggles over the meaning of the Revolution. The chief figure here is the historian François Furet, who – like Tocqueville before him – found lamentable the consequences of the French Revolution for his own *patrie*. Furet and his followers have sought to squelch the chronic instability produced by the shimmer of revolution and by the other abstractions promulgated by intellectuals. Herein, according to Furet and his epigones, lay the error of those led astray by the communist illusion, just as Tocqueville had seen in the French revolutionaries' penchant for abstraction the key to their excesses.[15]

Here it is perhaps worth noting that, for all their shared enthusiasm for the concept of totalitarianism, what one might call the 'young Tocquevilleans' around Furet differ sharply from Hannah Arendt – the inventor of the concept in this form – in their attitude towards the revolutionary heritage in modern political culture. The excesses of communism did not vitiate the idea of revolution for Arendt, who lionized the American version in which she found refuge from Nazism. In her comparative analysis of the American and French revolutions, Arendt lovingly invoked 'the revolutionary tradition and its lost treasure'. She remained committed, in a Jeffersonian vein, to the revolutionary tradition as an affirmation of 'man's' ability to escape the stagnation of unfreedom and of the quintessentially human capacity to 'start something new'. Indeed, one of the forms of that revolutionary creativity was the soviets or councils (*Räte*), which, Arendt noted in the 1960s, 'were to make their appearance in every genuine revolution throughout the nineteenth and twentieth centuries'. These 'spontaneous organs of the people' she regarded as having created 'a new public space for freedom which was constituted and organized during the course of the revolution itself', beyond and even against the designs of the leaders of the revolution (Arendt, 1963, 249). Interestingly, the idea of 'councils' was developed as an antidote precisely

14 Brogan notes this problem as well; see Brogan (2007), 270.

15 For Tocqueville's critique, see Tocqueville (1998 [1856]), Book III, Chapter One. For Furet's perspective, see Furet (1999).

to the dominance of bureaucratic elements, including intellectuals, in the workers' movement and its parties.[16]

Whether Tocqueville would have approved his admirer Hannah Arendt's enthusiasm for this revolutionary democratic institution may be doubted. Tocqueville took for granted that intellectuals could be legitimate political actors, and assumed that such involvement would temper their judgement and wean them off the airy abstractions of the *vita contemplativa*. Participation in politics would enhance critical capacity by giving it the necessary 'reality-check'. Presumably one can also gain from active participation some insights about political life that would be unavailable to the outside observer.

Meanwhile, however, the modern social sciences have come to be distinguished by the 'norm of disinterestedness', the expectation that the findings of scholarship should be as untainted as possible by the preferences and whims of the person doing the scholarship. This posture suggests maintaining distance from practical affairs, which are thought to bias one's views about social life. These ideas are most associated with Max Weber's understanding of objectivity and 'value neutrality', and have of course been subject to intense scepticism in recent years. Weber's views on these matters did not keep him from taking an active part in the affairs of his time; like Tocqueville, Weber was tremendously involved in the political life of his day, acting for example as an adviser to the negotiators of the treaty that ended the First World War and participating in the drafting of the Weimar Constitution (see Mommsen, 1984). Despite his insistence on objectivity in the course of scholarly work, Weber had no difficulty – indeed, he felt a responsibility for – taking part in serious politics. His view was that 'objectivity' entailed 'freedom from value judgements' combined with choices of research topics based on their 'valuc-relevance'.

Weber regarded politics as perhaps the supreme vocation of humankind, where the stakes were the highest imaginable. Recall his conclusion in 'Politics as a Vocation' that – contrary to the position sometimes maintained that he advocated a complete divorce between the ethics of conviction and responsibility – 'an ethic of ultimate ends [that is, of 'conviction'] and an ethic of responsibility are not absolute contrasts but rather supplements, which only in unison constitute a genuine man – a man who *can* have the "calling for politics"' (Weber, 1946, 127). Weber saw politics as a realm in which people's ultimate value commitments would battle it out in a contest for supremacy – the struggle of the 'warring gods' that hold human beings in their grip. Yet despite his heroic, agonistic view of politics, Weber also understood the need to attend to the details of policy. Raymond Aron would thus later write in praise of Weber that 'he was prepared at any moment to answer the question that disconcerts all our amateur politicians: "What would you do if you were a Cabinet minister?"' (Aron in Judt, 1998, 161).[17] Weber's views of the place

16 For a useful study, see Schneider and Kuda (1968).

17 Weber seems to have been very close to being named Reich Interior Minister by the Social Democratic President, Friedrich Ebert, but was ultimately passed over in favour

of politics in human life would seem to belie Wolin's claim about Tocqueville's status as the last influential theorist to have 'truly cared' about politics.

Tocqueville shared with Weber a stoic sensibility concerning the changes occurring in modern life and a sense of the profound importance of politics for human beings, combined with a regard for the details of political life. His trip overseas that served as the foundation of his classic *Democracy in America* was motivated by a desire (at least in part) to examine the novel developments in penal practice that were taking place in the United States at that time. *Democracy in America* itself was intended as an effort to show his countrymen what they had to anticipate from the democratic revolution that he was certain was sweeping the (Christian) world: 'I confess that in America I saw more than America; I sought there an image of democracy itself, of its penchants, its character, its prejudices, its passions; I wanted to become acquainted with it if only to know at least what we ought to hope or fear from it' (Tocqueville, 2000, 13). In the introduction to Volume Two, published five years later, he wrote that he intended not to unduly flatter 'democracy', which he was confident he could leave to others, but instead to call attention to its more disturbing aspects: '[B]ecause I was not an adversary of democracy … I wanted to be sincere with it' (Tocqueville, 2000, 400).

Yet Tocqueville's ambivalence about both democracy and America are unmistakable. Of the former, he fears the novel political malady of the 'tyranny of the majority', and of the latter he worries that it will produce artistic mediocrity and a stifling uniformity of thought. These perspectives are remarkably similar to Weber's central concerns, which in contrast to Tocqueville's Gallicized English liberalism come wrapped in the language of German Romanticism. Weber wrote of the 'Protestant ethic' and of the rationalization that it promoted as the avatar of a more 'reasonable' way of doing things. There is little doubt that he regarded legal-rational forms of organization and legitimacy as preferable from the point of view of efficiency and procedural fairness. Yet his recourse to Schiller's terms for the larger process it embodied – the 'disenchantment of the world' – bespoke Weber's contempt for a tendency in human life that would deprive it of its warmth and meaning. The rationalized world whose coming he diagnosed was by no means one in which he wanted to live: 'Not summer's bloom lies ahead of us, but rather a polar night of icy darkness and hardness, no matter which group may triumph externally now' (Weber, 1946, 128).

In contrast to Weber's doomsaying, Tocqueville seems relatively optimistic – though hardly cheery. He worried about the fate of politics in the 'levelled' world of democracy. He regarded modern intellectuals as playing a potentially disastrous role in politics because of their tendency towards abstract rationalism, whereas Weber viewed this as the unavoidable nature of the intellectual beast. But for all his concern about the future, Tocqueville lacked Weber's – or Marx's – Teutonic capacity for imagining catastrophe, whether in the 'polar night' or in the 'icy water of egotistical calculation'. If proper 'habits of the heart' could be found

of Hugo Preuss (see Mommsen 1984, 333).

or instilled, the future might be bright, or at least warmly glowing. Intellectuals might contribute to this enterprise, but only if they were sufficiently immersed in the political life of their societies to be able to distinguish 'pie in the sky' from the 'art of the possible'. It continues to be a difficult challenge, and Tocqueville's own peregrinations between the two worlds offers an exemplary instance of how the two can be combined. Still, in 'that distant epoch the writing of a masterpiece of political thought was deemed to be an excellent qualification for entry' (Brogan, 2007, 294) into the top ranks of political leadership. Such a trajectory is rather more difficult to imagine in our own day.

References

Arendt, Hannah (1958), *The Human Condition* (Chicago IL: University of Chicago Press).

Arendt, Hannah (1963), *On Revolution* (New York: Penguin).

Aristotle (1958), *The Politics of Aristotle*, ed. and trans. Ernest Barker (New York: Oxford University Press).

Bellah, Robert et al. (1985), *Habits of the Heart: Individualism and Commitment in American Life* (Berkeley, CA: University of California Press).

Brogan, Hugh (2007), *Alexis de Tocqueville: A Life* (New Haven, CT: Yale University Press).

Drescher, Seymour (2003), 'Who Needs Ancienneté? Tocqueville on Aristocracy and Modernity', *History of Political Thought* 24:4 (Winter), 624–46.

Durkheim, Emile (1973a), 'Individualism and the Intellectuals', in Bellah, Robert (ed.), *Emile Durkheim on Morality and Society* (Chicago, IL: University of Chicago Press).

Durkheim, Emile (1973b), 'The Principles of 1789 and Sociology', in Bellah, Robert (ed.), *Emile Durkheim on Morality and Society* (Chicago, IL: University of Chicago Press).

Furet, François (1981), *Interpreting the French Revolution*, trans. Elborg Forster (New York: Cambridge University Press).

Furet, François (1999), *The Passing of an Illusion: The Idea of Communism in the Twentieth Century*, trans. Deborah Furet (Chicago, IL: University of Chicago Press).

Gouldner, Alvin (1962), 'Introduction', in Durkheim, Emile, *Socialism*, ed. Alvin W. Gouldner (New York: Collier).

Habermas, Jürgen (1984), *Theory of Communicative Action*, vol. 1 (Boston, MA: Beacon Press).

Habermas, Jürgen (1987), *Theory of Communicative Action*, vol. 2 (Boston, MA: Beacon Press).

Habermas, Jürgen (1989 [1962]), *The Structural Transformation of the Public Sphere*, trans. Thomas Burger with the assistance of Frederick Lawrence (Cambridge, MA: MIT Press).

Mansfield, Harvey C. and Winthrop, Delba, 'Editors' Introduction', in Tocqueville, Alexis de, *Democracy in America*, trans. and ed. Harvey C. Mansfield and Delba Winthrop (Chicago, IL: University of Chicago Press), xvii.

Hecht, Martin (1998), *Modernität und Bürgerlichkeit: Max Webers Freiheitslehre im Vergleich mit den politischen Ideen von Alexis de Tocqueville und Jean-Jacques Rousseau* (Berlin: Duncker and Humblot).

Jackson, Kenneth (1985), *Crabgrass Frontier: The Suburbanization of the United States* (New York: Oxford University Press).

Judt, Tony (1998), *The Burden of Responsibility: Blum, Camus, Aron and the French Twentieth Century* (Chicago, IL: University of Chicago Press).

Kahn, Joseph (2002), 'Some Chinese See the Future, and It's Capitalist', *New York Times*, 4 May, A17.

Lukes, Steven (1985), *Emile Durkheim: His Life and Work. A Historical and Critical Study* (Stanford, CA: Stanford University Press).

Mann, Michael (1986), *The Sources of Social Power*, vol. 1 (New York: Cambridge University Press.

Marx, Karl (1963 [1852]), *The Eighteenth Brumaire of Louis Bonaparte* (New York: International Publishers).

Michels, Robert (1959 [1910]), *Political Parties: A Sociological Study of the Oligarchical Tendencies in Modern Democracy* (New York: Dover).

Mommsen, Wolfgang J. (1984), *Max Weber and German Politics, 1890–1920*, trans. Michael S. Steinberg (Chicago, IL: University of Chicago Press).

Offe, Claus (2005), *Reflections on America: Tocqueville, Weber, and Adorno in the United States* (Malden, MA: Polity).

Parsons, Talcott (1977), *The Evolution of Societies*, ed. Jackson Toby (Englewood Cliffs, NJ: Prentice-Hall).

Podhoretz, Norman (1979), 'The Adversary Culture and the New Class', in Bruce-Briggs, B. (ed.), *The New Class?* (New York: McGraw-Hill).

Putnam, Robert (2000), *Bowling Alone: The Collapse and Revival of American Community* (New York: Simon & Schuster).

Schneider, Dieter and Kuda, Rudolf (1968), *Arbeiterräte in der Novemberrevolution: Ideen, Wirkungen, Dokumente* (Frankfurt: Suhrkamp).

Schumpeter, Joseph (1942), *Capitalism, Socialism, and Democracy* (New York: Harper and Brothers).

Skocpol, Theda (1979), *States and Social Revolutions* (New York: Cambridge University Press).

Tocqueville, Alexis de (1848), 'Speech to the Chamber of Deputies', 27 January, quoted in Tocqueville, Alexis de (1971), *Recollections*, trans. George Lawrence (Garden City, NY: Anchor).

Tocqueville, Alexis de (1971), *Recollections*, trans. George Lawrence (Garden City, NY: Anchor).

Tocqueville, Alexis de (1985), 'Recollections', in Jardin, André (ed.), *Oeuvres completes III: Écrits et discourse politiques*, vol. 2 (Paris : Gallimard).

Tocqueville, Alexis de (1997), *Memoir on Pauperism*, with an introduction by Gertrude Himmelfarb (Chicago, IL: Ivan R. Dee).

Tocqueville, Alexis de (1998 [1856]), *The Old Regime and the Revolution*, ed. with an introduction by François Furet and Françoise Mélonio, trans. Alan S. Kahan (Chicago, IL: University of Chicago Press).

Tocqueville, Alexis de (2000), *Democracy in America*, trans. and ed. Harvey C. Mansfield and Delba Winthrop (Chicago, IL: University of Chicago Press).

Torpey, John (2006), 'Alexis de Tocqueville, Forgotten Founder', *Sociological Forum* 21:4 (December), 695–707.

Tucker, Robert (ed.) (1978), 'Introduction to Marx and Engels, *The Communist Manifesto*', in *The Marx-Engels Reader* (New York: W.W. Norton).

Weber, Max (1946), 'Politics as a Vocation', in Gerth, Hans and Mills, C. Wright (eds), *From Max Weber* (New York: Oxford University Press).

Wolf, Eric (1982) *Europe and the People Without History* (Berkeley, CA: University of California Press).

Wolin, Sheldon (2001), *Tocqueville Between Two Worlds: The Making of a Political and Theoretical Life* (Princeton, NJ and Oxford: Princeton University Press).

Chapter 9
Tocqueville's Dark Shadow: Gustave de Beaumont as Public Sociologist and Intellectual *Avant la Lettre*

Tom Garvin and Andreas Hess

Introduction

Gustave de Beaumont (1802–1866) was, with his friend and lifelong co-worker Alexis de Tocqueville (1805–1859), one of the best-known social and political commentators in the world during the period 1830–65. Both men had French gentry backgrounds, and were best described as liberals in a rather interesting French Catholic tradition; both of them lived in a France whose aristocracy had lost power and which was apparently destined to adopt democratic institutions in the near future as the ideas of the French Revolution, the English and Scottish Enlightenments and those of the American republic's founding fathers worked their way into French intellectual and popular culture. Both men did their most important work during the reign of Louis-Philippe (1830–48), both being legitimists and therefore somewhat at odds with the Orleanist regime. Tocqueville is best-known for his monumental two-volume treatise on the United States, published in French as *De la démocratie en Amérique*, and almost simultaneously in English translation, between 1835 and 1840.[1] The book, an instant classic, has never been out of print, and has become a key work for the analysis of American society, political culture and the historical significance of the United States as a new, non-European, world power. Beaumont was, and is, less well known, and it is often not fully realized how closely they worked together, proof-reading, rewriting and commenting on each other's work-in-progress. The two Frenchmen were passionate admirers of Anglo-American representative institutions and constitutional traditions, being both in the Anglophile tradition of Montesquieu. They believed that the Americans, in particular, had evolved and put into practical use a constitutional system involving semi-democratic participation and the exercise of human rights to an extent unparalleled in the world of the early nineteenth century. They admired this liberal democratic system despite such evidently scandalous features as race-based slavery and the expropriation of native populations. This Anglo-Saxon democratic

1 There are now a few modern translations available. Particularly good ones are Tocqueville (1994) and Tocqueville (2003).

liberalism was seen by both men as being at once ahead of its time and as being a harbinger of the political future of a Europe still ruled mainly by aristocracies and absolute monarchs. The two Anglophiles had an informal division of labour; even though they were of one mind in recognizing the political creativity of the Anglo-American tradition, Beaumont did his most important work on the truly disadvantaged, slaves and Indians in America and the impoverished inhabitants of Ireland, while Tocqueville's most mature and powerful work addressed the larger questions of the societal and political institutional conditions of America and France.

The German-Jewish poet Heinrich Heine, in exile in Paris, found it difficult to warm to Alexis de Tocqueville. It seemed to him that Tocqueville had an aristocratic arrogance and certainty unbecoming of an academic scholar. By way of contrast, he found Tocqueville's friend Beaumont to be a far more attractive and warm person. However, historians of ideas in general have never paid much attention to a German poet's opinions of two famous Frenchmen. Even today, Tocqueville is still celebrated as the political prophet, the time traveller, the man who predicted an inevitable long-term tendency towards democratization in conjunction with the creation of modern mass societies, the emergence of the United States and Russia as superpowers in the twentieth century and the dangers of racism in a shadowy future united Germany. Beaumont, on the other hand, is usually sidelined as the rather shadowy travel companion of modern democracy's intellectual seer.

However, a rather different picture emerges on further investigation. Historical documentation demonstrates that the two men were actually almost inseparable throughout most of their adult lives; they shared their observations and research and debated every aspect of any intellectual conversation either of them might have had with any third party; in effect, they constituted a two-man Department of Political Sociology. They discussed every scholarly line either of them had written, whether together or separately. The history of ideas knows very few examples of such intimate intellectual companionship. Benjamin Constant and Madame de Staël, Karl Marx and Friedrich Engels, and Theodor W. Adorno and Max Horkheimer come to mind; but even these examples don't really parallel the extraordinarily intimate intellectual friendship between Tocqueville and Beaumont.

Students of Tocqueville have often paid lip service to Beaumont's oeuvre, but it is seldom given adequate appreciation and analysis.[2] In what follows, a short

2 Up to the present day not one study, PhD dissertation or biography is available that analyses Beaumont's work comprehensively. At present, the best studies containing material on Beaumont are: Drescher, *Tocqueville and England* (1964); from the same author, 'Tocqueville and Beaumont: A Rationale for Collective Study' (1968), and Pierson, *Tocqueville in America* (1996 [1938]). Pierson has also published an essay which tries to portray Beaumont: *Gustave de Beaumont: Liberal* (1946). Further helpful information is contained in Jardin, *Tocqueville – A Biography* (1988). Jardin also edited the three-volume set of the *Correspondance d'Alexis de Tocqueville et de Gustave de Beaumont* (Jardin, 1967). A more thorough study, particularly using the Tocqueville and Beaumont material

account of Beaumont's life and work as a public sociologist and intellectual is given. Particular emphasis is also given to his special intellectual relationship with Tocqueville. The initial success of Beaumont's first two books, *The Penitentiary System of the United States* (1833) and *Marie, or Slavery in the United States* (1835), is seen as providing a major breakthrough for his literary and academic reputation. In the second section, we will discuss Beaumont's most successful, and arguably most important, book – his pioneering 1839 study of pre-Famine Ireland – in context. Here it is argued that, although the Ireland study was one of the first sociological best-sellers in France and has become an important source for Irish and other historians working on nineteenth-century Ireland, it remains an almost forgotten classic in the wider academic world, deserving rediscovery and appreciation.[3] In the Conclusion we will argue that Beaumont was, together with his companion Tocqueville, an early example of what we would call today a 'public sociologist' and a 'public intellectual'.

Parallel Lives: Gustave de Beaumont and Alexis de Tocqueville

Gustave de Beaumont de Bonninière was born on 6 February 1802 at Beaumont-la-Chartre in the Sarthe. Beaumont's parents and family were both of French aristocratic background, and the family had always been linked to the more enlightened circles of the French upper class. Indeed, Lafayette, the famous aristocratic soldier who had fought alongside Washington against the British during the American War of Independence, was related to Beaumont's family, and an early American connection. Not much is known of how Beaumont spent his childhood. His first appearance on the historical record as an adult is as a *juge auditeur* and then as a deputy public prosecutor at the court of Versailles. It was also at Versailles that Beaumont first met Alexis de Tocqueville, a fellow student who had been pursuing a similar legal career. The two young men shared more than just the fact that both came from similar aristocratic backgrounds and were aspirant lawyers. They clicked personally, intellectually and politically; a friendship soon developed, and in the following years the two developed their fabled habit of reading and studying together. Both had an interest in political economy and were particularly taken by the theories of Jean-Baptiste Say. Again, both of them attended the history lectures of François Guizot, the renowned liberal historian. They were particularly influenced by Guizot's arguments concerning the history and course of French civilization.

---

that is available in the Yale Beinecke Library, is called for; this chapter cannot, of course, be a substitute for such a study.

3 A new edition of this book is now available; see Beaumont (2006). This chapter is an elaborated version of the introduction to the 2006 edition. Additionally, the present text highlights the public dimension of the activities of Beaumont.

The July Revolution (1830) brought an end to the reign of Charles X, and both young men were faced with difficult decisions. They had been forced to take an oath of loyalty to the new regime of Louis-Philippe; after much soul-searching, the two friends finally decided to take the oath in order to secure their legal careers. Since Tocqueville and Beaumont were deeply worried about the possible intentions of the new regime, they also began to make contingency plans. Part of their plan was, quite simply, to take some time out by getting away from France. Beaumont had already written a short study of the French prison system. In this pilot study, he had adumbrated a further, more detailed, investigation into prison systems from a comparative perspective. To their astonishment, the two friends actually received funding for their project. The pair were commissioned to travel together to America with the purpose of investigating the new prison systems of the United States to find out to what extent they resembled the French system and if there were any innovations which the French authorities might profitably study. In April 1831, the two friends left Le Havre for America, where they were to stay until February 1832.[4] They first arrived in New York, and spent the first few weeks in the city and its environs. From New York they went to Boston, Philadelphia, Baltimore and Washington before returning again to New York. Two further excursions were also part of the trip, one to the Northwest and Canada, and another down the Mississippi river to New Orleans.

The trip turned out to be a success in more than one respect. The two friends managed to gather plenty of information about prisons and the American penitentiary systems. However, the most important result of their journey was the discovery that the comparison of prison systems also provided the key to a new, democratic 'philosophy'. They argued that the way a penitentiary system treats its prisoners reveals how a regime treats its individual citizens or subjects in general. American prisons apparently attempted at that time to turn criminals into good citizens rather than simply mete out retribution or vengeance. This enlightened attitude was the true revelation of the New World in the eyes of the two Frenchmen: American institutions, American *mores* and attitudes, a new democratic and egalitarian approach to social relations which had evolved in the young United States, showed France (and Europe) its hoped-for future.

On their return to France in the Spring of 1832, Beaumont immediately started writing their joint report. Tocqueville at first found himself unable to put his own thoughts into writing; however, he contributed to the final stages of the draft and supplied statistics and other useful data. In the meantime the news had spread to their joint boss, the French state, that the pair were suffering from an apparently incurable new spiritual disease: love of democracy. Both found themselves peremptorily dismissed from their duties as public prosecutors. However, since

4 A primary source is G.W. Pierson's almost day-by-day reconstruction of the trip in his study *Tocqueville in America* (Pierson, 1996 [1938]). Particularly interesting in Pierson's book is the list of acquaintances and contacts, among them John Quincy Adams and Daniel Webster. They also had one meeting with the then President, Andrew Jackson.

both remained registered at the bar, this decision does not seem to have threatened their career prospects in any major way. As it turned out, the dismissal actually did them no harm at all.

Early in 1833, their report was finally published. *The Penitentiary System of the United States and its Application to France* proved to be an immediate success (see Beaumont and Tocqueville, 1964 [1833]). Francis Lieber, whom Tocqueville and Beaumont had met on their American trip, had translated the American edition. The study was widely discussed, and was awarded the prestigious Montyon Prize. Second and third editions followed in 1836 and 1844. Furthermore, the book soon appeared in translations; it was particularly widely read and appreciated in America and Germany. *The Penitentiary System* created a snowball effect that prompted the two friends to carry their studies further. While Beaumont embarked on a new project, a novel about the more tragic aspects of their American experiences, Tocqueville was writing his monumental book on American democracy.

In retrospect, it seems that the year 1835 saw a breakthrough for the two friends. In the Summer of 1833, Tocqueville travelled to England for the first time.[5] He had hoped that the former mother country England would provide further insight and perhaps provide some kind of intellectual key to an understanding of how the young American republic had been shaped. To his disappointment, no clear clues emerged during his first trip across the Channel. Furthermore, he was apparently treated like a nobody. However, two years later, Tocqueville's ship had come in, and he was received very differently; the first part of *Democracy in America* had finally appeared in France, and a translation had been published in England.[6] The book caused a sensation. In London, the two friends met the translator of *Democracy*, Henry Reeve. Other contacts proved to be equally crucial for getting to know English society and its political system; in particular the help and advice of two eminent political economists, John Stuart Mill and Nassau William Senior, were central.[7]

Tocqueville and Beaumont continued their travels as far as Ireland, where they toured for six weeks.[8] The two friends used Dublin as a base, staying in the city for a few days before starting on a round trip that would bring them first to the south (Carlow, Waterford, Kilkenny), then the south-west (Cork, Killarney), the west (Limerick, Ennis, Galway, Castlebar) and then via the midlands (Longford) back to Dublin. They seem to have skipped the North of Ireland. At the end of their stay in Ireland, Tocqueville and Beaumont also attended a meeting of the

---

5 The notes and diaries from the two trips to the British Isles have been published posthumously in Tocqueville (1988).

6 For more details, see Drescher (1964).

7 For a more detailed account on the various intellectual influences – not all of them British – see Michael Drolet's excellent study *Tocqueville, Democracy and Social Reform* (2003).

8 A detailed reconstruction of this trip can be found in Larkin (1990) and Drescher (1964).

British Association for the Advancement of Science at Trinity College Dublin.[9] While travelling together, they also talked about their publication plans for the future. They agreed on two things. Firstly, they established that they would respect each other's publication plans and individual research interests. Beaumont would write on the unfulfilled promises of American democracy, the plight of African Americans and American Indians, and the colonial relationship between England and Ireland, while Tocqueville would focus mainly on America's political system and the prospects for both American and European democracy. Secondly, to prevent possible misunderstandings, overlapping of research effort or any intellectual turf war, they decided also that they would make a point of showing each other their work before publication.

The year 1835 not only saw Tocqueville's publication of the first volume of *Democracy in America*, but also the publication of Beaumont's *Marie, or Slavery in the United States*.[10] While *Democracy* looked mainly at America's political system, *Marie* was an attempt to take a closer look at the seamier side of American society. The two books have to be read as companion volumes in order to make complete sense of America, or rather, to grasp the two men's joint understanding of the country. *Marie,* like *Democracy in America*, was a huge success and was reprinted numerous times in French over the following decades. However, *Marie* remained almost unknown in America for over a century; American slavery was apparently a more popular topic in Europe, and to put it gently, the book did not harmonize well with American tendencies toward self-congratulation. The two books paid off in career terms; Tocqueville's tome got him elected to the French Academy of Moral and Political Sciences, thus emulating Beaumont's Montyon Prize.[11] The two friends also made a promising start to their political careers by being elected to the French Parliament.

---

9 Although it cannot be confirmed by any records available to the writers, it is probable that Beaumont met his future translator William Taylor (1800–1849) at this academic gathering. William Cooke Taylor was a writer and economist. Taylor had been educated at Trinity College Dublin, but later moved to London, where he became a contributor to the Whig–Liberal, reform-oriented weekly *Athenaeum*. Throughout his life he remained supportive of the Irish cause, following a liberal and reformist agenda and being particularly keen on furthering Irish higher education. He is also known as the founder of the Dublin Society for Statistical and Social Inquiry, which still exists. Two of his books dealt particularly with Ireland: *History of the Civil Wars in Ireland* (1831) and *Reminiscences of Daniel O'Connell by a Munster Farmer* (1847). His magnum opus was *The Natural History of Civilisation* (1840), in which he argued that mankind was created by God to be civilized, and that savagery is not a natural condition, but rather the product of ignorance.

10 For editions and translations of Tocqueville's *Democracy in America*, see note 1 above. Gustave de Beaumont's slavery book has been reissued recently in English; see Beaumont (1999 [1958]).

11 Their publishing triumphs were also accompanied by personal fulfilment; Beaumont married his cousin, Clémentine de Lafayette, the granddaughter of General Lafayette, while Tocqueville married an Englishwoman, Mary Motley.

During the summer of 1837, Beaumont travelled a second time to England and Ireland, this time on his own, to gather material for his Ireland project. Two years later, *L'Irlande* finally appeared as a two-volume study (Beaumont, 1839a). Taylor's translation of the book into English was published later that year.[12] It turned out to be an intellectual *tour de force*, and proved to be even more of a hit than his first two studies. During Beaumont's own lifetime, the book saw seven French reprints, and once again the author was awarded the Montyon Prize for his new book. Beaumont also became a member of the French Academy of Moral and Political Sciences.

Quite apart from their publishing record and their political and academic achievements, Tocqueville and Beaumont remained true liberals dedicated to social reform. Unlike many other liberals, however, they also remained internationalist; their opinions were not confined to internal French issues, and they argued publicly, for example, against the excesses and abuses of an emergent French colonialism. By now the two friends had perfected their division of labour, by which the two men acted as a team, complementing and supporting each other's efforts. Thus, for example, Tocqueville presented a report on the abolition of slavery to Parliament while Beaumont simultaneously presented a petition to the Chamber on behalf of the French Abolitionist Society. In 1841, they both travelled to Algeria, again an experience that would lead to both looking for more coherent and humane French policies in North Africa. Tocqueville and Beaumont were later to become members of the parliamentary commission on Algeria, and they always remained interested in the subject as long as their political careers lasted.[13]

The Revolution of 1848 ushered in the Second Republic. Tocqueville and Beaumont both became members of the new National Assembly, and both were selected to join the Constitutional Commission. In the following year, Beaumont was appointed Special Ambassador to the United Kingdom and became based in London, while Tocqueville became France's Minister for Foreign Affairs. However, this improvement in political status and achievement didn't last for very long. In 1851, after Louis Napoleon seized power and declared himself emperor, both men were simultaneously forced to resign. They were arrested and imprisoned for opposing Louis Napoleon's coup d'état against the Second Republic. Their arrests, and their almost comically prompt releases, marked their withdrawal from public affairs and the end of two remarkable political careers.

Tocqueville retreated to his home on the countryside and continued his intellectual reflections, *Souvenirs* (written in 1850–51, published posthumously

---

12 See Beaumont (1839b); for further information on a new edition of the English translation, see Beaumont (2006).

13 Their unique personal and intellectual friendship only once suffered a rather trivial crisis. The spat was caused by a disagreement about the editorial policies of *Le Commerce*, a newspaper that Tocqueville took a particularly strong interest in. However, there was a quick reconciliation.

in 1893)[14] and *L'Ancien Régime* (1856)[15] being the results. Beaumont was less fortunate, and found that he could not devote all his time to writing. He had to attend to financial matters out of economic necessity connected with a legally encumbered inheritance of his father-in-law, Georges de Lafayette; this unpleasant experience seems to have informed his quite strong grasp of Irish land law, the plight of Irish encumbered estates and the malign social consequences of the interaction of land law and indebtedness, as is illustrated rather vividly in his 1863 introduction to the seventh edition of *L'Irlande*. Occasionally, Beaumont managed to surface from his retreat. Thus, in 1854 he presented a longer meditation entitled *La Russie et les États-Unis* to the Academy of Moral and Political Science – once again the paper seems to have been in part the result of a long discussion with Alexis.

After Tocqueville's death in January 1859, Gustave began editing his friend's published and unpublished writings. Six volumes appeared between in the early 1860s.[16] Preoccupied as he was with these editorial efforts, Beaumont seems to have found less time to voice his concern for the oppressed and the excluded. Only once more would he succeed in making this concern public. Shocked and disappointed about British attitudes to the Irish tragedy after the Famine, he presented the Irish case (*Notice sur l'état présent de L'Irlande*) to the Academy of Moral and Political Science in 1863, and a longer version of this presentation was to become the introduction to the seventh edition of *L'Irlande* (Beaumont, 1863, i–lxxxiv).[17] The *Notice* is an old man's impassioned protest at the plight of Ireland combined with an optimism derived from, as ever, his somewhat uncritical admiration for the English constitution. As far as is known, this was Beaumont's last major public utterance before his death on 22 February 1866 in Paris.

Parallel Lives, Different Intellectual Passions

Tocqueville and Beaumont were intellectual equals; only history and circumstance have occluded Beaumont's very real intellectual eminence. Back in 1835, some time in the summer on their joint travels in England and Ireland, Tocqueville and Beaumont had carved out their respective intellectual territories and also reached an agreement concerning their respective future publication plans. As we have seen,

14 The first American edition is Alexis de Tocqueville, *Recollections* (1970); as pointed out above, *Souvenirs* was first published in 1893 and is now volume 12 of the *Collected Works* of the Gallimard edition (ed). J.P. Mayer, (1964).

15 The first American edition is Tocqueville, *The Old Regime and the French Revolution* (1969); the book was first published in Paris in 1856 (Michel Lévy Frères).

16 Tocqueville (1860–66); a rare two-volume selection of Beaumont's edited collection appeared in the US in 1862.

17 This post-Famine comment has now been translated into English and is part of the new Beaumont edition (see Beaumont, 2006, 379–403).

Tocqueville was to address the political systems and the development of modern democracies in France and the United States, while Beaumont was to investigate the less attractive side of the process, in particular by looking at America, Britain and Ireland. In the case of the United States, this meant the treatment of slaves and Indians; in relation to the British Isles, it meant dissecting the peculiar political arrangements and links that England had with Ireland.

It is exactly this joint agreement which throws light on the different political and intellectual preoccupations of the two friends. As demonstrated by the first publication on the American and French penitentiary systems (for which, despite common authorship, Beaumont had mainly been responsible), Beaumont was clearly more interested in the downside of modern democracy and the plight of the underdog, while Tocqueville was equally obviously fascinated by the possibly larger question of the future of democracy. The comparative study demonstrated that Beaumont understood himself as a liberal, but as also an advocate of the wretched of the earth: those who had either been omitted from, or who had been marginalized by, the democratic process. In *Marie*, a strange mixture of romantic narrative and critical political and sociological reflection, Beaumont had addressed the negative side of American society in particular. This concern with the victims of democratic or semi-democratic societies is perhaps what most clearly distinguishes Gustave intellectually and emotionally from Alexis. A similar sensitivity toward the weak occasionally shows through in Tocqueville's *Democracy*, but is never the main thrust of his discourse. In *Marie*, Beaumont persistently emphasizes the normative content of the Declaration of Independence, the Constitution and the Bill of Rights in the sense that all these founding documents had either presupposed or promised political equality. He was shocked by the contrast between their high aspirations and the rather grubby realities of American politics; he noted bluntly that the documents remained mere rhetoric when it came to the systematic dispossession of the Indians and the equally systematic mass enslavement of black people. Thus, it should not come as a complete surprise that the American edition of *Marie* took more than 120 years to appear in print (1958, to be precise), its re-publication coinciding, probably not by accident, with the emerging civil rights movement.[18] It is also only around the same time that it finally dawned on some that *Marie* and *Democracy* actually had to be regarded as companion volumes and needed to be studied together.

Of course, the American critics and reviewers who belatedly welcomed Beaumont's sociological novel had a point: *Marie* had to be interpreted as the much-needed corrective to Tocqueville's omissions in his *Democracy*; however, such late and posthumous success came at a price. While American critics praised Beaumont's book as a classic and as a forerunner to the emerging civil rights movement, they seemed quite unaware of the success his work on British rule in

18 On American self-criticism and intermittent angry awareness of the lack of congruence between American political ideals and the sometimes squalid and brutal realities of American life, see in particular Huntington (1981).

Ireland had enjoyed in Europe during his lifetime. *Marie* had been celebrated in France when it first appeared there. Viewed retrospectively, however, it was no match whatsoever for the book on Ireland.

The reasons for the Ireland book becoming a sociological bestseller are twofold; one explanation relates to form, the other one to content. In terms of form, the success of the Ireland study can be partly explained through Beaumont's unique way of presenting his material and findings that resembled very much what in contemporary social science would be called 'thick description' (Clifford Geertz). Beaumont's thick description consisted of a mix and wide range of readings and possible interpretations, usually derived from a broad variety of sources. Detailed note-taking, interviews with experts and other knowledgeable sources, direct observation, the collection and careful study of secondary sources such as journals, government reports, books and studies, as well as detailed notes from travel books and diaries – they all contributed to the final draft. Often tentative arguments and intellectual trial-balloons were sent to Tocqueville in the form of letters or reports, just to await his friend's response and to include or further elaborate on a given theme. In addition to the modern form of 'thick description', the success of *L'Irlande* could also lie in the structure of the book – the political constellation and history were described first, followed by a second part which looked at the present societal conditions; this scheme very much resembles the structure of Tocqueville's *Democracy in America*.

In terms of content, *Marie* had shed light on the problematic aspects of American democracy, *L'Irlande* had an obvious European context. The book made it starkly obvious that even the 'oldest democracy in the world', the United Kingdom, had, to put it mildly, a negative side. Of course, it could be argued, more or less *ad hominem* and quite unfairly, that Beaumont's study and its reception were mainly an expression of French national pride. It could even be argued that, by their enthusiasm for his study of the plight of the Irish, his French readers were showing an ancient antipathy toward *l'Albion perfide*. However, nothing could be further from the author's intentions. As we have seen, like Alexis and like their common intellectual predecessor Montesquieu, Beaumont showed a deep but perhaps somewhat uncritical admiration for the political system of the United Kingdom. Indeed, it is exactly this admiration that helps to explain the immediate success of his book on Ireland. In *L'Irlande*, Beaumont hits all the emotional registers, he weighs all the pros and cons, he appears to be Britain's advocate and uses all available arguments for the defence of the British government's policies in Ireland, but finally he gives up and concludes reluctantly that Ireland was to the United Kingdom what slavery was to the United States; Ireland was that ironic and tragic entity, a persecuted martyr nation in a free polity. His instinct for the underdog drove his impassioned preface of 1863. In fact, he has been accused of exaggerating the pre-Famine poverty of the Irish; while the potato was free of blight, the Irish were actually unusually well fed, it has been argued, and the Famine came like a bolt from the blue.[19]

However, there had been earlier failures, and 1847 followed two years of partial failure; the British Government had had some warnings from Mother Nature, *pace* Joel Mokyr. There has been no famine in Ireland since 1848, but prior to the Great Hunger, famine had been endemic on the island for over a century; back in 1740 one quarter of the population was carried away in a huge famine, and smaller starvations occurred every few years over the subsequent century. Near genocidal dying-offs had occurred on the island in the sixteenth and seventeenth centuries. Since 1900, it appears, perhaps rather weirdly, that the Irish are among the best-fed people on the planet.

Beaumont pursues two lines of argument in *L'Irlande*. In the first part, he outlines how over the course of nearly three centuries the English conquerors and the Anglo-Irish aristocracy ('the Ascendancy') that took over the island never quite legitimized themselves. Naturally, this tiny and fantastically privileged minority were going to be resented by the mainly folk-Catholic aboriginals, and even by people of lower status who happened to be Protestant by religion. However, this privileged minority attempted to constitute itself as the Irish nation *toute courte* in the eighteenth century, ignoring the teeming millions of men and women of no property below it with their covertly expressed collective ideology of dispossession and sullen dreams of *revanchisme*, commonly expressed in Gaelic prose, poetry and verse.[20] The Ascendancy essentially drifted between two extreme poles: social, political and religious indifference to the dispossessed native Irish on the one hand, and a passionate wish to exterminate Irish popery by a policy of proselytism on the other.[21] Thus, the English Ascendancy in the conquered island was never able to conceive of a majoritarian project which might have made it possible to assimilate the Catholic majority to its colonial polity, whether during the Cromwellian period, during the Restoration, during the period of Grattan's Parliament (1782–1800) or even during the period that was, as it turned out, the time of the Ascendancy's last chance: the early years of the parliamentary union of Britain and Ireland after 1800. Edmund Burke's famous pleas for religious tolerance fell on deaf ears, as did the more pragmatic private warnings of the Duke of Wellington. Furthermore, while the aristocracy in England was much more open and acceptant of the industrialization of Britain, in Ireland the landed Anglo-Irish aristocracy was reluctant or unable to get involved in such enterprise, with the usual exception of the north-east, where a true cross-class Protestant community

19 See Mokyr (1985), 6–29. The literature on the Irish famine is vast; however, see also Edwards and Williams (1962); Woodham-Smith (1962); O'Gráda (1998).

20 See O'Buachalla (1996) on both old Catholic aristocratic and popular Irish-speaking attitudes to the supposedly legitimate Catholic monarch of the Three Kingdoms, but a king also seen as *Séamus Cachach*, or 'Shitty Jimmy'.

21 For a vivid illustration of English proselytism and hatred of Catholicism in Ireland in the early nineteenth century, see Tonna (2004).

containing a significant Presbyterian tradition had grown up and developed a preoccupation with British-style modernization and industrialization. However, the mainly Scottish-derived plantation in Ulster did not have much impact on Irish society outside the north-eastern region of the island.

In the second part of his Irish study, Beaumont describes the political and social constellations that arose from this seemingly irresolvable dilemma. Again and again he stresses that through English colonization, Ireland had also been given all the constitutional tools to free herself from colonial oppression. Daniel O'Connell had grasped that fact as a young man, and for thirty years between 1815 and 1845 had wrested concessions from an unwilling Protestant ascendancy in both islands by means of a lethal, very Irish and brilliant blend of mass popular agitation, liberal political principles and constitutional argument; like the Irish poor, Beaumont admired the beloved Dan, 'King of the Beggars' and the charismatic leader of the emergent Irish democracy.[22] However, in the end Beaumont remained sceptical about the prospect of any real sea change in the powerful landed aristocracy of Ireland. It seemed to be too out of touch, too arrogant and too unwilling to learn from past mistakes; like the Bourbons, it learned nothing and forgot nothing. Repeatedly, he referred to the Irish aristocracy as being essentially a collective tyranny.

Much as Tocqueville had pointed unerringly to central and unique aspects of American social and political culture, Beaumont gave a thoroughgoing and vividly written diagnosis of the Irish disease. Despite his admiration for Anglo-Saxon constitutionalism, his book could possibly have been legitimately entitled, following de Tocqueville's famous title *De la démocratie en Amérique*, *De la tyrannie en Irlande*. The country was agrarian, the land was controlled by what he termed a 'bad aristocracy', an aristocracy hampered by being derived from a recent and remembered conquest, alien in nationality, language, religion and culture from the vast bulk of the underlying population. The landlords despised the lower orders, and the latter returned the compliment with a ferocious blend of covert contempt and hatred masked by an apparently genial subservience. This arrogant aristocratic tyranny used the law and the soldiery to enforce its exploitation of the vast majority, who defended themselves in the only way they could: by collective solidarity, secret combination, threats, assassination and mass agitation. This discredited ruling class, pathetically dependent on British support, was, by the time of the famine, politically illegitimate. It was also incompetent and helpless because of the vicious stalemate that dominated Irish property relations, a stalemate brilliantly described by Beaumont, particularly in his 1863 Introduction.

L'Irlande is, of course, very much a work of its time, and Irish historians and social scientists have revised and revised again Beaumont's diagnosis over the past century and a half. However, the basic thrust of the book has not really been shaken decisively by later works. In fact, if one looks at the work of modern Irish alleged

22 On this extraordinary Irish liberal democratic leader, see Trench (1986). See also O'Connell (1991); O'Ferrall (1985). The classic rehabilitation of O'Connell in the face of his hypernationalist republican detractors is O'Faoláin (1938), since reissued many times.

revisionists such as Roy Foster, Dermot Keogh or Tom Garvin, it is striking how much they have actually built on Beaumont's basic insights, perhaps unconsciously. *L'Irlande* cannot fairly be compared to *Démocratie*, because the two writers set themselves very different tasks. It could be argued that Tocqueville was time-travelling forwards, whereas Beaumont was looking to the future, but Ireland made him look into the deep Irish past; Beaumont had a tougher row to hoe.[23]

On reflection, however, the case of Beaumont and Ireland is more complicated than that of Tocqueville and America. What took the form of an early constitutional promise in America, to be realized only over generations and after civil war and a century of discrimination and political struggle, was fought for even more bitterly

---

23 Like most of de Tocqueville's prophecies concerning American democracy, most, but not all, of de Beaumont's prophecies concerning Ireland came to pass. The Irish Famine of the 1840s radicalized the Catholic majority further. It also caused the British government to finally write off the Irish Ascendancy. After 1850, Westminster tried to change horses in Ireland and side with the vast peasant-cum-farmer majority against the landlords. Following on O'Connell's precedent, a series of mass movements agitating for land reform and a native government ('Home Rule') emerged. Beaumont foresaw the land reform, and prophesied the emergence of an Ireland of small owner-occupier farmers, as duly happened in the period 1880–1903. However, he also expected the Irish to settle down after land reform as part of a British–Irish constitutional democracy. Strangely enough, he did not foresee the rise of a large, successful and vengeful Irish American community in the United States that willingly encouraged and financed Irish militant insurgents from 1865 on. Just after Beaumont's death, Irish veterans of the Union Army led the Fenian rising of 1867, which attempted to transform Ireland into an independent republic; these ex-soldiers were referred to respectfully in Ireland as 'the men with the square-toed [G.I.] boots'. A covert, and later overt, hatred of the British government continued to flourish in Ireland as well as in Irish America; the Famine had partially delegitimized the British state in Ireland. Beaumont never fully appreciated this fact, but of course, he could not have foreseen the calamity of 1914.

Because of the First World War, which destabilized most of Europe, Ireland descended, with much of the rest of the Continent, into revolution, civil war and sectarian pogrom after 1918. Eventually, an Irish independent democratic state emerged in 1922, shorn of the north-eastern counties with their very different culture and social structure. This new country rapidly evolved into a republican democracy of Catholic yeoman farmers with democratic institutions heavily influenced by both British and American prototypes. The landed ascendancy died out, leaving behind a formidable cultural heritage; the great houses of the aristocracy were burned down, turned into convents, used as schools or, eventually, converted into hotels, spas and golf clubs. Despite many backslidings, most of twentieth-century Ireland had achieved an ambivalent freedom, or as Michael Collins, the Irish revolutionary leader, famously put it in a presumably unconscious echoing of Beaumont, the freedom to achieve freedom. However, the sectarian curse of old Ireland lived on in Northern Ireland, and has yet to be clearly lifted from Ulster society. Still, in both parts of Ireland equal rights and liberty for all citizens were no longer revolutionary demands, but had gradually become practical achievements, in the south in the 1920s and in the north sixty years later. Versions of the English constitution worked in interestingly different ways in both parts of Ireland to enable a gradual liberalization and equalization of society to be engineered over the generations.

in a Europe that had to build democracy in the face of the stubborn resistance of ancient entrenched agrarian aristocracies with great social, cultural and intellectual power. However, the messenger should not be blamed for the bad news; Gustave de Beaumont, Ireland's Tocqueville, has given us a classic account of the painful birth pangs of Irish democracy, Ireland providing in miniature a model of the struggle for democracy against feudalism in Europe.[24]

Beaumont as a Public Sociologist and Intellectual *Avant la Lettre*

Beaumont certainly deserves to be rediscovered and given intellectual recognition by the English-speaking world; after all, he could easily be termed the discursive father of Irish sociology, and certainly a father of the wider field of comparative sociology. However, it is not only his publications – and, as we have argued, particularly the Ireland book – that needs to be rediscovered. Beaumont was also an early prototype and representative of what we today would call a 'public sociologist' or 'public intellectual'. Beaumont, and indeed Tocqueville, constantly moved back and forth between political engagement and sociological discovery. It is this back-and-forth movement between the two spheres, constantly informing each other, yet without reducing one dimension to the other, that is one of the most interesting aspects of Beaumont's and Tocqueville's public life. Modern reflection on the role of the public face of the social sciences often tends to forget that sociology's role should neither be reduced to becoming a mere intellectual stimulus or conceptual service station to practical politics, nor should politics be limited to merely translating and applying sociological insights. Particularly flawed in this respect seems to be Michael Burawoy's rather instrumental call for public sociology in his 2004 presidential address to the American Sociological Association.[25] It seems that Burawoy just made another attempt to rescue Marxist arguments for the twenty-first century.

In contrast to such instrumental reasoning, the crucial task is to bring sociology and politics into a critical dialogue with each other, but without making one sphere or field a simple instrument of the other. What is important is that there be some form of border maintenance between the two spheres. A call for public sociology that goes back to the liberal ideas of Beaumont and Tocqueville seems to us to be more inspiring and appropriate than going back to a monistic Marxist view that has no notion of how differentiated the modern civil sphere has become. (For an account of how differentiated the civil sphere has become and the role intellectual argument can play in it, see particularly Alexander's new study, *The Civil Sphere*, 2006.) Yet within the liberal approach that Tocqueville and Beaumont proposed,

24 For a comparative discussion of the much taken for granted but actually somewhat problematic birth of Irish democracy, see Garvin (1996).

25 See Burawoy's rallying calls 'Public Sociology: Contradictions, Dilemmas and Possibilities' (2004) and 'For Public Sociology' (2005).

we can also distinguish between two positions. In contrast to Tocqueville, who saw that democracy creates its own dilemmas while striving for equality, Beaumont's looks at and describes in detail what is often only hinted at and what remains conspicuously absent from his companion's account. Arguing in favour of liberal ideas and institutions, Beaumont was indeed the first public sociologist and intellectual who actually looked critically into the neglected dark side of the struggle for liberal democracy.

References

Alexander, Jeffrey C. (2006), *The Civil Sphere* (New York: Oxford University Press).

Beaumont, Gustave de (1839a), *L'Irlande – social, politique et religieuse* (Paris: Michel Levy Frères).

Beaumont, Gustave de (1839b), *Ireland – Social, Political and Religious*, ed. W.C. Taylor (London: Richard Bentley).

Beaumont, Gustave de (1863): *L'Irlande – sociale, politique, et religieuse*, 7th edn (Paris: Michel Levy Frères).

Beaumont, Gustave de (1999 [1958]), *Marie, or Slavery in the United States* (Baltimore, MD: Johns Hopkins University Press).

Beaumont, Gustave de (2006), *Ireland*, with a new introduction by Tom Garvin and Andreas Hess (Cambridge, MA: Belknap Press of Harvard University Press).

Beaumont, Gustave de and Tocqueville, A. de (1964 [1833]), *On the Penitentiary System of the United States and its Application to France* (Carbondale, IL: Southern Illinois University Press).

Burawoy, Michael (2004), 'Public Sociology: Contradictions, Dilemmas and Possibilities', *Social Forces* 82, 1603–18.

Burawoy, Michael (2005), 'For Public Sociology', *American Sociological Review* 70, 2–28.

Drescher, Seynour (1964), *Tocqueville and England* (Cambridge, MA: Harvard University Press).

Drescher, Seymour (1968), 'Tocqueville and Beaumont: A Rationale for Collective Study', in: Drescher, S. (ed.) *Tocqueville and Beaumont on Social Reform* (New York: Harper and Row), 201–17.

Drolet, Michael (2003), *Tocqueville, Democracy and Social Reform* (Houndmills: Palgrave Macmillan).

Edwards, R. Dudley and Williams, T. Desmond (eds) (1957), *The Great Famine* (New York: New York University Press).

Garvin, Tom (1996), *1922: The Birth of Irish Democracy* (Dublin: Gill and Macmillan).

Huntington, Samuel P. (1981), *American Politics: The Promise of Disharmony*, (Cambridge MA: Belknap Press of Harvard University Press).

Jardin, A. (ed.) (1967), *Correspondance d'Alexis de Tocqueville et de Gustave de Beaumont* (Paris: Gallimard).

Jardin, A. (1988), *Tocqueville – A Biography* (Baltimore, MD: Johns Hopkins University Press).

Larkin, E. (1990), *Alexis de Tocqueville's Journey to Ireland* (Dublin: Wolfhound Press).

Mokyr, Joel (1985), *Why Ireland Starved* (London: Allen and Unwin).

O'Buachalla, Breandan (1996), *Aisling Ghéar: na Stiobhartaigh agus an tAois Léinn, 1603–1788* ['Sharp Vision: The Stuarts and the Intellectuals, 1603–1788'] (Dublin: Clochomhar).

O'Connell, Maurice R. (ed.) (1991), *Daniel O'Connell: Political Pioneer* (Dublin: Institute of Public Administration).

O'Faoláin, Seán (1938), *King of the Beggars: A Life of Daniel O'Connell, the Irish Liberator, in a Study of the Rise of Irish Democracy (1775–1847)* (London: Nelson).

O'Ferrall, Fergus (1985), *Catholic Emancipation: Daniel O'Connell and the Birth of Irish Democracy* (Dublin: Gill and Macmillan).

O'Gráda, Cormac (1998), *The Black '47 and Beyond: The Great Irish Famine in History, Economy and Memory* (Princeton, NJ: Princeton University Press).

Pierson, G.W. (1946), 'Gustave de Beaumont: Liberal', *Franco-American Review* I:37, 307–16.

Pierson, G.W. (1996 [1938]), *Tocqueville in America* (Baltimore, MD: Johns Hopkins University Press).

Tocqueville, Alexis de (1860–66), *Oeuvres complètes D'Alexis de Tocqueville*, ed. Gustave de Beaumont (Paris: Michel Lévy Frères).

Tocqueville, Alexis de (1862), *Memoirs, Letters, and Remains*, ed. Gustave de Beaumont (Boston, MA: Ticknor and Fields).

Tocqueville, Alexis de (1969), *The Old Regime and the French Revolution* (New York: Doubleday).

Tocqueville, Alexis de (1970), *Recollections*, ed. J.P. Mayer and A.P. Kerr (New York: Doubleday).

Tocqueville, Alexis de (1988), *Journeys to England and Ireland*, ed. J.P. Mayer (New Brunswick, NJ: Transaction).

Tocqueville, Alexis de (1994), *Democracy in America*, trans. George Lawrence, ed. J.P. Mayer (London: Fontana Press).

Tocqueville, Alexis de (2003), *Democracy in America*, trans. Gerald E. Bevan, ed. and introduced by Isaac Kramnick (London: Penguin).

Tonna, Charlotte Elizabeth (2004), *Irish Recollections* (Dublin: University College Dublin Press); first published as *Personal Recollections* (1841).

Trench, Charles Chenevix (1986), *The Great Dan* (London: Triad Grafton).

Woodham-Smith, Cecil (1962), *The Great Hunger: Ireland 1845–1849* (London: Hamilton).

Chapter 10

French Sociologists and the Public Space of the Press: Thoughts Based on a Case Study (*Le Monde*, 1995–2002)

Laurent Jeanpierre and Sébastien Mosbah-Natanson

Introduction

Recent studies in comparative history tend to support the hypothesis of a specifically French national mode of engagement of the intellectual professions and of their place in the social structure (see Charle, 1996). It is in France, as is well known, that, at the time of the Dreyfus Affair at the end of the nineteenth century, the neologism 'intellectual' was coined and that a heterogeneous social group, made up of thinkers and writers, used it to oppose the traditional elites, in particular those in possession of economic power (see Charle, 1990, 163–82). For a long time, being an intellectual in France was based on the fact of speaking out in public in the name of universal values, using a legitimacy acquired in a specific professional field of the intellectual world, as in the case of Zola upon his famous publication of 'J'accuse' (1898). Other forms of intervention by professional intellectuals have undoubtedly been developed over the last century. But this initial model of engagement has been maintained in contemporary national public life. In this chapter we ask how it is socially structured and organized today. This chapter deals more particularly with the public engagement of sociologists in France. It considers one aspect of this issue: stances taken in newspaper op-ed columns. We focus on the op-ed columns of only one large daily newspaper, *Le Monde*, between 1995 and 2002.[1] In the French political and public context, the year 1995 witnessed the intense engagement of certain intellectuals with social movements of the time, a mobilization that has already been the subject of sociological analysis (see Duval et al., 1998; Legavre, 1999). Therefore, it appeared that this year and the studies formerly carried out could serve as a first point of comparison which would be of relevance for our own results, seeking to treat a longer time span.

On the basis of this case study, we shall firstly situate the commentary of sociologists in relation to that of the other intellectual professions. Then, the main factors determining the behaviour of French sociologists in *Le Monde* over recent years will be analysed. Finally, we aim to identify the traits – in

1 For a comparison between the French and the Italian case, see Lettieri (2002).

particular the themes – that may characterize the modes of intervention of French sociologists in the national daily press.

Methodology

In order to evaluate the position and role of sociologists in the contemporary French public sphere, we decided to carry out an analysis of the interventions in debates in the daily newspaper *Le Monde*. Using the newspaper's CD–ROMs, we constructed a database containing the opinions published in the 'Horizons-Débats' pages between 1995 and 2002. For the most part, these pages publish columns, similar to the 'op-ed' pages of Anglo-American newspapers.[2] There is no freedom of access to the column, which is in fact managed by one editorial journalist who selects columns on the basis of proposals received. She or he is actually the gatekeeper or even the producer of the op-ed section. Personalities gain the right to write in it, and through this, attain the status of public intellectual. The words published in the opinion pages must, furthermore, be individually or collectively signed, or taken responsibility for in the name of a group. In the newspaper studied, individual bylines must also be followed by a title or post. This signature takes on the role of a veritable 'discourse on discourse', and allows for the representation made by the intellectuals of their position in the social space, and on this occasion the public sphere, to be situated.[3]

The articles which appeared in the opinion pages of *Le Monde* can be broken down and analysed in terms of the following intellectual professions: economists,[4] writers, historians,[5] philosophers, political scientists, psychologists,[6] sociologists.[7]

2 These commentaries, solicited or selected by the newspaper, were also supplemented by some less frequent pages of interviews under the same general op-ed format and called *Horizons-Entretiens* ('interviews'). They also reflect the representation that the newspaper constructs of people with the most legitimacy to have their words published.

3 On the social role of the signature, see Fraenkel (1992).

4 We have excluded signatories of texts with the title 'lecturer in economic sciences' and probably underestimated the number of economists who do not work in higher education or scientific institutions, but rather for banks or insurance companies. We have also excluded business, management or finance professionals. Intellectuals with multiple affiliations (a Professor of Economics and Business, for instance) were included with the economists.

5 Historians of art and of science were excluded from the study. In the French university system, their training and recruitment follow different patterns from those of historians.

6 In addition to psychologists and teachers of psychology, we included psychoanalysts and psychotherapists. We did not take psychiatrists into account, as their primary training in medicine is further away from the human and social sciences that are the focus of our study.

7 Ethnologists and anthropologists were not included. A first survey of the database of columns allowed us to see that these professions were always less well represented than those we selected for inclusion in this study.

The first selection was made on the basis of 'self–presentations', in the Goffmanian sense, chosen by the authors themselves (see Goffman, 1959 [1956]). It is not unusual to observe intellectuals changing self-presentation on the basis of circumstance or the 'cause' being defended.[8] In all of the professional fields selected, professors and the holders of various teaching positions at secondary or tertiary levels, as well as students, were added from the outset wherever their disciplinary affiliation was indicated. In order to limit the omission of professionals in the social and human sciences, we also specifically added people with an affiliation to the *Centre national de la recherche scientifique* (CNRS) or the *École des hautes études en sciences sociales* (EHESS) and explicitly coming from disciplines in the social sciences which appear in the public organigrams of these institutions or of their research centres.[9] This means that while self-presentation remained the criterion for the professional categorization of position that prevailed, it was also crossed, during the primary phase of the study, with another criterion: affiliation to teaching and research in social science institutions.

In order to avoid any suspicion of professional ethnocentrism or bias, we applied this last criterion most rigorously to sociologists themselves. The number of interventions they made was therefore slightly underestimated. During the study's second phase, we excluded from the final breakdown those who presented themselves as sociologists or as holding a title or an equivalent position but having never appeared in a scientific journal of the discipline in recent decades.[10] Taking into account the proximity in France between sociology and political science, the same restrictive criterion had also to be applied to political scientists. In several cases, it was difficult to determine if people belonged to one discipline or the other, as instances of cross- and dual affiliations were rather frequent. In the same way, columnists who declared themselves teachers of 'political sociology' were classified in both disciplines, and consequently counted twice.

In addition to the margins of error regarding the breakdown of intellectual professions contributing to op-ed sections, a further limitation of our study, related

8 Therefore, in the relatively numerous cases of dual self-definitions ('philosopher and writer', 'sociologist and historian'), we decided to classify the author under all the fields she or he claimed to represent. We therefore from the outset prevented ourselves from judging the legitimacy of the self-definitions given. As a result, multiple self-definitions do not figure more heavily in any field in particular.

9 Other institutions were added in the case of political scientists – the *Fondation nationale des sciences politiques* (FNSP), the *Centre d'études et de recherches internationales* (CERI) and the *Centre d'étude de la vie politique française* (CEVIPOF). To be sure, our breakdowns tend to underestimate specialists of cultural regions. It appeared to us that their disciplinary skills, as sociologists, political scientists, geographers, historians, economists or anthropologists, were secondary to their knowledge of a specific territorial domain.

10 The appearance of signatories in disciplinary journals was evaluated on the basis of information taken from two databases of social science articles, the Social Science Citation Abstracts (since 1963) and a French language scientific database, while recognizing the limitations of these tools.

to the specific nature of the newspaper selected as a case study, must be underlined. The daily newspaper *Le Monde* was set up in 1945 following the liberation of France.[11] After *Le Figaro*, it has the second largest print run, at around 400,000 copies, of the French national daily press (yet it is the most widely distributed priced daily, at 389,249 copies in 2003). It also has the largest readership, at an average two million per day (2,129,000 in 2003 as against 1,302,000 for *Le Figaro* and 901,000 for *Libération*, *Le Monde's* two principal competitors).[12] In Europe, the newspaper has been in partnerships with *El Pais* in Spain and the British *Guardian*. It is sometimes compared to the German *Frankfurter Allgemeine Zeitung*. Politically to the Centre-Left, the newspaper's readership is more highly educated than its national or regional competitors. The first national daily to be read among students, 66 per cent of *Le Monde* readers are under 35 years old and have been in higher education (as against 41 per cent among the under-35s generally). *Le Monde* is also the general national daily that is most widely read among high earners (those earning more than 52,000 euros a year). Executives, those in the intellectual professions and small businessmen represent 42 per cent of the readership as against 43 per cent of workers, employees and retired people. However, more than 50 per cent of readers come from an executive household, and on average, the readership earns a higher income. In short, the readership of *Le Monde* has, on average, both a higher economic and a higher cultural capital than that of other daily newspapers and of the French population at large. The hypothesis may be made that *Le Monde* has a greater capacity to mobilize for op-ed the intellectual professions, or the representatives of the dominant groups among its readership, than do other dailies.

The *Le Monde* Op-ed: A Panorama

The above is partly confirmed by a survey carried out by a citizen association on the op-ed sections of the daily during 2003 (using a similar methodology to our own). Among the 710 columns published in 2003 (representing a little more than 2.25 opinion pieces daily), more than 45 per cent come from the university, research, art or culture worlds as against 29.2 per cent from the political and 4.6 per cent from the economic fields (see Appendix 10.1; see also Désintox, 2004, 15). However, access to an opinion column printed on the first page and continued within the newspaper is more frequent for personalities from the economic and political worlds (see Désintox, 2004, 21). Although the dominant classes are privileged in the op-ed section of *Le Monde*, it is the subordinate sector within

11 On the history of *Le Monde*, see Eveno (2001); Cohen and Péan (2003).

12 Released by the publishers of *Le Monde* in a supplement to the newspaper, Saturday 5 June 2004. The majority of the figures in this paragraph are taken from a European survey of the national daily press, EuroPQN, 2003/2004. In France, the largest daily print run of a daily newspaper is that of the regional daily *Ouest-France*, at 783,000 copies.

these classes, namely the intellectual professions, that most often contribute to it. Indeed, they are over-represented with respect to their place in French society on the one hand, but certainly also with respect to their place among the newspaper's readership (see Désintox, 2004, 24–5).

Other traits are also characteristic of the op-ed section of this large French national daily newspaper. In terms of space, as well as in terms of the number of annual interventions, the columns carry greater weight than do the letters to the editor (Désintox, 2004, 24). According to the newspaper's ombudsman, the rate of selection for publication of the latter is around 3 per cent, probably much higher than for columns, although it is impossible at this stage to know the precise figures for their rejection. Within both, interventions by men are hugely over–representative at 80 per cent (see Désintox, 2004, 24). All of these data confirm the fact that the *Le Monde* op-ed is a universe with specific social rules: a relatively autonomous social world that is neither the simple reflection of the social structure of the country within which it is published nor of the social structure of its readership.

This relative autonomy of the *Le Monde* op-ed can be seen, for example, through its openness to columns originally written in foreign languages. Using calculations made for 2003, a little more than 10 per cent of all columns published annually are translated from a foreign language (see Désintox, 2004, 24). Our study shows that the proportion of intellectuals of foreign origin (or, to a very small extent, French intellectuals working abroad) is clearly higher, and remains relatively stable between 1995 and 2002 at around 30 per cent. This relative openness of the *Le Monde* columns to foreign intellectuals (or those well known abroad) varies across disciplines: for the period we have looked at, it appears that there is most openness towards writers, political scientists and historians (see Appendix 10.2). In contrast, the columns of *Le Monde* less regularly invite foreign economists or sociologists despite the fact that the newspaper was recently voted the second daily read by European 'opinionmakers', after *The Financial Times*,[13] and that these professions may appear to be more international than the former.[14] Two alternative hypotheses can follow from the above: European public space cannot as yet be said to exist; or if it does, it may be witnessed in the columns of the largest national newspaper.[15] On the other hand, while there are sociologists in

13 Information taken from the publishers of *Le Monde* in a supplement to the newspaper, Saturday 5 June 2004.

14 The internationalisation of scientific exchange does not, however, entail the disappearance of national borders between disciplinary fields. To be convinced of this fact, it is sufficient to calculate the proportion of articles translated from foreign languages in the various scientific journals of any of the social scientific disciplines. It will be obvious that the columns of *Le Monde* are generally more open to non-French interventions than are scientific journals that remain structured along national lines.

15 On the history of the European public space, see Requate and Schulze-Wessel (2002).

Europe with the role of public intellectual, it is more probable that they would be better known in the countries in which they work (or from where they originate) than in other European Union countries.[16]

The Legitimate Intellectual Professions in the Columns of *Le Monde*

According to our sample of 1,505 columns written by intellectuals in *Le Monde* between 1995 and 2002, writers are the most highly represented group. Columns by writers in the newspaper are almost twice as numerous as those by any other intellectual professions. However, university professors and researchers altogether dominate the *Le Monde* op-eds when compared to writers. Historians and philosophers, attached in France to the Faculty of Arts and Humanities, intervene as often as sociologists or political scientists. Within the social sciences, psychologists write more than three times less often than other professions; economists are a little less represented than sociologists and political scientists, who over the period studied are those who intervened most often in *Le Monde* (for all the results referred to in this paragraph, see Appendices 10.3 and 10.4).

These first results demonstrate both the significance and the inertia of the structures inherited from the French intellectual field within the press and the so-called public sphere. The words of the writer, whose mastery has long reigned over French intellectual life,[17] always dominate in the newspaper in quantitative terms. The division among intellectual professions within the columns of *Le Monde* partly reflects the rise of the social sciences within French universities since the end of the 1960s, but older disciplines such as philosophy or history are also well represented. The position of economists, relatively weaker than that of other social scientists, is furthermore an indication above all of the delay with which the columns of *Le Monde* have reflected the contemporary balance between the scholarly disciplines. On the other hand, however, this is also the result of the

16 The number of interventions by foreign sociologists in the columns of *Le Monde* is too small, even in the period of eight years considered, to be representative of the international prestige of one personality or another. Ulrich Beck, Wolf Lepenies and Alan Wolfe have all intervened twice while those who have intervened once include Zygmunt Bauman, Daniel Bell, Anthony Giddens and Jürgen Habermas. The regular intervention of Francophone sociologists (and intellectuals), in particular from Switzerland or Quebec (such as Régine Robin), but also from several North African and African countries, should be noted.

17 Despite the republican alliance between science and democracy, in France there is an attachment to the literary definition of educational culture that, from 1900 to the present day, stands in often conscious opposition to the German representation that privileged the scientist-scholar (*Gelehrte*) over the writer or the unaffiliated intellectual – irremediably separating between the two groups – and that sees professors as being in the service of the governing elites to which they naturally belong; see Pinto (1984), 26; Charle (1990), 231–2, and esp. Ringer (1992).

daily's orientation, that legitimates forms of knowledge receiving less attention among elites. It is undoubtedly herein that the institution of the op-ed, at least at *Le Monde*, has inherited from the critical tradition of the French intellectual: it intervenes as a counterweight to dominant opinion, or rather to the dominant means of producing opinions.[18]

The hierarchy of intellectual professions represented in *Le Monde* columns is in fact neither a reflection of the morphological developments of the various disciplines within higher education nor of the recognition gained by each from the institutions of the state. It is the product of journalists' construction of hierarchies within the intellectual field (see Pinto, 1981, 1994 and 2002). Another way of treating this legitimacy of the various intellectual professions within the specific public space constituted by the op-ed section of *Le Monde* is to analyse the interview questions asked by journalists themselves for the clarification, outside of the op-ed, of issues raised by current affairs. Our study shows that, for such analytical interviews, sociologists are approached more often by *Le Monde* journalists than are philosophers, university-based economists or researchers. Even if one includes economists from banks or economic organizations, the discipline is only slightly better represented than sociology. This means that when those from a given intellectual field are selected, *Le Monde* journalists tend to favour sociology over economics, and the latter over the humanities, which is less the case in the op-ed section (see Appendix 10.5). Sociology is a highly legitimate discipline for *Le Monde*, while this does not seem to be the case in all other dailies or in the public sphere in general (see Tavernier, 2004).

Before turning to those sociologists who take on the role of public intellectual and to the specific nature of this group in France, it is useful to return to the degree of international openness of these professions now that we have a better understanding of the legitimacy of each within *Le Monde*'s columns. There is a strong correlation between the weight they carry within the columns and the degree of their internationalization: in other words, the more legitimate a profession is in the eyes of the op-ed editors, the more it seems to be open to the participation of foreign intellectuals. Sociology represents a separate case due to the fact that, among the disciplines which are becoming more and more legitimate in the op-eds, it appears to be the least open to those of non-French origin. This poses an obstacle to the Europeanization of public debates, or at least to their sociological treatment. For this reason, we shall now turn to attempting to better understand the milieus in which those sociologists frequently participating in public debates exist.

---

18 This statement must be relativized because, beyond its columns, *Le Monde* has privileged economists' opinions by creating a weekly supplement dedicated to economics that we did not take into account in our study. During the period studied, the national daily cancelled another weekly supplement on social issues.

The Nature of the French Public Sociologist

A first means of examining this milieu is to create a list of the top-ranking sociologists who intervene in the *Le Monde* op-ed section (see Appendix 10.6). By only selecting those who have written, individually or collectively, *more than twice in eight years*, we obtained a restrictive group of around twenty persons.[19] The result is almost the same for philosophers (see Appendix 10.7). In other words, there is a strong concentration of intellectuals participating in public debates at the top of the hierarchy. As in the case of the scientific field and most of the fields of cultural production, the public sphere of the press is structured by what Robert Merton has called the 'Matthew effect': there is a threshold of media recognition on the basis of which symbolic capital accumulates itself (see Merton, 1968 and 1988).

What traits are characteristic of the French public sociologist? They mainly tend to be male, three-quarters of columns having been written by men. It is even more probable that they will be attached to a Parisian institution: sociologists from the provinces less frequently write for *Le Monde* than do those from other countries. The columns do little more than accentuate the centralized nature of French sociology; 78 per cent of its research centres are based in the Paris region (see Godelier, 2002). Finally, the public sociologist is generally over 40 years old: there is no means of accessing public opinion before having passed the tests posed by the field. The institution to which one belongs seems, furthermore, to be an important variable in the legitimization of participation in public debates. Among the twenty or so sociologists we selected, a majority come from the CNRS and the EHESS, although the former represent only a little over a third of all French sociologists (see Godelier, 2002). They are full-time researchers rather than professors[20] and they come from relatively new institutions as opposed to the *Grandes Ecoles* (elite higher education institutions), or the *Collège de France*.[21] On the basis of the list of top-ranking sociologists intervening in *Le Monde* from 1995 until 2002, either in columns or interviews, the significance of a specific network emerging from the research centre founded at the EHESS by the sociologist Alain Touraine in 1981, the *Centre d'analyse et d'intervention sociologique* (CADIS), which houses five of the twenty most publicized researchers (Touraine, Wieviorka, Le Bot, Khosrokhavar and Louis), can be observed.

As in the rare cases of studies on public intellectuals in other countries (see for example Posner, 2003 [2001], 167–220), it may be seen that there is a very weak

19 As an indication, at the time of the study there were a little over 950 sociologists in France, of which 600 were lecturer-researchers (professors) and 350 full-time researchers; see Godelier (2002), 26.

20 On the structuring nature of this opposition between 'professor' and 'researcher' in the history of French sociology, see Heilbron (1985).

21 The same results would emerge from the observation of political scientists. They intervene most often in electoral debates, on the one hand, and in international affairs, on the other.

correlation between the scientific capital of an intellectual and his/her legitimacy in the public sphere of the press (see Appendix 10.6). Top-ranking sociologists in our study have published much less in national or international scientific journals than in the *Le Monde* columns in the period under consideration. This negative correlation can be witnessed to an even greater degree among the most public philosophers (see Appendix 10.7). This type of correlation may well constitute a law in the relations between the intellectual field and the public sphere. This is what explains the fact that the philosopher Jacques Derrida or the sociologist Pierre Bourdieu, known publicly and among the scientific community abroad, were in fact at the bottom of the top-ranked list of public intellectuals in France, particularly because their interventions were most of the time part of collective articles of petitions.

In the same way, the sociologists most highly represented in the columns of *Le Monde* are not those with the highest initial educational capital. Among our sample of public sociologists, those educated at the elite *École Normale Supérieure* are less well represented than those from mainstream universities, and in particular the *Institut d'Études politiques* (IEP), a private, independent higher education institution that trains future high civil servants, politicians, journalists and researchers in political science. Writing a column in *Le Monde* – a significant proportion of its journalists having been educated at the IEP – seems to be more easily accessible to those following similar educational paths.

The majority of the sociologists most prolific in the *Le Monde* columns also have a high status position within education or research – a professorship or directorship of research or studies. Therefore, although some scientific capital is necessary in order to access the columns, it is not necessary to gain more in order to remain there and increase one's importance. It is as if, having reached a threshold authorizing intervention, there is a mechanism in operation that converts the resources accumulated in the scientific field for use in the public sphere. In France, and probably in other Western countries, one should thus distinguish between two careers that require a minimal amount of scientific capital: that of the public intellectual, and that of the scholar or university professor.

The analysis of the interventions of these twenty French public sociologists (108 columns) allows, furthermore, for the distinction to be made between two modes of participation in the public debate. A first group of 'generalists' (those whom Bourdieu and Passeron once wrote off as 'universal specialists'; see Bourdieu and Passeron, 1963), intervene on all – or nearly all – topics without mobilizing specific skills or resources (Alain Touraine, Edgar Morin, Michel Wieviorka).[22] Here, the sociologist reproduces the norms of behaviour of the public intellectual

22 Alain Touraine and Edgar Morin conquered the columns at the time of the events of May 1968, of which they were the real time interpreters. With Raymon Aron, they were among the only sociologists to intervene in the national press, interpreting events as they unfolded. On intellectuals and the press in May 1968, see Brillant (2003), 195–203 and 307–31.

figures of the past, such as writers or philosophers. Another type, or particular sub-type, is represented by the spokesperson (or the 'organic' sociologist, as Gramsci would have said) who represents the position taken by a party (as in the case of Michaël Löwy, or on this occasion, Michel Wieviorka and Alain Touraine), a trade union or a collective to which she or he generally belongs. This type of figure stands in contrast to that – in the minority – of the specialist public sociologist who takes a stance in the public sphere on subjects within which she or he has developed competency and scientific recognition (such as Didier Fassin on public health, Yvon Le Bot on Chiapas, Laurent Mucchielli on delinquency, Pierre Merle on the education system, François de Singly on the family and Dominique Wolton on the media).[23]

This division is probably not specific to sociology. Indeed, since the 1970s it has accompanied the legitimization process of the social sciences within the public sphere of the press so that the traditional figure of the Dreyfusard intellectual, the 'universal intellectual', in France has by now entered into competition with that of the 'specific intellectual' (see Foucault, 1977 [1972]). However, because the social institution of the op-ed and the former figure are historically linked, it is normal that the latter remain in the minority, no doubt appearing more within expertise and counter-expertise. An analysis of the themes of intervention of public sociologists in *Le Monde* between 1995 and 2002 can allow for this first brief typology to be concluded and considered.

The Themes of Sociological Intervention

In fact, among the more than 250 columns by sociologists (or including sociologists, in the case of collectively authored articles of petitions) that we selected for the period 1995–2002, those treating international affairs dominate significantly, representing at least 15 per cent of all interventions.[24] It is within this domain that foreign sociologists most often intervene (Beck on Germany, Giddens on the UK, Wolfe on the United States). Over this period, particular attention was paid by French sociologists to the consequences of the Algerian war, to reflections on American society and politics, and to the Israeli–Palestinian conflict, and so on.

---

23 A confirmation of this classification can be found in Tavernier (2004) (esp. ch. 4) that, drawing from a study based on 3500 media discourses where sociologists have been mobilized by the national French daily press (*Le Monde, Le Figaro, Libération*), distinguishes three figures among sociologists who intervene publicly: the spokesperson, the expert and the scholar. These also include sub-types. The spokesperson may be a reader, a witness or an activist in a collective. The expert can represent a professional, institutional or practical competency (as when, for example, the editor of an official report is concerned).

24 Once the body of the study is enlarged, over time and to other publications, we shall carry out a coding and a more precise statistical analysis of columns written by sociologists.

Domestic politics is the second theme on which sociologists intervene, whether they critique or support one or another party-political line (generally on the Left for most of the public sociologists of *Le Monde*), or whether they intervene at times of elections or propose general reflections on the subject of representative democracy. Certainly, in these two domains, the structure of the newspaper's op-ed section and the themes it favours[25] impose upon the position taken by sociologists and social science specialists in general (see Appendix 10.8).

If we exclude interventions with no specifically defined object, with a very general discourse on the nature of French society or modernity, the specific theme that most attracts sociological attention is that of the family, sexuality or private life, to which can also be added the issue of gender. It will be necessary to verify since when this theme was imposed and ask whether this domination may last beyond the contextual effects that, during the period under observation, brought it to the fore of the French media scene.[26] The public sociologist at the top of our ranking, Eric Fassin, is a specialist in such topics. He shares the same working methods and professional ethos as the national daily newspaper journalist. Following the theme of family, gender and sexuality come the themes of (1) religion and secularism (*laïcité*), (2) immigration, (3) social movements, and (4) employment, business, poverty, social class and economics, slightly ahead of education and the environment. These are all recurrent themes in French public debates, but their respective importance still depends on context. If we add to columns on international affairs those that deal with national political affairs, in 2003, for example, more than 80 per cent of columns were concerned with a theme of current affairs (see Désintox, 2004, 29–31).

The commentaries written by sociologists in *Le Monde* between 1995 and 2002 also often deal with debates on the subject of sociology itself, but also science (particularly due to the Sokal affair) and university or research policy. Such debates are often added to by a series of tributes (to Pierre Bourdieu, for example) or by profiles of well-known sociologists and theorists (Castoriadis, Foucault, and so on). Here, sociologists represent their profession, their university or research in general. The universalizing norm that determines the nature of the op-ed section is nevertheless so strong that it was relatively rare, for example in 2003, to see professors or researchers intervening on issues surrounding public higher education and research policy (see Désintox, 2004, 43).

---

25 In 2003, more than 45 per cent of the columns in *Le Monde* treated the subject of international politics; see Désintox, 2004, 29–31.

26 This period witnessed important debates on the issue of homosexual parenting and the transformation of the family following the institutionalization by the state (law passed on 15 November 1999) of a form of civil union, the PACS (*Pacte civil de solidarité* – Civil pact of solidarity). There are other studies that confirm the significance taken on by these themes in recent years in public debate and the importance of the reference made to sociology when they are dealt with by a newspaper; see Tavernier (2004).

The op-ed section is not a space for unrestricted writing. It is constructed in reference to other sectors of the public sphere and of the press itself. They demand the universalization of a cause or of a particular point of view, as is the case for readers' letters.[27] Furthermore, in the same year, more than half of *Le Monde* op-ed columns participated in the denunciation or support of a given cause. A further fifth expressed normative positions (see Désintox, 2004, 38–9). Certain themes or standpoints thus provoke knock-on effects, veritable 'controversies': one opinion leads to several others, in a chain reaction in which rhetorical skills take over from scientific capability. The analysis of the *Le Monde* op-ed columns for 2003 thus confirms that it is rare, at around 15 per cent of interventions, for researchers or professors to transmit or intervene on the basis of their knowledge of a specific theme, to play the role of the expert rather than that of the scholar or spokesperson, constrained to speak only in general terms (see Désintox, 2004, 43). Whatever social-professional background these intellectuals mobilize, the op-ed section, more than a century after the Dreyfus Affair, favours the position of the 'universal intellectual'.

Synthesis of Results

In France, the world of the public intellectual therefore remains dominated by 'universal specialists'. The institution of the newspaper op-ed column has brought about a particular model of the intellectual, emerging since the end of the nineteenth century from the literary field or the humanities, as in the case, for example, of Sartre. Our study suggests that while the social structure of columns written in the national daily press has probably changed over the last decades, their discursive constraints have mostly remained the same.

Once an actor takes a stand within the columns, the principles of his or her intervention lose, almost completely, their relationship to those of their discipline. Where scientific capital is accumulated to a large extent according to specialization (scholarly sociological associations today account for some fifty sub-disciplines in France; see Godelier, 2002, 26), the symbolic capital attached to column-writing is primarily achieved by means of universalization. This first tension is added to by a further one for scholars, between the normative constraint of neutrality attached to scientific activity and the constraint of engagement that has historically dominated the op-ed. These dual constraints lead to the definition of four possible roles that public sociologists in France must fulfil, as must their colleagues coming from other disciplines of the social or natural sciences (see Table 10.1).

It is uncertain in this context whether disciplinary affiliation is the most important social property in order to better understand how intellectuals who intervene in the press. Beyond the frequent recourse to dual self-definitions, we

27 On this demand for the generalization of all public intervention, see Boltanski et al. (1984).

Table 10.1 The system of constraints of public sociologists

	Specialization	Generalization
Neutrality		
Commitment		

also noted the importance in the presentation of one's title (professor) and research institution among the most public of intellectuals. Interviews carried out with public sociologists also revealed the importance of a reference to a given school of thought in their identity-construction and for resolving the tensions inherent in their position (see Tavernier, 2004, ch. 8, 9 and 10). Sociologists' opinion is often formed in the name of activist affiliations, party politics or trade union organizations. In short, it is therefore not only the legitimacy of sociology in the public sphere that is at stake when sociologists write columns; there is a whole set of other social properties that define the public intellectual's identity.

Sociology has certainly become, in the written press, a resource in the construction of increasingly active public debates, particularly in *Le Monde*, where *in the op-ed section alone*, it appeared to have served as a counterweight, along with other social sciences, to the hegemony of economics as a mode for problematizing and constructing public issues. This might be not only a specific trait of the case under study, but also a national characteristic, in that comparison with other countries, in particular the United States, would reveal that the discipline of sociology enjoys a much weaker legitimacy in the public space of the press. Family and sexuality, social movements, the organization of labour, education, cultural policy and the media are, in France, the domains that are prioritized in the public interventions made by sociologists who intervene as experts, rather than as spokespersons or scholars. On all of these themes, nevertheless, it is the scientific skills gained at the national level that predominate: authors of non-French origins are absent; the framework used for problematizing the issues is rarely a European one, at least when not imposed by the political agenda.

A debate has begun during recent years in the United States on the modes of sociologists' intervention in the public sphere. To these ends, the columns of a large daily newspaper are one of the possible sites in which sociologists may invest. The study we carried out of a French op-ed section reveals the limitations of such an investment. Without having even evoked the question of its social influence or legitimacy *vis-à-vis* the readers of daily newspapers, the writing of columns by sociologists subordinates them to rules made externally to their world and which force them to abandon both their habits and their skills.

References

Boltanski, Luc with Darre Yann and Schilz, Marie-Ange (1984), 'La dénonciation', *Actes de la recherche en sciences sociales* 51 (March), 3–40.

Bourdieu, Pierre (1984), *Homo Academicus* (Paris: Minuit).

Bourdieu, Pierre and Passeron, Jean-Claude (1963), 'Sociologues des mythologies et mythologies de sociologues', *Les Temps modernes* 211 (December), 998–1021.

Brillant, Bernard (2003), *Les clercs de 68* (Paris: PUF).

Charle, Christophe (1990), *Naissance des intellectuels* (Paris: Minuit).

Charle, Christophe (1996), *Les intellectuels en Europe au XIXè siècle. Essai d'histoire comparée* (Paris: Le Seuil).

Chenu, Alain (2002), 'Une institution sans intention: la sociologie en France depuis l'après-guerre', *Actes de la recherche en sciences sociales* 141–2, 46–59.

Cohen, Philippe and Péan, Pierre (2003), *La face cachée du* Monde (Paris: Mille et une nuits).

Désintox (Association de citoyens contre la désinformation) (2004), *Du bon usage des tribunes du* Monde, La désinformation – La preuve, dossier 4, Paris.

Duval, Julien, Gaubert, Christophe, Lebaron, Frédéric, Marchetti, Dominique and Pavis, Fabienne (1998), *Le 'décembre' des intellectuels français* (Paris: Liber-Raisons d'agir).

Eveno, Patrick (2001), *Le journal* Le Monde*, une histoire d'indépendance* (Paris: Odile Jacob).

Foucault, Michel (1977 [1972]), 'Intellectuals and Power: A Conversation Between Michel Foucault and Gilles Deleuze', in *Language, Counter-memory, Practice* (Cornell: Cornell University Press), 205–17.

Fraenkel, Béatrice (1992), *La signature. Genèse d'un signe* (Paris: Gallimard).

Godelier, Maurice (2002), *L'état des sciences de l'homme et de la société en France et leur rôle dans la construction de l'espace européen de la recherche* (Paris: Ministère de la recherche).

Goffman, Erving (1959 [1956]), *The Presentation of Self in Everyday Life* (New York: Doubleday Anchor).

Heilbron, Johan (1985), 'Les métamorphoses du durkheimisme, 1920–1940', *Revue française de sociologie* 26, 2–3, 203–37.

Legavre, Jean-Baptiste (1999) 'Les intellectuels dans l'espace public. Les lectures journalistiques des pétitions de novembre–décembre 1995', in François, Bastien and Neveu, Erik (eds), *Espaces publics mosaïques. Acteurs, arènes et rhétoriques des débats publics contemporains* (Rennes: Presses universitaires de Rennes), 209–28.

Lemieux, Cyril (1996), 'L'objectivité du sociologue et l'objectivité du journaliste: convergences, distinctions, malentendus', in Feldman, J., Filloux, J.-C., Lecuyer, B.-P. et al., *Ethique, épistémologie et sciences de l'homme* (Paris: L'Harmattan), 147–63.

Lettieri, Carmela (2002), *Formes et acteurs des débats publics contemporains. Les tribunes publiques de la presse quotidienne en France et en Italie* (thèse soutenue à l'Université Paris II sous la direction de Rémy Rieffel, Paris).

Merton, Robert K. (1968), 'The Matthew Effect in Science', *Science* 159, 56–63.

Merton, Robert K. (1988), 'The Matthew Effect in Science II: Cumulative Advantage and Symbolism of Intellectual Priority', *Isis* 79, 606–623.

Pinto, Louis (1981), 'Les affinités électives. Les amis du *Nouvel Observateur* comme "groupe ouvert"', *Actes de la recherche en sciences sociales* 36–7, 105–124.

Pinto, Louis (1984), 'La vocation de l'universel. La formation de la représentation de l'intellectuel vers 1900' *Actes de la recherche en sciences sociales* 55, 23–32.

Pinto, Louis (1994), 'Le journalisme philosophique', *Actes de la recherche en sciences sociales* (March), 25–38.

Pinto, Louis (2002), 'L'espace public comme construction journalistique. Les auteurs de "tribune" dans la presse écrite', *Agone* 26–7, 151–82.

Posner, Richard A. (2003 [2001]), *Public Intellectuals: A Study of Decline* (Cambridge, MA: Harvard University Press).

Requate, Jörg and Schulze-Wessel, Martin (eds) (2002), *Europäische Öffentlichkeit. Transnationale Kommunikation seit dem 18. Jahrhundert* (Frankfurt am Main: Campus).

Ringer, Fritz K. (1992), *Fields of Knowledge. French Academic Culture in Comparative Perspective 1890–1920* (Cambridge and Paris: Cambridge University Press and Editions de la MSH).

Sirinelli, Jean-François (1990), *Intellectuels et passions françaises. Manifestes et pétitions au XXè siècle* (Paris: Fayard, réed. Gallimard, coll. Folio).

Tavernier, Aurélie (2004), *Paroles d'experts: rhétoriques journalistiques de recours aux paroles extérieures,* Le Monde, Libération, Le Figaro. *Journaliste et sociologue, la construction d'un référentiel* (thèse soutenue à l'Université de Lille III sous la direction de Bernard Delforse, Lille).

Appendix

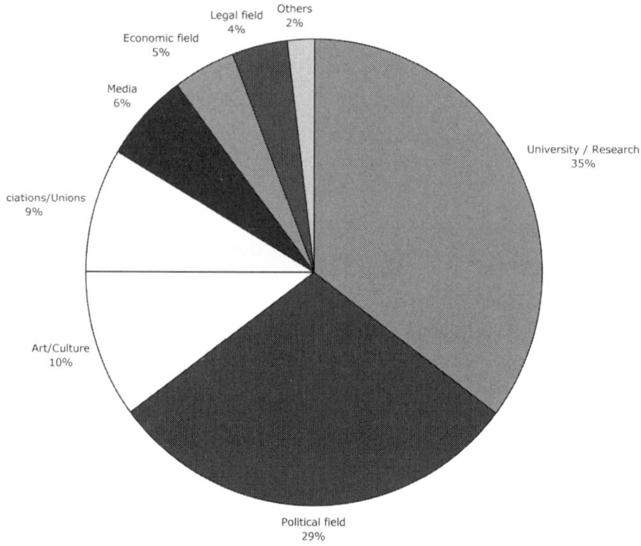

Figure 10.1 Professional origins of op-ed writers, *Le Monde*, 2003

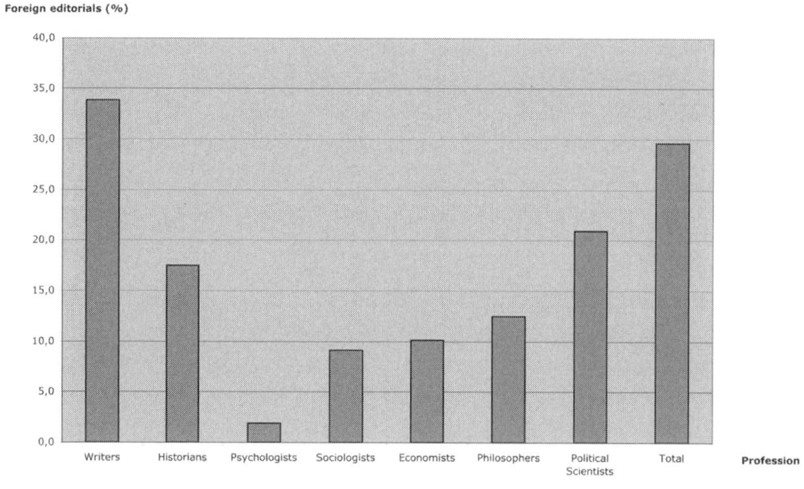

Figure 10.2 Op-ed pages in *Le Monde*, 1995–2002, rate of foreign columns

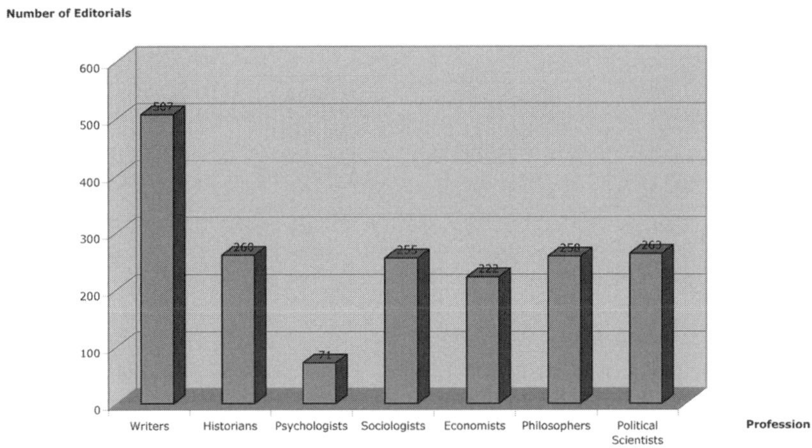

Figure 10.3 Op-ed columns in *Le Monde*, 1995–2002: The hierarchy of legitimate intellectual professions

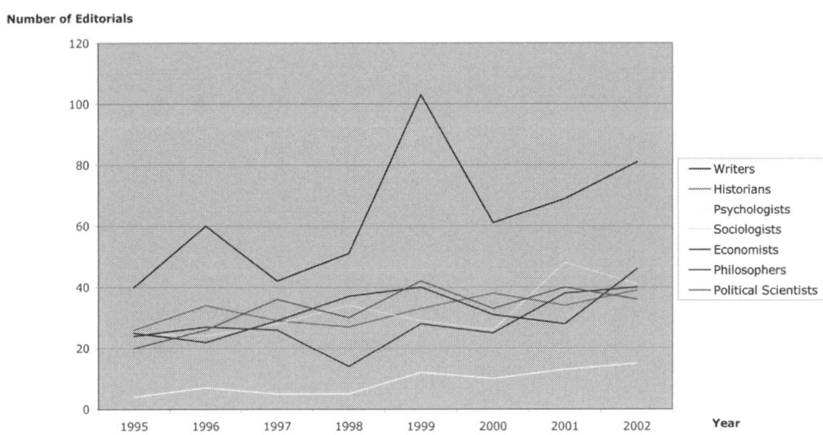

Figure 10.4 Op-ed columns in *Le Monde*, 1995–2002: The evolution of legitimate intellectual professions

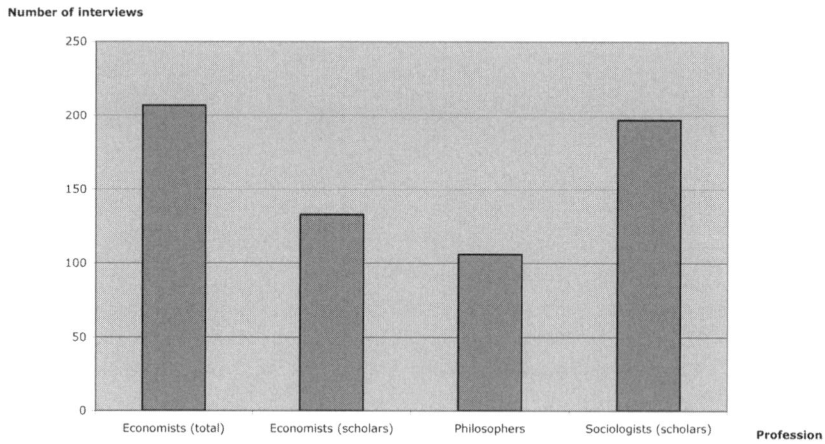

Figure 10.5 Interviews in *Le Monde*, 1995–2002: The hierarchy of legitimate intellectual professions

	Scholarly Citations (Sociological Abstracts)	Op-Eds		Analytical Interviews
Eric Fassin	18	13	Bertrand Hervieu	5
Alain Touraine	222	11	Irène Théry	4
Edgar Morin	48	11	Monique Dagnaud	4
Shmuel Trigano	11	9	Fahrad Khosrokhavar	4
Henri-Pierre Jeudy	8	6	Jean-Pierre Le Goff	4
Bruno Latour	120	6	Dominique Pasquier	4
Michel Wieviorka	108	6	Christian Baudelot	3
Monique Dagnaud	10	5	Stéphane Beaud	3
Dominique Wolton	5	5	Philippe Breton	3
Philippe Breton	10	4	Margaret Maruani	3
Denis Duclos	20	4	Dominique Monjardet	3
Didier Fassin	26	4	Alain Touraine	3
Yvon Le Bot	5	4	Michel Wieviorka	3
Pierre Bourdieu	446	3		
Fahrad Khosrokhavar	23	3		
Marie-Victoire Louis	5	3		
Michaël Löwy	183	3		
Pierre Merle	17	3		
Laurent Mucchielli	31	3		
François de Singly	23	3		

Figure 10.6 Ranking of public sociologists, *Le Monde*, 1995–2002

	Op-Eds
Alain Finkielkraut	23
Régis Debray	11
Robert Redeker	11
Alain Etchegoyen	10
Daniel Bensaïd	8
André Glucksmann	6
Bruno Mattéï	6
Etienne Balibar	5
Monique Canto-Sperber	5
Blandine Kriegel	5
Elizabeth Badinter	4
Jacques Derrida	4
Tariq Ramadan	4
Alain Badiou	3
Geneviève Fraisse	3
Denis Kambouchner	3
Yves Michaud	3
Yvon Quiniou	3

Figure 10.7 Ranking of public philosophers, *Le Monde*, 1995–2002

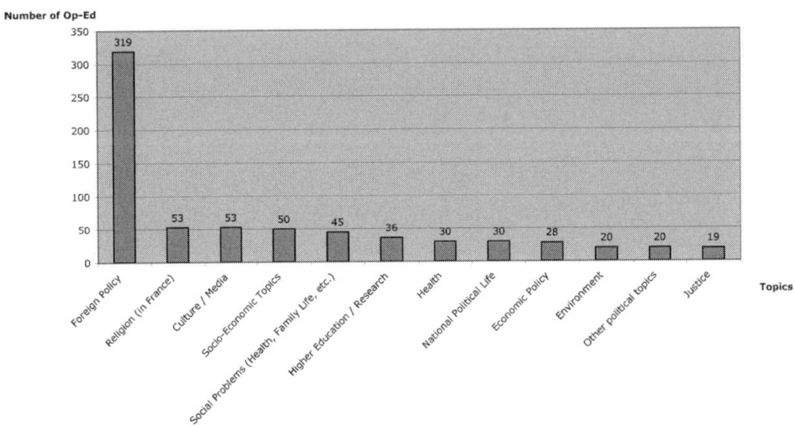

Figure 10.8 Hierarchy of topics in *Le Monde* op-ed, 2003

Chapter 11
You Only See What You Reckon You Know: Max and Marianne Weber in the United States of America at the Turn of the Twentieth Century

Dirk Kaesler

America, you are so much better off than Germany. Or, to be more precise: American women are so much better off than German women. That's what the wife of a German professor reports to her female friends at home:

> Understanding what it means for *civilised people* to keep a private household of today without servants is only possible by seeing it for yourself. Only when spending some time in a household like this, you will be able to understand that, for example, cleanliness is an enormous luxury. One can only applaud educated American women for their ability to still preserve their intellectual identity in such a household, and for being astute and active and not afflicted with a narrow field of vision as opposed to some exemplary housewives in Germany, who elevate their house work to some kind of religious cult and perceive the pursuing of activities beyond their domestic duties or even a continuing education as some kind of flagitious polytheism. It seems to me that Americans consider the household as a means to an end and not – just like the Germans do – as an *end in itself.* …
>
> Of course, the capacity of American engineering to compensate for the lack of servants is high above our own. Demands for individual habitations, however, result in increased aspirations for privately owned houses. 80 percent of detached houses are still made of wood and are available as prefabricated houses for 8 to 12.000 German Marks. They are all equipped with central heating, gas cookers and coal gas, cold and hot water pipes in the kitchen as well as in the bathrooms and bedrooms. The kitchen always adjoins the dining room.
>
> But American *husbands* are willing to do just as much as technology does to ease women's requirements. Instead of having their wives attending upon their everyday needs according to good old German customs – rumour has it that there are some German married men who still have their wives setting up every single piece of their dress for them and who would never remove a stain off their frock! – American men are more than willing to assist in the household: they take care of the heating service, shine their boots and clean their rooms. Many couples do the dishes together in the mornings

> or evenings. As soon as the children outgrow their swaddling clothes, they are urged to perform certain tasks as well, such as dusting, sweeping or making the beds. Thus, they are learning to help themselves and to assist in the household at a very early age. Even the sons of university presidents have to sweep the sidewalk and clean the windows.
>
> There is of course a large number of women neither pursuing a job nor having to keep house on their own, who spend their time as lovely 'ornamental plants' in select company, invest time and money to spangle their appearance, fill theatre and concert halls and graze intellectual comfit at one of the countless popular public lectures.
>
> I have also met childless women who live with their husbands in a boarding house and who are 'busy' the whole day long with dusting their rooms, endless conferences with their dress makers, afternoon teas or other important and useful things. I felt the ungodly desire to foist six children upon them. (Weber, 1905, 177–8)

What you just read was a short extract from Marianne Weber's extensive *Travel Experiences* published in the *Centralblatt des Bundes deutscher Frauenvereine* ('Newspaper of the Coalition of German Women's Associations') in Spring 1905. This short sample is entertaining enough to read, but does not tempt one to present a whole volume full of travel reports depicting the many impressions Max and Marianne Weber gained on their three-month journey through the United States of America (see Figure 11.1).

On 20 August 1904, the passenger liner *Bremen* hoisted anchor in Bremerhaven. On 19 November 1904, the two voyagers from Heidelberg watched the Manhattan skyline slowly vanishing into mist of that winter day. The couple had spent three months and 12 days in the United States, during which they had covered a hard and exhausting route from New York to Niagara Falls, from St Louis – their official destination – to Chicago.

After attending the Congress of Arts and Sciences within the framework of the Louisiana Purchase International Exposition, Max Weber journeyed on in a westward direction to Oklahoma on his own. He then met Marianne Weber in Memphis before they went southwards to New Orleans. Together they travelled to the north, passing Tuskegee, Atlanta, Mount Airy, Washington, DC, Philadelphia and Boston before heading back to New York, where they stayed another two weeks.

Instead of presenting a lot of usually amusing anecdotes, I shall focus on the essential experiences and ideas Max and Marianne Weber gained during their trip through the United States.

Most interpretations assume that it was Weber's observations, experiences and impressions gained in America that prompted his belief in the idea of the Protestant work ethic and rational economic capitalism (*rationaler Betriebskapitalismus*) being effectively linked. A careful examination of the outcome of Weber's journey for his sociological research shows that this well-known assumption cannot be confirmed.

Weber had sent the first part of his manuscript for 'The Protestant Ethic and the Spirit of Capitalism' – which was to be published in the first issue of the 20th volume of the *Archiv für Sozialwissenschaft und Sozialpolitik* – to his publisher in

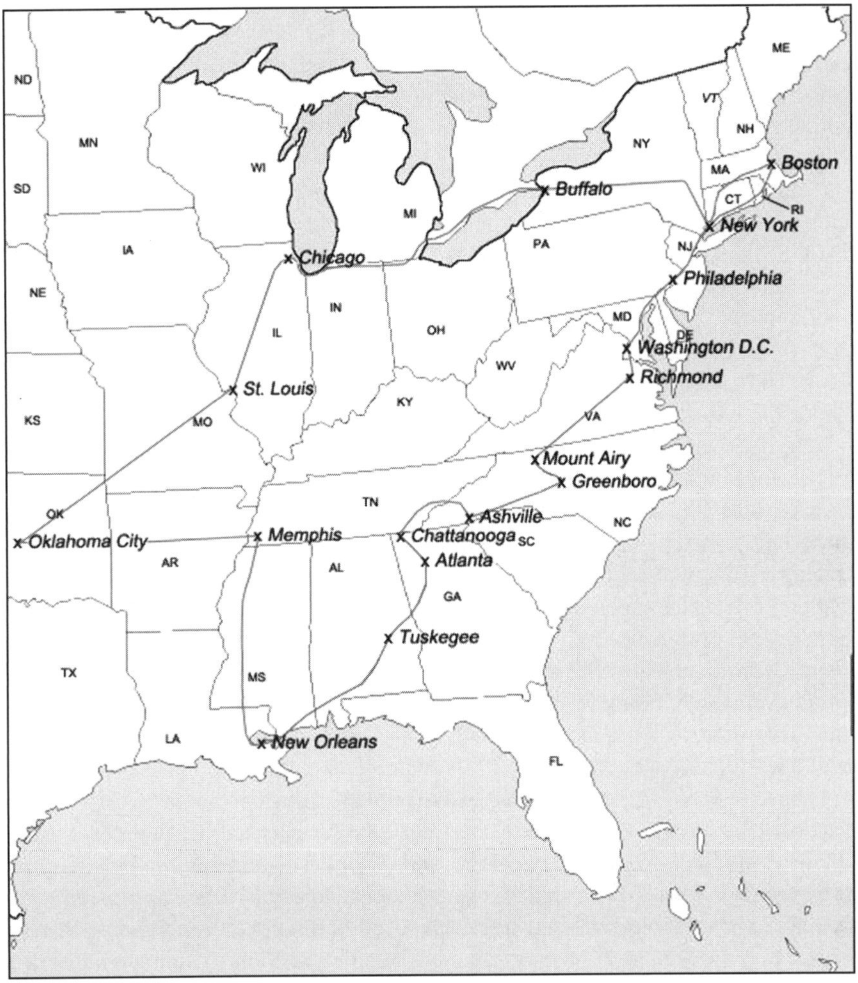

Figure 11.1 Weber's itinerary, 1904

Tübingen, Paul Siebeck, several months before boarding the *Bremen*. The printed issue itself was published in November 1904, when Weber was still in New York. It would only have been possible for Weber to include his experiences of America in the second part of his article, to be published in March 1905. Analysing the text for any correlations between his thesis before and after his trip overseas, it is noticeable that there are no changes whatsoever, neither in detail nor in general. One could interpret this as proof of an immutable attitude in Weber's famous text, which founded his reputation in the Anglo-American countries. One can conclude furthermore that the legendary 'Weber thesis' certainly didn't need a prolonged visit to the United States. He had it all worked out long before he visited America.

Apart from the prime motive for his trip to the New World, which was an extremely profitable invitation to St Louis, the question remains what Weber was searching for on his trip and how exactly he applied the outcomes of his search within his subsequent work. In my reading, Weber was looking for three aspects in particular: an increasing secularisation of life, development of an unstoppable bureaucratization, and tendencies towards an 'aristocratization' of American society. According to Weber's notion, these three trends would eventually displace 'genuine Americanism' and therefore abet a rapid development towards Europeanization.

Keeping in mind the whole of Weber's work and its development, it is noticeable that Weber's American experiences had had considerable influence on his scholarly work. His reasoning on religion, sciences, universities, democracy and political leadership was strongly influenced by his impressions of the New World.

The following quote taken from Weber's Munich lecture in November 1917 on 'Science as a Vocation', where he elaborated on various analogies to America, points to his basic message: 'Permit me to take you once more to America, because there one can often observe such matters in their most massive and original shape' (Weber 1967b, 149). Weber believed that the 'massive and original shape of such matters' he saw in America was no longer apparent in Europe, and especially in Germany, but only appeared in elaborately distorted and advanced form. Weber's vision of modernity – which his wife Marianne breathlessly reported on in Chicago – was a vision of a future *European modernity*. And it was this European modernity that, according to Weber's gradually arising vision, was bound to dominate the whole world, and even America.

Thus, it was not America that was destined to define modern reality, but Europe! Gazing into the womb of the future, it was not an emerging democratic country, hardly burdened by history and tradition, and high in potential of undreamed-of possibilities that Weber had seen. In fact, he had witnessed – or thought to have witnessed – an American society growing old very fast, a society whose unbowed energy, intensity of labour, sportive fighting, pioneering spirit and childlike naivety would not last for long. The alleged departure towards an unknown future would finally cause social and mental states to lead back to their origin, to Europe, the Old World, where the immigrants had come from. The domination of bureaucratic machinery, the overall power of social control, tendencies towards social 'aristocratization' as well as the failing integration of the Afro-American community into the American majority society would in the end debunk the illusionary dreams of a free society of equal people. Unlike many of his contemporaries who conceived America to be Europe's antithesis, Weber stated a peculiar synthesis which involved America's reputed distinctiveness slowly fading away. American innocence would be replaced by European refinement, American pragmatism by European intellectualism, American energy by European world-weariness, and American moralizing by the European need for compromise.

From Weber's point of view, all these processes – especially in the religious field – were highly influenced by his own fellow countrymen who had immigrated to America, the German-American community, in whose circles he and his wife had moved almost throughout their entire stay in the US. Several observations confirmed Weber's notion of the German-Americans undermining the religious traditions of the Yankees: in the commitment to the Lutheran vicarage in North Tonawanda by the German-American community, in the doubtful attitude of Weber's relatives in North Carolina, who attended a Baptist christening and expressed their disapproval by 'disrespectfully spitting out', and in the German-Jewish freethinking circles of Brooklyn, about which he wrote to his mother: 'It is hard to say how great the indifference is at this time; that it has increased – particularly because of the Germans – is rather certain. But the power of the church communities is still tremendous as compared to our Protestantism'(Weber 2003, 289).

When Weber was back at his desk in Heidelberg's Schlossstrasse 73 around Christmas of 1904, he had brought with him a multitude of memories on encounters and experiences which were to colour his subsequent work. In what follows, I will try to give a brief summary of Weber's American gains.

At the time Weber travelled to America, he had just finished his examining the 'cultural meaning' (*Kulturbedeutung*) of Protestant ethics. One could assume, therefore, that he would continue his research in this area during his three-month stay in America. But that was not the case at all. It seems that Weber's emotional interest in the problem itself had weakened. Then again, his fast-paced calendar of events and meetings cut his timing fine and left no time for further research.

Recapitulating what had been Max and Marianne Weber's particular interests in America, one can summarize that they were concerned with the problems of a society of immigrants, ethnicity and race, ranks and social stratum, questions of gender politics, education, religion and democracy. People engaging in institutions of social politics and education were in the centre of their interest. The Webers were particularly keen to understand the current development of social reforms in America.

Max Weber was interested in questions of social politics, work relationships, the agrarian constitution, and the methods of religious groups and educational institutions. Among the many people he had met and who had been of vital importance to him were W.E.B. Du Bois and Booker T. Washington, who both held leadership positions within the black community, the Pragmatist philosopher and psychologist William James from Harvard University, and the economist Edwin Seligman from Columbia University. One of his most important interlocutors in the Indian territory was Robert Latham Owen, who had been elected Senator for Oklahoma shortly after Weber's visit. Weber didn't neglect one opportunity to visit reformatories, schools, colleges and universities of all kinds. He listed libraries for material he could use for his research on the religious groups in America. He was particularly interested in the question of the differences between American educational institutions and their affiliated institutions in Germany. Apart from educational institutions, Weber also visited religious events of different denominations, such as the Quakers, the Baptists and the Christian Scientists; he had been deeply impressed by the service of the Afro-American preacher Walter

H. Brooks in Washington, DC, not to mention the famous baptism in Brushy Fork Pond at Mount Airy which made history in world sociology.

Marianne Weber focused her interest on the leading women of the American feminist movement, on the Settlement Houses movement as well as on educational institutions established for women. She met the later Nobel Prize winner Jane Addams and her assistants at the legendary institution of Hull House in Chicago. She visited the elite colleges for women in Bryn Mawr and Wellesley. In the society circles of New York, she met women of German-American families.

In the following, I shall focus on the main scholarly outcome of Weber's journey to America, which might be organized in six main ranges of topics. These thematic contexts can all be provided with the same headline. It is my view that it was due to Weber's journey to America that his idea of the universal, unstoppable and fateful rationalization of all areas of life obtained his most distinctive formulation.

But before Weber had been able to depict an overall picture, he identified the following six detailed patterns.

Americans Are Not that Religious After All

During his travels through America, Weber focused his interest on two issues closely affiliated to each other. Due to Weber's pre-existing scepticism about the allegedly intense religiosity of the American people, he always sought out evidence of the secularization of American society. He tried to detect a social development that would lead to an increasing number of contemporary people shaping their lives and worldviews independently from religious or ecclesiastic classification systems.

It was his aim – and one of the reasons for his direct and indirect preoccupation with America – to connect this development to an unstoppable Europeanization of the still young American society. There was no direct connection between the journey and his essays on the cultural meaning of Protestant ethics, which he had started to write before he went to America. Weber had only secondary interest in the matter, and mentioned things that he would have to check if he visited America a second time. But there was neither a sequel of his Protestant Ethic nor a second trip to America.

As mentioned, Weber used every opportunity during his three months in America to attend religious services as an observer. He was less interested in the religious or theological contents than in the capacity of collectivization and socialization originating from the respective religious practice. Weber's interest was not in religion as faith, not even in the coherence of theological statements, but in the organizational forms of churches, and especially in the social role of the various Protestant sects. That was his sociological 'discovery', which, as a consequence, expanded into his 1906 essay on 'Churches and Sects in North America' (Weber, 2002). This he begins with the striking sentence:

> Only the most superficial visitor to the United States could fail to notice the strong growth of community life within the Church there. The permeation by the Church of the whole of life, however, which was an integral part of true 'Americanism', is today everywhere being undermined by rapid Europeanization. (Weber, 2002, 203–4)

Weber illustrates this strong thesis with anecdotes about the formalities of the University of Chicago allowing the possibility of alternating charging of church services and seminar participation, about the allegedly standard question about ecclesiastical affiliation in order to check credit worthiness, and about a German ear, nose and throat specialist in Cincinnati who receives unasked information on their sect memberships from his patients. Weber does not just expose the literal, purely utilitarian meaning of such religious mass practice, but also states its rapid break-up:

> In conversation with Europeans, the 'modern', or would-be modern, American gradually becomes embarrassed when the subject turns to matters relating to the Church in his country. However, such embarrassment is a recent phenomenon for the genuine Yankee, and the 'secularisation' of life has still not gone very deep within Anglo-American circles. The exclusiveness of these circles, and ... part of their superiority in the struggle for existence, rests on these 'remnants'. In fact, it is almost an understatement to talk of 'remnants' when we are dealing with what remains one of the most powerful elements in their whole conduct of life [*Lebensführung*], an element which affects their life in a way that must seem us grotesque and frequently repellent. (Weber, 2002, 204)

It is well known that Weber not only believed in the gradual dissolution of a specific American religiosity, but also in its functional replacement by a diverse culture of various associations. In his contributions on 'Churches and Sects' written for the *Frankfurter Zeitung*, one can find the sober phrase, that it is the 'cool objectivity of sociation' stimulating the individual 'to find his precise place in the purposeful activity [*Zwecktätigkeit*] of the group' (Weber, 2002, 213). Social placement of people is what sects are primarily concerned with, according to Weber, not religious matters.

Weber's own worries – being the modern and religiously 'unmusical' person he was – to visit a country where he might be confronted with lived religiousness of Italian imprint proved to be unfounded. Whereas in the case of Italy he had been able to calm himself by reference to his own theory of a direct link between Catholicism and the magic of popular belief, he might very well have become quite uneasy by feeling guilty about his own religious incompetence had he encountered a tradition of seriously religious Protestantism. But now, facing a secularization of life and realizing that it was all really about upgrading social, and especially economic, opportunities, Weber was relieved and began to feel able to deride Germany's merely 'nominal Christianity' (*Namenschristentum*) that he himself was part of.

During the three months of his American journey Weber was busily searching for hints to prove the existence of a weak religiosity in the United States. In America, Max and Marianne Weber emerge as representatives of a German anti-church attitude which was widespread in Protestant bourgeois circles of late Wilhelmine Germany. Max and Marianne Weber neither went to church regularly nor did they believe in the dogmas of Christian belief. Altogether, Weber's increasing interest in sociological questions of religion went hand in hand with his growing distance from Christianity.

Modern Capitalism in America is Much More Brutal than in Germany

The art historian Johannes Leo, who attended one of Max Weber's Heidelberg public lectures in January 1905, provided a summary of Weber's overall impression on his journey. In this lecture, according to Leo, Weber elaborated in flowery detail on the 'great development, originating in the Puritan-liberal spirit of the Pilgrims and considerably influencing the formation of society as well as the material advancement of the United States from a colony to an economic and political great power' (Leo, 1963, 17). As can be seen throughout his work, Weber often created theories out of things he had read, heard or experienced himself. His notions then created a picture of 'the laws of life dominating the becoming and growing of people and nations' (Leo, 1963, 17). The most important subject arising from the manifold experiences gained during the Summer and Autumn months of 1904 was the analysis of the widespread social consequences of modern capitalism, which were self-evident and very impressive for Weber to witness.

Consider his depiction of the bankruptcy of a trolley company in Chicago. This company risked four hundred passengers being killed or crippled in trolley accidents, and took the risk of having to pay damages rather than bearing the cost of new trolley cars. Living in the late Wilhelmine Empire where social legislation prevented the worst excesses of the impact of capitalism on the agrarian and industrial sector of the German economy, the actuality of a capitalism sticking at nothing was striking to Weber. Taking into account several conversations with the women of Hull House, it is likely that Weber recognized the inhuman character of modern rational economic capitalism in America for the first time. This development does not, in Weber's opinion, indicate the Americanization of Europe, but rather the Europeanization of America, as the 'spirit' of capitalism was not originally an American, but a European product.

Altogether, Weber conceived modern rational capitalism as characteristic of modern occidental rationalism. The geographic cultural area that this 'occident' would designate had been described in contradictory terms by Weber. In many of his texts, he generally describes it as Europe, but sometimes also as Western and Northern Europe or Europe along with Northern America, which he conceived as Europe's virgin soil. Beyond these ambiguous statements, the essence of Weber's theory was phrased during an argument with Eduard Meyer in 1906, namely the 'whole "modern", Christian-capitalist constitutional "culture" of today *deriving from Europe*' (Weber, 1968, 257). Weber's conception of the history of mankind implied universal changes that started in Europe as some kind of glowing core of an active volcano that pours its lava over the rest of mankind. The collective term for these changes, beyond semantic contradictions, was rationalization, which was initially an occidental-European phenomenon before it turned into a transatlantic and later a universal one.

Keeping in mind Weber's whole work, one will understand his notion of an Europeanization of American society being part of Western European-American capitalism. From this point of view, American society seems to be more natural, forming something like a 'premature Europe', which would inevitably reach European conditions. Reading his depictions, especially about his experiences in the Indian territory, it is evident that he perceived the destruction of genuine 'Yankeeism' as a loss, including the dissolution of religiousness caused by the 'victory' of secularization of life.

One can say that Weber's experiences gained in America were the key to his research programme as stated in his 1917 article 'The Meaning of 'Ethical Neutrality' in *Sociology and Economics*: 'European and American social and economic life is "rationalized" in a specific way and in a specific sense. The explanation of this rationalization and the analysis of related phenomena is one of the chief tasks of our disciplines' (Weber, 1949, 34).

Bureaucracy Will Soon Be an All-dominant Force in the US as Well

The third issue emerging from the outcome of Weber's journey included his 'observation' of bureaucracy's unstoppable victory in all areas, especially within the domains of the state, the economy and the political parties. These areas in particular made Weber believe he had looked into 'the womb of the future' (Weber, 1993, 558), even though this was not America's future in particular, but a general future following a European direction of development. Weber's point of view was that the American form of bureaucracy as witnessed by him was only a preliminary stage to an all-dominant system of regularizing life which had already prevailed in Germany, or more precisely, in the kingdom of Prussia. His comments at a conference held by the Verein für Sozialpolitik in Vienna in 1909 illustrate this opinion: Weber was totally in despair because of the passion for bureaucracy that some of his German colleagues pursued. He compared the bureaucratic machinery of Germany to those of other countries, especially that of America.

Weber was committed to the implication of this deplorable but inevitable trend, mentioning the problem again and again in a series of articles written in April–June 1917 for the *Frankfurter Zeitung*. In particular his contribution 'The Authority of Officials and Political Leadership' contains the most significant formulation of the problem and also refers to the American situation. Weber contends that Germany's outmatching performance on the rational organization of all realms of life – that is to say the rational, manufacturing, professional and bureaucratic organization of factories, of the army as well as of the whole of German society – will soon encroach upon the United States, not least because of the First World War.

According to Weber's slogan 'the future belongs to bureaucratization', a kind of universal bureaucratization that would soon prevail as a medium for a modern and rational way of life, 'All of the world's bureaucracies would end up like this. Outlasting the war was the key for our advantage' (Max Weber, 1984, 462–3). That is also part of Weber's thoughts in his piece 'The Re-structuring of Germany's Parliament and Government' from 1917/18, where he evokes the dark image of bureaucracy's victory by constantly keeping American developments in mind:

> It is a *living machine of clotted mind*, portraying bureaucratic organisation with its specialism of professional and skilled work, its classification of competence, its regulations, and its hierarchical relations of obedience. United with the dead machine, it promotes the establishment of a cage forged by future dependence, waiting for the people to be captured without resistance just like fellahs in Old Egypt, captured because of *a rational administration and accommodation of officials being the last and sole value to decide on the direction of their affairs*. (Weber, 1984, 464)

Weber's notion of the unstoppable triumph of bureaucracy was not as definite as it may seem, considering the following reservation formulated in *Economy and Society*:

> it must also remain an open question whether the power of bureaucracy is increasing in the modern state in which it is spreading. The fact that bureaucratic organization is technically the most highly developed power instrument in the hands of its controller does not determine the weight that bureaucracy as such is capable of procuring for its own opinions in a particular social structure. The ever-increasing 'indispensability' of the officialdom, swollen to the millions, is no more decisive on this point … Whether the power of bureaucracy as such increases cannot be decided a priori from such reasons. (Weber, 1978, 991)

Bourgeois Democracy Has No Chance in America Either

The fourth thematic complex summarizing the outcome of Weber's journey could be headed by the question of whether or not American society was able to constitute a realistic alternative to the developments in Europe. Did America offer an effective solution to overcome the processes of control spread by capitalism, bureaucratization, secularization, reification and depersonalization? Was it able to offer alternative ways to contain the absurdity of modern rational economic capitalism accrued from rationalization?

These questions can be boiled down to the question on whether American society would be capable of arousing new hope for a true 'bourgeois society'. Was there any evidence suggesting that this 'young' nation provided more room for a society in which the bourgeois citizen would dominate, and not the aristocracy nor the proletariat? Could there be a political development of a self-confident bourgeoisie that would be much stronger than in Old Europe, a bourgeoisie willing and able to resist the forefront of state machinery's power with its administrations and political parties merely staffed by a small powerful minority? Was America a role model for the successful implementation of the 'Puritan-liberal spirit of the Pilgrims', capable of feeding Weber's hopes for a true bourgeois and liberal democracy?

For these questions, America would have been a great disappointment for Weber, as it had been to several of his fellow countrymen joining him on his journey. But since Friedrich Kapp, a fatherly friend of Weber's, had supplied him with detailed information long before he had left for America, Weber already had a keen sense of American democracy's shady side on arrival. It is clear that Weber didn't cherish any illusions on that matter. American society, still bound to ancient democracy, was unable either to provide a convincing perspective to overcome the 'steely cage of victorious capitalism' or to push open the gateway to political freedom for the bourgeois individual. In a country where the profit motive had been 'inexorably unleashed' and 'often took on the character of sport' (Weber, 2002, 121), a convincing alternative perspective was not likely to evolve.

Altogether, Weber conceived the process of Europeanization as an increasing bureaucratization of state democracy and of the organization of political parties. He expected an increasing tendency towards 'corporate "aristocratisation" as opposed to pure plutocracy' (Weber, 1967c, 310). As for religion, he predicted an increased indifference caused by Europeanization.

As a consequence of Weber's observations and talks in the US, he established the concept of a 'plebiscitarian democracy of leadership', considering not only ancient and pre-modern examples, but especially the bosses of the American political parties themselves as well as 'municipal dictators' of the big cities of America. It was mainly due to his observations in America that he came to establish the ideal type of a (plebiscitary) 'democracy of leadership' involving 'machines', which he elaborated on in his Munich speech in 1919 on 'Politics as a Vocation':

> In order to be a useful apparatus, a machine in the American sense – undisturbed either by the vanity of notables or pretensions to independent view – the following of such a leader must obey him blindly. Lincoln's election was possible only through this character of party organization … This is simply the prize paid for guidance by leaders. However, there is only the choice between leadership democracy with a 'machine' and leaderless democracy, namely, the rule of professional politicians without a calling, without the inner charismatic qualities that make a leader. (Weber, 1967a, 113)

America is Still an Equal Society

Previous passages have already pointed out a fifth complex processing of the outcome of Weber's journey which could be described as the encounter with an egalitarian and rather republican society. This was an issue of great importance, not only to Weber, but to everybody in the German Empire dealing with America prior to the coming of the First World War.

A 25-page-long entry in the *Brockhaus Encyclopaedia* of 1898 starts with the sentence 'United States of America, Northern American liberal states, frequently just called United States or Union, the biggest republic of history' (*Brockhaus Konversationslexikon*, 1898). That sentence alone would probably have been a solid reason for a liberal social scientist coming from the monarchical empire of Germany to visit the United States. Visiting this republic, Weber witnessed a society with enormous powers of assimilation:

> Concerning the already mentioned condition of Northern America I want to state only one thing. The enormous power of assimilation embraced by the Yankees – which has probably come to an end regarding the high number of immigrants and a decreasing birth-rate – is not based on racial qualities, but their system of child education. Just like the whole lives of genuine Americans, child education as well is controlled by the principle of autonomy and exclusive associations and clubs gaining their members only by means of a ballot. The specific American character is generated by enforced autonomy teaching even the very youngest schoolboys to hold their ground in life. (*Verhandlungen des Zweiten Deutschen Soziologentages vom 20.–22. Oktober 1912 in Berlin*, 1913, 190–91)

In speaking of a republican society, Weber's interest was not just in political dimensions, but the question of whether American society featured a social stratification that was different to Germany's. Weber was specifically interested in the reasons for the impressive self-esteem of the American working class – one that was very different when compared to the rather underdeveloped self-esteem of the German workforce.

Note an amendment from Marianne Weber, who felt a good deal less doubtful about the corporate equation of American society than her husband. In her reports on the working girls' clubs in Chicago and New York, she also draws general sociological comparisons between American and German society, especially by taking into account the clothes of American women. Max Weber, a German professor who usually wore knickerbockers or dinner jackets during his American sojourn, was presumably lacking this very special point of view. What he observed at the pool table, Marianne Weber experienced in the company of American women:

> I was attending a talk in a club in New York and was deeply moved by the warden's canny and warm-hearted manner to encourage the girls to speak their minds about

a rather abstract matter. But the essence of these types of coalitions is sticking to a democratic spirit: to cherish the equality of people affiliated to different professions and to acknowledge every respectable work as being socially equal. An accurately graded hierarchy of ranks, as prevailing in Germany, bars officials, businessmen, the military as well as liberal professionals from dealing with each other impartially. Moreover, this hierarchical order narrows interactions between different kinds of dependant employees and manual workers: the cook feels to outrank the chambermaid, the chambermaid feels to outrank the nursemaid. The saleswoman feels superior to the milliner and the seamstress, the cashier and the correspondent on the other hand feel superior to the saleswoman because of better education and higher salaries. The same 'corporate' shading applies for differently paid workers of the industrial branch. Looking down on somebody seems to be part of sustaining one's self-esteem in Germany!

...

The striving of every man and woman in America for being able to dress according to a certain standard, namely those of the propertied class, as well as the fabulous talent of all circles to adopt the social graces of the educated is a trait of enormous democratising power. It is characteristic for immigrated unpropertied women from Italy, Poland, and Germany not to wear hats, for no American woman of any social class, for example a chambermaid, would dare to show her face on the streets without wearing a hat. But if, for example, a factory worker and a commercial clerk were able to afford the same kind of clothing, both women were to feel equal and ready to share their leisure-time for joint recreation. And if one were able to sit next to a lady in the theatre wearing appropriate clothes and demonstrating good manners, one would not at all be out of place. An elegant hat, a nice blouse, gracefulness and 'savoir vivre' – these are the main ingredients for American women of the working and dependant classes. Decent clothing is, nevertheless, essential for both sexes in the struggle of life, for example when applying for a job of any kind. The outward appearance and a certain way of dressing oneself makes it easy to recognise a 'gentleman' or a 'lady', and it is this will for recognition one has to respect. But an all-dominant trend towards the craving of luxurious clothes yielding moral and economic danger and reducing the main focus of personal judgement to peripheral appraisal can, of course, not be denied. (Weber, 1905, 187–8)

Negroes Do Not Smell

Closely connected to Weber's pessimistic estimation of the future prospects for a republican and egalitarian society in America was his rating of a racially classified society as witnessed in the United States. Weber associated his own observations with various experimental analyses conducted in his time as well as with references to the similarity between American and ancient plantation economy and the fatal consequences of slave supply 'running dry'.

Weber's meetings with the leading figures of the then Black Movement in the United States show that he was very much aware of racial issues. On the other hand, it becomes clear that Weber was vehemently denying and fighting every form of biologistic or racist justification for the social differences between Caucasians, Afro-Americans and Native Americans.

Weber's examination of contemporary racial issues hits its peak in a public discussion he had with the 'race scholar' Alfred Ploetz during the first convention of the German Sociological Association in Frankfurt in 1910, a discussion one could bluntly headline 'Negroes do not smell', in which, once again, Weber referred to his experiences gained in America:

> Contrary to common opinion, it is not true for the social situation of Whites and Negroes in Northern America being solely ascribed to racial qualities. It is possible in all probability that ancestral qualities are of equal and maybe strong influence. To what extent and especially to what sense is not yet established. Gentlemen, it has not just been stated in Dr. Ploetz's magazine by notable gentlemen that the difference between Whites and Negroes is based on 'racial instincts'. I would ask for any evidence on these instincts and their effects. They are, among other things, said to become manifest in the inability of White persons to 'smell' or rather stand Negroes. I am able to rely on my own nose; I have no experience of anything like that whatsoever. I was struck that Negroes exhale the same smell as the Whites and vice versa. I can further refer to a scene happening every day in the Confederate States, displaying a lady on a carriage holding the reins and having a Negro sitting closely next to her, shoulder to shoulder, without her nose suffering from it. The notion of Negroes exhaling a certain smell is, as far as I am concerned, an invention by the Union in order to give an explanation to the renewed renunciation of the Negroes. If we, gentlemen, were able to paint people black, these people would also be in a parlous and peculiar position as soon as they were in the company of Whites. Any evidence on the specific relations of races there being based on inherent instincts has so far not yet been reliably produced … (Verhandlungen des Ersten Deutschen Soziologentages vom 19.–22. October 1910 in Frankfurt am Main, 1911, 154)

Conclusion

I am going to conclude this chapter by taking stock of the outcome of Weber's journey to America for the whole of his scholarly and journalistic work. From a current point of view, one can state that Weber, due to his astute analytical skills, drew a picture of the United States which is still valid today. Adhering to the notion of a mammoth, polymorphic and manifold American society with all its ethnic, social and religious fractions and frictions being ideally divided into two entities – into a 'democratic nation' tending to shape up mainly as urban, secularized, female and coloured, and into a 'republican nation' tending to shape up mainly as rural, godly, male and white – one may conclude that Weber has not only become acquainted with these two American nations, but also recognized and understood their intrinsic tensions.

His notion of America being 'not a formless sand heap of individuals, but rather a buzzing complex of strictly exclusive, yet voluntary associations' (Weber, 1967b, 310) can still be used as a penetrating description of the United States, even though the observed exclusiveness of these groups has been under permanent attack, not least because of jurisdictional support. Concerning an unstoppable Europeanization of America, Weber's appraisal seems less convincing. Aforementioned changes to justify his arguments, such as the increase of secularized religious attitudes in favour of an increasing indifference, can so far not be supported by empirical examination. In this sense, Weber's bias proves to be particularly misleading. But concerning his claim for an increasing bureaucratization of democracy and party organization, an increasing trend towards corporate 'aristocratization', and the apparently unstoppable global superiority of the United States in economic, military and political matters, it is difficult not to admit the accuracy of Weber's analyses of the society he had witnessed during the three months in America. One can of course disagree on paraphrasing these trends as an Europeanization of American society, as well as perceiving modern rational economic capitalism as being a monopolistic and unrivalled form of organizing the economy and society of the United States.

Samuel Huntington's notion of American society running the risk of a permanent collapse because of the threat to its unity caused by immigrants from Central and South America, especially from Mexico, sounds like the current echo of Weber's ideas on the termination of the so-called genuine 'Yankeeism', not least under German-American influence. The extensive destruction of a social order based on an Anglo-Saxon Protestant system of values completing these cataclysmic changes might give definite proof of Weber's visionary capability.

Weber, like most of us, was searching for affirmations of his own knowledge when travelling, and in this respect, was 'discovering' what he already believed to know. But it was Weber's predictive vividness that clearly distinguished his vision of the universal sub-processes indicating an unstoppable rationalization of all parts of human life from other 'grand narratives' of his time and our own.

In a hundred years from now, in the year 2104, people may know more about the lasting significance of Weber's analyses of 1904 to his readership then. For us, living at the beginning of the twenty-first century, his analyses ought to initiate lively discussions in any case.

References

Brockhaus Konversationslexikon (1898), 14th edn (Leipzig, Berlin and Vienna: Brockhaus Verlag).

Leo, Johannes (1963), 'Erinnerungen an Max Weber', in *Max Weber zum Gedächtnis. Materialien und Dokumente zur Bewertung von Werk und Persönlichkeit*, ed. René König und Johannes Winckelmann (Cologne and Opladen: Westdeutscher Verlag).

Verhandlungen des Ersten Deutschen Soziologentages vom 19.–22. Oktober 1910 in Frankfurt am Main (1911) (Tübingen: Mohr-Siebeck).

Verhandlungen des Zweiten Deutschen Soziologentages vom 20.–22. Oktober 1912 in Berlin (1913) (Tübingen: Mohr-Siebeck).

Weber, Marianne (1905), 'Was Amerika den Frauen bietet. Reiseeindrücke von Marianne Weber', *Centralblatt des Bundes deutscher Frauenvereine* 23:1 (March).

Weber, Marianne (2003), *Max Weber: A Biography*, trans. and ed. Harry Zohn with a new introduction by Guenther Roth (New Brunswick, NJ and London: Transaction Publishers).

Weber, Max (1949), 'The Meaning of "Ethical Neutrality" in Sociology and Economics', in *The Methodology of the Social Sciences*, ed. and trans. Edward A. Shils and Henry A. Finch (New York: Free Press).

Weber, Max (1967), 'Science as a Vocation', in *From Max Weber: Essays in Sociology*, ed. and trans. with an Introduction by H.H. Gerth and C. Wright Mills (London: Routledge and Kegan Paul).

Weber, Max (1967a), 'The Protestant Sects and the Spirit of Capitalism', in *From Max Weber: Essays in Sociology*, ed. and trans. with an Introduction by H.H. Gerth and C. Wright Mills (London: Routledge and Kegan Paul).

Weber, Max (1967b), 'Politics as a Vocation', in *From Max Weber: Essays in Sociology*, ed. and trans. with an Introduction by H.H. Gerth and C. Wright Mills (London: Routledge and Kegan Paul).

Weber, Max (1968), *Gesammelte Aufsätze zur Wissenschaftslehre*, ed. Johannes Winckelmann, 3rd edn (Tübingen: Mohr-Siebeck).

Weber, Max (1978), *Economy and Society: An Outline of Interpretative Sociology*, ed. Guenther Roth and Claus Wittich (Berkeley, CA: University of California Press).

Weber, Max (1984), 'Parlament und Regierung im neugeordneten Deutschland. Zur politischen Kritik des Beamtentums und Parteiwesens', in *Zur Politik im Weltkrieg. Schriften und Reden 1914–1918*, ed. Wolfgang J. Mommsen in collaboration with Gangolf Hübinger (Tübingen: Mohr-Siebeck).

Weber, Max (1993), 'Der Nationalstaat und die Volkswirtschaftspolitik', in *Landarbeiterfrage, Nationalstaat und Volkswirtschaftspolitik. Schriften und Reden 1892–1899*, ed. Wolfgang J. Mommsen in collaboration with Rita Aldenhoff, 2nd edn (Tübingen: Mohr-Siebeck).

Weber, Max (2002), 'Churches and Sects in North America: An Ecclesiastical and Socio-political Sketch', in *The Protestant Ethic and the 'Spirit' of Capitalism and Other Writings*, ed. and trans. with an Introduction by Peter Baehr and Gordon C. Wells (London and New York: Penguin).

Chapter 12
Towards a Sociology of Intellectual Styles of Thought: Differences and Similarities in the Thought of Theodor W. Adorno and Jürgen Habermas

Stefan Müller-Doohm

The social figure of the intellectual is without doubt one of the most significant cultural innovations of the nineteenth century. Ever since the Dreyfus Affair in the France of the Third Republic, when Émile Zola created a sensation with the publication of his open letter 'J'accuse' in the widely read newspaper *L'Aurore*, people have classified certain thinkers as intellectuals on the basis of the nature of their public interventions in writing and speech.[1]

From this point on, intellectuals began to form themselves into a social group, and with their manifesto of 1898, they created an initial statement about the way in which they viewed themselves (see Gilcher-Holtey, 1997).[2] This process of constituting themselves was accompanied by a (sociologically highly relevant) controversy which centred not least on a question that even today has not been satisfactorily resolved: what are the specific features of a speaking and writing practice that lead, for example, in the case of a literary figure like Zola not simply to literary recognition and fame, but mark him out over and above this as an

1 The provocative title 'J'accuse' was chosen not by Zola, but by the editor in chief of *L'Aurore*, Georges Clemenceau, who correctly foresaw the eye-catching effect it would have, and who, with Zola's agreement, printed it in a banner headline above the text: 'It was only through this action on the part of the press that the public became informed about the accusations of spying levelled at Dreyfus in 1894 … The intervention of intellectuals in the topical events of the day played an equally important part …' (Essig, 2000, 173ff.).

2 Jacob Taubes notes: 'The "Manifesto of the Intellectuals" of 1898 in the midst of the Dreyfus Affair was essentially the product of the École Normale Supérieur and it laid the foundations for the "republic of professors" that represented the Third Republic in the first decades of the twentieth century. The Dreyfus Case had divided public opinion in France: on the one side were ranged the forces of the ancien régime, the church and the army; opposing them were the representatives of the revolutionary tradition, the intellectuals … In consequence, in France the intellectuals have continued to this day to identify with the left more consistently than elsewhere …' (Taubes, 1996, 327f.).

intellectual? What are the functions of these additional, specifically intellectual, activities of a writer or artist in the cultural and political space of a society?

Taking the historically significant case of Zola's 'J'accuse' as our starting point, we can assert that the intellectual may be regarded as the personified instance of a public critique of social ills and abuses that have been suppressed or ignored by the majority. If that is so, one of the tasks of a sociology of the intellectuals is to clarify the particular defining features of this critique. What form of critique can be described as the form of criticism specific to intellectuals? Is it subject to historically conditioned changes in styles or patterns of thought,[3] in the same way as the intellectual according to Bourdieu has always needed, and continues to need, to reinvent himself ever since he emerged on the historical scene (see Hillmann, 1997, 185ff.; Bourdieu, 1992, 185ff.)?

Such questions as these are evidently unavoidable in a sociology of intellectuals. Against that background, the intention here is to examine two different intellectual styles of thought that have come to form independent types of public critique: the intellectual practices of Theodor W. Adorno and Jürgen Habermas. Following the analysis of the typical features of the styles of thought of these representative intellectuals, who regularly intervened in public debates, the attempt will be made to identify the general patterns underlying divergent forms of intellectual critique. This will enable us to shed light on the function of intellectual practice for the public sphere in a liberal democracy, so as finally to be able to discuss the crucial question, the one in the forefront of our attention: does the intellectual form of critique possess a function in public discourse that is specific to intellectuals, one that is determined by an intellectual style of thought?

Solidarity with the Intellectual at the Moment of His Fall: Contradictions between Adorno's Diagnosis of the Intellectual and the Task of Critique in the Public Sphere

Adorno undoubtedly regarded himself as the quintessential intellectual. He attempted to give an account of the paradoxes of the situation of the intellectual on the level of theory, even though he was simultaneously convinced that the intellectual was destined to disappear. His view of the intellectual had been sharpened by an experience of exile that had lasted over fifteen years, something that led him to speak of himself as one of the 'professionally homeless' (Adorno and Mann, 2002, 49). By this he wished to imply that the intellectual owes the intransigent nature of his criticism to the fact that 'one no longer feels at home anywhere; but then, of course, someone whose business is ultimately demythologization should hardly

3 By 'style of thought', what is meant is the unity of the critical outlook of an intellectual like Adorno or Habermas, while 'patterns of thought' has been used to refer to the synthesis of distinct modes of argumentation.

complain too much about this' (Adorno and Mann 2002, 62).[4] In his most personal book, the *dialogue intérieur* of *Minima Moralia*, he thematizes the dilemmas of the role of the intellectual in late-bourgeois society. The intellectuals who fall between two stools are both 'the last enemies of the bourgeois and the last bourgeois' (Adorno, 1974, 26). They are a part of the very thing they combat so strenuously. Moreover, according to Adorno, even though the practice of intellectuals thrives on their illusion-free exposure of dubious political trends and problematic social conditions, that same practice increasingly displays elements of standardization: 'What intellectuals subjectively fancy radical, belongs objectively so entirely to the compartment in the pattern reserved for their like, that radicalism is debased to abstract prestige, legitimization for those who know what an intellectual nowadays has to be for and what against' (Adorno, 1974, 206).

On the one hand, the intellectual allows himself the luxury of independent thought, and hence feels able to criticize existing circumstances from within the free space to which he is confined. But because he remains at the level of mere reflection while insisting on his independence, he ends up squandering the privileged situation of someone who is only able to criticize because of his social position and intellectual status. On the other hand, the very fragile position of the intellectual who merely criticizes cannot be stabilized in the long run by simply deciding to intervene in practical affairs, but only by 'inviolable isolation'. For the intellectual who leaves his ivory tower in full knowledge of what he is doing and in order to take an active part in politics runs the risk of condoning the inhuman aspects of politics. This does not mean that the only sensible solution is to remain aloof in the ivory tower. On the contrary, 'the detached observer is as much entangled as the active participant ... His own distance from business at large is a luxury which only that business confers' (Adorno, 1974, 26). In view of the hopelessness of this situation, nothing remains for the intellectual but the minimalist moral counsel 'to deny oneself the ideological misuse of one's own existence' (Adorno, 1974, 27). With this recommendation, which amounts to an expression of solidarity with the intellectual at the moment of his failure, Adorno falls back in quite a conventional manner on the idea of intellectual integrity. That is to say, he reminds us not to regress to a position below our own theoretical insights into the social pressures to conform, and therefore advises us to resist co-option by practical interests on principle, even where these might be of service to our own cause. The integrity of the intellectual implies a strictly 'ascetic attitude towards any unmediated expression of the positive' (Adorno and Mann, 2002,

4 Although Adorno was one of the severest critics of Karl Mannheim's sociology of knowledge and his conception of ideology, the two men share a number of striking features in their diagnosis of the situation of the intellectual. Where Adorno situated the intellectual in a no man's land, Mannheim had coined the formula of the free-floating intellectual. As early as the *Heidelberger Briefe* of 1921, he described intellectuals as 'the scattered crowd ... with no firm ground beneath their feet ... The question of who is to be included in this caste is one that can only be decided on an individual basis' (Karadi, Vezér and Lukács, 1985, 75).

128), an attitude that Adorno has referred to as a basic motif of his philosophy. For this reason, he took a sceptical view of the kind of politically motivated commitment that was practised by philosophers like Sartre or artists like Brecht in the service of progressive or revolutionary goals. As the figureheads of a political movement, such intellectuals would 'from sheer despair about violence short-sightedly go over to a violent praxis' (Adorno, 1992, 86). Joining in out of a sense of commitment is in Adorno's eyes for the most part no more than 'parroting what everybody is saying, or at least what everybody would like to hear' (Adorno, 1992, 93). So he constantly reiterates that it cannot be the task of the intellectual to transmit a positive meaning by offering an interpretation of the world or by taking up the cudgels on behalf of a political programme. For 'political reality is sold short for the sake of that commitment; and that decreases the political impact as well' (Adorno, 1992, 84).

It follows that if the role of the intellectual cannot lie in engaging with practical politics because Adorno's philosophical principle of determinate negation contains the view that 'The goal of real praxis would be its own abolition' (Adorno, 1998b, 267), we may legitimately enquire how he solved this dilemma in his own practice as an intellectual. In other words, how did he resolve the contradiction between his emphatic demand for an interventionist mode of thought that transcends mere contemplation (see Seel, 2005; Heidbrink, 2004) on the one hand, and his insistence upon abstention from political action on the other?

To answer this question, it is illuminating to recall Adorno's own intellectual practice, since this was of particular importance for the discourse relating to the past and the question of guilt in the Germany of the post-war period.

Shortly after his return to Frankfurt am Main from exile in America, he ventured to start speaking of the rope in the country of the hangman, in full awareness of what he was taking on (see Müller-Doohm, 2005, 380ff.); he provoked the literary public with the statement that first appeared in 1951 to the effect that 'To write poetry after Auschwitz is barbaric.' It was perfectly clear to him that in making this statement, he was venturing into the public realm. He went one step further, consciously exposing himself to the full glare of publicity in the late 1950s and early 1960s when he published such essays as *The Meaning of Working through the Past*, *Combating Anti-Semitism Today* or *Education after Auschwitz*. At a time when anti-Semitic outbursts were common in Germany, Adorno, both as philosopher and sociologist, put his academic reputation on the line so as to alert German public opinion to the dangers of a resurgence of National Socialism. He said at the time: 'I consider the survival of National Socialism *within* democracy to be potentially more menacing than the survival of fascist tendencies *against* democracy' (Adorno, 1998, 90).

In this way, Adorno assumed the role of intellectual in public lectures and countless radio talk shows, in which he tirelessly insisted that democracy would only have a chance of surviving in Germany if Germans were to succeed in working through the past. The discourse about the past started off hesitantly in the first half of the 1960s, triggered by such events as the Eichmann trial in Israel and the Auschwitz trials in Frankfurt, but it finally did get slowly under way. Adorno took on the role of the intellectual who makes an appeal to the citizens of an increasingly politicized public sphere. At the level of theory, he defines this function of intellectual enlightenment as 'a turn towards the subject, the reinforcement of a person's self-consciousness' (Adorno, 1998c, 102). His aim is to use theory to shake up public opinion with the aid of provocative statements. The public should be made to face up to the reality of Auschwitz and everything the name stands for. This is his imperative, and he tirelessly insists on it in order to break down the prevailing silence. He positions himself, therefore, as a nay-sayer, a troublemaker, who consciously runs the risk of breaking taboos (see Kramer, 1996, 513ff.). With his criticism of the different forms of resistance to making German guilt the focus of explicit debate, he played a significant part in enabling genuine discussion to emerge about the past and about the function of democracy. He not only helped to ensure that the normative values of the democratic constitution would form the object of public debate, but was also one of the chief actors who may be credited with responsibility for a second founding of the republic, an intellectual founding (see Albrecht et al., 1999; Bonacker, 1999, 170ff.). In this way, by means of what he called 'interventions', Adorno became an important stimulus for the processes involved in shaping public opinion.

This cursory glance back at Adorno's intellectual practice during the 1950s and 1960s shows that the contradictions in the definition of the intellectual on which he reflected were then resolved in his own dogged interpretation of the role of the intellectual. He intervened in particular situations without committing himself to a long-term, politically based involvement in public affairs. For all the empathy implicit in the critical spirit, he maintained his distance from the representatives of political power as well as from day-to-day politics. Because he was convinced that ultimate catastrophes had to be thought through, he refused to embrace particular political programmes based on ethical convictions. On the contrary, he embodied the idea of the intellectual as a dissident as far as both practical politics and the public sphere are concerned. But even as a strict nay-sayer, his criticism of such matters as the defective democratic consciousness of post-war Germans was still addressed to a public at large, or more generally, to the community of those capable of understanding what he was saying. It is true that, as an intellectual, Adorno struck a fundamentally anti-consensual note, one that even entered the language he uses, and this tone was in harmony with his distance from actual politics and the establishment in public life. Nevertheless, the dissident energy he generated ended up in an intellectual practice that both avoided the pitfalls of political commitment and was conscious of the need for the courage to stand by one's convictions (see Adorno, 1997a, 132). 'The individual who thinks must take a risk', as Adorno phrased it (Adorno, 1997a, 132), and he went beyond this, asserting that, as intellectual dissidents, philosophers must 'make the moral effort to say what they think is wrong on behalf of the majority who cannot see for themselves or else will not allow themselves to see out of a desire to do justice to reality' (Adorno, 1973). In this way, Adorno takes part in public discourse from a vantage point outside time and space, and thus appears in the public sphere as someone estranged from common opinions, and hence as someone who opposes pressures to conform in every sphere. This gives rise to ways of seeing that radically question hitherto accepted views such as the possibility of poetry after Auschwitz, not least because of Adorno's consciously chosen trope of hyperbole in both concrete diagnosis and linguistic expression (see Duttmann, 2004a, 32ff.). His non-conformism is the soil from which arise the impulses that guide Adorno's intellectual practice. He pleads vehemently for the need to come to terms with the past and to seize the opportunities offered by a democratic constitution, while in the same breath he warns that the realm of politics and the political public sphere is a mere façade. Nevertheless, in his role as intellectual he avails himself of the opportunities provided by the media of this pseudo-public sphere.[5] To be an active intellectual, the philosopher must refuse all compromises in his thinking, but he must necessarily live with the dilemma summed up in *Minima Moralia* with the words: 'Whatever the intellectual does is wrong' (Adorno, 1997a, 133). As a dissident estranged from common opinions, to get things wrong or to be accused of doing so is a risk that Adorno willingly accepted, in accordance with his own maxim: 'The almost impossible task is to let neither the power of others, nor our own powerlessness, stupefy us' (Adorno, 1997a, 57).

Jürgen Habermas as Public Intellectual

Like Adorno, Habermas represents a specific type of intellectual practice. Even though he was preoccupied from early on with the relations of theory to practice, and has continually returned to this theme, he only makes marginal comments on the role of the intellectual in modernity. In fact, it is only in his essay on Heinrich Heine of 1986 that he makes the intellectual the specific object of reflection. His restraint with regard to the theoretical definition of the intellectual is all the more striking as Habermas is rightly regarded as the most influential intellectual of first the Bonn and then the Berlin republic. His reputation as a fighter has assumed global dimensions since the time of the great initiative in May 2003 when he took the

5 The same dilemma characterizes Adorno's concept of the public sphere. On the one hand, the public sphere is a constructive aspect of democracy: 'It is something to be brought into being in accordance with the political conception of democracy, which presupposes mature citizens who are well informed about their own essential interests' (Adorno, 1997a, 533). On the other hand, as an institution, the public sphere has detached itself from human subjects and made itself independent: 'The right of human beings to a public sphere has turned into supplying them with a public sphere' (Adorno, 1997b, 534). Thus, in his practice as an intellectual, Adorno laid claim to the public sphere, while at the same time criticizing it for having sold out to market forces: 'The public sphere is bad not because it is too much but because it is too little; if it were complete, if what is said did not distract us from the essentials that remain unsaid, all would be in its proper place' (Adorno, 1997b, 535).

lead. This initiative was published simultaneously in a variety of leading dailies; it consisted of a plea for an independent Europe as opposed to a hegemonic America, and for a global society on the basis of co-operating multilateral institutions. From its opening lines, it makes clear Habermas's own view of his practice as an intellectual. He conceives of it as a discursive contribution to the public of a deliberative democracy that is capable of making an appropriate response.

The function of the intellectual who 'marshalls rhetorically polished arguments in defence of injured rights and suppressed truths, in favour of overdue innovations and delayed reforms' (Habermas, 1985, 51) is in Habermas's view, historically, an essential component of the constitution of a politically functioning public sphere. 'Public sphere' here is understood as the 'medium and intensifier of a democratic will. Here the intellectual finds his rightful place' (Habermas, 1985, 51). When the intellectual speaks out in the public sphere, he leaves his professional role behind him. Nevertheless, for the practical philosopher and critical social theorist who is concerned with the truth of practical questions, there are affinities between his political valuations and his theoretical assumptions. Take the case of the *Theory of Communicative Action*, which is concerned to demonstrate that the goal of mutual understanding is built into the everyday communication situation. It is self-evident that one consequence of this consists in providing practical proof that this communication is a productive force. The task is to show in concrete terms that the power of communication is able to determine the political culture, and that it can be an influential factor alongside money and administrative power. Despite this affinity between intellectual practice and the paradigmatic importance of reaching an understanding, Habermas regards the intellectual as no more than an active citizen who, together with other citizens, engages in politics as a sideline, admittedly without being invited to do so and without political mandate. His commitment is driven by a sense of 'responsibility for society as a whole' (Habermas, 1985, 52) rather than the ambition of obtaining political power for himself. The intellectual has no wish to acquire a strategic influence on the political power struggle as such. Inspired by the wish to communicate, that is, to reach an understanding, he desires to influence the autonomous and pluralist public sphere. The citizen gains the status of an intellectual not as a professional expert, but as the participant in a discourse who is especially good at what others might do equally well, namely advance compelling arguments. It follows that the recognition of an intellectual as an intellectual results from the quality of his arguments, which have to prove their worth as impulses for public debate through the cut and thrust of discussion. In this process, intellectuals do not seek to impose interpretations. On the contrary, 'addressees must have the unambiguous opportunity to accept or reject interpretations that they are offered in appropriate circumstances, i.e. without coercion. Enlightenment that does not terminate in insight, i.e. in uncoercively accepted interpretation, is not enlightenment at all' (Habermas, 1981, 327).

Connected with the task of practical enlightenment is the idea that the intellectual is the guardian of those universalist principles that constitute the normative substance of modernity, that is to say, the substance of democratic societies. These principles owe their existence to the fact that the 'project in which a community of free and equal human beings has been able to empower itself' (Habermas, 1992) has succeeded in proving itself historically and establishing itself. This theoretical definition of the intellectual is entirely in harmony with Habermas's own intellectual practice, which has put its stamp on the history of mind in recent decades through a whole series of interventions in the shape of articles, journalistic statements, open letters and discussions with leading politicians. These include:

- his insistence on a radical reform of the universities and his controversy with the actionism of the student movement in the mid-1960s;
- the so-called historians' debate in the mid-1980s when a number of historians attempted to question the uniqueness of Nazi crimes;
- the debate about civil disobedience as a calculated violation of the rules, and about the notion of a loyalty towards the constitution (*Verfassungspatriotismus*) as an attitude that should replace nationalism and 'communities of fate';
- his criticism of the Gulf War and the way it was presented in the media;
- his intervention on the question of whether the GDR should freely join up with the Federal Republic after the fall of the Berlin Wall, or be annexed;
- his statements on the Kosovo crisis and on the propriety of military intervention in order to prevent a genocide;
- his vigorous contributions to the debate on the ethical questions arising from reproductive medicine and cloning;
- his recent utterances on American violations of international law in the second Iraq War.

What do all these exemplary forms of intellectual practice have in common? Four characteristics can be identified: normativity, discursivity, changeability and fallibility.

First, intellectual practice extends its activity to everything concerning questions of the just life (not the good one) that belong within the decision-making capabilities of all human beings. As an intellectual, Habermas expresses a moral, and hence an implicitly political, attitude that is based on a highly developed sense of justice: existing practices in politics, art and society are made the objects of debate in the light of normatively established and grounded judgements. His point of reference is always the universalist principles of a constitutional democracy, its republican self-understanding of constitutional loyalty.

Second, his interrogation is based on the assumption that it is possible to differentiate between true and false arguments, to advance good reasons discursively, reasons that are addressed to hearers who are of sound mind and that make an appeal to the sensibilities of people involved in the formation of public opinion and policy. The meaning and purpose of the public debates initiated by Habermas is to generate discursivity, to provide a model for the public use of reason.

Third, the interpretations that constantly enquire after the common interest of all contain an implicit drive towards at least long-term practical change, the expectation that where existing power structures can be shown to be illegitimate, they can also be broken.

Fourth, Habermas nowhere implies that his intellectual intervention owes anything to privileged insights into the secrets of what makes society tick. On the contrary, as he himself has noted, his approach is unusually exposed to the risk of error. His conception is incompatible with the idea of the intellectual as the mediator of meaning and interpreter of the universe: 'The thinker as a form of life, as vision, as expressive self-presentation – that is no longer viable' (Habermas, 1985, 207).

Thus, intellectual practice survives as a translating function; it is confined to the translation of complex problems in the specific value spheres of science, law, art and so on into the language of daily life. Intellectual competence culminates in this mediating function that consists in what might be called speaking numerous languages, in appropriating the knowledge of various expert cultures while making no claim to expertise oneself; it consists, in Habermas's own words, 'in advancing, in an enlightening way, the processes in which a life-world seeks to understand itself by relating its experience to a totality' (Habermas, 1988, 26).

Two Different Intellectual Styles of Thought

For both Adorno and Habermas, the provocative background to their philosophy and social theory is provided by the catastrophes of our century of extremes. This shared background should not blind us to the obvious fact that they belong to two different generations. In the case of the older man, what was constitutive for his way of thinking was the persecution at the hands of the totalitarian state, exile, the loss of his own culture and language in a foreign land. In the case of Habermas, the crucial experience was the replacement of a criminal social system by a democratic constitution.[6] Their different historical positioning on either side of the great rupture in civilization is not the least important factor in determining the distinct modes of practical critique in Adorno and Habermas which then emerge in their differing practice as intellectuals. In Adorno's case, critique is the whole of his thought: the determinate negation of existing reality through the medium of language. Critique operates by way of the conscious use of hyperbole. For all his distrust of the imperative of solidarity and the frenetic activity of the action men who are committed on all fronts, Adorno rarely let an opportunity pass to criticize defective conditions – whether through talks, public debates or radio and television talk shows (see Boll, 2005, 163ff.) on topics as far apart as musical culture, the theatre, education or the mass media. He articulated his criticism in

6 We can perhaps differentiate the two thinkers by saying that Adorno was the philosopher of the Holocaust, while Habermas's philosophy is that of the post-Holocaust era.

an unusually provocative way; it drew its force from his paradoxical attempt to change the falseness of the false by means of unconventional and hence effective interpretations. This form of critique is sustained by his conviction that changes for the better are possible, and are therefore not entirely futile, even in the negative totality of the administered world. Only from this vantage point does intellectual critique makes sense as a possible mode of behaviour: as resistance to 'everything that is merely posited, that justifies itself by the fact that it exists' (Adorno, 1998a, 282). In this way, Adorno's critical negativity expresses on the one hand a general philosophical contradiction to society as it exists, and on the other hand a concrete form of intervention as a public intellectual. This practical critique is designed to enable him to demonstrate that 'the possibility of what is better' (Adorno, 1974; see also Heidkamp, 2000) arises from this dissident behaviour. The changes envisaged by this critique are concerned both with the destructive nature of the civilization process, the threatened destruction of the human species, and with the utopian substance of a 'right life', for which Adorno uses the concept of 'non-identity'.

For Habermas, critique relates to social practices that are judged in the light of moral principles and norms whose own rationality is, of course, open to critical scrutiny. Critique begins concretely with social institutions, and sheds light on the degree of structural violence that has accumulated in them. Adorno had operated extraterritorially, as it were, from where he issued warnings about the dangerous potential of flawed historical and cultural trends and sought to preserve his equilibrium through a negative and ostentatiously evaluative critique. For his part, Habermas's starting point is that of a participant who focuses on illegitimate forms of political power in society; he opposes decisionism in all its forms. In his transcendent social critique, Adorno's starting point is the position-less position of a no man's land (see Müller-Doohm, 2005, 91ff.). Habermas, in contrast, criticizes society from within society itself.

In order to clarify the differences between these two forms of critique, I should like to recall a distinction introduced by Habermas in an essay on Walter Benjamin – albeit with a certain shift of meaning. In that essay, he draws a distinction between a consciousness-raising and a rescuing critique (Habermas, 1998, 336). The notion of a 'rescuing critique' not only encapsulates important aspects of Benjamin's intentions, but also tells us something about the particular nature of Adorno's conception of the intellectual. Needless to say, Adorno's critique amounts to more than the expression of a moral idiosyncrasy. And in the context of historical experience, he was undoubtedly justified in formulating his maxim that the whole is untrue. His critique as determinate negation in fact arises from his sense of despair about the course of history of which he felt himself to have been a victim (see Müller-Doohm, 2003, 169ff.). For this reason, the critique he carried out as a public intellectual who did not seek political commitment in the sense of joining in, can be described as being driven by the idea of rescuing or redemption. This gesture of 'all or nothing' was an attitude Adorno illustrated with a quotation from Christoph Dietrich Grabbe which he frequently referred to: 'For nothing but despair can save us now.'

Consciousness-raising criticism, in Habermas's hands, may indeed be born of despair, but it springs from a confidence in the emancipatory potential of democratic institutions; it banks on the good sense of active agents who desire to reach an understanding. Consciousness-raising critique is in fact addressed to such agents. It is the product not of the subjective impulse of despair, but of indignation. The point at which indignation about the violence done to solidarity and justice is resolved is the understanding that has been reached discursively. Thus a consciousness-raising critique is not an objectively superior form of knowledge, it is not formulated from an external vantage point, but arises from an internal view of one's own culture. It starts from the internal symptoms of communication that has been systematically distorted. For a consciousness-raising form of criticism there are no ultimate answers, because this type of intellectual practice is an open-ended, fallible process of argumentation that has to be constantly renewed.

Prospect: Continuity Amid the Changes in Intellectual Styles of Thinking

The comparison between Adorno and Habermas shows sufficiently clearly that the older representative of Critical Social Theory embodies an anti-consensual style, makes use of hyperbole[7] and looks to the productive force of negation for salvation. In contrast, the protagonist of the linguistic turn in Critical Theory puts his trust in the illuminating force of non-coercive argument, in the productive force of communication. He appeals to the norms of a participatory and deliberative democracy. Adorno's style of thought as an intellectual culminates in a form of critique that is not primarily or exclusively based on argument. Instead, it can properly be described as gestural in the sense of the gesture 'Oh, I see.' The gesture that signals '"Oh, I see" makes possible a seeing and a comprehension in the actual process of recognition' (Duttmann, 2004a, 52). It aims to open our eyes to injustice, suffering and delusion by exaggerating the case. It is connected to Adorno's 'evaluative negativism', which represents the foundation of his philosophy, social theory and intellectual practice (Heidbrink, 2004, 110).

In contrast, we can speak of a 'normative negativism' (Heidbrink, 2004, 101) in connection with Habermas. This points to an intellectual practice whose significant characteristic is the use of argument, the public attempt to reach an understanding on controversial issues. The antithetical unconditionality of Adorno's form of critique as dissent corresponds to Habermas's insistence upon discursive justification, intersubjective argumentation, as practised by intellectuals who may be regarded as a specific category of free and equal citizens. The mobilization of good or even better reasons, which is what characterizes Habermas's form of criticism, culminates in a consensus, in other words, in an agreement not to accept

7 'Adorno has a highly positive view of exaggeration, of hyperbolic radicalization, without however going so far as to hypostatize hyperbole' (Duttmann, 2004b, 50; see also Duttmann, 2004a, 39ff.).

what may be deemed false, or alternatively, to concur with whatever appears to deserve recognition after scrupulous inspection.

> While the normative social critic appeals to principles capable of being universalized, the evaluative social critic relies on authentic value judgements. His diagnosis of the present is rooted not in objective reasoning but in personal reasons which for their part are embedded in his own life history and the particular features of his age. (Heidbrink 2004, 101)

Despite these differences between Habermas and Adorno as far as their intellectual styles of thought and their approaches to criticism are concerned, it seems possible to discern a common pattern in their practice as intellectuals.

First, neither man seems to have been predestined to become an intellectual, either by birth and origins or even by their profession as academic philosophers and sociologists. We can say of neither man that his intellectual style of thought is the product of his chief or secondary professional activity. Thus, intellectual criticism is not a part of his professional equipment. We may say instead that the willingness to draw attention to oneself in public by appearing as a critic seems rather to arise from a moral stance and a sense of responsibility towards one's own conscience that is anything but common, and that is therefore culturally striking. Even if Adorno and Habermas are rightly included among the intellectual elite, such an ascription is not of decisive importance for their practice as intellectuals, and even less so for their critical method. They did not speak out simply because as academics they felt qualified to do so.

Second, one quality they share is that their critical activity as intellectuals is different from their scholarly criticism. The language they use as intellectuals is different from the highly characteristic language used by philosophers and sociologists. This can be seen very clearly in the different modes of expression cultivated by both Adorno and Habermas when speaking to fellow academics on the one hand, and in the world of journalism and the media on the other. When they spoke as intellectuals, both men used different versions of a nuanced educated language that, for all its dissonance and polemicizing, was concerned with effective communication.

Third, critique as a form is triggered by external causes: in other words, it is situational and restricted in time; it is a controversial statement on urgent problems of social existence that is capable of opening up new ways of seeing or of drawing attention to matters that have been previously overlooked. As regards linguistic presentation, it makes use of rhetorical tropes, dramatization, polemics, irony and generalization.

Fourth, the intellectual style of thinking employed by both Adorno and Habermas represents a kind of balancing act between autonomy and partisanship. On the one hand, both men leave no doubt about the fact that their critical interventions are not tied to any platform, and this explains why they find a public willing to listen. On the other hand, intellectual critique is an activity that is located in the bear pit of conflicting political interests.[8] It always contains value judgements, since the historically changing forms of contempt for humane forms of mutual recognition (of being able to be different without fear, unimpaired intersubjectivity) constitute a constantly changing stumbling block. As far as the contents of the intellectual critique of Adorno and Habermas are concerned, what they have in common is that they both spell out the repressive consequences of structural violence and political domination. Where Adorno places his hopes in the sensibilities of his addressees, in their capacity for empathy, Habermas appeals to politically anchored and culturally acknowledged fundamental values, and at the same time reminds society of its disregard of these normative guidelines.

If we inquire into the function of an intellectual style of thought for the public sphere, we uncover a further, somewhat surprising feature that is common to the two men. It is true that for Adorno, what is crucial is the process of negation that has dissent as its goal, while Habermas's form of critique is inspired by the idea of communication which – in the best case – can culminate in agreement. But in both men, the appellative function of intellectual critique, whether it addresses morally sensitive subjects, as in Adorno's case, or a politically functioning public sphere, as with Habermas, points to the agonal positionality of the intellectual style of thought. Agonality, the battle for meaning, is the defining feature of the intellectual style of thought which finds expression wherever commonly accepted views, convictions, institutional preconceptions and tendencies become the objects of contestation. As an agonal form, intellectual critique is an 'incompetent but legitimate form of criticism' (Lepsius, 1964, 88). It follows that agonality is an interpersonal characteristic of the intellectual style of thought.[9] It may make its appearance in finely graded and highly divergent versions: in Adorno's case, as agonality with the goal of dissent, in that of Habermas, as agonality with the goal of deliberation.

Translated by Rodney Livingstone

8 In this way, 'intellectual autonomy and political commitment form the two complementary structural elements that constitute the role of the intellectual' (Hillmann, 1997, 80).

9 It may be suggested at this point that a precise hermeneutic analysis of intellectual styles of thought from the standpoint of different forms of agonality would be desirable. This would require a clarification of the concept of agonality as well as the development of a theoretical underpinning of the differences between its different forms. At this point, the concept of 'agonal pluralism' contains considerable potential that needs to be explored further (see Mouffe, 1997).

References

Adorno, Theodor W. (1973), *Negative Dialectics*, trans. E.B. Ashton (London: Routledge and Kegan Paul).

Adorno, Theodor W. (1974), *Minima Moralia: Reflections from Damaged Life*, trans. Edmund Jephcott (London: NLB).

Adorno, Theodor W. (1992), 'Commitment', in *Notes to Literature*, vol. 2, trans. Shierry Weber Nicholsen (New York: Columbia University Press).

Adorno, Theodor W. (1997a), 'Notes on Philosophical Thinking', in *Catchwords*, trans. Henry W. Pickford (New York: Columbia University Press).

Adorno, Theodor W. (1997b), 'Meinungsforschung und Öffentlichkeit', in *Gesammelte Schriften*, vol. 8 (Frankfurt: Suhrkamp), 532–46.

Adorno, Theodor W. (1998a), 'Critique', in *Critical Models*: *Interventions and Catchwords*, trans. Henry W. Pickford (New York: Columbia University Press).

Adorno, Theodor W. (1998b), 'Marginalia to Theory and Praxis', in *Critical Models*: *Interventions and Catchwords*, trans. Henry W. Pickford (New York: Columbia University Press).

Adorno, Theodor W. (1998c), 'The Meaning of Working Through the Past', in *Critical Models*: *Interventions and Catchwords*, trans. Henry W. Pickford (New York: Columbia University Press).

Adorno, Theodor W. and Mann, Thomas (2002), *Briefwechsel 1943–1955*, ed. Christoph Gödde and Thomas Sprecher (eds), (Frankfurt: Suhrkamp).

Albrecht, Clemens, Behrmann, Günther C., Bock, Michael, Homann, Harald and Tenbruck, Friedrich H. (1999), *Die intellektuelle Gründung der Bundesrepublik* (Frankfurt and New York: Campus).

Boll, Monika (2005), *Nachtprogramm. Intellektuelle Gründungsdebatten in der frühen Bundesrepublik* (Münster: Lit).

Bonacker, Thorsten (1999), 'Theodor Adorno – Die Zukunft des Erinnerns', in Fröhlich, Claudia and Kohlstruck, Michael (eds), *Engagierte Demokraten. Vergangenheitspolitik in kritischer Absicht* (Münster: Westfälisches Dampfboot), 170–84.

Bourdieu, Pierre (1992), *Les règles de l'art* (Paris: Edition du Seuil).

Duttmann, Garciá (2004a), *Philosophie der Übertreibung* (Frankfurt: Suhrkamp).

Duttmann, Garciá (2004b), *So ist es* (Frankfurt: Suhrkamp).

Essig, Rolf-Bernhard (2000), *Der offene Brief. Geschichte und Funktion einer publizistischen Form von Sokrates bis Günter Grass* (Würzburg: Königshausen and Neumann).

Gilcher-Holtey, Ingrid (1997), 'Menschenrechte oder Vaterland? Die Formierung der Intellektuellen in der Affäre Dreyfus', *Berliner Journal der Soziologie* 7, 61–70.

Habermas, Jürgen (1981), 'Die Utopie des guten Herrschers', in *Kleine politische Schriften I bis IV* (Frankfurt: Suhrkamp).

Habermas, Jürgen (1985), *Die neue Unübersichtlichkeit* (Frankfurt: Suhrkamp).

Habermas, Jürgen (1988), *Nachmetaphysisches Denken* (Frankfurt: Suhrkamp).
Habermas, Jürgen (1992), *Faktizität und Geltung* (Frankfurt: Suhrkamp).
Habermas, Jürgen (1998), *Philosophisch-politische Profile* (Frankfurt: Suhrkamp).
Heidbrink, Ludker (2004), 'Die Grenzen kritischer Negativität', in Ette, Wolfram, Figal, Günter, Klein, Richard and Peters, Günter (eds), *Adorno im Widerstreit. Zur Präsenz seines Denkens* (Freiburg and Munich: Alber), 98–120.
Hillmann, Henning (1997), 'Zwischen Engagement und Autonomie: Elemente für eine Soziologie der Intellektuellen', *Berliner Journal für Soziologie* 7, 71–86.
Karadi, Èva; Vezér, Erszébet and Lukács, Georg (1985), *Karl Mannheim und der Sonntagskreis* (Frankfurt: Sendler).
Kramer, Sven (1996), 'Wahr sind die Sätze als Impuls …', *Deutsche Vierteljahresschrift für Literaturwissenschaft und Geistesgeschichte* 70, 501–23.
Lepsius, M. Rainer (1964), 'Kritik als Beruf. Zur Soziologie der Intellektuellen', *Kölner Zeitschrift für Soziologie und Sozialpsychologie* 16:1, 75–91.
Mouffe, Chantal (1997), 'Inklusion/Exklusion. Das Paradoxon der Demokratie', in Weibel, Peter and Žižek, Slavoj (eds), *Inklusion/Exklusion* (Vienna: Passagen).
Müller-Doohm, Stefan (2003), *Adorno: A Biography*, trans. Rodney Livingstone (Cambridge: Polity Press).
Müller-Doohm, Stefan (2005), 'Thinking from No-Man's-Land', *Studies in Social and Political Thought* 11, 91–103.
Müller-Doohm, Stefan (2008), *Jürgen Habermas. Leben, Werk, Wirkung* (Frankfurt: Suhrkamp).
Seel, Martin (2005), *Adornos Philosophie der Kontemplation* (Frankfurt: Suhrkamp).
Taubes, Jacob (1996), 'Die Intellektuellen und die Universität [1963]', in Assmann, Aleida and Assmann, Jan et al. (eds), *Vom Kult zur Kultur. Bausteine zu einer Kritik der historischen Vernunft* (Munich: Fink), 319–39.

Chapter 13
Women as Public Intellectuals: Kerstin Hesselgren and Alva Myrdal

Per Wisselgren

'Public intellectual' is a term that is *en vogue*. Over the last few years, often in relation to the debates on the roles and functions of academics in the changing relationship between higher education, media and the public, the conceptual figure of the 'public intellectual' has appeared more and more frequently. When the English magazine *Prospect* published a special issue on the theme in July 2004, it was immediately followed up by polyphonic comments in the daily newspapers. A series of new books on the theme has appeared (for example, Posner, 2001; Small, 2002; Melzer, Weinberger and Zinman, 2003). New academic courses with the term in their titles are being arranged. Special professorships and centres for advanced studies have been established to enhance the role of the public intellectual. Meanwhile, in a quite different sphere of thought, in one of the bulletins of the Federal Reserve Bank of Dallas, the economist Milton Friedman is described as a prominent 'public intellectual' (Formaini, 2005). Apparently, almost everyone seems to agree that public intellectual is a good thing to be, and a resource of common importance which society at large benefits greatly from.

Having reached this level of popular usage and the status of a positive catchword, it comes as no surprise, in what has been described as our list-making culture, that there now also exist several rankings for the most important public intellectuals of our time. In one of these lists, Michel Foucault is ranked as number one, followed by Pierre Bourdieu, Jürgen Habermas and Jacques Derrida (Posner, 2001, 212); in another, the linguist and political activist Noam Chomsky is placed at the top (*Prospect*, 2005). As always when qualities are being quantified and ranked numerically, this draws our attention to the criteria used or tacitly presupposed. But they do also raise questions about the glaring absence of women. Apparently, in these lists as well as in more general discussions, the 'public intellectual' tends to be a man. Why is that so? Is it because women tend to be ignored as public intellectuals? Or is it because there actually are fewer of them? And in that case, what is meant with being a 'public intellectual' in the first place?

By taking these questions under consideration, the aim of this chapter is to argue for the need for a more gender-sensitive understanding of public intellectuals. The first section problematizes the concept 'public intellectuals' in itself by pointing at its inherent ambiguity, historical situatedness and gendered bias. In the second section, this discussion will be substantiated empirically by analysing and contextually comparing two of Sweden's most prominent intellectual women of the early twentieth century, Kerstin Hesselgren and Alva Myrdal. In that context, their relations to the historically changing spheres of higher education, social reform and the public will be especially focused upon. The main argument developed in the final discussion is that at least a part of the answer to the question about the lack of women among public intellectuals is to be found in these very spheres with their traditionally gendered barriers.

What is a 'Public Intellectual'?

In one sense, the public intellectual is a new phenomenon. As a term, 'public intellectual' is a neologism – some would even say a pleonasm, arguing that an intellectual *per se* is a public person – which originated in the predominantly American discussion on the declining role of intellectuals – and which has entered common usage in European English only recently, but still not in most other languages, including French, German and Swedish (Small, 2002, 1–2). But, as often is the case with these sorts of popular terms, the suggested definitions vary considerably. Depending on the positions and the perspectives of the authors, as well as the main arguments made, the public intellectual is sometimes described as somebody 'who ceremoniously disdains and turns his back on society – the better to serve it' (Melzer, 2003, 11), on other occasions as 'intellectuals who opine to an educated public on questions of or inflected by a political or ideological concern' (Posner, 2001, 2). However, in none of these definitions is it obvious what distinguishes the 'public intellectual' of our time from the more well-known classical 'intellectual'. Instead, it is significant that the terms are often used interchangeably (Melzer, 2003, xi). In that sense, what is new in the discussion is not so much its subject or the definitions, but the addition of the prefix 'public'. But, who is then 'the intellectual'?

By and large, the same observation – on the diversity and disagreement on the definition of the concept – can be made on the already vast and likewise rapidly expanding literature on 'intellectuals' (for example, Said, 1993; Fuller, 2005; Collini, 2006). There is far from being any consensus about the proper and more precise meaning of the term. 'The intellectual' is, however, and in contrast to 'public intellectual', not a new term, as commented in the introduction, but a concept with a well-documented history, originating in the context of the French Dreyfus Affair in the 1890s. An additional point in this context is that the term was not coined by Émile Zola, but by the anti-Dreyfusards as a *pejorative* signifier for what they regarded as the rootless (*déracine*) and anti-nationalist aspects of Zola's and the other Dreyfusards' free-floating, cosmopolitan and dissident style of thought (Liedman, 2003, 271).

Ever since then, discussions on intellectuals have mirrored the *ambiguity* of the term as an empirical category, its positive and negative connotations, its contextual dependencies on national and cultural traditions, and its inherent tensions between its different central components. Hence, some authors have emphasized the *professional identity* among academics, writers, journalists, teachers and so on, others the *public* mission and the political engagement in the issues of the time. Some point at the *independent* and cosmopolitan style of thought of the restricted few, others at the intellectual's *representational function* in relation to contemporary social movements.

The approach taken in this chapter is not to stick to one definition of the 'true nature of the intellectual' and disqualify the others, but on the contrary, to emphasize the historically and contextually changing preconditions for people to act and identify themselves as intellectuals (cf. Connell, 2007, 3). Analytically, I will do this by distinguishing between two opposing ideal typical definitions of the intellectual. On the one hand, we have the 'free-floating intellectual', the disinterested outsider who has the courage and integrity to criticize any authority, at whatever personal costs and consequences. On the other hand, we have the pragmatic and constructive intellectual, who emphasizes that it is necessary to 'reach out' and actively contribute to the change of order of things.

The two definitions are opposite, in the sense that a positive valuation of one standpoint is usually combined with a negative one of the other. Hence, while intellectuals in the first camp regard themselves as independent and autonomous, they are often critical of others for isolating themselves in the Ivory Tower. On the other hand, while the intellectuals in the second camp want to identify themselves as socially engaged, pragmatic realists, they are sometimes being portrayed as market-oriented 'jetsetters' flying from one political leader to another all over the world to discuss subjects of worldly concern.

What both these ideal typical extremes have in common, however, is that they are deeply concerned with questions about the roles, functions and uses of social knowledge, and related issues in the overlapping field between the spheres of learning, policy and the public. Another thing that they have in common is that these topics are usually discussed from within, from the insider's perspective, since most intellectuals themselves usually have a formal higher education, participate in the public debate and exert some kind of influence on the political sphere. For that reason, I suggest, it is plausible to analytically situate the different types of public intellectuals within a framework of a tripartite, historically changing, relationship between the academic sphere, the political sphere and the public sphere.

With such a framework, it will also be possible to develop a more gender-sensitive understanding of the institutional preconditions that circumscribe the spheres of action of 'public intellectuals'. Empirically, this will be done by focusing on women with explicit intellectual ambitions and considering in what sense they may qualify as public intellectuals, but also by analysing their actions and their experiences in their historically situated contexts in general, and in relation to the educational, the political and the public spheres in particular.

Kerstin Hesselgren, Alva Myrdal and their Historical Contexts

The two intellectuals chosen for this purpose are the Swedish women Kerstin Hesselgren and Alva Myrdal. The most important reasons for choosing them are fourfold. First, both of them had explicit intellectual ambitions, showed distinction in their own fields, were well versed and good at communicating their ideas, and opined on questions of political concerns – and in that sense would qualify as 'public intellectuals' according to the most commonly expressed criteria (cf. *Prospect*, 2004, 22). Second, they had a similar basic agenda – to propagate social reforms based on social research in the name of modernization and social welfare, especially on issues related to women's experiences – where both of them actively and explicitly mediated between the spheres of education/research, reform/politics and the media/public, and hence make a good case for a contextual comparison. Both of them were also regarded as outstanding women in public life in their own lifetime (Wetterstrom, 1936, 7–10). Of similar importance, however, is the third reason, that they belonged to two different generations and were partly active during different phases of the first half of the twentieth century, and hence make it possible to discuss the *changing* conditions for women intellectuals *over time*. Fourth, both Myrdal and Hesselgren are well-known figures in the Swedish context, which means that they offer not only good empirical sources, but also a growing body of literature to draw on in this context. Still, however, there does not exist any comparative study of their achievements as public intellectuals.

Methodologically, it is worth clarifying at the outset that I am not primarily interested in whether Hesselgren and Myrdal were typical of women of their time more generally. On the contrary, there are a good many reasons for arguing for their unique and exceptional qualities. The purpose is instead to use their cases as heuristic tools for discussing the *conditions* for women to act as public intellectuals. In that respect, the biographical studies will be chronologically limited. In Hesselgren's case, her achievements in the first two decades of the twentieth century will be emphasized, while in Myrdal's case, her activities in the 1930s and 1940s will be especially focused upon (although their trajectories were chronologically parallel during six decades, and actually crossed each other a few times).

The following questions structure the presentations: (1) What do today's images of Hesselgren and Myrdal look like, and what does earlier research say about them? (2) What were their social and educational backgrounds? (3) How can one portray them as social researchers and social reformers? (4) In what sense, more exactly, can they be described as 'public intellectuals'? (5) Did their positions as 'public intellectuals' change over time?

Kerstin Hesselgren and the Early Twentieth Century

In the Swedish context, Kerstin Hesselgren (1872–1962) is primarily known as one of the very first women to enter the Swedish Parliament (*Riksdag*) directly after universal suffrage had been introduced in 1921. As a symbol for that historical moment, the image of her has almost reached the status of an icon, whose positive heritage most people want to share. For example, when the Swedish Research Council established the so-called Kerstin Hesselgren Chair in 1987, a prestigious guest professorship which since then has been awarded annually to an excellent woman scholar from abroad, the name was chosen to commemorate Hesselgren's 'outstanding public service [and] her expertise in social policy and work on women's rights, as a pioneer of the women's movement, and for her commitment to the cause of international peace' (Swedish Research Council, 2004). However, strangely enough, there has been no proper biography written about Hesselgren. Instead, the standard account being at hand is a book written by her former colleagues and close friends (Hamrin-Thorell et al., 1968). And her reputation is still more or less one-sidedly focused on her political achievements, where she is usually described as a liberal pioneer – despite the fact that she did not join the liberal party until in 1934 (Lindblad, 2002). Meanwhile, her role as a social researcher has attracted remarkably little attention. However, an important point in this context is that Hesselgren herself – in a way typical of the time – regarded social research and social reform as intimately and inseparably interwoven (cf. Hedin, 2002, 209–11).

She was also typical of her generation of social researchers, in the sense that what originally drew her attention to the rapidly expanding field of social knowledge was her deep concern for the widely debated social issues of her time, and the conviction that social reform ought to be based on systematic social investigations. But unlike her male equals – among which we find the first generation of Swedish academic social scientists such as Gustaf Steffen in sociology and Knut Wicksell and Gustav Cassel in economics (Wisselgren, 2000, 210–34) – Hesselgren never attained any established position in the higher education system.

Instead, it is instructive from the point of gender to follow Hesselgren's broad, not to say winding, educational background. Brought up in a well-to-do upper-middle-class home – as the daughter of a conservative district medical officer and a liberal-minded housewife – she was initially educated at home by governesses. After that, she followed different courses in nursing and household economics and was certificated as both a barber-surgeon and school kitchen teacher before she went abroad to Bedford College in London, from which she received a degree as a sanitary inspector in 1905 (Hamrin-Thorell et al., 1968, 46–60). The trajectory leading to this diploma may give the impression that Hesselgren was hesitant and irresolute about her own future. My point is, however, that the winding nature of her educational training rather bears witness to Hesselgren's thirst for learning, as well as to the many locked doors that met those women who looked for appropriate opportunities to channel their commitment to social issues in the contemporary system of higher education. In that sense, it is significant that Hesselgren went abroad, to England, where the system – unlike in Sweden – included specially designed women's colleges, but also that the Bedford department which educated sanitary inspectors later developed into the Department of Social Studies (Drewry and Brock, 2001, 313–16).

Directly after her return to Sweden – with her unique diploma as sanitary inspector in her portfolio of merits – Hesselgren began her career as a social researcher. During the decade to come, she passed through several of the most important institutions in the rapidly expanding field of social knowledge-production. First, she joined the newly created Centralförbundet för socialt arbete (CSA, 'Central Association for Social Work'), a kind of Swedish equivalent to the English Charity Organization Society, where she belonged to the inner circle of the organization, and as such was heavily involved in most of its many social research initiatives (Wisselgren, 2006). In 1906, Hesselgren was recruited to carry out a minor study on the female emigrants in the context of the huge, state-supported so-called 'Emigration Survey' (*Emigrationsutredningen*) which was set up that year and during the next seven years produced a 900-page final report and no less than 20 volumes of supplementary reports (Hesselgren, 1908).

After her social research projects for the CSA and the Emigration Survey, Hesselgren turned into a Sanitary Inspector (in 1906) and School Kitchen Inspector (in 1909), before she was employed in 1912 by the newly created Socialstyrelsen ('National Board of Health and Social Welfare'), where she became the first female Factory Inspector in Sweden, a post which she stayed in for two decades. This did not, however, mean that she changed track; she continued to work as social researcher and reformer in her professional role as inspector. As the head of the Female Factory Inspectorate with its staff of assistants, Hesselgren during the following decades initiated no less than fifty investigations and thousands of minor inspections in different factories all over Sweden (Åkerblom, 1998). And when the Institutet för socialpolitisk och kommunal utbildning och forskning ('Social Institute') in Stockholm was set up in 1921 – which pioneered the academic training of social workers and in the following decades developed into an institutional stronghold for academic social research in Sweden – Hesselgren became one of its most loyal lecturers and examiners, besides her activities as a member of the Swedish Parliament (Thörn, 1997, 256).

So in what sense was Hesselgren a 'public intellectual'? In the context of the development of an early social policy intelligentsia in Sweden, Hesselgren has been grouped together with a number of contemporary male and female philanthropists, municipal officeholders, civil servants, social teachers and writers under the heading of a so-called 'liberal humanitarian welfare intelligentsia', characterized by its blend of secular liberalism and social-Christian humanitarianism (Olsson, 1993, 86–7). But she was also steadily anchored in the contemporary women's movement (Frangeur, 2003, 92).

In addition to this, I would like to underline the practical orientation of Hesselgren's social thought. She was from early on aware of the need for social investigations, but also of the importance of disseminating the social knowledge produced to a larger audience and turning this knowledge into practical action, where research and reform were always intricately interwoven. In that sense, Kerstin Hesselgren's rather unnoticed achievements as a social researcher fit well into a specific type of public intellectuals, which in the Swedish context can be characterized as 'practical movement intellectuals' – individuals deeply engaged in public issues, whose practically oriented deeds have left historical tracks not so much in the form of elaborated theoretical thoughts documented in thick books, but rather as practical contributions in the building of anonymous institutions – and partly for that reason have tended to be disregarded by traditional intellectual historians (Ambjörnsson and Sörlin, 1995, 7–12). Hence, it is no coincidence – but another important part of the argument – that many of these practically oriented public intellectuals were women.

Quite naturally, however, Hesselgren's political duties expanded rapidly, and consequently took up more and more of her time. In spite of that, the research-reform nexus remained an important component in her social thought. An important forum in that context, where research and reform efforts could be combined, was offered by the state-governed investigations, where Hesselgren was repeatedly commissioned as a social expert. But she also continued to keep close contact with the steadily growing women's movement, where she often acted as a network-builder who united women from different classes and political parties (Frangeur, 2003, 97). She was also one of the prime movers behind both the first union for social workers (Östlund, 2001; Carlson, 2006) and the so-called Fogelstad group, a small but influential group of women arranging courses and seminars for other women to fulfil their new citizenship (Eskilsson, 1991).

When in the late 1930s a special Committee on Women's Work was set up by the government to investigate the role of women in the job market, it is significant that Hesselgren, who had actively agitated for social reforms based on careful social investigations, often with a focus on women's issues and with an open mind to compromises over the political party lines, was appointed to the chairmanship (SOU, 1938). But it is also significant that the secretary by her side on that committee was Alva Myrdal, a social democratic woman thirty years younger, who shared Hesselgren's commitment to research-based reform in the area of women's rights.

Alva Myrdal and the Inter-war Period

Although they belonged to two different generations, Alva Myrdal and Kerstin Hesselgren have much in common. Like Hesselgren, Alva Myrdal (1902–1986) is extremely well known in the Swedish context. Unlike Hesselgren, however, Myrdal's reputation stretches far beyond the national borders. One reason for this is certainly that she received the Nobel Prize in 1982 for her diplomatic work on nuclear disarmament, another that her husband also received a Nobel Prize, in economics in 1974. As the only spouses to have won Nobel Prizes for their achievements in separate fields, they have also been recognized as an extraordinary creative couple (Abir-Am, 1995, 272). In Sweden, however, Alva and Gunnar had already become known as 'the Myrdal couple' after having published their co-authored and extremely influential book *Kris i befolkningsfrågan* ('Crisis in the Population Question') in 1934, which is usually regarded as one of the ideological pillars of the Swedish welfare state project. Ever since then, Alva Myrdal has been a public figure whose private life has attracted common interest.

In the last two decades, however, the historical conceptualization of the modern Swedish welfare project has been the object of a critical re-evaluation process, where not least the legacy of Alva Myrdal has been contested (Hirdman, 1989; Runcis, 1998). To this process, her own children have contributed by giving their own – partly contradictory – biographical accounts of their mother, and more recently, these issues have attracted renewed interest after the rich private correspondence between Alva and Gunnar was opened to the public in 2000 (see, for example, Hederberg, 2004; Hirdman, 2006). Still, however, Alva Myrdal is primarily known as a politician – like Hesselgren. But Myrdal was also a social researcher, who authored a number of books and large numbers of pamphlets, articles and reviews. Her bibliography, which only covers the period up until 1961, includes 491 entries (Terling, 1987). However, unlike Hesselgren, her significance as a social researcher has more recently begun to attract increasing interest (see, for example, Nilsson, 1994; Ekerwald, 2000; Holmwood, 2000; Lyon, 2004).

As a woman committed to social research, there were several gender barriers to overcome. Brought up in a well-to-do lower-middle-class home, as the oldest daughter to a father with socialist sympathies and a bourgeois mother with traditional ideas about what a girl should and should not do, Alva had to struggle for her education. Although she ached to continue her studies after elementary school, all traditional avenues were blocked. The public *gymnasium* in her hometown, Eskilstuna, was only for boys. After two years of near-constant arguing, Alva did, however, manage to convince her father to persuade the local town school board to arrange private courses at *gymnasium* level for Alva and a few other girls – not for free, however, and separated from the existing *gymnasium* building. After having compressed the last two years of studies into one and attained her matriculation with the highest honours, she aimed for university studies (Bok, 1991, 35–48).

Her dream was to become a doctor, but she soon realized the lack of realism in that project and decided to aim for a more conventional woman's job as a librarian instead. After all, Myrdal commented in retrospect, 'the main thing for me was to come to the university' (quoted in Buttimer, 1987, 15). There, first at Stockholm University College and later at Uppsala University, she took courses in Literature and Nordic Studies, but after a while her focus changed to psychology and pedagogy. Encouraged by the Professor of Pedagogy, Bertil Hammer, she started to work on a thesis aimed at a positive critique of Freud's dream theory (Myrdal, 1929c). But when Hammer suddenly died and was replaced by Rudolf Anderberg, who was not only critical of Freud but regarded his theories as unworthy of any academic attention, Myrdal was once again barred from continued studies (Bok, 1991, 95–6).

At that moment, Alva had already met Gunnar and accompanied him on his stipend trips to England and Germany. During these trips, Alva not only helped Gunnar to translate his dissertation, but was also offered a possibility to deepen her interest in child education. Even more important as a formative experience was their joint trip to America in 1929–30 as Rockefeller Foundation research fellows (Jackson, 1990, 59). While Gunnar was working on his critical study of the foundations of neoclassical economics (Myrdal, 1930), Alva's aim with the trip was, according to her own formulation in the application, 'to specialize my studies in the direction of social psychology, a branch which is until now almost exclusively an American science', in order to 'prove competent for holding an academic lecturership in psychology and theoretical pedagogics' (Myrdal, 1929a).

But Alva's research interests were not restricted to the social psychological area. Together, Gunnar's economic network contacts and Alva's social psychological ones overlapped and were extended in each direction. In a letter to a friend, Alva explained the dialectical result of their collaboration: 'An economist + a social psychologist, united in marriage and authorship, makes naturally and easily a sociologist' (Myrdal 1929b). Of special importance for this collaborative approach and their new sociological research interests were Dorothy Swaine and W.I. Thomas, who lived, worked and performed as an intellectual couple, and were engaged in research and policy issues closely related to the interests of Alva and Gunnar, and with whom they developed a close and long-lasting relationship (Lyon, 2001, 231). Filled with new impressions, they saw a future role for themselves as social scientists and public intellectuals when they returned to Sweden (Carlson, 1990, 42).

Back in Sweden, the Myrdals were drawn into politics, and from that moment on began to perform as public intellectuals. They joined the Social Democratic Worker's Party, and soon became practically and ideologically involved in the social reform movement. Alva Myrdal became vice-chairman of the newly established Swedish branch of the Yrkeskvinnors Klubb ('Working Women's Association'), a member of the editorial board of the Social Democratic women's journal *Morgonbris*, and was soon regarded as one of the central authorities in the women's movement. Meanwhile, Gunnar became one of the leading figures in avant-garde social policy circles, revolving around the so-called *acceptera* group and the journal *Spektrum* (Hirdman, 2006, 166).

However, their definite breakthrough as public intellectuals came, as mentioned, with their co-authored book *Crisis in the Population Question* (1934), where they formulated the steadily declining population as a crucial issue of national importance, and proposed a family-centred social policy where the state was the instrument to put things on a new course, and hence managed to open up common ground for both radical reformers and conservatives (Myrdal and Myrdal, 1934). The book was received in a way that probably no other book has been in Sweden in modern time: the first edition quickly sold out, and was soon followed by several new editions, including a special 'people's edition', as well as special study circles and radio debates based on the book, and no less than 30 volumes of press cuttings (Andersson, 1998, 15). From that focal point of the contemporary public debate, the step was not very far into the centre of Swedish political life. Gunnar was recruited to the large Population Commission set up by the parliament, and Alva was soon enlisted in the same commission as an expert (Wisselgren, 2008).

In retrospect, Alva Myrdal characterized the decade and a half following *Crisis* as 'a period filled by preaching the social gospel' (quoted in Buttimer, 1987, 15). At the beginning of that period, she was primarily concerned with issues of children's welfare and women's rights, but gradually her scope of tasks widened to the areas of education, international issues, peace and disarmament (Andersson, 2003, 14–15). In 1949, she was recruited to New York to head the UN Department of Social Affairs. After that, her international career took off, and was followed first by another top job in Paris, where she directed the UNESCO Department of Social Sciences, and then a six-year period in India, Ceylon, Burma and Nepal as Sweden's first woman ambassador, several other commissions of trust, a period as a member of the Cabinet, intense work on disarmament, crowned by the Nobel Prize in 1982, and followed by several periods as a visiting research fellow abroad (Thullberg, 1989, 161).

Was Alva Myrdal a public intellectual? And if so, in what sense, more precisely? According to the general criteria mentioned earlier – distinction in her own field of knowledge coupled with an ability to communicate well to generalist audiences on issues of political concern – the answer is definitely yes. As an opinion-maker, she was probably one of the most important voices of twentieth-century Sweden (Mral, 1994). She was also one of the leading figures of the inter-war generation of social democratic social policy intellectuals (Tilton, 1991, 145). Her more fundamental *Leitmotiv* was not restricted to the party political agenda, however, but based on an inner conviction to always fight for social justice (Bok, 1991, 43). The practical aspects were accordingly, in a way that bears resemblance to Hesselgren's case, emphasized. Knowledge was for Myrdal a means for doing, not contemplating (Hirdman, 1992, 117). This credo, transferred to the field of social knowledge, meant that social research and social reform were and should be intimately interwoven.

But did she identify herself as an intellectual? Although Alva Myrdal often expressed her sympathy for social justice, participated in the public debate, praised the importance of learning and higher education, and emphasized the symbiotic relationship between social research and reform, she very seldom spoke explicitly about intellectuals. One such rare occasion was when, after their homecoming to Sweden, she wrote a letter to their American friends and told them about her and Gunnar's new circle of friends, which she enthusiastically described as:

> young radical people who want to be free to criticise anything – they don't care about their careers – but who are not going to be just *intellectuals* making a show, but keeping together as a group because they want to be constructive. They are all *experts* in different fields and probably the most outspoken group in this country, being at the same time absolutely free from all petty considerations of what is done and what is not said and so on. (Myrdal, 1932; my italics)

What is remarkable in this context, however, is that the term 'intellectuals' – when taken into closer consideration – is actually not used in a positive way, as a position or style of thought that Alva Myrdal identified herself with. Instead, what Myrdal pointed out was that her friends were *not only* 'intellectuals making a show', but a group of knowledgeable experts who wanted to be constructive. This use and connotation of the term was in no way unique for Myrdal. For example, one of her contemporary colleagues, the modernist author and journalist Ludvig Nordström, who from today's perspective would also qualify as a public intellectual, explicitly described 'the intellectuals' as a backward-looking and introspective group of people who had long since lost contact with modern reality (Nordström, 1937, 32). The historical point to be made in this context is, of course, not that Nordström was thinking about social reformers such as Alva Myrdal, but that he wanted to emphasize the importance of constructive and future-oriented action, symbolized by the pragmatic engineer rather than the detached intellectual, a standpoint which Alva Myrdal – named after Thomas Alva Edison – sympathized with, and exactly for that reason, did not identify herself as an 'intellectual' in that sense.

In a similar way, Gunnar Myrdal used the term pejoratively. For instance, when, as the new editor of the social democratic journal *Tiden* (in March 1945), he defended the government's neutrality policy against the critique delivered by a group of academics, journalists and authors, Myrdal described them as 'intellectuals':

> The group is small and fragmented. What it is all about is a group of *isolated intellectuals* who experienced the neutrality during the War as a mental trauma. Some of them are writing in the newspapers, which may give the impression that they are more important than they actually are. What they miss however are sound contacts with common people's organizations, and they are of course in lack of any political significance. (Myrdal, 1945, 133; my translation and italics)

But it is also important to keep Alva's and Gunnar's individual opinions apart. As intellectuals, they were not identical. Gunnar was in several ways more like the classical male intellectual who identified himself as a detached researcher observing the world from above. While Alva emphasized the importance of practical political action on the democratic grass-root level, Gunnar during his period as a member of the parliament was 'longing back to disinterested work again, where I am neutral and skeptical' (quoted in Lyon, 2001, 230). Hence, when they went on their second journey to the US in 1938, there were two different minds observing the country. While Gunnar expressed with relief, 'Now we are free researchers again, independent of the masses and mass-people in the shapes of political representatives' (quoted in Hatje, 1974, 45; my translation), Alva was more fascinated by Roosevelt's pragmatism – 'almost the *opposite* to what we usually have in mind when we speak about an *intellectual*' – and the way Roosevelt had succeeded in enrolling young academics as experts and transforming their 'negative intellectual radicalism' into a 'practical idealism' (Myrdal and Myrdal, 1941, 144, 243; my translation and italics; cf. Jackson, 2003, 68).

Women as Public Intellectuals: Concluding Discussion

What do these accounts of Kerstin Hesselgren and Alva Myrdal say about women as public intellectuals? Is it possible to generalize from their experiences? In some ways, apparently not. Hesselgren and Myrdal were – like all individuals – unique. As women, they were in many respects exceptional for their time rather than typical, and in that sense it is not possible to regard them as representatives for women more generally. Nevertheless, it is possible to draw a few more far-reaching conclusions. As two intellectual women with similar agendas – to improve the conditions for other women as well as for the population at large by initiating social policy reforms based on social research – their biographical experiences can be used heuristically to unveil some of the gendered conditions circumscribing those women who attempted a public intellectual endeavour. In that sense, their trajectories bear witness to more general patterns, which supersede the individual and the exceptional, in the historically changing relationship between the three spheres of social research, political reform and the public.

As stated in the introduction, most discussions on the role of intellectuals are also discussions about the social functions and uses of knowledge, and in that respect the systems of education and higher education constitute two fundamental institutions in the sphere of learning and research. In that context, it is worth noting that both Hesselgren and Myrdal – despite the fact that they belonged to the growing middle class, where learning and education were encouraged – had problems quenching their thirst for knowledge. Because of their gender, their parents had to arrange private education outside the public *gymnasium* system – which remained closed for girls until in 1928 – to make it possible for them to take their exams. Having managed to sidestep that barrier, however, another obstacle marked the entrance to the higher education system. Although women had been formally eligible to enter Swedish universities since 1871, the academic world remained highly segregated for a long time afterwards, implying that the intellectual sphere as such was regarded as masculine territory (Rönnholm, 1999). Unlike Hesselgren, Myrdal did, however – one generation later – enter the Swedish academic sphere, although in the end she had to abandon her dissertation plans.

More important for both were their international educational experiences – Hesselgren's from Bedford College and Myrdal's from the US. During their years abroad, both of them developed a deep commitment to empirical research and social investigations. To channel these interests, however, both had to go outside the academic sphere, to the private sphere and organizations such as the CSA, and the public sphere with its governmental investigations. In that way, Hesselgren managed to make an indeed remarkable career crowned by the job as a kind of 'research director' for the Female Factory Inspectorate – in a period when most positions in the public sphere, including the state universities, were still closed for women. Unlike Hesselgren, Myrdal for a long time worked in a full-time permanent post and had to pursue her social research on a 'freelance' basis – although, of course, economically, her position as a professor's wife was safe. In that context, and compared to her male equals among social researchers, of whom most had a professorship behind them, including Gunnar, it is remarkable that it was not until in 1951, when Alva Myrdal was appointed the directorship of the UNESCO Department of Social Science, that her recognition as a social researcher was accompanied by an appropriate position.

However, neither Hesselgren nor Myrdal are especially well known today as social researchers. Instead, both of them are primarily recognized as politicians – Hesselgren as one of the pioneering women in the Swedish parliament, and Myrdal as one of the ideological founders of the Swedish welfare state. Both of them were also offered wider scope for action within the political sphere than within the academic social scientific one. Although they had their ideological bases in the most influential political parties of their time – Hesselgren in the Liberal Party and Alva in the Social Democratic Party – their party political allegiances were in several respects of minor importance. Instead, both of them acted relatively free of party ties. Hesselgren did not become a formal member of the Liberal Party until 1934, and was re-elected in 1926 on a combination of Social Democratic and Liberal votes, while in Myrdal's case it is well documented how she actively worked across party lines to reach constructive solutions. Their reform efforts were also directed towards social issues in general, and those concerning women in particular, primarily such as they appeared in public life, but also within the domestic sphere. Significant in this respect is Hesselgren's and Myrdal's close and successful collaboration in the important Women's Work Committee during 1935–38, which in the end resulted in a new law in the area of gender equality, unique of its kind, which for the first time restricted employers' ability to discriminate and dismiss women because of marriage or pregnancy (Frangeur, 1998, 246).

As intellectual women active in the traditionally male-dominated public sphere, Hesselgren and Myrdal were forerunners who widened the sphere of action for other women, both as role models and by articulating problems from women's point of view and improving the actual conditions. And there was certainly much to be done. Although Hesselgren personified the successful result of the decade-long struggle for women's political rights, several other formal obstacles remained to be challenged. It would, for example, take another half-decade before women were eligible to take up posts within the state-governed sphere, including the academic one – but still with some restrictions which were not abolished until 1949 (Markusson Winkvist, 2003, 47, 208). But there were also cultural barriers to overcome. Any woman attempting to be an intellectual had to cross the traditionally gendered boundary between the private and the public spheres (Landes, 1998, 9–10).

Considering these legal and cultural restrictions, it is no coincidence that both Hesselgren and Myrdal were focusing especially on issues related to women's emancipation in their strivings for general social welfare. As women with intellectual ambitions, both had personally experienced several of these injustices because of their gender, and as Myrdal explained, it was basically these experiences that made her identify not only with other women, but also with the underprivileged and the downtrodden in general (Buttimer, 1987, 14–15). From such a perspective, it was important for both Hesselgren and Myrdal that a deepened theoretical understanding of society, based on research, should be followed up by practical reforms, but also that both of them tended to emphasize the reform side in the research–reform nexus.

Reconnecting this comparison between Hesselgren and Myrdal to the two ideal types of intellectuals outlined in the introduction to this chapter, it can be concluded that neither of them identified themselves as classical free-floating intellectuals. For both of them, 'intellectual' was still a pejorative term, with connotations of isolation, elitism, and idealistic and theoretical introspection. On the contrary, they emphasized the importance of political engagement and pragmatic democratic solutions, public mission and political engagement in the social issues of their time. Anchored in the women's movement as they were, it is more plausible to describe them as movement intellectuals who articulated a female point of view and who, by way of their expert function, strived for social reforms from within.

In so far as the public intellectual is defined – explicitly or implicitly – as an academic going public and permeating the political sphere, it is important to remind oneself that it has for historical institutional reasons been unlikely that those intellectuals should be women, since there have been formal and cultural barriers to overcome in every single respect: in the spheres of education and higher education, in the political sphere in Sweden up until 1921, and in the culturally gendered public sphere. In all these respects, Hesselgren and Myrdal were exceptional rather than typical, in the sense that they managed to make careers as public intellectuals anyway, although they – also for historical reasons – did not identify themselves as such.

Acknowledgements

This chapter was originally produced within the project '*Analysing and Overcoming the Sociological Fragmentation in Europe' (ANOVASOFIE), funded by the European Commission, DG Research, Sixth Framework Programme, Citizens and Governance in a Knowledge Based Society, Contract no. CIT2-CT-2004-506035.* Other parts of the work have been sponsored by the Bank of Sweden Tercentenary Foundation and the Swedish Research Council. An earlier version of this chapter was published in the series of working reports (no. 30, in 1996) from the Office for the History of Science, Uppsala University.

I am grateful for many stimulating discussions throughout the whole research process with Hedvig Ekerwald, the co-ordinator of the Swedish part of the EU-project, and for important comments from Stellan Andersson, Annika Berg, Anders Ekström, Marika Hedin, Ragnvald Kalleberg, Stina Lyon, Ulla Manns and Jennifer Platt.

References

Abir-Am, Pnina G. (1995), 'Collaborative Couples Who Changed the World', in Pycior, H.M., Slack, N.G. and Abir-Am, P.G. (eds), *Creative Couples in the Sciences* (New Brunswick, NJ: Rutgers University Press).

Åkerblom, Annika (1998), *Arbetarskydd för kvinnor* (Uppsala: Department of economic history).

Ambjörnsson, Ronny and Sörlin, Sverker (eds) (1995), *Obemärkta* (Stockholm: Carlsson).

Andersson, Stellan (1998), 'On the Value of Personal Archives', paper presented to the Gunnar Myrdal Centennial Seminar, Stockholm, 2–4 December.

Andersson, Stellan (2003), 'Alva Myrdal 1902–1986', *Arbetarhistoria* 106–7, 12–15.

Bok, Sissela (1991), *Alva Myrdal* (Cambridge: Perseus Publishing).

Buttimer, Anne (1987), 'From an Interview with Alva Myrdal', in Terling, B., *Alva Myrdal: An Annoted Bibliography 1932–1961* (Stockholm: Alva och Gunnar Myrdals stiftelse).

Carlson, Allan C. (1990), *The Swedish Experiment in Family Politics* (New Brunswick, NJ: Transaction Publishers).

Carlson, Benny (2006), 'Hesselgren, van Kleeck and the IRI', Historisk tidskrift 126:2, 215–35.

Collini, Stefan (2006), *Absent Minds* (Oxford: Oxford University Press).

Connell, Raewyn (2007), 'The Heart of the Problem', *Sociology* 41:1, 11–28.

Drewry, Gavin and Brock, Jenny (2001), 'Social Studies and Social Science', in Crook, J.M. (ed.), *Bedford College* (Egham: Royal Holloway and Bedford New College).

Ekerwald, Hedvig (2000), 'Alva Myrdal', *Acta Sociologica* 43, 343–52.

Eskilsson, Lena (1991), *Drömmen om kamratsamhället* (Stockholm: Carlssons).

Formaini, Robert L. (2005) 'Milton Friedman', *Economic Insights* 7, <http://www.dallasfed.org/research/ei/ei0202.pdf>, accessed 7 March 2005.

Frangeur, Renée (1998), *Yrkeskvinna eller makens tjänarinna* (Lund: Arkiv förlag).

Frangeur, Renée (2003), 'Kerstin Hesselgren och kvinnorörelsen 1925–1955', in Witt-Brattström, E. and Lennerhed, L. (eds), *Kvinnorna skall göra det!* (Huddinge: Södertörns högskola).

Fuller, Steve (2005), *The Intellectual* (Cambridge: Icon).

Hamrin-Thorell, Ruth, Widemar, Ingrid Gärde, Myrdal, Alva and Bergman, Malin (1968), *Boken om Kerstin Hesselgren* (Stockholm: P.A. Norstedt and Söner).

Hatje, Ann-Katrin (1974), *Befolkningsfrågan och välfärden* (Stockholm: Allmänna förlaget).

Hederberg, Hans (2004), *Sanningen, inget annat än sanningen* (Stockholm: Atlantis).

Hedin, Marika (2002), *Ett liberalt dilemma* (Stockholm/Stehag: Symposion).

Hesselgren, Kerstin (1908), 'Kvinnliga emigranter under år 1907', in *Emigrationsutredningen, Bilaga VII* (Stockholm: P.A. Norstedt and Söner).
Hirdman, Yvonne (1989), *Att lägga livet tillrätta* (Stockholm: Carlssons).
Hirdman, Yvonne (1992), *Den socialistiska hemmafrun* (Stockholm: Carlssons).
Hirdman, Yvonne (2006), *Det tänkande hjärtat* (Stockholm: Ordfront).
Holmwood, John (2000), 'Three Pillars of Welfare State Theory', *European Journal of Social Theory* 3, 23–50.
Jackson, Walter A. (1990), *Gunnar Myrdal and America's Conscience* (Chapel Hill, NC: University of North Carolina Press).
Jackson, Walter A. (2003), 'Alva Myrdals kritik av amerikansk politik', *Arbetarhistoria* 106–7, 62–73.
Landes, Joan B. (ed.) (1998), *Feminism, the Public and the Private* (Oxford: Oxford University Press).
Liedman, Sven-Eric (2003), 'De intellektuella i Sverige och Frankrike', in Kylhammar, M. and Battail, J.-F. (eds), *På väg mot en kommunikativ demokrati?* (Stockholm: Carlssons).
Lindblad, Linnéa (2002), 'Kerstin Hessselgren', in Holmberg, H. (ed.), *Liberala pionjärer* (Uppsala: Uppsala Publishing House).
Lyon, E. Stina (2001), 'The Myrdals and the Thomases 1930–1940', in Mucha, J., Kaesler, D. and Winclawski, W. (eds), *Mirrors and Windows* (Torun: Nicholas Copernicus University Press).
Lyon, E. Stina (2004), 'Writing about Alva and Gunnar Myrdal's Contribution to Sociology', *International Journal of Social Research Methodology* 7, 323–43.
Markusson Winkvist, Hanna (2003), *Som isolerade öar* (Stockholm/Stehag: Symposion).
Melzer, Arthur M. (2003), 'What Is an Intellectual', in Melzer, A.M., Weinberger, J. and Zinman, M.R. (eds), *The Public Intellectual* (London: Rowman and Littlefield).
Melzer, Arthur M., Weinberger, Jerry and Zinman, M. Richard (eds) (2003), *The Public Intellectual* (London: Rowman and Littlefield).
Mral, Brigitte (1994), *Alva Myrdal och medierna på 30-talet* (Uppsala: Avdelning för retorik).
Myrdal, Alva (1929a), 'Application to the Rockefeller Foundation, 28 February 1929', vol. 1.1.1, Labour Movement Archives and Library, Stockholm.
Myrdal, Alva (1929b), 'Letter to Else-Merete and Alf Ross, 20 December 1929', vol. 3.1.2, Labour Movement Archives and Library, Stockholm.
Myrdal, Alva (1929c), 'Utkast till en kritik av Freuds drömlära', vol. 4.1.1, Labour Movement Archives and Library, Stockholm.
Myrdal, Alva (1932), 'Letter to Eve and Arthur Burnes, 12 October 1932', vol. 3.1.2, Labour Movement Archives and Library, Stockholm.
Myrdal, Alva and Myrdal, Gunnar (1934), *Kris i befolkningsfrågan*, 2nd edn, reprint (Nora: Bokförlaget Nya Doxa, 1997).
Myrdal, Alva and Myrdal, Gunnar (1941), *Kontakt med Amerika* (Stockholm: Bonniers).

Myrdal, Gunnar (1930), *Vetenskap och politik i nationalekonomien* (Stockholm: Norstedts).
Myrdal, Gunnar (1945), 'Utrikespolitisk enighet', *Tiden* 3, 129–37.
Nilsson, Jan Olof (1994), *En virvel i den moderna strömmen* (Stockholm: Symposion).
Nordström, Ludvig (1937), 'Den dumme svensken – farväl', *Vecko-Journalen* 52, 24–5, 30–32.
Olsson, Sven E. (1993), *Social Policy and Welfare State in Sweden* (Lund: Arkiv).
Östlund, David (2001), 'Kerstin Hesselgren och personalkonsulenterna', unpublished manuscript.
Posner, Henry A. (2001), *Public Intellectuals*, 2nd edn (Cambridge, MA: Harvard University Press, 2003).
Prospect (2004), 'Britain's Top 100 Public Intellectuals?', *Prospect* (July), 22–5.
Prospect (2005), 'Top 100 World Public Intellectuals?', *Prospect* (October), 24–6.
Rönnholm, Tord (1999), *Kunskapens kvinnor* (Umeå: Department of Historical Studies).
Runcis, Maija (1998), *Steriliseringar i folkhemmet* (Stockholm: Ordfront).
Said, Edward (1993), *Representations of the Intellectual* (London: Vintage).
Small, Helen (ed.) (2002), *The Public Intellectual* (Oxford: Blackwell).
SOU (1938), *Betänkande ang. gift kvinnas förvärvsarbete m.m.*, SOU 1938:47.
Swedish Research Council (2004), 'The Kerstin Hesselgren Chair', <www.vr.se/humsam/index.asp?id=385anddok_ id=4727>, accessed 23 April 2004.
Terling, Barbro (1987), *Alva Myrdal: An Annoted Bibliography 1932–1961* (Stockholm: Alva och Gunnar Myrdals stiftelse).
Thörn, Kerstin (1997), *En bostad för hemmet* (Umeå: Department of History of Science and Ideas).
Thullberg, Per (1989), 'Myrdal, Alva', in *Svenskt Biografiskt Lexikon*, vol. XXVI (Stockholm: Norstedts).
Tilton, Tim (1991), *The Political Theory of Swedish Social Democracy* (Oxford: Clarendon Press).
Wetterstrom, Ingrid (1936), 'Swedish Women in Public Life', *The American Swedish Monthly* (October), 7–10.
Wisselgren, Per (2000), *Samhällets kartläggare* (Stockholm: Symposion).
Wisselgren, Per (2006), 'CSA och det sociala kunskapsfältets gränser', in Swärd, H. and Egerö, M.-A. (eds), *Ligga till last* (Lund: Gleerups).
Wisselgren, Per (2008), 'Reforming the Science-Policy Boundary', in Eliaeson, S. and Kalleberg, R. (eds), *Academics as Public Intellectuals* (Newcastle: Cambridge Scholars Publishing).

Chapter 14
How Hayek Managed to Beat Lazarsfeld: The Different Perception of Two Sub-fields of Social Science[1]

Werner Reichmann and Markus Schweiger

Introduction

On 17 September 2005 the Austrian newspaper *Die Presse* reported on a strange event in Germany. In front of a Berlin theatre, a three-metre-high 'depression barometer' had been installed that informed the German people about its current emotional state. A red liquid in a cylinder made of plastic provided an indicator to show the emotional state of Germans. The average the value indicated for July 2005 was 33.1 points out of a possible 100. If Germans had been in the best possible mood, the depression barometer would have recorded zero. The 'depression index' is re-computed every day and based on a standing Internet survey. The aim of those who created this depression barometer is ambitious. They would like to see their barometer gain equal worth to current business cycle indicators and the *Geschäftsklimaindex*.[2] However, we do not believe that this aim can be reached in the foreseeable future. The explanation for our scepticism about the likely success of opinion research like the depression barometer, psephology, social survey research – or, in short, applied social research – in comparison with business cycle research is the topic of the argument which follows.

The two important questions that inform our thesis are: (a) Which factors make a field of scientific work popularly successful and publicly respected? (b) Why is there a gap in public perceptions between applied economics and applied social research, and why especially in Austria? We argue that this is for four reasons:

1. There are differences in the perception of two respective scientific communities.

---

1 Research underlying this chapter was financed by the FWF (Nr. P16999). We are grateful to Christian Fleck, Johanna Muckenhuber, and Keith Doubt for constructive comments, and to the participants of the 'Public Intellectuals in Europe – European Public Intellectuals: Sociological Perspectives' international symposium at the Geary Institute, UCD Dublin in October 2005.

2 For more information, see <http://www.depressionsbarometer.de>.

2. Although taking place almost at the same time, the process of institutionalization of both applied sub-fields differs considerably.
3. The different political engagement of the founding fathers of those two fields in Austria led to a paradoxical situation: those thinkers who tried to influence political decisions in the 1920s by establishing research departments are not now taken seriously by policymakers, but those who proclaimed political detachment at the time of founding their departments now have an important influence over economic policymaking.
4. Public reception of the two academic fields was influenced by discipline knowledge and engagement, and by the textual continuity/discontinuity with the respective disciplines.

To investigate these four dimensions we will use a comparative approach.

We will first describe the biographical connections of Hayek with business cycle research and of Lazarsfeld's activities in the field of applied social research. Secondly, we refer to some case study research on the development and reception of these two academic fields in Austria. We will compare two institutions: the Österreichisches Institut für Konjunkturforschung (ÖIfK, 'Austrian Institute of Business Cycle Research') and the Österreichische Wirtschaftspsychologische Forschungsstelle (WPFS, 'Austrian Research Unit for Economic Psychology'). Both were the first institutions which dealt with applied research in their disciplines. We will try to explain the gap between business cycle research and social research by comparing the reception of both scientific fields in different public spheres. Finally, we will analyse this comparative case along dimensions which have been shown to influence the position of a scientific field in society.

Hayek versus Lazarsfeld: Biographical Comparison

Most of our readers will not be familiar with the link between business cycle research and Friedrich A. Hayek. Hayek was born in 1899 in Vienna into a bourgeois Viennese family. About his origins, he writes:

> If my father's parents, however proud of their gentility and ancestry, lived in modest circumstances, my mother's parents, the von Juraschecks – although from a 'younger' family and ennobled over a generation later – were definitely upper-class bourgeois and wealthier by far. (Hayek, 1994, 39)

Thus, Hayek grew up in a liberal environment without any substantial material worries. After finishing school and joining a field artillery regiment in March 1917, Hayek returned to Vienna in 1918 and started to study at the University of Vienna. After having received his PhD in law, he worked as a research fellow of

Ludwig Mises in the so-called Abrechnungsamt[3] in 1921 (see Hayek, 1994, 6). A few years later, Hayek travelled to the United States, mainly to further his studies. After his return, he soon became the first director of the ÖIfK, newly founded in 1926. As we will see later, the visit to America played an important role in the foundation of the Business Cycle Research Institute. However, in 1931, Hayek again left Austria in order to give a series of invited guest lectures at the London School of Economics. He remained in Britain until 1950.

During the 1930s in Britain, John Maynard Keynes was the most renowned economist. This explains why Hayek seemed to have been somewhat marginalized during this period. The most important output during this time was *The Road to Serfdom* (1944), which was widely recognized by a broader public, but largely ignored by the profession of economists. Hayek notes about this time:

> After *The Road to Serfdom*, I felt that I had so discredit myself professionally, I didn't want to give offense again. I wanted to be accepted in the scientific community. To do something purely scientific and independent of my economic view. I thought I could do it in a summer term and turn it into a decent English exposition, but of course it took well over three years. (Hayek, 1994, 152f.)[4]

The book was a big popular success. Hayek was invited to the United States in the Spring of 1945 for a lecture tour which resulted in the offer to become the Chair of Social and Moral Sciences at the Committee on Social Thought at the University of Chicago. Hayek remained in Chicago for a little over ten years, and left the city in 1962 after having been offered a position at the University of Freiburg in Germany, where he remained for the rest of his life.[5] In 1974, Hayek received the Nobel Prize in Economics, jointly with the Swedish economist Gunnar Myrdal. Hayek died in 1992.

The particular point that we would like to focus on more closely concerns Hayek's relationship to business cycle research. As one of the founding fathers of the Austrian Institute of Business Cycle Research, he was the first to import this from the United States to Austria. His colleague Mises notes that as the first director of the institute, Hayek performed well:

> Some time after his return to Vienna, he was entrusted with the management of a newly founded scientific institution, the Austrian Institute of Business Cycle Research. He did a brilliant job in this field, not only as an economist but also as a statistician and an administrator. (Mises, 1962b)

3 'Office of Accounting'. This office was responsible for accounting for Austria's war debts from the First World War.

4 Hayek is referring to his work on *The Sensory Order* (1952).

5 There was a short interlude at Salzburg, but this seems not to have been a happy experience (see Hayek, 1994).

Mises here hints at the increasing significance of statistics for the social sciences, and he describes Hayek as both a good economist and a brilliant statistician. For Hayek, economics and statistics were significantly connected and of equal importance. In his autobiographical dialogue, the author tells the reader about the things which impressed him most during his first stay in the United States and about how his interests were caught by 'newly developed techniques for the statistical analysis of economic time series' (Hayek, 1994, 7). Hayek notes:

> Still, he [Ludwig Mises] gave me the job, and so for the next five years – interrupted by a visit to America – I was working under him, and then I brought back from America a new idea of great predictions, the sort of thing which the Harvard economic barometer had developed in the 1920s. Mises helped me to create in the same building an institute for pursuing this type of research. (Hayek, 1994, 67)

A few weeks before the founding of the new institute, Hayek published an article in the weekly economic newspaper *Der Österreichische Volkswirt* ('The Austrian Economist'). In this article, he argued for the necessity and advantages of such an institute for dealing with empirical economics. He affirmed the need to develop and use new empirical and statistical methods – which he had learned in the Unites States – and argued that these were important not only for scientific reasons, but also because a better knowledge of the economic situation in Austria would soon lead to a better international rating of the Austrian economy and thus to an increase in foreign investments (Hayek, 1926, 49).

As we have pointed out, business cycle research was from its very beginning connected to the use and improvement of statistical – or quantitative – methods and to its perceived utility for the broader public through an improvement in the national economy. This view was emphasized by The Royal Swedish Academy in a press release justifying its awarding Hayek the Nobel Prize:

> Particularly, his theory of business cycles and his conception of the effects of monetary and credit policies attracted attention and evoked animated discussion. He tried to penetrate more deeply into the business cycle mechanism than was usual at that time. Perhaps, partly due to this more profound analysis, he was one of the few economists who gave warning of the possibility of a major economic crisis before the great crash came in the autumn of 1929. (The Royal Swedish Academy of Science, 1974)

We thus conclude that while Hayek today is well known for his contribution to a broader theory of economics and for his arguments in favour of liberalism in economic and social affairs, he also did important work in the economic empirical sub-field of business cycle research.

Paul F. Lazarsfeld was born in 1901 in Vienna, a member of the same generation as Hayek. After completing his PhD in mathematics in 1924, he studied a post-doctoral course in France and later worked as a teacher in Vienna. In 1933, he emigrated from Austria to the US, taking up a Rockefeller Fellowship. Due to the difficult political circumstances at home, he managed to get the fellowship extended, and finally decided not to return to Austria. From 1939 to 1971, Lazarsfeld worked at Columbia University in New York, where he led the Bureau of Applied Social Research. Until the end of his life, he worked as a sociologist, during his lasts years at the University of Pittsburgh. Lazarsfeld died in New York in 1976.[6]

Lazarsfeld's scientific approach to sociology developed under the influence of at least four factors. The first was his own socialist political orientation, which, in opposition to Hayek, was an important influence on the development of his scientific approach. He grew up in an assimilated Jewish family which 'was well known in Viennese radical socialist circles. A frequent visitor to the Lazarsfeld household was for example Friedrich Adler (Kern, 1982, 162).[7] As a member of the socialist students' movement, he wanted to disseminate the 'spirit of socialism' to the social public at large (Kern, 1982, 162). Lazarsfeld was actively engaged in social and educational work with working-class youngsters, and with the training of unemployed people. For him, social empirical research should be founded on socialist philosophy. The spheres of science and politics were not sharply delineated. Lazarsfeld always stressed the normative component of research activities. In 1960, Lazarsfeld wrote in the Foreword to the second edition of *Die Arbeitslosen von Marienthal* that his motivation to conduct social research derived from changes and reforms in Viennese social and educational policy in the 1920s. Lazarsfeld saw his social research activities as integral to the onset of a new socialist age (Jahoda, Lazarsfeld and Zeisel, 1960, xiiif.).

Second, during Lazarsfeld's time in Vienna, and later during his early years in the US, his socialist background and interest in public education were often seen as inconsistent with his commercial research projects. At a time when 'social research had no established institution, not in Germany, nor in Austria.' (Kern, 1982, 166), Lazarsfeld successfully gained commercial funding for his social research. One of the main tenets of his approach was to create a bridge between pure scholastic research and the social application of scientific methods and knowledge.

The third factor which contributed to Lazarsfeld's intellectual development was his close contact with the Department of Psychology at the University of Vienna, for which he worked as temporary *Assistent*. Charlotte and Karl Bühler, who were at the time joint heads of this department, provided Lazarsfeld with the opportunity to develop his own ideas regarding empirical and quantitative work. The department was empirically oriented, and tried to oppose the 'speculative and

6 Biographical accounts are not unanimous in giving the location of Lazarsfeld at his death. One author, Morrison (1976), writes that he died in Paris. All other biographical commentaries agree that he died in New York.

7 Friedrich Adler was the son of Victor Adler, who was the founder of the Austrian Social Democratic Party. Friedrich Adler was also a leading activist in this movement and in the Labour and Socialist International.

romanticizing' ideas of Othmar Spann,[8] Professor of Economics and Sociology at the University of Vienna (Kern, 1982, 163). Furthermore, the Bühlers shared Lazarsfeld's political perspective. The scientific and political symbiosis between Lazarsfeld and the Bühlers helped to establish a platform for applied social research, and led to the foundation of the Austrian Research Unit for Economic Psychology. However, the difficult employment situation at the University of Vienna made an academic career in Austria unlikely.

Finally, the fact that Lazarsfeld was well trained in mathematics had an important influence on his social scientific work. Teaching statistics courses came easily to him. His combined interests in social psychology and mathematics proved ideal for developing an applied quantitative approach to social science, and led to the publication in 1929 of a textbook, *Statistisches Praktikum für Psychologen und Lehrer* ('Statistical Training for Psychologists and Teachers') (see Lazarsfeld, 1929).

Although Hayek and Lazarsfeld had different political and intellectual interests and aims, both developed empirically and quantitatively oriented research programmes. Also, they both believed that the outcomes of their work should have an influence in the public sphere, and should ideally be understood by and inform the public at large.

The political circumstances of the time also contributed to the development of the applied social sciences. Austria was sharply politically divided between different ideologies, and between the federal states and the capital, Vienna. These divisions were interlinked. In 'red' Vienna, the Social Democratic Party with support from the industrial working class had developed its own political 'culture' affecting almost every aspect of life in the city.[9] In contrast, the rural federal states were dominated by the Conservative Party and Catholicism. The conflict between these irreconcilable political forces[10] led to civil war in 1934. The defeat of the left paved the way for what has been termed Austro-fascism. Unlike Lazarsfeld, the young Hayek was not involved in either side of the major political movements. Not a socialist, neither did he have a political relationship with the conservative Catholic movement. Hayek writes:

> By the age of fifteen, I had convinced myself that nobody could give a reasonable explanation of what he meant by the word 'God' and that it was therefore as meaningless to assert a belief as to assert a disbelief in God. (Hayek, 1994, 41)

---

8 Othmar Spann (1878–1950) was at the time Professor at the University of Vienna and one of the proponents of a so-called *Ständestaat*.

9 The Social Democratic administration of Vienna was popularly described as affecting life 'from the cradle to the grave'.

10 The German term describing this sense of 'political force' is *Lager*, which means more than just political party affiliation. Each 'camp' tried to provide all vital services for its supporters, but also to define culture in more general terms, leaving two profoundly antagonistic ideologies.

The only political engagement – which was not as extensive as that of Lazarsfeld – was during his student years:

> In fact, even I, although I've never since belonged to a political party, was along with my friends organizing a German Democratic party when I was a student in 1918–21, in order to have a middle group between the Catholics on one side and the socialists and communists on the other side. (Hayek, 1994, 53)

The main support for business cycle research during this turbulent period came from the more liberal side of the Viennese bourgeoisie, a non-aligned middle group between the conservatives and the socialists. However, it was Mises and Lazarsfeld who maintained the connections with politics and policymakers, not Hayek.

The Austrian Case

Institutionalization Compared

The institutionalization of business cycle research began in the early 1920s in the United States. As we have pointed out, Hayek learned a lot about this economic sub-field during his stay in New York, particularly through his contact with Wesley Clair Mitchell. At the time, Mitchell was one of the most important contributors to the development of quantitative economics. He has been called, perhaps somewhat exaggeratedly, 'the greatest American economic scholar of the twentieth century. Because of Mitchell's work, economics can now fairly claim to be called a "science"' (Berle, 1953, 169). In 1913, Mitchell wrote the first book that used the term 'business cycle research' in the sense that it is still referred to in economics today (cf. Mitchell, 1913). Mitchell became the first Director of the US National Bureau of Economic Research, founded in 1920 (Fabricant, 1984, 1; Rutherford, 2005, 110). Thus, the institutionalization of business cycle research first took place in the US, from where it spread to Europe, where several similar institutes were founded, such as the Deutsches Institut für Konjunkturforschung in Berlin (1925) and the Institut für Weltwirtschaft in Kiel (1926).[11]

In 1926, the era of business cycle research also began in Austria. In the beginning, such research was undertaken by a very small institute, the Österreichisches Institut für Konjunkturforschung. The board of the institute[12] was considerably larger than its working office. At its start in January 1927, only Hayek and a secretary were

11 The Institut für Weltwirtschaft was originally founded as the Königliches Institut für Seeverkehr und Weltwirtschaft in 1914, and was renamed in 1926. All the institutes mentioned still exist (see Kulla, 1996; Coenen, 1964; Beckmann, 2000)

12 Further information will be provided in the section on the political reception of business cycle research.

employed by the new institute. This somewhat paradoxical situation was the result of its being constituted as a *Verein*, a typical Austrian form of institution in which almost all activities take place under the umbrella of one institutional setting working within limited legal rules. There are thus varied types of *Vereine*, each with a different focus, ranging from football, environmental protection and politics to more academic activities such as business cycle research. In contrast to other non-university scientific institutions in Austria at the time, the institute had a small but secure financial basis and also a fixed office, and permanent, albeit few, staff. Much of the resources were provided by the Viennese Chamber of Commerce, which became the main supporter during the institute's first years.

Beyond the creation of a formal organization with a permanent financial base, the establishment of a new scientific sub-field is also seen to depend on the creation of a specialist journal (Shils, 1975, 72). Six months after the official start of the institute, the first issue of the so-called *Monatsberichte* ('Monthly Bulletin') was published. This journal provided the most important opportunity for publishing the institute's scientific work. From the start, the journal has contained articles addressing the same topic areas.[13] This continuity has helped enable researchers to undertake focused work within a defined area of business cycle research. Alongside its monthly journal, the institute also edited a series of books, Beiträge zur Konjunkturforschung ('Contributions to Business Cycle Research'). The theoretical work of the institute, such as later famous works by Hayek and Morgenstern,[14] was first published in this series. However, the institutionalization of a new field of research also depends on network opportunities and wider research discussions. Research fellows of the institute held their own scientific seminars, to which interested outsiders were invited. The *Privatseminar*, arranged by Ludwig Mises,[15] became a bi-weekly event at the Vienna Chamber of Commerce.

Business cycle research in Vienna reached a high degree of institutionalization. The factors mentioned above were responsible for the success of the institute, its continuity and its broad acceptance in the public sphere. Over time it grew rapidly, and many famous Austrian economists worked under its auspices, including Oskar Morgenstern, Fritz Machlup, Abraham Wald and Gottfried Haberler.

13 The topics which have been mentioned since 1927 are economic data for foreign countries, economic values for Austria, foreign trade, interest rates, labour market, industrial production, values for agriculture, food, traffic, national budget, prizes, and wages. Over the years, social security and environmental problems, two 'younger' but politically up-to-date topics, were added. In exchange, problems of food are not considered in later volumes of the journal; in Austria, they have been solved for many decades.

14 Oskar Morgenstern (1902–1977), Austrian economist, Director of the Österreichisches Institut für Konjunkturforschung from 1931 to 1938, when he emigrated to the US. There he contributed, together with John von Neumann, mainly to the application of game theory in economics.

15 For an interesting description of the seminar, see a short paper written by Gottfried Haberler, <http://www.mises.org/misestributes/haberler.asp>, accessed 28 September 2005.

In contrast, the story of the founding of the WPFS is different. Its foundation and research work were less institutionalized and less systematically managed. For those wishing to establish a new applied sub-field of sociology, then called social psychology, the circumstances were more chaotic. In the Foreword to the first edition of the famous Marienthal study, Lazarsfeld and Jahoda did not even mention the WPFS. However, in the second edition, published in 1960, Lazarsfeld wrote that the Marienthal study was published by the institute (Jahoda, Lazarsfeld and Zeisel, 1960, xiv). This is interesting for two reasons.

First, some research and work on social psychology, opinion polls and small surveys – in every case quantitatively oriented work on social psychology – had already being done *before* the establishment of the institute. The source of research funding at that time is hard to track down, and neither is there a clear date for the founding of the institute. Kern (1982) states that the Forschungsstelle was founded 'around 1927' (Kern, 1982, 165), while Morrison thinks that Lazarsfeld founded it 'in 1925' (Morrison, 1976, 8). Lazarsfeld himself wrote that the WPFS opened 'around 1927' (Lazarsfeld, 1960, 274). Lazarsfeld's own version of events must be doubted. Fleck (1990) argues that a young researcher in the position of Lazarsfeld could never have founded such an organization within the framework of an Austrian university. Fleck further points out that the connections between the Department of Psychology at Vienna University and Lazarsfeld were less close than Lazarsfeld presented them. The bureaucratic records of the University of Vienna contain no evidence that Lazarsfeld worked or taught there at the time. Fleck states that the Forschungsstelle was opened in 1931 (Fleck, 1990, 159ff.) because this is the year of official registration for the institute as a *Verein*. For our purposes, the exact date of the establishment of the institute is not essential, but the confusion surrounding this event and the differing information given about the founding year are indicative of the lack of historical clarity of the specific organizational status of the Forschungsstelle.

Second, the names given to the two compared institutes are indicative as to their public orientation. Lazarsfeld intended – as Hayek did (see above) – to offer his own work for broader public use. The names of both institutes suggest a programme that was intended to give shape to economic and policy debates.

In an interview, Marie Jahoda, another founding member of the WPFS, remembered the work environment there. According to her, it was never possible to manage the Forschungsstelle as a commercial company. Regular book-keeping, the use of criteria relevant to the running of profit-oriented organizations, and an effective management structure were not adhered to (Jahoda in Kern, 1982, 166f.). Furthermore, even though the WPFS was founded with a strong connection to the Department of Psychology, it obviously had no permanent office or rooms. This suggests a very low degree of institutionalization, and shows clearly its contrast with the organizational structure of the Austrian Institute of Business Cycle Research. Lazarsfeld wrote in 1968 about the low level of institutionalization of the WPFS:

> The Vienna Center was a sequence of improvisation and the basic elements of a research organization developed only slowly. In spite of a number of external formalities it never fused into a stable organization. It was only when I came to the University of Newark that the different components … could be integrated into some kind of an institutional plan. (Lazarsfeld, 1960, 287)

The financial base of the institute was precarious, and its rules for financial accounting fell short of what might have been expected, as Lazarsfeld himself has pointed out:

> For instance, after I left Vienna for my American fellowship, many financial difficulties seem to have become apparent. I received numerous letters, especially from the Bühlers, cursing me for the financial embarrassments I had created for them. … [T]here can be little doubt that I left behind a rather chaotic situation, even if the sums involved seem rather small by today's standards. (Lazarsfeld, 1960, 310)

Fleck (1990, 167) lists four different scientific works which were published by the WPFS: The famous Marienthal study, a study of scholars at the *Volkshochschule*,[16] a report on the needs of radio listeners, and a report on the relationship between authority and education. Two of them are dated after 1933, the year Lazarsfeld left Austria for the US. Despite their different content, they share the methodology of an empirical approach. Jahoda also hints at other early attempts at the WPFS to conduct empirical social research, such as her own attempt to research the social life of vagrants.

The fact that the WPFS had no permanent journal or book series is another indication of the low level of institutionalization of the institute. Until now, there exists no Austrian journal that deals seriously with applied social science[17] that can compare, for example, with the American *Public Opinion Quarterly*.

In contrast to the Institut für Konjunkturforschung, three facts stand out that distinguish the Wirtschaftspsychologische Forschungstelle: its late official formation, its unorganized management structure, and the absence of a periodical journal or book series. It was these institutional differences that explain the further development of the new sub-disciplines.

Intra-scientific Reception

As we mentioned above, Lazarsfeld was only a part-time lecturer at the University of Vienna. But his engagement with the WPFS, which could be seen as being part of the Department of Psychology, gave him access to academic life. In contrast,

16 The *Volkshochschule* is a form of adult education based on social democratic principles still in existence in Austria.

17 The name of the journal, *Angewandte Sozialforschung*, suggests that it is a journal for applied social research. In effect, it deals more with epistemology, methodology and logic.

however, the Institute of Business Cycle Research was never formally connected to the University of Vienna, but only very loosely in practice. The only relationship was in the training of so-called *Privatdozenturen*, non-tenured lectureship posts held at the university by select members of the institute[18].

Business cycle research was a very new field of research within economics, and as such it provided a good opportunity for young researchers to work in a new field and to earn a reputation. Conducting business cycle research gave them the chance to pursue an academic career, in Austria as well as abroad. However, in Austria there was only one organization where fellows of the institute were linked together with academics from the university, the so-called Nationalökonomische Gesellschaft. The head of this society was Hans Mayer, Professor at the University of Vienna. Ludwig Mises, Friedrich Hayek and – later – Oskar Morgenstern held other leading positions within the society.

In contrast, the fellows of the Forschungsstelle were not very deeply integrated into the Austrian academic system, though they had some contacts – or today we would say weak ties – to other business cycle researchers outside Austria. Starting with Hayek's visit to the United States, these young researchers continued to establish connections and networks. They travelled a lot, especially in Europe, and the whole community was international in outlook. A few conferences about business cycle research were held before the beginning of the Second World War, some of them in Vienna. As one of our interviewees pointed out, it was unusual at that time for Austrian scientists to have intensive international scientific contacts.

Although it was not possible to carry out any regular study or gain a degree at the Viennese Business Cycle Research Institute, there were quite a number of students and foreign fellows working there. They formed another part of the network, most of them attending the *Privatseminar* run by Mises.

From its beginning, business cycle research was widely accepted in the international scientific community of economists, although it was not an established university subject in most countries at this time. Acceptance by the scientific community can be seen as fundamental to acceptance by policymakers and the broader public. In this instance, it led to a strong and influential position in society beyond the academy. For both public spheres – policymakers and the broader public – business cycle research seemed to offer answers to prevalent questions and to offer hope of insights of value for the future. Their work and results were respected as enriching the development of economic reasoning.

18 As explained by Mises: '*Privatdozent* is an institution unknown to the universities of the Anglo-Saxon countries. A *Privatdozent* is ... admitted as a private teacher at the university. He does not receive any payment from the government; actually he has only the very unimportant right to receive the fees paid by his students. Most *Privatdozents* made the equivalent from their fees of about $5.00 or $10.00 a year. Therefore they had to find some other means of making a living in whatever way they wanted. As for me I served as economic adviser to the Austrian government's Chamber of Commerce' (Mises, 1962a).

The intra-scientific reception was completely different for Lazarsfeld and the WPFS. Lazarsfeld notes:

> Quite possibly the emergence of empirical social science will one day be considered an outstanding feature of the twentieth century. But its birth has not been without travail. Hardest have been its struggles with what we shall call the classical tradition. (Lazarsfeld, 1957, 39)

In 1957, Lazarsfeld explained the problems of having his empirical quantitative approach accepted in the social science community. He used the example of empirical ways of analysing the concept of 'public opinion'. Having introduced the concept, he found himself confronted with 'violent attacks' and 'complaints' by representatives of what he labelled 'the classical tradition' (Lazarsfeld, 1957, 40). First, traditionalists complained about a lack of definition of the research subject. Some traditionalists argued that 'when the pollsters use the term public opinion they do not know and cannot say what they mean' (Lazarsfeld, 1957, 41). Second, the pollsters were also seen as only having a microscopic view on the social world and as simply analysing opinions regarding particular current events, not the 'quasi-permanent sentiments' which underlie them (Lazarsfeld, 1957, 45). Third, the pollsters were seen as adopting a pseudo-objective and simplistic position with respect to the complex relationship between changing climates of opinion and political action. Modern opinion polls misleadingly purported to provide 'objective facts' as guidelines for action.

Lazarsfeld challenged such criticisms with counter-arguments and illustrative empirical case analysis. However, the criticisms raised against Lazarsfeld's approach are in contrast with the lack of similar serious attacks against business cycle research. The measure at the centre of business cycle forecasts is the Gross Domestic Product (GDP). This also presents a microscopic view of the economy at a particular time. Business cycle researchers have always emphasized that they provide the facts as measured, and claim no responsibility for how the outcomes of such measures are to be used by politicians and policymakers.[19] But Hayek's early work was not criticized by the classical community of economists with the same vehemence as that of Lazarsfeld. This new applied field of sociology as developed at the Forschungsstelle had to struggle against resistance from its own larger scientific community. In contrast, business cycle research was largely spared from such critical discipline arguments.

Economics and sociology are the 'mother-disciplines' of the disciplinary sub-fields discussed here. As disciplines, they differ in many respects, but one important difference stands out in this context. For economists, it seems to be completely

19 We could find many more problems with the GDP, and the business cycle researchers we spoke to are all aware of all those problems. They agreed with us in criticizing the excessive use of GDP, but argued that it is a very media-friendly value: short, concise, and easy to understand – maybe too easy.

clear what economics is about. In contrast, sociologists continue to quarrel about the 'substance' of what 'the social' could be. There is no consensus about the main object of investigation or over epistemological concerns. The different positions taken by the 'mother-disciplines' with respect to the development of these new applied sub-fields could be seen as one additional factor that influenced their contrasting developments, especially in the German-speaking countries.

Political Reception

The Early Years

The political reception of the two scientific sub-fields deliberated in this analysis has two different dimensions. One dimension could be called 'acceptance' – the results of the scientific process are accepted and applied by policymakers. They are accepted if taken for granted, and not accepted if systematically doubted. The Austrian Institute of Business Cycle Research was widely accepted by the whole political spectrum, despite being founded at the periphery of the Viennese Chamber of Commerce. One indicator of this acceptance is the constitution of the Ausschuss, the management board of the institute. Its task was the financial management of the institute and the appointment of a scientific executive of the institute. Also, the president of the Ausschuss represented the institute to the wider public. Taking a closer look at the constitution, we can observe a few interesting patterns. Members of the Ausschuss were not nominated because of their individual skills, but because of their roles as chairmen or employees of other institutions. These institutions – like the Chamber of Commerce or the Chamber of Employees – were thus in effect members of the institute, which allowed them to nominate the members of the Ausschuss. The second pattern to note is that the membership of the Ausschuss was comprised of employers' as well as employees' institutions. However, the majority of the board was made up of representatives of employers' organizations or of finance capital. There were ten institutions in the Ausschuss, and nine of them came from organizations representing capital. The employees' institution membership came from the Viennese Chamber of workers and employees.[20] Secondly, several ministers of the government commissioned studies on particular topics or asked the staff for consultancy assistance. One of the reasons why ministers consulted the staff at the institute was that there were not many economists working as part of the civil service. Most of the ministry staff members were lawyers without any deeper knowledge of economics. The

20 The other nine members were: the Viennese Chamber of Commerce, the Styrian Chamber of Commerce, the Austrian Federal Reserve, the Association of the Austrian Industry, the Association of Austrian Banks and Bankers, the Conference of agriculture Associations, the Association of the Mercantile Community, the Viennese stock exchange and the Austrian Railways.

continuing political involvement of the WIFO[21] is reflected in the fact that its fourth director, Hans Seidel, became *Staatssekretär*[22] in the Ministry of Finance after he left his position at the WIFO.

Both potentially supporting dimensions, acceptance and political involvement, were not realized by the WPFS nor other institutions which undertook applied social research. To be sure, there could have been political reasons for this lack of contact. Lazarsfeld's lack of influence could be seen to be due to his connection with social democracy. In the political constellation of the late 1920s and early 1930s, this may have limited his chances of obtaining research grants from the state. But although his social democratic convictions were strong, his political engagement did not extend to involvement in the social democratic movement as part of the political regime. The non-acceptance of the research results of the Forschungstelle calls for other explanations.

The Present

If we look to the political reception of the Austrian Institute of Economic Research today, we see that things have not changed. Quite the contrary, this institute's involvement in political processes grew, and is now fully institutionalized. The institute became an 'official' institution of business cycle research and economic consultancy in Austria. Fellows of the institute are represented on many different political decision-making organs. At the zenith of the Austrian *Sozialpartnerschaft*[23] in the 1970s and 1980s, the Austrian Business Cycle Institute became a substantial player in Austrian policymaking. The institute produced official economic forecasts for the country which were used to support the planning of the federal budget or for negotiations between employees and employers. Neither the labour unions nor employer organizations doubt the forecasts of the institute, and they accept them as the basis for negotiations. However, this consensus was somewhat weakened over recent decades, paralleling the decline of the *Sozialpartnerschaft.* But on the whole, it is still alive and the political role of the institute remains important.

Business cycle research became highly influential in other countries too, such as through the Sachverständigenrat zur Begutachtung der gesamtwirtschaftlichen

21 The Austrian Institute of Economic Research (WIFO) is the direct successor of the Austrian Institute for Business Cycle Research founded in 1926.

22 *Staatssekretär* is the second-highest political position in an Austrian ministry.

23 The *Sozialpartnerschaft* is an Austrian institution whose main task is to link policy and the economy together. On various boards of the *Sozialpartnerschaft*, members of unions and employers' organizations meet regularly and negotiate about various topics. Together with long periods of major coalitions between the Conservative and Socialist Party, the country was divided between these two sides. This institution has lost influence over the last fifteen years as a consequence of Austrian membership in the EU and the rightward swing of Austrian policy since 2000.

Entwicklung[24] in Germany. The main task of this institute is to provide an analysis of the current economic situation and to advise the German government and other bureaucratic institutions on economic questions. Other examples can be found in the United States, where the National Bureau of Economic Research and the Council of Economic Advisers play important roles in the political consultation process. Business cycle research can be shown to have become a very important player in the political and economic policymaking process in many Western countries. Much of the economic evidence and expertise is provided by institutes such as the ones described above.

Lazarsfeld's WPFS had no equivalent success in Austria. However, there exist some institutions and organizations in Austria that undertake polls and surveys on a wide range of social and political topics. Their clients include political parties which need forecasts or opinion polls, companies which want to know about trends in consumer behaviour, and bureaucratic institutions in need of census surveys. We can sum up all those activities as instances of applied social research. In some ways, they are in the tradition first founded by Lazarsfeld's approach to quantitative empirical social research. However, in contrast to the results of business cycle research, there is a distinctive 'never trust polls' mentality about the outcomes of this kind of social research in Austria. For example, politicians only use opinion polls that support their own position. When the results of such polls are in opposition to their own political point of view, they normally use protective strategies. The first is to explain that the study or the opinion poll is financed by their political opponent, and thus suspect. Occasionally, politicians present their own poll which shows different results. Secondly, they look only at those parts of the results which support their argument. The third strategy used by policymakers is that of doubting survey and opinion polls in general. Sometimes business cycle forecasts fail. But politicians and policymakers still believe in them, and there seems to be a social agreement among them to treat the results of applied economists seriously, but to doubt the work of applied sociologists.

Conclusion

Both Hayek and Lazarsfeld were path-breaking scholars who contributed greatly to the development of their respective disciplines, yet the disciplinary sub-fields they founded faced contrasting receptions at their point of origin in Austria. Our argument here has been that new ideas need structural, political and individual support to gain ground and leave a mark.

What are the most important conclusions to be drawn from the comparison between the applied sub-fields of economics, as exemplified by the work of Hayek, and that of sociology as developed by Lazarsfeld? As we have seen, Hayek

24 For further information, see <http://www.sachverstaendigenrat-wirtschaft.de/index.php>, accessed 28 September 2005.

started his scientific career in Vienna under the eyes of Ludwig Mises. Lazarsfeld started his with the Bühlers. At the beginning of both of their careers, neither had a strong connection with the established universities, although Lazarsfeld had a slight advantage here over Hayek. Both created and administered research institutes in Vienna which aimed to conduct empirical research, and both also tried to earn money by doing so. Both their institutes tried to be open to the non-academic world, and both of them also tried to reach out with their work to the public. Lazarsfeld and Hayek both emigrated at an early stage in their career. Hayek's scientific career got under way with his entry to the UK, after which he also held various academic positions in other countries. Lazarsfeld's work also became highly respected from the moment he started working in the US. It can be said that both their intellectual perspectives were made in Austria, but that their intellectual careers took off elsewhere. With so many similarities in terms of the starting position of these two young scholars, why is the perception of both of the sub-disciplines they created so different?

To answer this question, we tried to look at the differences between these two emerging sub-disciplines. First, Lazarsfeld did not manage to establish a journal to deal with applied empirical social research in Europe. In the US, *The Public Opinion Quarterly* was founded in 1937. It was the first scientific journal to deal with issues of applied social science, opinion polls and psephology. Nothing comparable was established in Europe at the time. The Austrian Institute of Business Cycle Research managed to publish a monthly journal that continues with somewhat similar contents up to the present day. As a result, everyone knows what business cycle research is about. In comparison, the textual discontinuity of empirical applied social research left a confused image of what this sub-field is all about.

The conditions for sub-disciplinary continuity can also be found in the process of institutionalization of research institutes. Whereas the Austrian Institute of Business Cycle Research had a clear structure, a permanent financial base and permanent staff from the beginning, it is not even historically clear when the more loosely organized Wirtschaftspsychologische Forschungstelle was founded. The latter occupied no office space, and those who worked there were without permanent connections to a university or other established research organizations.

A further reason for the difference in public perception, we have argued, related to different modes of political engagement of the two institutes, presenting us with a paradox: Lazarsfeld, who created an institute to provide a scientific basis for a social democratic policymaking, is today of lesser policy significance, whereas Hayek, who was not politically engaged, is today a source of major influence on economic policymaking across the world.

The process of institutionalization of academic disciplines does not only depend on individual actions. Individual scientists can create and take control, for instance by initiating a journal or ensuring a formal institutional basis for the sub-field, but there are structures which are beyond the influence of individuals, such as political circumstances or the prevalent general scientific trends in the scientific community.

In both sociology and economics, an applied empirical sub-field developed at nearly the same time. The comparison of the development of those two sub-fields brings to light similarities and differences, continuities and discontinuities. Each sub-field over time faced a very different reception by the scientific community, in the political sphere and with the public. Because of the nature of its institutionalization processes, it was business cycle research that became more widely successful and politically entrenched in Austria than applied empirical research. Business cycle research also gained earlier international scientific recognition, as well as international policymaking relevance and application. In summary: when it comes to the creation of influential disciplinary sub-fields, Friedrich A. Hayek can be said to have 'beaten' Paul F. Lazarsfeld, and applied economics can be shown to have 'beaten' applied quantitative empirical social research.

References

Beckmann, Ulf (2000), *Von Löwe bis Leontief – Pioniere der Konjunkturforschung am Kieler Institut für Weltwirtschaft* (Marburg: Metropolis-Verlag).

Berle Jr, Adolf A. (1953), 'Wesley Clair Mitchell: The Economic Scientist', *Journal of the American Statistical Association* 48:262, 169–75.

Coenen, Étienne (1964), *La 'Konjunkturforschung' en Allemagne et en Autriche 1925–1933* (Louvain: Éditions Nauwelaerts).

Fabricant, Solomon (1984), 'Toward a Firmer Basis of Economic Policy: The Founding of the National Bureau of Economic Research', <http://www.nber.org/nberhistory/sfabricantrev.pdf>.

Fleck, Christian (1990), *Rund um Marienthal: Von den Anfängen der Soziologie in Österreich bis zu ihrer Vertreibung* (Vienna: Verlag für Gesellschaftskritik).

Hayek, Friedrich A. (1926), 'Die Bedeutung der Konjunkturforschung für das Wirtschaftsleben', *Der Österreichische Volkswirt* 19:2, 46–49.

Hayek, Friedrich A. (1944), *The Road to Serfdom* (London: Routledge).

Hayek, Friedrich A. (1952), *The Sensory Order* (Chicago, IL: University of Chicago Press).

Hayek, Friedrich A. (1977) 'Zur Gründung des Institutes', in *50 Jahre WIFO* (Vienna: Verein Österreichisches Institut für Wirtschaftsforschung).

Hayek, Friedrich A. (1994), *Hayek on Hayek: An Autobiographical Dialogue* (Chicago, IL: University of Chicago Press).

Jahoda, Marie, Paul F. Lazarsfeld and Zeisel, Hans (1960), *Die Arbeitslosen von Marienthal – Ein soziographischer Versuch*, 2nd edn (Allensbach: Verlag für Demoskopie)

Kern, Horst (1982), *Empirische Sozialforschung – Ursprünge, Ansätze, Entwicklungslinien* (Munich: Beck).

Kulla, Bernd (1996), *Die Anfänge der empirischen Konjunkturforschung in Deutschland 1925–1933* (Berlin: Duncker and Humblot).

Lazarsfeld, Paul F. (1929), *Statistisches Praktikum für Psychologen und Lehrer* (Jena: Verlag von Gustav Fischer).

Lazarsfeld, Paul F. (1957), 'Public Opinion and the Classical Tradition', *The Public Opinion Quarterly* 21:1, 39–53.

Lazarsfeld, Paul F. (1960), 'An Episode in the History of Social Research: A Memoir', in Fleming, Donald and Bailyn, Bernard (eds), *Intellectual Migration: Europe and American 1930–1960* (Cambridge, MA: Belknap Press of Harvard University Press).

Mises, Ludwig von (1962a), 'The Austrian School of Economics at the University of Vienna', <http://www.mises.org/etexts/misesaustrian.asp>, accessed 7 September 2005.

Mises, Ludwig von (1962b), 'Tribute to F.A. von Hayek by Ludwig von Mises', paper presented at a banquet in Hayek's honour, Chicago, 24 May 1962, <http://www.mises.org/misestributes/misesonhayek.asp>, accessed 9 August 2005.

Mitchell, Wesley C. (1913), *Business Cycles* (Berkeley, CA: University of California Press).

Morrison, David E. (1976) 'Paul Lazarsfeld 1901–1976: A Tribute', *Österreichische Zeitschrift für Soziologie* 2:3, 7–9.

Rutherford, Malcolm (2005), '"Who's Afraid of Arthur Burns?" – The NBER and the Foundations', *The History of Economic Thought* 27:2, 109–39.

Shils, Edward (1975), 'Geschichte der Soziologie – Tradition, Ökologie und Institutionalisierung', in Parsons, Talcott, Shils, Edward and Lazarsfeld, Paul, *Soziologie – autobiographisch – Drei kritische Berichte zur Entwicklung einer Wissenschaft* (Stuttgart: Ferdinand Enke Verlag).

The Royal Swedish Academy of Science (1974), 'Press Release: The Sveriges Riksbank (Bank of Sweden) Prize in Economic Sciences in Memory of Alfred Nobel' for 1974', 9 October, <http://nobelprize.org/economics/laureates/1974/press.html>, accessed 9 August 2005.

Wacker, Alois (1998), 'Marie Jahoda und die Österreichische Wirtschaftspsychologische Forschungsstelle – zur Idee einer nicht-reduktionistischen Sozialpsychologie', *Psychologie und Geschichte* 8:1/2, 112–49.

Conclusion

Revisiting the Concept of the Public Intellectual

Howard Davis

The social scientists writing in this collection have responded to the recent reawakening of interest in intellectuals with a defence of the concept and a range of provocative and practical insights into their public role. The search for an understanding of the place of intellectuals is one of the distinctive features of the early twenty-first century social sciences after a period of relative neglect of the subject. It is a response to the growth of higher education, the research funders' challenge to be 'relevant', the marketization of arts and literature, uncertainty about the public or publics being addressed, as well as scepticism towards the media as disseminators of serious ideas. The burgeoning literature is pervaded by a sense of growing complexity and uncertainty. But more fundamentally, there is a sense of deterioration, deficiency, even crisis, and the feeling that the 'class' of intellectuals has lost something, be it a certain distinctiveness, the ability to speak with authority, or the right to have a hearing. The contributions to this volume have offered an exceptional range of material for thinking this through, including the cases which show the differences between the current and previous generations of intellectuals. Their diagnosis of the changing status of intellectuals generally resists the broad narrative of decline or the impoverishment of the public sphere, and provides a counterpoint to a number of other contributions to the debate (for example, Furedi, 2004; Goldfarb, 1998; Small, 2002). The perspective is from the social sciences, but it does not advocate a role for the public engagement from the point of view a particular discipline (a prime example of which is Burawoy's influential plea for a public sociology). Helpfully, the contributions draw attention to the positioning of particular intellectuals in the post-Cold War, post-secular, postmodern world. These are themes that any contemporary discussion of the public intellectual needs to address.

This chapter does not aim to be a review, let alone provide a summary or conclusion to all the contributions. As a sociological response to the ideas of international social theorists and fellow sociologists, the chapter revisits the concept of the public intellectual with a small selection of theoretical and empirical questions in mind. They are a continuation of the debate in the spirit of the volume as a whole. The relative disuse of the term 'intellectual' (and the relative lack of research and debate in the social sciences between the height of the Cold War and now) is explained in the distinction made in the Introduction between 'old' and 'new' and the discontinuities between them in the second half of the twentieth century. It is clear that there *is* discontinuity, that today's intellectuals survive, if at all, in a social context that is more differentiated and global, in a communications setting that is almost completely media-saturated, and in a field of knowledge and ideas that is increasingly de-aligned from established political and philosophical traditions. Put simply, the three themes of sociology, communications and culture help to explain the strengths and weaknesses of intellectuals in their public role today. At the same time, they also represent the pressure points of individual experiences. They highlight where intellectuals can stand, how they can speak, and what they can say.

The expression 'public intellectual' is an important clue to the problem. The prefix 'public' suggests, not that intellectuals could communicate without some form of public to address, but that their relationship to a *general* public has changed. The role of academics and writers, once a small minority which could be perceived as having elite status and likely to be accorded the authority associated with elite institutions, has for long been eroded by the waves of expansion of the new class (Gouldner, 1979), the service class (Goldthorpe, 1982) or the knowledge class, depending on the definition, which developed through the relative and absolute growth of the professional and managerial occupations and the large-scale expansion of higher education in particular. Higher education is far more significant than private employment or the state service, because it was traditionally associated with more egalitarian, libertarian and (sometimes) radical ideas (Rootes, 1995). At least it provided a relatively protected environment for these features to exist. To enter higher education was to enter a space protected economically and politically from the direct influence of the state (a precondition for autonomy and freedom of ideas) and generally free from political domination, albeit the institutions were culturally conformist until the temporary turbulence of the 1960s.

The prominent examples of 'old' intellectuals cited in this volume, from Socrates to Tocqueville to Weber, were politically minded philosophers and humanist scholars who transcended their particular social origins and intellectual traditions. They forged new disciplines, movements and key concepts. They have remained influential in their different ways because they articulated for their time and in a universal language the opportunities and limitations of democratic discourse around the general condition of society. The examples in this volume show how their successors face demanding new conditions where no aspect of the relationships between intellectuals and their publics can be taken for granted. The authors are not tempted to minimize or treat the intellectual as another kind of specialist. In fact, there is a consensus that the public intellectual has no less important a role than in the past.

In very different ways, the first three contributions or 'provocations' address a common theme: the condition which allows intellectuals to make public pronouncements that do not simply replicate the prevailing discourse or add to it through incremental changes to policy and practice, which is the overwhelming contribution of most professionals in higher education, the professions and what have recently come to be known as the 'creative industries'. What makes their presentations provocative from the perspectives of civil society (Alexander), gender (Evans) and moral discourse (Zulaika), respectively, is the implication that even when the authority of ideas has been undermined by the narrowing of frames of reference for expertise, the legitimization of public (lay) opinion, and the rise of mediatized celebrity, the public intellectual has a distinct and necessary place in the public sphere. But what evidence is there of a credible place for pronouncements that challenge expert opinion from a non-expert position or criticize society without any claim to be representative? After all, intellectuals are known to be more susceptible to ideology and fashion than most.

In locating the issue in the context of a theory of civil society, Alexander aims to reconcile the commitment of the intellectual to universalism (truth) with their particular attachments to society, politics and culture. He dismisses the image of the free-floating intellectual, but advocates a role for one who performs 'as if' the role exemplified freedom, independence and universality. The basic frame offered here suggests that public intellectuals can and should continue to be important, prophetic carriers of the discourse of civil society, mediating between its twin tendencies to promote emancipation and repression. They perform repairs on civil society through their advocacy of reform, revolutionary change or restoration. Alongside the familiar iconic figures of the Western democratic and revolutionary traditions, Alexander strikingly includes Osama Bin Laden as a new incarnation of the public intellectual, in this case one committed to repairing the solidarity of a traditional form of Islam.

In this way, Alexander shifts the familiar emphasis on intellectuals as 'central democratic actors' (Goldfarb, 1998, 1) or 'democracy's helpers' (Kenny, 2004, 89) to intellectuals giving a variety of performances which highlight the complexity of the civil society, where, alongside the cultivation of civility, there is the possibility of the public intellectual who opposes or seeks to destroy the very narratives of (Western) civil society. The case of Al Qaeda is distinct from the revolutionary Marxist intellectuals who condoned violence but proclaimed their revolutionary doctrines (whether in Western or non-Western societies) as the true successors to Enlightenment and the fulfilment of capitalism's destiny. When the intellectual is not simply an iconoclast but performs as a potential destroyer of the kind of world which made the role of intellectual possible in the first place, there is a contradiction even more disturbing than the one between revolutionary ideology and the society it proposes to transform through violent means. Are we to consider the pronouncements of terrorists using the rhetoric of Islam as an expression of global civil society? Auer notes that it was East European intellectuals who showed more reliable political judgement of state socialist power and violence than those who did not experience it from inside. The public intellectual who takes a stance on international terrorism should consider the implications of this. Rather than abstract models of international security or ethical principles, the starting point can be to understand the experience of innocent minorities (for example, European Muslims) who are seen as guilty by association.

The theme of terror is taken up by Zulaika, who poses some difficult questions for any public intellectual whose attempt to articulate a rational critical understanding of terrorism is conditioned by their own social embeddedness in a society divided by terrorism. His focus is on the Basque and Spanish intellectuals for whom the stance on terrorism is a defining issue or test. The case is a particular one, but the so-called 'global war on terror' confronts any intellectual with a similar, though usually less personal, question. It can, of course, become unexpectedly personal to anyone, as the media academic John Tulloch describes in his survivor's account of the 7 July attack in London (Tulloch, 2006). The similarity between Zulaika's question and the question for any public intellectual is the need to find a subject position which can express through rational language and universal concepts experiences that are beyond everyday contemplation. By taboo, silence or demonization, they are ruled out of normal discourse. Zulaika's answer as an anthropologist and ethnographer is instructive: he concentrates less on the structural preconditions or personal motivations of those who organize and carry out acts of terror than on the possibility of these experiences being written. His suspicion of interpretation is based on the view that 'discourse makes reality', and that the discourses of experts, politicians and the media obscure more than they reveal. His inspiration, significantly, comes from the fiction of Albert Camus, and the sense that to witness (in both senses of the word) is the proper response of the public intellectual to what cannot naturally be said or is impossible to fit into an established frame of reference.

Of course, terror has been a regular feature of nationalist and extreme Left and Right politics for generations. 'Old' public intellectuals have engaged with the phenomenon from a range of expertise: historical, sociological, legal, philosophical and ethical. But they have difficulty, as Zulaika shows, especially in their own society, in overcoming the distance which society itself creates as a form of self-protection. The quest for understanding is made more complicated by the extension of terrorism to the world stage, where it comes to be seen as a 'seamless' threat in the absence of a clear political narrative. Some depict it as a new form of totalitarianism, but as Rabinbach cautions in his chapter, the complexities of Islam and the effects of international policies and interventions should prevent us from resorting to old concepts that were applied to European conflicts. Twentieth-century public intellectuals had the defining issues of fascism and communism, the Holocaust, the Cold War and genocide to challenge their concepts of reason, common humanity and progress. But they were sustained by coherent ideological frameworks, audiences who implicitly understood them, and institutions that underpinned their public role. Western 'Sovietologists', for example, could accept positions and funding in higher education and yet maintain their critical distance from Cold War ideology. Recent experience in the UK about the scientific contribution to the government's counter-terrorism strategy shows that researchers are expected to have a more explicit commitment to the top strategic priority of making 'a world safe from global terrorism and mass destruction' (FCO, 2003). According to professional bodies, some calls have been made for research linked to possible UK government interventions in the internal affairs of foreign countries. The theme of terrorism, while only explicit in one of the contributions to this volume, usefully highlights one of the relatively new defining issues for contemporary public intellectuals. Certainly, there are other pressing themes, for instance the consequences of globalization or climate change, but they do not challenge civil society in such a fundamental way. Suicidal terror on 11 September 2001, as Gray puts it, 'destroyed the West's ruling myth' – the belief in modernity as the single progressive expression of Enlightenment values (Gray, 2003, 1). Exaggerated this may be, but the damage done and the repair needed has to be acknowledged.

This volume opens up and contributes helpfully to other areas of contemporary concern, notably the issue of gender and the legacy of feminism over the modern period. In her 'provocation', Evans chooses writers rather than academics to examine the gendered dynamic of intellectual life. No longer primarily an issue about women's right to speak or their access to the platforms where they can be heard, the discussion nevertheless reminds us that access to the public sphere involves a key dilemma, because presence there continues to be gendered. If a woman intellectual (there can be no doubt of their existence) accepts the abstract universal criteria of public discourse, it means abandoning what is distinct in her experience of gender. On the other hand, to speak from a feminine standpoint and claim a specific kind of authority is to risk marginalization. For men in a patriarchal society, as Simone de Beauvoir so powerfully argued, no choice is necessary, because the universal and the particular coincide. A similar structure of argument can be applied to public intellectuals speaking from subordinate ethnic, class, religious or minority national positions.

A great strength of this volume is that it allows the general statements in the 'provocations' to be compared with specific cases. To support his argument for a more gender-sensitive understanding of public intellectuals, Wisselgren presents a case study of two prominent Swedish intellectuals (who he says would have seen themselves as practical researchers, reformers and politicians rather than intellectuals). The examples of Hesselgren and Myrdal both show that opportunities for education, institutional recognition and advancement of women in Sweden in the first half of the twentieth century were beset with obstacles. Gender inequality and exclusion were the norm in higher education, research and politics. That these barriers were successfully overcome by both women is, of course, a tribute to their exceptional qualities. However, they were helping to forge a more democratic society, and their success is linked to the growing strength of civil society in Sweden and the relative openness of the social democratic regime after 1932 to applied research and expert contributions to policy. Their standing nationally and internationally represents another solution to the dilemmas faced by women intellectuals. They identified with women's emancipation, but not at the expense of general social reform. They were politically engaged, but not purely on male terms. Their 'performance' as public intellectuals was shaped less by the classical idea of the intellectual than by the convergence of the academic, political and public spheres in Sweden, which allowed them to claim recognition as insiders and experts in their fields. This case study surely has continuing relevance as a pointer to the conditions of civil society which may help to promote the equality of women and men as public intellectuals without denying gender.

All of the perspectives in this volume, whether they relate to classical, 'old' or 'new' public intellectuals touch on the issue of the relationship between intellectuals and their publics, and the enlarged scope of communication from national to the international and the global level. While the boundaries of history, geography, politics and language still allow us to speak meaningfully of 'American', 'European' or 'East European' intellectuals, for example, these boundaries have been weakening, and will weaken further. There is the potential for new communicative spaces to emerge. Outhwaite examines the case in favour of the category of 'European public intellectuals'. His lists, offered in a spirit of scepticism because many of the names could equally well be presented in lists of national or world figures, are used to support the notion found in Eder (2005) that there is an emergent Europeanization of public life. In another phrase, he describes his selection as 'transnationally recognized European intellectuals', echoing the idea that European institutions and processes generate complex spaces for interaction and communication that are additional to the nations and relations between nations. The present state of the European polity, economy and culture begs the question: are European developments linked with an emergent public sphere in which public intellectuals play a distinctively 'European' part? The loss of public confidence in the European project, reflected in anxieties about the constitution, enlargement and migration, make this a very topical question. Outhwaite chooses to answer it with empirical evidence from media structures, drawing on media ownership and the diffusion of media content across Europe. The relative lack of Europe-wide media is notable if it is taken to mean content produced by transnational European organizations, consumed in common formats, and designed to communicate on matters affecting the European public as a whole. The data on this is taken by a good number of media theorists to indicate the weak development of a European communications space. However, the removal of barriers in media markets through the 1989 European Directive was designed to open up competition, not to create integrated European media. Speculation at the time was misdirected at the possible implications for content, underestimating the resistances from language, culture on the one hand and the immense power of global American media on the other. The greatest impact was felt in the freer movement of media production facilities, finance and formats. It is hardly surprising, therefore, that Outhwaite concludes that there is very slow progress towards Europe as a 'communicative community'.

His conclusion is premature because it starts with media institutions and products rather than communication *per se*. All of the public intellectuals he lists undoubtedly communicate through a wide variety of different media: books, journals, periodicals and newspapers, lectures, speeches, television debates and radio interviews, and increasingly through the Internet. They are generally competent in at least two European languages, travel frequently, and have their work translated. Their regular contacts and communication with other countries inform their ideas. It is therefore unhelpful to depict the European public sphere in terms of communications through newspapers and periodicals with a European reach. Empirical evidence for the existence of a pan-European communicative space linking intellectuals and their publics would include the dissemination and patterns of readership of key works (in the original or in translation), participation in forums designed for specific publics (movements and communities of interest), as well as material spread through Websites and citizen networks. News reporting, as Outhwaite acknowledges, does not have to be transnational in production or format to contribute to European public debate. In short, the health of the European public sphere does not depend on, and should not be judged on, the extent of convergence in media regulation or the trans-frontier integration of markets. Deploying concepts from Habermas, the evidence will neither be found in the media system increasingly dominated by the commercial imperative nor in the life-world dominated by the imperative to entertain, but in the space between where opportunities arise for intellectuals and their publics to act: 'The way [intellectuals] interact with and react against the media, indeed act through the media, makes it possible for them to both promote civility … and to subvert consensus' (Goldfarb, 1998, 211).

In her chapter, Lyon ranges widely to explore the types of 'connectivity' between intellectuals, their publics, civil society and the state. Public intellectuals have most often depended on sponsorship from the state, which uses their services for ideological legitimization or technical support. She cites the Myrdals in this context, and other cases described in this volume can be understood in a similar way. For European scientists and academics, if not for writers, this sponsorship through public funding is the norm. Lyon notes the tendency for the power of the state to direct the forms of knowledge that intellectuals create, particularly when the rhythms of policymaking do not allow the luxury of waiting for full information. Similarly, in education, where knowledge is delivered as a modularized product, it is often detached from its social and cultural origins. The connection to the state is mainly responsible for the much-lamented decline and ambivalence in public intellectual life, but it is not the whole story. In contrast to this connection, there is civil society, which Lyon describes in terms of greater autonomy and choice for the intellectual (who may, of course, serve the state as well). But she also sees the play of ambiguity in intellectuals' participation in civil society: when involvement is linked to specific or local interests or a particularistic movement, the partisan commitment diminishes the scope of the public platform. The application of universalistic principles to particular causes may cloud or distort the universal vision. Lyon's comments on the connections to the public counter the cynical view of media power with a positive assessment of the advance of communications technologies. They sometimes allow public intellectuals to control their own platforms through owning publishing outlets, or to generate programme and publishing ideas which attract technical support and sponsorship.

Lyon is optimistic that public intellectuals can take advantage of the connections which bring legitimacy from the state, democratic support from civil society and a hearing from the general (media) public.

Others might consider the individual trajectories of well-known public intellectuals, including some that Lyon mentions herself, and conclude that these conditions are rarely met. If a public intellectual is someone who applies intellectual activities for a whole community in a way that is accessible to members of the community and open to challenge, it is the writer or creative worker rather than the academic who is more likely to fit the type. Indeed, there is a neglected area of connectivity which corresponds closely to the so-called creative industries – not in their entirety, but in the form of key cultural intermediaries such as editors or directors. Usually affiliated to profit-making organizations, though sometimes freelance, they nevertheless have a commitment to communicate their creative intellectual work to the general public, and may be the first to describe what is currently happening in society and culture. A new generation of public intellectuals may be emerging which is less conditioned by ideological and political configurations.

This volume is a sturdy defence of the public intellectual, both as a theoretical concept to explain the processes of the civil-public sphere and as a practical demonstration of the value to society of intellectuals who transcend their specialisms with creativity and civil courage (Misztal, 2007) in order to 'speak the truth to power'. As a sociological analysis of the position, status and activities of the public intellectual, the series of cases suggests some interesting conclusions. The 'old' public intellectuals have an intimate relationship to politics, but their styles do not, on the whole, belong to deliberative democracy. The 'new', modern intellectuals are more embedded in the practice of research in an institutional setting. Their contributions to politics are mainly indirect, through the policy process, but their reception is quite discipline-specific (as the contrasts between the economist Hayek, the sociologist Lazarsfeld and the policy research of the Myrdals show). The reasons for this may still be relevant today, as the reputation of economics remains far higher in government circles and the media than the reputation of sociology, for example. An analysis of this phenomenon across a wider range of disciplines would show how reception is shaped by the institutional structure of the field, by the characteristics of the theory, and by the patterns of engagement with politics. The issue can be extended to areas well beyond the focus of this volume. A fuller picture would include the impact of public intellectuals who are scientists, writers, cultural intermediaries and certain religious figures. The postmodern public intellectual exemplified by Bauman or Žižek is a 'new' type with characteristics that are more free-floating and where connectivity is stronger in relation to the media and the public than to the state and civil society. The pull of celebrity combined with lower levels of public trust in academic authority contributes to the ambiguity of this position. Ultimately, however, sociological analysis of public intellectuals in any period must be about what they say as well as what they do, the ideas, the truth as told, as well as the role.

References

Burawoy, Michael (2005), 'For Public Sociology', *American Sociological Review* 70 (February), 4–28.

Eder, Klaus (2006), 'Making sense of the public sphere', in Delanty, Gerard (ed.), *Handbook of Contemporary European Social Theory* (London: Routledge), 333–46.

Foreign and Commonwealth Office (FCO) (2003), *UK International Priorities: A Strategy for the FCO*, Cm. 6052 (London: Stationery Office).

Furedi, Frank (2004), *Where Have All the Intellectuals Gone?* (London: Continuum).

Goldfarb, Jeffrey C. (1998) *Civility and Subversion: The Intellectual in Democratic Society* (Cambridge: Cambridge University Press).

Goldthorpe, John (1982), *Social Mobility and Class Structure in Modern Britain* (Oxford: Clarendon Press).

Gouldner, Alvin (1979), *Intellectuals and the Rise of the New Class* (London: Macmillan).

Gray, John (2003), *Al Qaeda and What it Means to be Modern* (London: Faber and Faber).

Kenny, Michael (2004), 'Reckless Minds or Democracy's Helpers? Intellectuals and Politics in the Twentieth Century', *Contemporary Political Theory* 3, 89–103.

Misztal, Barbara (2007), *Intellectuals and the Public Good: Creativity and Civil Courage* (Cambridge: Cambridge University Press).

Rootes, Chris (1995), 'A New Class? The Higher Educated and the New Politics', in Mahieu, Louis (ed.), *Social Movements and Social Classes* (London: Sage/ISA).

Small, Helen (ed.) (2002), *The Public Intellectual* (Oxford: Blackwell).

Tulloch, John (2006), *One Day in July: Experiencing 7/7* (London: Little, Brown).

Index